Palgrave Studies in Democracy, Innovation, and Entrepreneurship for Growth

Series Editor
Elias G. Carayannis
The George Washington University
Washington, DC, USA

The central theme of this series is to explore why some areas grow and others stagnate, and to measure the effects and implications in a trans-disciplinary context that takes both historical evolution and geographical location into account. In other words, when, how and why does the nature and dynamics of a political regime inform and shape the drivers of growth and especially innovation and entrepreneurship? In this socio-economic and socio-technical context, how could we best achieve growth, financially and environmentally?

This series aims to address such issues as:

- How does technological advance occur, and what are the strategic processes and institutions involved?
- How are new businesses created? To what extent is intellectual property protected?
- Which cultural characteristics serve to promote or impede innovation? In what ways is wealth distributed or concentrated?

These are among the key questions framing policy and strategic decision-making at firm, industry, national, and regional levels.

A primary feature of the series is to consider the dynamics of innovation and entrepreneurship in the context of globalization, with particular respect to emerging markets, such as China, India, Russia, and Latin America. (For example, what are the implications of China's rapid transition from providing low-cost manufacturing and services to becoming an innovation powerhouse? How do the perspectives of history and geography explain this phenomenon?)

Contributions from researchers in a wide variety of fields will connect and relate the relationships and inter-dependencies among (1) Innovation, (2) Political Regime, and (3) Economic and Social Development. We will consider whether innovation is demonstrated differently across sectors (e.g., health, education, technology) and disciplines (e.g., social sciences, physical sciences), with an emphasis on discovering emerging patterns, factors, triggers, catalysts, and accelerators to innovation, and their impact on future research, practice, and policy.

This series will delve into what are the sustainable and sufficient growth mechanisms for the foreseeable future for developed, knowledge-based economies and societies (such as the EU and the US) in the context of multiple, concurrent and inter-connected "tipping-point" effects with short (MENA) as well as long (China, India) term effects from a geo-strategic, geo-economic, geo-political and geo-technological set of perspectives.

This conceptualization lies at the heart of the series, and offers to explore the correlation between democracy, innovation and growth.

More information about this series at
http://www.palgrave.com/gp/series/14635

João J. M. Ferreira · Sérgio J. Teixeira ·
Hussain G. Rammal
Editors

Technological Innovation and International Competitiveness for Business Growth

Challenges and Opportunities

palgrave
macmillan

Editors
João J. M. Ferreira
Department of Management and Economics & NECE Research Unit in Business Sciences
University of Beira Interior
Covilhã, Portugal

Hussain G. Rammal
UTS Business School
University of Technology Sydney
Sydney, Australia

Sérgio J. Teixeira
Higher Institute of Administration and Languages
Research Centre—ISAL
Funchal, Portugal

NECE—Research Unit in Business Sciences
Funchal, Portugal

ISSN 2662-3641 ISSN 2662-365X (electronic)
Palgrave Studies in Democracy, Innovation, and Entrepreneurship for Growth
ISBN 978-3-030-51997-1 ISBN 978-3-030-51995-7 (eBook)
https://doi.org/10.1007/978-3-030-51995-7

This Palgrave Macmillan imprint is published by the registered company Springer Nature Switzerland AG
The registered company address is: Gewerbestrasse 11, 6330 Cham, Switzerland

Praise for *Technological Innovation and International Competitiveness for Business Growth*

"Engaging, informative and challenging. Contributors present a wide and diverse range of studies that offer new insights into the relationship between technological innovation and international competitiveness, raising questions for debate and opening pathways for future research. A must read for scholars of international business."

—Patrick Dawson, *Professor of Organizational Change at Newcastle Business School, Northumbria University and Emeritus Professor of Management at the University of Aberdeen*

"There are few things more critical to managers, organizations and national governments than technological innovation as a means to achieving international competitiveness. This is especially relevant in the current global crisis of pandemic, stagnant economies, international discord and other looming crises such as climate change and famine. I know of few other teams that can inform us on these crucial issues more effectively than the authors of this important text."

—Leyland Pitt, Ph.D., Dennis F. Culver *EMBA Alumni Chair of Business and Professor of Marketing, Beedie School of Business, Simon Fraser University, Vancouver, Canada*

"Companies around the world are interested in improving performance and growing their businesses. The application of new technologies has always been a powerful way to achieve these objectives. But such applications must be done correctly and strategically, because failed efforts can be crippling to an organization. Editors Ferreira, Teixeira, and Rammal have assembled some of the world's best scholars to shed light on this important area. This scholarly and practical book will inform 21st century innovation, entrepreneurship, and strategy researchers, provide guidance to industry leaders and practitioners, and make a significant contribution to humanity's shared interest in harmonious and productive international business activities."

—Patrick J. Murphy, Ph.D., *Goodrich Chair and Professor, University of Alabama at Birmingham, USA*

"In a world of ever-changing competitive landscapes epitomized by the recent Covid-19 pandemic, this edited book provides a timely overview of the state-of-the-art literature on technological innovation and international competitiveness. The book is both eclectic and homogenous in its treatment of the multilevel, multifaceted drivers of technological innovation and international competitiveness. As business uncertainty reaches unseen new levels, policymakers both at firm, industry and national levels will need to develop new business models capable of moving goods, services and even people across geographic borders in novel ways. Technological innovation will play a pivotal role in this endeavor and this book will serve as a pivotal starting point for anyone – scholar, manager, or policymaker – to educate themselves on the topic. If you only read one book this year on how technological innovation may help your company to succeed internationally in a world of upheaval – this should be it!"

—Bo Bernhard Nielsen, *Professor of Business Strategy at Sydney University and Professor of International Business at Copenhagen Business School*

"Nowadays, technological innovation and international competitiveness are more than ever interesting and relevant topics for organizations. How do innovation, technology and competitiveness contribute to corporate growth? What are the challenges of technological innovation and international competitiveness? What is the relationship between technological innovation and business growth? These are just some of the critical questions that will be addressed in this book. This book offers a solid and eclectic approach and provides a shared vision for understanding the key issues surrounding this fascinating field of knowledge."

—Sascha Kraus, *Durham University Business School, UK*

"This book explores one of the most important areas in the innovation literature, that which connects technological innovation with firm competitiveness. Through fourteen chapters, organized around four broad groups, the book takes us from a managerial perspective to the industry, and to the macro or national level, of how these two themes interlock and interplay in determining business growth. It is a timely contribution, given the Covid-19 world in which business have to deal with, in which technological innovations would be likely determinant not just for firm survival but for growth."

—Soumodip Sarkar, *University of Evora, Portugal*

Contents

List of Contributors

İbrahim Semih Akçomak Middle East Technical University, Ankara, Turkey

Ahmad Arslan Department of Marketing, Management & IB, Oulu Business School, University of Oulu, Oulu, Finland

Bouchaib Bahli Information Technology and Management, Ryerson University, Toronto, ON, Canada

Serkan Bürken OSTIM Technical University, Ankara, Turkey

Silveli Cristo-Andrade Fucape Business School, Vitoria, ES, Brazil

Marina Dabić University of Zagreb, Zagreb, Croatia;
Nottingham Trent University, Nottingham, UK

Tugrul U. Daim Portland State University, Portland, OR, USA

Cristina I. Fernandes Department of Management and Economics & NECE Research Unit in Business Sciences, University of Beira Interior, Covilhã, Portugal

Sara Fernández-López Department of Finance and Accounting, Universidade de Santiago de Compostela, Santiago de Compostela, Galicia, Spain

João J. M. Ferreira Department of Management and Economics & NECE—Research Unit in Business Sciences, University of Beira Interior, Covilhã, Portugal

Ronnie Figueiredo Business School (FCES), Universidade Europeia (UE) & NECE-UBI, Lisbon, Portugal

José Manuel Guaita Martínez Universitat Politècnica de València, Valencia, Spain

Pia Hurmelinna-Laukkanen Department of Marketing, Management & IB, Oulu Business School, University of Oulu, Oulu, Finland

Minnie Kontkanen School of Marketing & Communications, University of Vaasa, Vaasa, Finland

Emerson Wagner Mainardes Fucape Business School, Vitoria, ES, Brazil

Mohammed Marthed Portland State University, Portland, OR, USA

José María Martín Martín International University of La Rioja, Logroño, Spain

John McManus Stoke-on-Trent, UK

Ricardo Kalil Moraes Rio de Janeiro Federal University, Rio de Janeiro, Brazil

Manuel Ángel Nogueira-Moreiras Department of Finance and Accounting, Universidade de Santiago de Compostela, Santiago de Compostela, Galicia, Spain

Parth Patel Newcastle University Business School, Newcastle University, Newcastle upon Tyne, UK

Adith Pérez University of Santander, Valledupar, Colombia

Vanessa Pertuz University of Santander, Valledupar, Colombia

Hussain G. Rammal UTS Business School, University of Technology Sydney, Sydney, Australia

Domingo Enrique Ribeiro Soriano University of Valencia, Valencia, Spain

David Rodeiro-Pazos Department of Finance and Accounting, Universidade de Santiago de Compostela, Santiago de Compostela, Galicia, Spain

María Jesús Rodríguez-Gulías Department of Business, Universidade da Coruña, A Coruña, Galicia, Spain

Matti Saari School of Marketing & Communications, University of Vaasa, Vaasa, Finland

José Antonio Salinas Fernández University of Granada, Granada, Spain

Minna Saunila School of Engineering Science, LUT University, Lahti, Finland

Tania Sebastian VITSOL, Vellore Institute of Technology, Chennai, India

Santoshi Sengupta School of Management, Graphic Era Hill University, Bhimtal, India

Ranjana Singh-Nagpal School of Social Sciences—Centre for Studies in Social Management, Central University of Gujarat, Gandhinagar, India

Tihana Škrinjarić Department of Mathematics, University of Zagreb, Zagreb, Croatia

Arilda Teixeira Fucape Business School, Vitoria, ES, Brazil

Sérgio J. Teixeira Higher Institute of Administration and Languages, Research Centre—ISAL, Funchal, Portugal;
NECE—Research Unit in Business Sciences, Funchal, Portugal

Pedro Mota Veiga Escola Superior de Educação de Viseu - Instituto Politécnico de Viseu e Universidade Católica Portuguesa & NECE-Research Unit, Covilhã, Portugal

Peter F. Wanke Rio de Janeiro Federal University, Rio de Janeiro, Brazil

Sawlat Zaman Newcastle University Business School, Newcastle University, Newcastle upon Tyne, UK

List of Figures

List of Tables

CHAPTER 1

Introduction: Technological Innovation and International Competitiveness for Business Growth—State-of-the-Art

João J. M. Ferreira, Sérgio J. Teixeira, and Hussain G. Rammal

1.1 Introduction

Technological innovation is a critical driver for the development of international competitiveness and for determining ways to improve business efficiency, performance, and competitiveness on a global scale

J. J. M. Ferreira (✉)
Department of Management and Economics & NECE Research Unit in Business Sciences, University of Beira Interior, Covilhã, Portugal
e-mail: jjmf@ubi.pt

S. J. Teixeira
Higher Institute of Administration and Languages, Research Centre—ISAL, Funchal, Portugal
e-mail: sergio.teixeira@isal.pt

NECE—Research Unit in Business Sciences, Funchal, Portugal

J. J. M. Ferreira et al. (eds.), *Technological Innovation and International Competitiveness for Business Growth*, Palgrave Studies in Democracy, Innovation, and Entrepreneurship for Growth,
https://doi.org/10.1007/978-3-030-51995-7_1

(Antonio et al., 2020; Ferreira, Fayolle, Fernandes, & Raposo, 2017; Klímová, Žítek, & Viturka, 2017; Kurtishi-kastrati, 2016). The relationship between technological innovation and international competitiveness is one of the most intensively researched topics in the literature on corporate growth (Coad & Rao, 2008; Hussain & Ismail, 2015; Jianmin & Li, 2020). Penrose's growth theory (1959, 1965) explains how innovation activities act as a source of knowledge resources that, in turn, enhances the growth and competitiveness of companies.

Some contemporary studies argue that having natural resources appears not to be an essential element when analyzing the factors of competitiveness and power of countries in the international arena (Amorós, Fernández, & Tapia, 2012; Chen, Yin, & Mei, 2018; Jung, Lee, Hwang, & Yeo, 2017; Zaichenko, 2018). Innovation and internationalization are now more interconnected. The knowledge acquisition and learning by organizations across national boundaries is considered to be critical for sustained innovation and growth (Cantwell, 2017). Bagheri, Mitchelmore, Bamiatzi, and Nikolopoulos (2019) found an inverted U-shaped relationship between technological innovation and international firm performance among small-and-medium enterprises (SMEs). Technological innovation was found to positively mediate the effect of internationalization orientation on international firm performance, and managers can improve international performance by incorporating technological innovation activities in their strategic decisions (Bagheri et al., 2019).

The search for understanding technological innovation and international competitiveness has led to different approaches in the context of business growth influenced by innovation factors and practices (Chabowski & Mena, 2017; Kurtishi-kastrati, 2016; Neutzling, dos Santos, de Barcellos, & Land, 2015), and technology (Efrat, Hughes, Nemkova, Souchon, & Sy-Changco, 2018; Kim & Kim, 2013; Neutzling et al., 2015; Oelze & Habisch, 2018; Wilde, Cox, Kelly, & Harrison, 2017). In response to increased competition resulting from globalization, companies are seeking to leverage their innovation and technology

H. G. Rammal
UTS Business School, University of Technology
Sydney, Sydney, Australia
e-mail: hussain.rammal@uts.edu.au

practices by developing international partnerships (Bakhru, Behera, & Sharma, 2018; Ketelhöhn, Artavia, Arce, & Umaña, 2015; Frange & Verdier, 2011; Ye, Xiao, & Zhou, 2019).

Innovation activities increase opportunities for company growth. Thus, endogenous growth models (Aghion & Howitt, 1992; Geroski, 1999; Hausman, Hall, & Griliches, 1984; Howitt & Aghion, 1998; Klette, Møen, & Griliches, 2000; Lucas, 1978) show that an irregular pattern of innovation and R&D spending leads to an irregular pattern of growth. In active learning models (Ericson & Pakes, 1995; Pakes & Ericson, 1998), companies learn from their experiences and improve their level of efficiency by investing in innovation.

To analyze the existing literature on Technological Innovation and International Competitiveness for Business Growth, we identified the critical studies published through a search in the Web of Science (WoS) database. Figure 1.1 shows the evolution of the number of published articles and citations, over time, by the two significant areas defined, Technology Innovation and International Competitiveness. The first study in this area was published in 1981, with a more marked evolution of publications from 2009 onwards. The total number of publications in this area

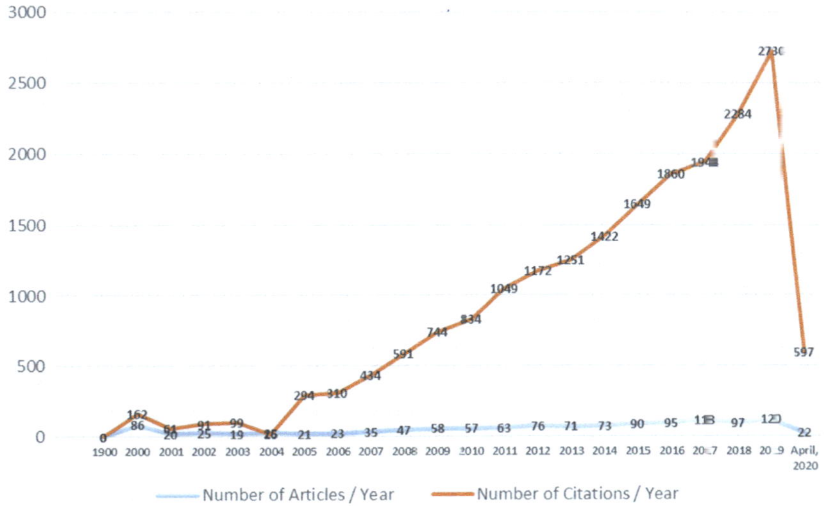

Fig. 1.1 Evolution of the number of publications and citations/year

totals 1241, with the highest number of articles published in the years 2017 and 2019.

Table 1.1 presents a summary of the Top 25 publications most cited and most relevant to the articles identified.

1.2 An Integrative Mapping of the Literature

Using the VOSviewer Software, and applying the selection method based on titles and summaries, the option of 'full counting' was chosen. With a minimum number of 100 occurrences per term, 280 terms were identified with greater relevance, so when analyzed, it was possible to identify the areas with a higher density of clusters and how they relate to each other (Fig. 1.2).

Table 1.2 shows the 10 most influential authors in the study area, with the highest number of citations. The results show that Malerba, F. is the most influential author in this field of research with 358 citations, followed by Constantini, V. (202 citations), Sinkovics, R.R. (136 citations), and Crespi, F. (78 citations).

Figure 1.3 shows the most significant network of affiliations (with more citations) in this area of research.

The results show that the University of Nottingham with 710 citations has the highest number of citations, followed by the University of Sussex (202 citations), Tsinghua University (144 citations), and Peking University (113 citations). In terms of countries with the most significant influence in this area of knowledge (Table 1.3), measured by the number of citations, the United States leads this field, followed by England, Italy, Finland, China, and Germany.

An analysis based on the co-occurrence of keywords led to the identification of six thematic clusters: (i) red cluster (56 items); (ii) green cluster (37 items); (iii) dark blue cluster (36 items); (iv) yellow cluster (25 items); (v) pink cluster (22 items); and (vi) light blue cluster (86 items). These clusters are illustrated in Fig. 1.4.

These clusters highlight the antecedents and outcomes of technological innovation and the theoretical perspectives used to study this topic.

Table 1.1 Top 25 most cited articles in the study area

#	*Authors*	*Journal*	*# citations*
1	Gold, A.H., Malhotra, A., Segars, A.H. (2001)	*Journal of Management Information Systems*	1527
2	Autio, E., Sapienza, H.J., Almeida, J.G. (2000)	*Academy of Management Journal*	1252
3	Zhu, K., Kraemer, K.L. (2005)	*Information Systems Research*	530
4	Tallman, S., Jenkins, M., Henry, N., Pinch, S. (2004)	*Academy of Management Review*	430
5	Walter, A., Auer, M., Ritter, T. (2006)	*Journal of Business Venturing*	449
6	Mudambi, R., Navarra, P. (2004)	*Journal of International Business Studies*	434
7	Zhu, K., Kraemer, K.L., Xu, S. (2006)	*Management Science*	420
8	Frost, T.S., Birkinshaw, J.M., Ensign, P.C. (2002)	*Strategic Management Journal*	377
9	Zahra, S.A., Garvis, D.M. (2000)	*Journal of Business Venturing*	344
10	Narasimhan, R., Kim, S.W. (2002)	*Journal of Operations Management*	334
11	Simonin, B.L. (2004)	*Journal of International Business Studies*	304
12	Maskell, P., Malmberg, A. (1999)	*European Urban and Regional Studies*	297
13	Guan, J., Ma, N. (2003)	*Technovation*	260
14	Phene, A., Almeida, P. (2008)	*Journal of International Business Studies*	241
15	Bingham, C.B., Eisenhardt, K.M. (2011)	*Strategic Management Journal*	229
16	Schneider, M.R.;, Schulze-Bentrop, C., Paunescu, M. (2010)	*Journal of International Business Studies*	222
17	Yalcinkaya, G., Calantone, R.J., Griffith, D.A. (2007)	*Journal of International Marketing*	203
18	Zhu, K., Dong, S., Xu, S.X., Kraemer, K.L. (2006)	*European Journal of Information Systems*	195
19	Lall, S. (2001)	*World Development*	178
20	Malerba, F., Orsenigo, L. (1996)	*Research Policy*	177
21	Chittoor, R., Sarkar, M.B., Ray, S., Aulakh, P.S. (2009)	*Organization Science*	160

(continued)

Table 1.1 (continued)

#	*Authors*	*Journal*	*# citations*
22	Bartholomew, S. (1997)	*Journal of International Business Studies*	159
23	Teng, Bing-Sheng (2007)	*Journal of Management Studies*	139
24	Costantini, V., Mazzanti, M. (2012)	*Research Policy*	138
25	Montealegre, R. (2002)	*Organization Science*	133

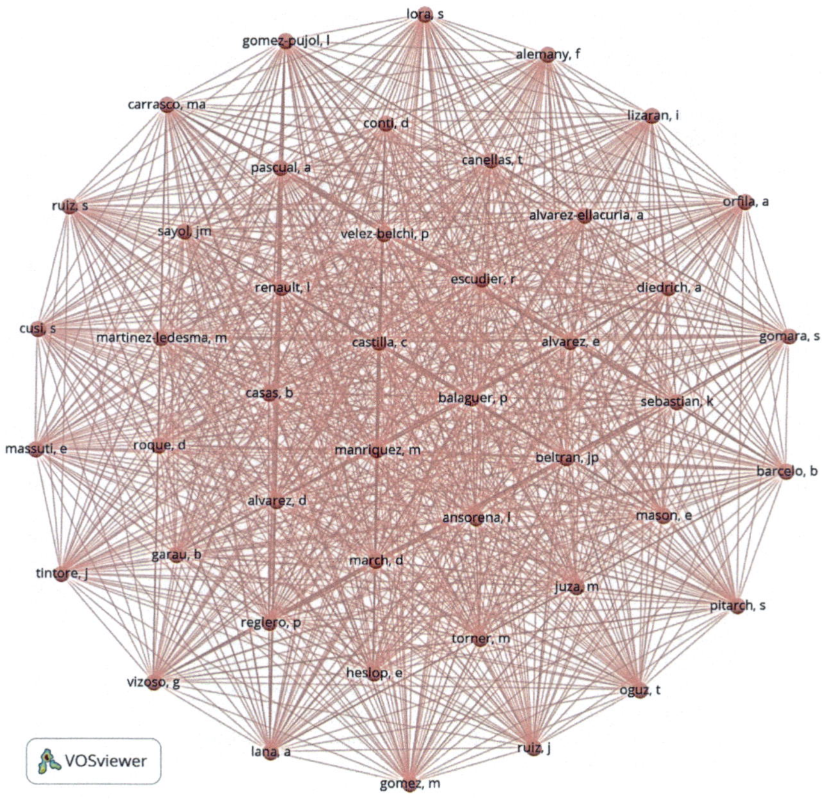

Fig. 1.2 Network of most influential authors in the area

Table 1.2 Top 10 most influential authors in this area of studies

#	*Authors*	*Citations*	*Documents*
1	Malerba, F.	358	4
2	Constantini, V.	202	4
3	Sinkovics, R.R.	136	5
4	Crespi, F.	78	4
5	Porter, A.L.	51	4
6	Kordos, M.	41	8
7	Huang, Y.	25	4
8	Chen, J.	3	4
9	Zhang, J.	1	4
10	Danilova, E.A.	0	4

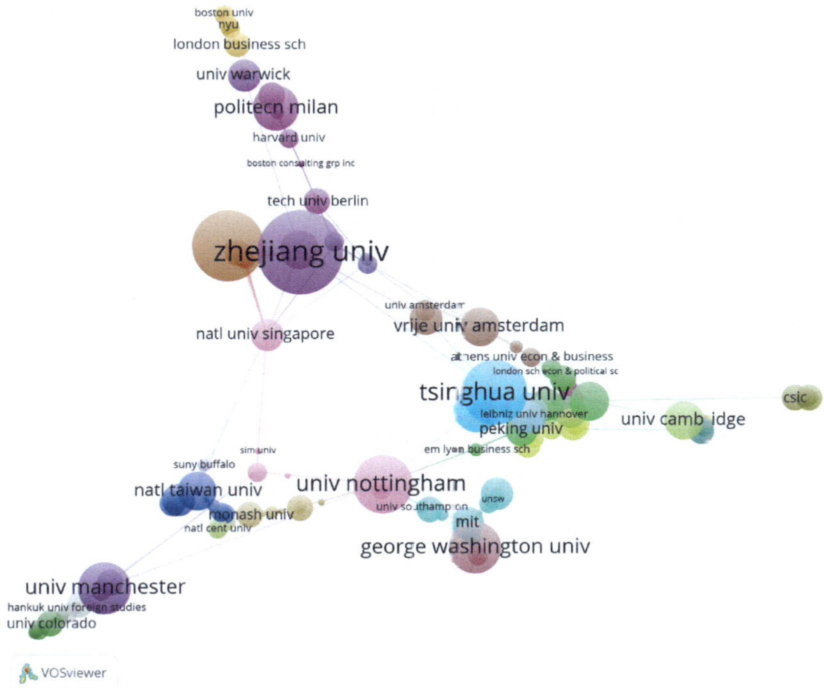

Fig. 1.3 The network of most influential universities/institutions in the area

Table 1.3 Top 10 countries with the most citations in this area of studies

#	*Country*	*Citations*	*Documents*
1	U.S.A	9554	172
2	England	3029	83
3	Italy	1582	74
4	Finland	1387	23
5	China	1141	224
6	Germany	1141	42
7	Denmark	900	11
8	Spain	884	74
9	Canada	806	27
10	Sweden	694	18

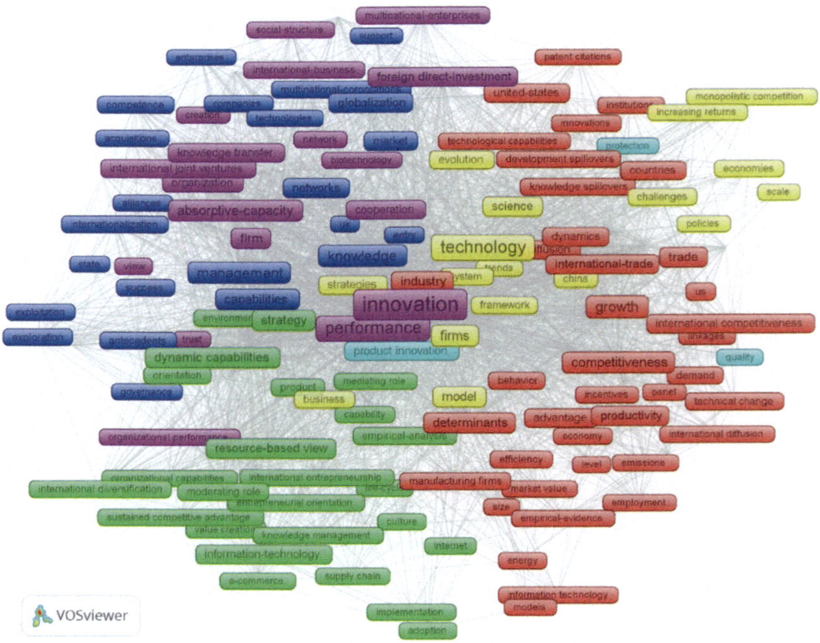

Fig. 1.4 Clusters of keywords co-occurrence

1.3 Overview of the Book Chapters

This book is structured in four parts and includes fourteen chapters. The first part, entitled 'Bridging technological innovation domains , consists of the following three chapters.

Chapter 2, titled 'Technological Innovation and Exports: Effects on Firm Growth' by Rodríguez-Gulías, Fernández-López, Rodeiro-Pazos, and Nogueira-Moreiras, explores the effect of exports and technological innovation of growth firms. The chapter highlights the role of a set of innovation measures revealing the impact on firm growth.

Chapter 3 by McManus titled 'How Do Innovation and Technology and Competitiveness Contribute to Business Growth', conceptualizes how innovation, technology, and competitiveness impact business growth. This contribution shows how these concepts are linked to issues related to business globalization.

Chapter 4, titled 'International Growth and Social Media Competitiveness of Small Software Firms' by Saari, Kontkanen, Arslan, and Hurmelinna-Laukkanen, focuses on how social media can become a competitiveness source and enrich international growth of small technology firms. The authors offer some important theoretical and managerial implications for this knowledge field.

The second part of the book focuses on the 'Dynamics of international business competitiveness', and consists of the following three chapters.

Fernandes, Veiga, Ferreira, Teixeira, and Rammal in Chapter 5 titled 'The Impact of Innovation and Entrepreneurship on Competitiveness' assess ways in which innovation impacts on competitiveness and how the effects of entrepreneurship shape and fashion competitiveness. Using estimations of dynamic panels from Eurostat regional data, the study pursues to address the gap in the literature concerning the measurement of innovation and entrepreneurship, and its influence over competitiveness at the European Union NUTS 2 regional level.

In Chapter 6, 'Internal Barriers for the Brazilian Economy to Achieve External Competitiveness', Teixeira, Cristo-Andrade, and Mainardes analyze the performance of the Brazilian economy. Based on a comparison with other countries, the authors argue that the technological gap and the lack of competitiveness of the Brazilian economy is the result of choices that led it to institutionalize the misallocation of resources.

Chapter 7, titled 'Social Sustainability on Competitiveness in Tourism Industry: Towards New Approach?' by Martín, Martinez, Fernández, and

Soriano, uses a literature review to study competitiveness in the Tourism Industry. They argue that social sustainability linked to the development of tourism and the support of the local population is critical for the competitiveness of tourism destinations.

The third part, 'Refining the technological innovation and business growth link', is constituted by three chapters.

Chapter 8, titled 'Reframing Technological Innovation Capabilities: Empirical Evidence and a Framework for Study' by Saunila, Pertuz, and Pérez, discusses the micro-foundations of technological innovation research by defining the technological innovation capabilities and their relationship to a firm's competitiveness.

Chapter 9 by Figueiredo and Bahli discusses the linkage between the three pillars of the Spinner Model in the extant literature. The study, titled 'Service Business Growth: A Spinner Model Approach', identifies some main themes relating to knowledge creation, knowledge transfer, and innovation. The authors encourage practitioners and researchers to support business growth through the Spinner innovation model approach.

Chapter 10, titled 'Evaluating R&D Efficiency of Selected European Countries: A Dynamic Analysis for Period 2007-2017' by Škrinjarić, measures the (in)efficiency of R&D expenditures and innovation policies of 30 selected European countries and shows a robust ranking system of the most efficient countries in the R&D area.

The last part of the book, designed by 'Empirical case studies', comprises of the remaining five chapters.

Chapter 11, titled 'Middle-Technology Trap: The Case of Automotive Industry in Turkey' by Akçomak and Bürken, focuses on whether the success in the Turkish automotive manufacturing industry stimulated technological learning and to what extent the sector has gained R&D and innovation capabilities over the years. Some mechanisms are identified that explain how the automotive industry collapsed into a middle-technology trap on the borders of a weak innovation system and strong global value chains.

Chapter 12, titled 'Kaiser Permanente Internet of Things Roadmap' by Daim, Mohammed, and Dabić, focuses on the Internet of things for one of the largest healthcare organizations in the United States, Kaiser Permanente. This case illustrates how to compete with other healthcare organizations and take advantage of the fast growth opportunity in the sector.

Moraes and Wanke, in Chapter 13, titled 'BNDES' Impact on the Steel Industry's Efficiency: A Two-Stage Malmquist Model Usage', use a Malmquist Index decomposition and robust nonlinear robust regression to evaluate how the Brazilian National Development Bank impacts the performance of the steel industry.

In Chapter 14, 'Fostering Business Growth and Innovation through Internationalization: The Interesting Illustration of the Indian IT Industry', Sengupta, Patel, and Zaman detail the history of information technology, and illustrate the emergence of the Indian IT industry. The chapter explains the process by which firms in the Indian IT industry successfully internationalized to foster business growth, which led to its global dominance of the sector.

The final chapter, titled 'Decoding Management Practices of Women Entrepreneurs with or without Technological Skills in Emerging Economies: Evidence from India' by Singh-Nagpal and Sebastian, focuses on the possession of knowledge and technological skills in women entrepreneurs. This study evidences the path for future researchers to explore ICT entrepreneurial ecosystem that is responsive to the requirements of women entrepreneurs.

1.4 Conclusion

This introductory chapter provides a state-of-the-art review on the topic of Technological Innovation and International Competitiveness for Business Growth, based on insights from the analysis of the literature using bibliometric techniques. This methodology allowed an integrative mapping of scientific publications and intellectual structures related to this theme.

In general terms, this chapter emphasizes the role of technological innovation and international competitiveness in business growth, highlighting its distinctive characteristics that are explored and discussed in the various contributions (chapters) that make up this book.

The chapters address several topics, including (i) the challenges of technological innovation and international competitiveness; (ii) knowledge, innovation, and creative skills as technology solutions to create high value for businesses internationally; and (iii) the contribution of innovation, technology, and smart strategies to business growth.

This book is thus one of the first to relate, in a broader sense, the micro (manager/entrepreneur and company), meso (industry), and macro (country) levels that affect technological innovation and international competitiveness and play a growing critical role for business growth in the global market.

Acknowledgements The authors would like to acknowledge and thank NECE—Research Unit in Business Sciences funded by the Multiannual Funding Programme of R&D Centres of FCT—Fundação para a Ciência e a Tecnologia, under the project 'UID/GES/04630/2020' and ISAL Research Centre.

References

Aghion, P., & Howitt, P. (1992). A model of growth through creative destruction. *Econometrica, 60*(2), 323–351.

Amorós, J. E., Fernández, C., & Tapia, J. (2012). Quantifying the relationship between entrepreneurship and competitiveness development stages in Latin America. *International Entrepreneurship and Management Journal, 8*(3), 249–270.

Antonio, J., Fernández, S., Serdeira, P., María, J., Martín, M., Antonio, J., & Martín, R. (2020, January). Determinants of tourism destination competitiveness in the countries most visited by international tourists: Proposal of a synthetic index. *Tourism Management Perspectives, 33,* 100582.

Bagheri, M., Mitchelmore, S., Bamiatzi, V., & Nikolopoulos, K. (2019). Internationalization orientation in SMEs: The mediating role of technological innovation. *Journal of International Management, 25*(1), 121–139.

Bakhru, K. M., Behera, M., & Sharma, A. (2018). Entrepreneurial communities and family enterprises of India: An overview of their emergence and sustained growth. *Journal of Enterprising Communities-People and Places in the Global Economy, 12*(1, SI), 32–49.

Cantwell, J. (2017). Innovation and international business. *Industry and Innovation, 24*(1), 41–60.

Coad, A., & Rao, R. (2008). Innovation and firm growth in high-tech sectors: A quantile regression approach. *Research Policy, 37*(4), 633–648.

Chabowski, B. R., & Mena, J. A. (2017). A review of global competitiveness research: Past advances and future directions. *Journal of International Marketing, 25*(4), 1–24.

Chen, J., Yin, X., & Mei, L. (2018). Holistic innovation: An emerging innovation paradigm. *International Journal of Innovation Studies, 2*(1), 1–13.

Efrat, K., Hughes, P., Nemkova, E., Souchon, A. L., & Sy-Changco, J. (2018). Leveraging of dynamic export capabilities for competitive advantage and performance consequences: Evidence from China. *Journal of Business Research, 84,* 114–124.

Ericson, R., & Pakes, A. (1995). Markov-perfect industry dynamics: A framework for empirical work. *Review of Economic Studies, 62*(1), 53–82.

Ferreira, J. J., Fayolle, A., Fernandes, C., & Raposo, M. (2017). Effects of Schumpeterian and Kirznerian entrepreneurship on economic growth: Panel data evidence. *Entrepreneurship and Regional Development, 29*(1–2), 27–50.

Geroski, P. (1999). The Growth of Firms in Theory and in Practice, No 2092, CEPR Discussion Papers, C.E.P.R. Discussion Papers.

Hausman, J., Hall, B., & Griliches, Z. (1984). Econometric models for count data with an application to the patents-R&D relationship. *Econometrica, 52*(4), 909–938.

Hussain, M. H. M., & Ismail, H. N. (2015). Understanding the morphology in the form of business expansion: Perspective of small tourism firm in coastal resort destination. *International Journal of Built Environment and Sustainability, 2*(4, SI), 269–277.

Howitt, P., & Aghion, P. (1998). Capital accumulation and innovation as complementary factors in long-run growth. *Journal of Economic Growth, 3,* 111–130.

Jianmin, W., & Li, Y. (2020). Does factor endowment allocation improve technological innovation performance? An empirical study on the Yangtze River Delta region. *Science of the Total Environment, 716,* 137107.

Jung, S., Lee, J.-D., Hwang, W.-S., & Yeo, Y. (2017). Growth versus equity: A CGE analysis for effects of factor-biased technical progress on economic growth and employment. *Economic Modelling, 60,* 424–438.

Ketelhöhn, N., Artavia, R., Arce, R., & Umaña, V. (2015). The Central American competitiveness initiative. *Competitiveness Review, 25*(5), 555–570.

Kim, W., & Kim, H. (2013). Regional development strategy for increasing cultural tourism business in South Korea. *Asia Pacific Journal of Tourism Research, 18*(6), 534–548.

Klette, T., Møen, J., & Griliches, Z. (2000). Do subsidies to commercial R&D reduce market failures? Microeconometric evaluation studies. *Research Policy, 29*(4–5), 471–495.

Klímová, V., Žítek, V., & Viturka, M. (2017). The 20th Jubilee Colloquium on Regional Sciences: A Conference Report. *Review of Economic Perspectives, 17*(2), 209–215.

Kurtishi-kastrati, S. (2016). Do foreign direct investments accelerate economic growth ? The case of the Republic of Macedonia Veland Ramadani *Leo-Paul Dana Vanessa Ratten. *International Journal Competitiveness*, *1*(1), 71–78.

Lucas, R. (1978). Asset prices in an exchange economy. *Econometrica, 46*(6), 1429–1445.

Neutzling, D. M., dos Santos, M. S., de Barcellos, M. D., & Land, A. L. (2015). Value creation from internationalization of Sugar Cane by-products:

A multi-stakeholder view of artisanal cachaça production. *Review of Business Management, 17*(55), 890–910.

Oelze, N., & Habisch, A. (2018). Responsible supply chain implementation—Are multinational companies gods and small and medium sized enterprises oxen? *Journal of Cleaner Production, 179*, 738–752.

Pakes, A., & Ericson, R. (1998). Empirical implications of alternative models of firm dynamics. *Journal of Economic Theory, 79*(1), 1–45.

Penrose, E. T. (1959). *The theory of the growth of the firm*. New York: Oxford University Press.

Penrose, E. T. (1965). *Economics and the Aspirations of Le Tiers Monde*. London: University of London.

Prange, C., & Verdier, S. (2011). Dynamic capabilities, internationalization processes and performance. *Journal of World Business, 46*(1, SI), 126–133.

Wilde, S. J., Cox, C., Kelly, S. J., & Harrison, J. L. (2017). Consumer insights and the importance of competitiveness factors for mature and developing destinations. *International Journal of Hospitality & Tourism Administration, 18*(2), 111–132.

Ye, S., Xiao, H., & Zhou, L. (2019). Small accommodation business growth in rural areas: Effects on guest experience and financial performance. *International Journal of Hospitality Management, 76*(December 2017), 29–38.

Zaichenko, S. (2018). The human resource dimension of science-based technology transfer: Lessons from Russian RTOs and innovative enterprises. *Journal of Technology Transfer, 43*(2), 368–388.

PART I

Bridging Technological Innovation Domains

CHAPTER 2

Technological Innovation and Exports: Effects on Firm Growth

María Jesús Rodríguez-Gulías, Sara Fernández-López, David Rodeiro-Pazos, and Manuel Ángel Nogueira-Moreiras

2.1 Introduction

Creating fast-growing innovative and global firms has become the cornerstone of European policies for promoting regional growth (Coad, Segarra, & Teruel, 2016), especially in environments characterised by high levels of competitiveness. As a result, stimulating exports and innovation remains a priority on the agenda of institutions aiming to enhance

M. J. Rodríguez-Gulías (✉)
Department of Business, Universidade da Coruña, A Coruña, Galicia, Spain
e-mail: maria.gulias@udc.es

S. Fernández-López · D. Rodeiro-Pazos · M. Á. Nogueira-Moreiras
Department of Finance and Accounting, Universidade de Santiago de Compostela, Santiago de Compostela, Galicia, Spain
e-mail: sara.fernandez.lopez@usc.es

D. Rodeiro-Pazos
e-mail: david.rodeiro@usc.es

J. J. M. Ferreira et al. (eds.), *Technological Innovation and International Competitiveness for Business Growth*, Palgrave Studies in Democracy, Innovation, and Entrepreneurship for Growth,
https://doi.org/10.1007/978-3-030-51995-7_2

sustained regional growth and development (European Commission, 2014).

There is a burgeoning body of literature that investigates the determinants of firm growth (see Coad, 2009). In this domain, particular emphasis is devoted to the importance of innovation for sales growth (see Nogueira, Fernández-López, Rodríguez-Gulías, Vivel-Bua, & Rodeiro-Pazos, 2019). The most widely accepted hypothesis is that successful innovators outgrow non-innovators. However, solid evidence on the effect of innovation activities on firm growth remains inconclusive and dependant on the profile of innovators (Coad, 2009; Nogueira et al., 2019; Romano, 2019; Spescha & Woerter, 2019) and on business cycle (Spescha & Woerter, 2019). Similarly, research on export activities and firm growth has flourished in the last 30 years (Lu & Beamish, 2006; Park & Jang, 2010), to the point of considering export as a growth-enhancing strategy (Di Cintio, Ghosh, & Grassia, 2017; Fuertes-Callén & Cuéllar-Fernández, 2019; Du & Temouri, 2011).

In spite of the significant literature on the aforementioned topics, previous research has sometimes overlooked that successful development of both activities requires a high level of resource, preventing financially constrained firms from carrying out these activities. In this respect, small firms are more likely to choose resource-constrained strategies than larger firms (Variyam & Kraybill, 1993), particularly in what refers to how much they invest in innovation (Pangarkar, 2008). Additionally, concerning internationalisation, small companies differ from their larger counterparts in risk perception, capabilities and speed of decision-making (Svetličič, Jaklič, & Burger, 2007). One route to address this gap in the literature is to acknowledge the key role of firm size in the effect of innovative and export activities.

This chapter aims to tackle the above-mentioned issues: (1) whether innovation affects sales growth; (2) whether exporting affects sales growth and (3) whether such effects depend on firm size. By applying the dynamic panel data methodology to a sample of 3267 Spanish manufacturing firms over the period 2004–2014, we study whether the effect of innovation and exports on firm sales growth depends on firm size. In so doing, we contribute to a better understanding of the strategies that shape firm growth.

Answering these questions is especially relevant in countries such as Spain, where SMEs traditionally show low levels of both innovation and export activities. Thus, the Spanish economy provides an interesting context for such an analysis. The percentage of innovative enterprises in Spain in 2014 was 36.4%; in the European Union, it was 49.1% (Eurostat, 2018). In 2016, only 21 Spanish companies were among the 1000 European firms with more research and development (R&D) investment (Hernández et al., 2018). Moreover, during the economic crisis, public and private resources available to support innovation were drastically cut. As a result, the R&D effort of Spanish firms in 2016 was half the European average (COTEC, 2017). In contrast, the government seems to have opted for a national strategy to foster exports as the main vehicle to counterbalance the negative effects of the drop in the country's demand caused by the economic downturn of 2007. Nevertheless, the export sector in Spain has some important limitations, where exports are highly concentrated in a few large companies (Durán, 2014) and the smaller companies, which represent a higher percentage in Spain than in other economies, are generally less productive than European companies (Mora Sanguinetti & Fuentes, 2012). These data reinforce the idea that Spain's export sector is still weak (Dones Tacero, Heredero de Pablos, & Ruesga Benito, 2017). In this context, gaining insights into innovation and exporting outcomes for firms will allow for better-designed policies aimed at supporting job-creating firms.

This chapter contributes to the literature in three ways. Firstly, it provides insight into the influence of exports and innovation activities on sales growth conditioned by the firm size. Secondly, a wide set of innovation measures, including both innovative inputs and outputs, is employed to know what innovation activities are more growth-enhancing. Thirdly, the above-mentioned characteristics of Spain make it an interesting context to identify lessons applicable to other similar countries.

This chapter is organised as follows. Section 2.2 summarises the relevant literature. Section 2.3 explains the data and the variables, as well as the estimated econometric model. Section 2.4 presents the empirical findings. Finally, Sect. 2.5 draws out the main conclusions, limitations and future research lines.

2.2 Literature Review: Innovation, Exports and Sales Growth

The relationship between innovation and growth is one of the most intensively researched relationships in the literature on the firm growth (Bianchini, Pellegrino, & Tamagni, 2015; Coad & Rao, 2008).

Similarly, the effect of exporting behaviour on firm growth has long interested economics and academics (Di Cintio et al., 2017).

Regarding innovation growth literature, different streams have indicated that firms' innovation activities enhance the opportunities for growth. Thus, at a macro-level of analysis, the endogenous models of growth (Aghion & Howitt, 1992; Geroski, 1999; Hall, Griliches, & Hausman, 1984; Klette & Griliches, 2000; Lucas, 1978; Pakes & Ericson, 1998) outline that an erratic pattern of R&D spending and innovation leads to an erratic pattern of growth. In active learning models (Ericson & Pakes, 1995; Pakes & Ericson, 1998), firms learn from their experiences and can only improve their level of efficiency by investing in innovation, so these activities would be key to improving efficiency and growth. Also, for Penrosean growth (Penrose, 1959) innovation activities, acting as a source of knowledge resources, can increase firm growth.

While theoretical approaches acknowledge the role of innovation as growth-enhancing for firms, the empirical literature does not fully support the theoretical expectations. Thus, when firm growth is measured in terms of sales growth, although most studies find that innovators grow faster (Bianchini et al., 2015; Cassia, Colombelli, & Paleari, 2009; Coad & Rao, 2008; Coad et al., 2016; Colombelli, Haned, & Le Bas, 2013; Corsino, 2008; Corsino & Gabriele, 2010; Cucculelli & Ermini, 2012; Czarnitzki & Delanote, 2013; Demirel & Mazzucato, 2012; Falk, 2012; Mazzucato & Parris, 2015; Na & Kang, 2019; Nogueira et al., 2019; Segarra & Teruel, 2014; Spescha & Woerter, 2019), a non-negligible number of papers either yield the opposite relationship (Freel, 2000; Freel & Robson, 2004; Grabowski, Vernon, & DiMasi, 2002) or fail to find a significant effect of innovation on sales growth (Bottazzi, Dosi, Lippi, Pammolli, & Riccaboni, 2001; Geroski, 1995; Geroski, Machin, & Walters, 1997). Additionally, a recent strand of the literature insists on the need of identifying the different profiles of innovators to disentangle the effect of innovation on firm growth. Thus, Romano (2019) finds that product and process innovation yield firm growth in 'high complex innovators' both singularly and jointly, while the same effect in other kinds of innovators requires that both innovations realise jointly. Spescha and Woerter (2019) also conclude that firms relying on non-R&D innovations are more sensitive to business cycle than non-innovative firms.

Drawing on previous theoretical models, as well as on the evidence mostly found, we propose that firms developing innovation activities outgrow non-innovative ones, regardless if they are measured by innovative inputs (i.e. R&D expenditure) or innovative outputs (i.e. patents, product innovation, process innovation, commercial innovation and organisational innovation).

Hypothesis 1 Innovation activities positively influence firms' sales growth.

Participation in international markets is often viewed as a requisite for firm growth (Chen, Zou, & Wang, 2009; Di Cintio et al., 2017; Du & Temouri, 2011). The burgeoning work on the internationalisation-growth relationship has stressed exporting as one of the main channels of firms' international activities (Lu & Beamish, 2001, 2006), it being relatively faster, easier and lesser risky to operate in foreign markets compared to foreign direct investment (Lu & Beamish, 2006). International competition increases the efficiency of firms (Du & Temouri, 2011) and, in particular, the growth of exporting firms is faster than firms operating only in domestic markets (Falk & Hagsten, 2018; Lu & Beamish, 2006). Exports positively contribute to firm growth not only due to their direct effects on sales, but also through indirect effects such as the development of new capabilities and experience, as well as the possibility of achieving economies of scale in firms whose local market is small (Fuertes-Callén & Cuellar-Fernández, 2019) or suffering an economic recession

Exports are considered an important channel to boost firms' sales, for both established and young and small enterprises (Shrader, Oviatt, & McDougall, 2000). Thus, a survey of 54 firm-level studies, including data for firms from 34 countries, published between 1995 and 2006, shows that exporting firms are more productive than non-exporters (Wagner, 2007), and Becchetti and Trovato (2002) show that the access to export markets positively affects SME employment growth. Requena Silvente (2005) shows that, for a sample of UK small firms between 1994 and 2000, exporters (regular, irregular and new) have higher sales per worker than non-exporters. Similarly, Filatotchev and Piesse (2009) find that export intensity is positively associated with the sales growth of newly listed firms. Fuertes-Callén and Cuellar-Fernández (2019) highlight that export was the strategy that enabled Spanish manufacturing firms to growth over the period 2008–2014. Furthermore, Hölzl (2009) concludes that exports are important for high-growth firms using the export to sales ratio. Hernandez and Nieto (2016) indicate that exporters increase sales growth when also undertaking international supply operations, especially when both—inward and outward international operations—take place in the same foreign country.

Stemming from previous arguments, we propose the following hypothesis:

Hypothesis 2 Export activities positively influence firms' sales growth.

Taken together, the above-mentioned studies mostly indicate a positive effect of exporting and innovation on firms' sales growth. Nevertheless, both relationships depend to a large extent on the amount of resources that firms can allocate to these activities which, in turn, depends on the firm size. In this respect, previous research has overlooked how the effect of innovation and exporting is conditioned by firm size.

Although firm innovation increases growth opportunities, it also creates instability, to the point that, as noted in Coad and Rao (2008), the growth driven by innovation can only be a matter of chance. In other words, innovation has a high level of risk with can be transformed into better results for firms or losses if these activities are not successful (Coad & Rao, 2008; Segarra & Teruel, 2014). It is usually easier for larger firms to take such risks than it is for small ones. Thus, Demirel and Mazzucato (2012) conclude that the growth of large firms is affected by R&D intensity, but SMEs must be persistent with innovation activities to achieve a positive effect in growth. Colombelli et al. (2013) prove that innovative companies grow more than 'non-innovative', but in this case, a stronger positive effect of innovation is found in small firms. One possible reason for the inconclusive relationship between innovation and firm growth in the small firms can rely on the fact that many SMEs under-report their innovation activities (Saridakis, Idris, Hansen, & Dana, 2019).

Concerning export activities, there are also some risks linked to expanding into international markets, especially for financially constrained firms, which is frequently the case with small to medium sized enterprises (SMEs). Thus, large firms have better access to financial and non-financial resources (Svetličič et al., 2007). Similarly, they are able to benefit of standardisation of products and services to a greater extent than small companies by reducing the production costs and having better performance (Bagheri, Mitchelmore, Bamiatzi, & Nikolopoulos, 2019; Reçica, Hashi, Jackson, & Krasniqi, 2019). In contrast, human resources of SMEs tend to have less managerial knowledge and experience of foreign markets (Taylor & Taylor, 2014). Smaller companies are also more affected by

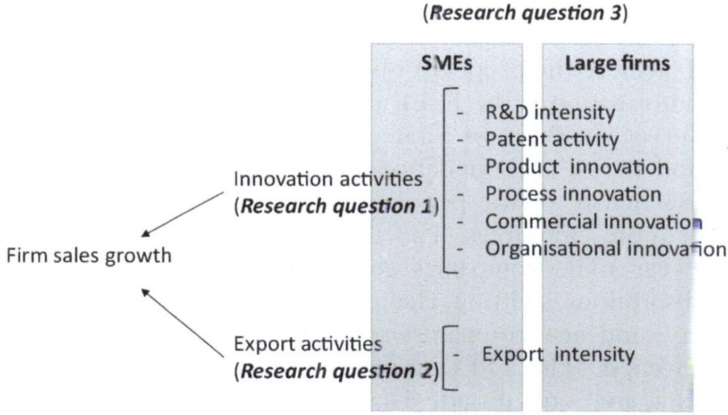

Fig. 2.1 Summary of research questions

the risk of export activities due to the relatively greater impact of failure compared to larger ones (Reçica et al. 2019; Svetličič et al., 2007). Nevertheless, the growth of the former benefits more from exporting than the growth of the latter. The underlying rationale for this higher benefit in terms of sales growth relies on the fact that large companies tend to be more diversified than small ones, that is, a greater share of their sales is already dependant on economies suffering low growth rates sometimes, so their growth could be hampered (Coad, 2009). Additionally, small companies benefit from higher speed of decision-making (Svetličič et al., 2007) compared to large ones due to the lack the agility to adapt to market changes of the latter (Bagheri et al., 2019).

To summarise, we tackle these issues in this chapter (Fig. 2.1): (1) whether innovation affects sales growth (Hypothesis 1); (2) whether export affects sales growth (Hypothesis 2) and (3) whether such effects depend on firm size.

2.3 Methodology

This section is dedicated to defining the sample and the variables used, as well as the strategy of estimation and the specification of the econometric models used in the multivariate analysis.

2.3.1 The Data and Sample

In order to achieve the proposed objectives, the dataset employed as the source of information is the ESEE (*Encuesta sobre Estrategias Empresariales*, or Survey on Business Strategies). Sponsored by the Ministry of Industry and the SEPI Foundation since 1990, the survey is designed to be representative of the population of Spanish manufacturing firms with 10 or more employees. The ESEE is an unbalanced panel, given that each year some companies cease providing information (due to mergers, absorptions, splitting, changes to non-industrial activity, or stopping activity) and new companies enter the survey in order to preserve representativeness. The ESEE contains accounting data, technological activities data, and foreign trade data, among others.

The original sample was formed of 5304 Spanish manufacturing companies observed over the period 2004–2014. However, 2037 firms were discarded because of the lack of data referring to innovation activities and sales. As a result, the final unbalanced study sample contained 20,244 observations corresponding to 3267 companies.

2.3.2 Definition and Measurements of the Variables

As mentioned, the dependent variable is annual growth rate of firms' sales. The growth rates are calculated in the usual way as the log-differences of size (Coad, 2009):

$$\text{Growth}_{i,t} = \ln\left(S_{i,t}\right) - \ln\left(S_{i,t-1}\right)$$

where $S_{i,t}$ and $S_{i,t-1}$ represent the deflated sales for the firm i in the period t and $t - 1$, respectively. The price effect on the measurement of the dependent variable was taken into account following Coad and Rao (2008). We used the gross domestic product (GDP) deflator based on 2010.

Concerning the independent variables, the main explanatory ones are those referring to firms' internationalisation and innovation activities. Whereas internationalisation activities are measured through the firm's export intensity (EXPORT_INT), six variables are used as a proxy for innovation activities. In so doing, a more complete view is offered of innovation activities carried out by firms. Moreover, as Saridakis et al. (2019) note, while most empirical studies measure innovation in terms of R&D,

patents and technological innovation, small firms are more likely to undertake a softer type of innovation. Hence, we consider the R&D intensity (R&D_INT), the patenting activity (PATENTS) and different kinds of innovation activity carried out by firms (product (PRODINN_D), process (PROCINN_D), commercial (COMINN_D), and organisational innovation (ORGINN_D). Whereas the first could be considered as an innovative input, the remaining have frequently been viewed as innovative outputs by the literature on innovation and firm growth.

Also, firm size is a key explanatory variable for the analysis, since one of the research questions addressed by this chapter is whether the effects of internationalisation and innovation activities depend on firm size. In this respect, the ESEE database comprises a random sample of small companies (with 10–200 employees) and an exhaustive sample (all firms are requested to participate) for large firms (with more than 200 employees). Based on this classification, the dummy variable EMP_D takes the value 1 for the latter group of firms (large firms) and 0 for the former one (SMEs).

In order to control for several aspects common in similar studies, we include additional explanatory variables: delayed sales growth, size, age, technological level, and legal form of firm, measured as shown in Table 2.1, are used as control variables.

2.3.3 Strategy of Estimation and Model Specification

The proposed model to analyse the links between exports and innovation activities and firm sales growth is the following:

$$GROWTH_{i,t} = \beta_1\ L.GROWTH_{i,t} + \beta_2\ L.LNTURNDEF_{i,t} + \beta_3\ EMP\_D_{i,t} + \beta_4\ AGE\_D_i + \beta_5\ HIGTHTECH\_D_i + \beta_6\ PUBLICLIAB\_D_i + \beta_7\ EXPORT\_INT_{i,t} + \beta_8\ R\&D\_INT_{i,t} + \beta_9\ PATENTS_{i,t} + \beta_{10}\ PRODINN\_D_{i,t} + \beta_{11}\ PROCINN\_D_{i,t} + \beta_{12}\ COMINN\_D_{i,t} + \beta_{13}\ ORGINN\_D_{i,t} + \alpha_i + \lambda_t + \varepsilon_{it}$$

where α_i is the individual effect or the time-invariant firm-specific fixed effect; λ_t measures the effects of macroeconomic variables that are common to all firms and that change over time by the time dummy variables; and ε_{it} is the random disturbance.

To estimate the proposed model, we use panel data methodology. Particularly, we estimate the models by applying the Arellano-Bond system GMM estimator (Arellano & Bond, 1991), and, more specifically, the user written command *xtabond2* for Stata (Roodman, 2006). Three

Table 2.1 Definitions of independent variables and predictions

Group	*Factor*	*Variable*	*Measures*
International activities	Exports intensity	EXPORT_INT	Export turnover/Total turnover
Innovation activities	R&D intensity	R&D_INT	R&D expenditure/Total turnover
	Patents	PATENTS	No. of patent applications and utility models
	Innovative outputs	PRODINN_D	1 if the firm has introduced product innovation and 0 otherwise
		PROCINN_D	1 if the firm has introduced process innovation and 0 otherwise
		COMINN_D	1 if the firm has introduced commercial innovation and 0 otherwise
		ORGINN_D	1 if the firm has introduced organisational innovation and 0 otherwise
Firm-specific characteristics (Controls)	Delayed growth	L.GROWTH	Annual growth rate of firms' sales delayed one year
	Size	L.LNTURNDEF	Natural logarithm of the deflated total turnover lagged one period
		EMP_D	1 for companies with more than 200 employees and 0 otherwise

(continued)

Table 2.1 (continued)

Group	*Factor*	*Variable*	*Measures*
	Age	AGE_D	1 if the firm was created before 1985 and 0 otherwise
	Technological level	HIGHTECH_D	1 for the firms in high-medium technology sectors according to the Eurostat classification[a] and 0 otherwise
	Legal form	PUBLICLIAB_D	1 for public limited liability companies and 0 for private limited liability

[a]Eurostat uses the aggregation of the manufacturing industry according to technological intensity and based on NACE Rev. 2 at two-digit level

issues were considered in making this choice. Firstly, unlike cross-sectional analysis, panel data allowed us to control the unobservable heterogeneity (α_i). Secondly, the dynamic panel data methodology allows us to deal with the endogeneity problem. The endogeneity problem is likely to arise since the dependent variable (firm sales growth) might also explain some independent variables in the model (innovation, for example). Thirdly, it also allows to consider the delayed dependent variable (L.GROWTH) in the right-hand side of the equation. In so doing, the possible serial correlation is taken into account (Colombelli et al., 2013; Geroski et al., 1997), since the firm's future growth could be explained in part by the current level of growth.

2.4 Empirical Results

2.4.1 Univariate Analysis

Table 2.2 reports the summary statistics of dependent and independent variables.

The average sales of sampled companies over the period of analysis is 69 million euros, with an average negative annual growth rate of –2.7%. Therefore, in average terms, the sales of Spanish manufacturing firms have experienced significant decline throughout the decade considered. Going

Table 2.2 Descriptive statistics for the dependent and independent variables

Variable	*Obs.*	*Mean*	*Std. Dev.*	*Min.*	*Max.*
SALES[a,b]	20,244	6.92e+07	3.30e+08	5389	7.62e+09
GROWTH[c]	16,974	−0.027	0.296	−3.976	7.866
EXPORT_INT	20,220	0.216	0.284	0	1
R&D_INT	20,181	0.008	0.092	0	12.412
PATENTS	20,235	0.511	6.415	0	314
PRODINN_D	20,244	0.190	0.392	0	1
PROCINN_D	20,244	0.319	0.466	0	1
COMINN_D	14,936	0.195	0.396	0	1
ORGINN_D	14,936	0.219	0.414	0	1
EMPLOYEES [d]	20,244	213.036	703.562	1	14.400
AGE_D	20,244	0.495	0.500	0	1
HIGHTECH_D	20,244	0.356	0.479	0	1
PUBLICLIAB_D	20,244	0.529	0.499	0	1

Notes [a]In euros, [b]Not deflated, [c]Not in logs, [d]Number of people

deeper in the analysis of sales growth, Fig. 2.2 shows its evolution over the period 2004–2014.

With regard to international activities developed by the sampled firms, Table 2.2 shows that, in mean terms, exports account for 21.60% of sales over the period 2004–2014. Concerning innovation activities, the

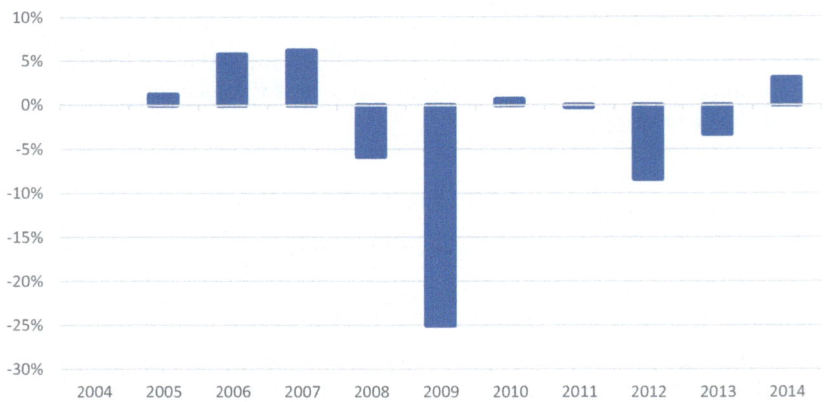

Fig. 2.2 Evolution of the average annual growth rates (2004–2014)

Table 2.3 Correlation matrix

	GROWTH	*R&D_INT*	*PATENTS*	*EXPORTS_INT*
GROWTH	1			
R&D_INT	−0.0383*	1		
PATENTS	0.0161*	0.0458*	1	
EXPORTS_INT	0.0739*	0.0405*	0.0361*	1

Note This table shows the Pearson correlation coefficients for the continuous variables considered in the empirical analysis. $*p < 0.05$, $**p < 0.01$, $***p < 0.001$

R&D intensity indicates that R&D expenditure accounts for 0.80% of turnover and the average number of patent applications is 0.5. Regarding the different types of innovation, Table 2.2 shows that the percentage of innovative companies in product innovation is about 19%. For process innovation, the results are a bit higher, with a percentage of innovators near to 32%. In turn, commercial and organisational innovators account for 19.5 and 21.9% of firms, respectively.

In Table 2.2 it can also be observed that almost half of the companies in the sample were started from 1986 onwards, 35.6% operate in the medium to high technology sectors, and nearly 53% are public limited liability companies. Additionally, the figures show that the mean number of employees is 213, in spite of the fact that over 78% of the sampled firms could be considered an SME (with less than or equal to 200 employees).

Finally, Table 2.3 shows the correlation matrix for the dependent variable and the independent continuous variables considered in the empirical analysis.

2.4.2 *Multivariate Analysis*

Table 2.4 presents the results of the GMM estimations of the sales growth for the complete sample and for both subsamples resulted in dividing the full sample by firm' size (EMP_D): SMEs subsample and large companies subsample.[1]

[1] To provide greater robustness to the estimates obtained through GMM, alternative estimates were made using the random effects (RE) estimators, the results obtained were qualitatively similar to those obtained with GMM.

Table 2.4 Estimation of the sales growth: GMM

	Full sample	*Small companies*	*Large companies*
EXPORT_INT	0.213***	0.272***	0.060
	(0.053)	(0.054)	(0.061)
R&D_INT	−0.698	−0.662	−0.337
	(0.424)	(0.358)	(0.528)
PATENTS	0.001*	0.002	0.001*
	(0.000)	(0.002)	(0.001)
PRODINN_D	−0.005	0.024	−0.006
	(0.015)	(0.020)	(0.021)
PROCINN_D	0.058***	0.043**	0.035*
	(0.013)	(0.016)	(0.018)
COMINN_D	0.020	0.033	0.010
	(0.015)	(0.020)	(0.023)
ORGINN_D	0.005	0.027	0.014
	(0.015)	(0.020)	(0.018)
L.GROWTH	0.047	−0.069	0.041
	(0.032)	(0.038)	(0.063)
L.LNTURNDEF	0.005	0.043***	−0.052**
	(0.010)	(0.012)	(0.018)
EMP_D	−0.003		
	(0.003)		
AGE_D	0.001	0.002	−0.000
	(0.001)	(0.001)	(0.002)
HIGTHTECH_D	−0.003*	−0.005***	0.003
	(0.001)	(0.002)	(0.002)
PUBLICLIAB_D	−0.003*	−0.008***	−0.000
	(0.001)	(0.002)	(0.002)
CONS	0.000	−0.655***	0.985**
Year dummies	Yes	Yes	Yes
No. of observations	12,766	9600	2889
No. of firms	2629	2129	612
No. of instruments	180	188	186
F test	31.78***	23.06***	12.33***
AR(1) test	−12.21***	−9.65***	−5.11***
AR(2) test	−1.450	−2.800**	−0.940

Note Corrected standard errors (Windmeijer, 2005) are presented in parentheses. *$p < 0.05$; **$p < 0.01$; *** $p < 0.001$ In all models the absence of second-order serial correlation (AR (2) test) is accepted, except the model related to sales in small companies

A positive effect of patents (PATENTS) and process innovation (PROCINN_D) on firm growth has been found, validating Hypothesis 1. However, R&D intensity (R&D_INT), product innovations (PRODINN_D), commercial innovations (COMINN_D) and organisational innovations (ORGINN_D) seem to have no influence on business growth. These results indicate that only some innovation activities play a key role in enhancing firm growth. More specifically, process innovation s require companies to apply technology to a reduction in the cost of producing existing products, and product innovations require that firms study customer needs and then design and manufacture a product for them (Ettlie, Bridges, & O'Keefe, 1984). In turn, patents also reflect innovative outputs that are legally protected and give rights to the use of an invention, which can be used as advantage for the companies, even if there is no conclusive result in the empirical studies (Hall & Harhoff, 2012). In any case, previous findings stress the idea that the effect of innovation on growth differs in terms of economic significance, depending on the different measures of innovation activities undertaken (Coad, 2009; Coad and Rao, 2008; Nogueira et al., 2019; Romano, 2019; Spescha & Woerter, 2019).

The company's export intensity (EXPORT_INT) positively influences its growth, confirming Hypothesis 2. These results are similar to those of Filatotchev and Piesse (2009), Geroski (1995), Hölzl (2009), Requena Silvente (2005), Robson and Bennett (2000), Roper (1997), and Wakelin (2001): the higher the export intensity of firm, the higher its sales growth. Moreover, consistently with Fuertes-Callén and Cuellar-Fernández (2019), the estimates suggest that exporting was the strategy that enabled the growth of the Spanish manufacturing firms in the aftermaths of the great recession.

In order to test whether the obtained effects of innovation and exporting depend on firm size, the proposed model was run for the subsamples of SMEs and large firms. Whereas process innovation positively affects sales growth regardless of firm size, patents are positively associated with growth in large firms. Patents involve substantial short-term costs which cannot be afforded by those with less access to financial resources, such as small entrepreneurial firms (Hall & Harhoff, 2012). In contrast, exporting intensity is positively associated with sales growth only in the sample of SMEs. Coad (2009) gives a potential explanation in the fact that larger firms are more present in international markets and so the greater market share includes also areas with low potential growth; SMEs can instead focus on areas with high potential.

As for the rest of the determinants of growth, the previous estimates also reveal other important findings. Whereas delayed sales (L.LNTURNDEF) fail to be significant for the whole sample, they show significant effects when the model is run for the subsamples. Thus, lagged sales are positively related to present sales growth in SME, while the opposite is found in large firms. These results suggest that SMEs grow more than large companies, rejecting Gibrat's Law (1931).

Concerning the technological level of the sector (HIGHTECH_D), the estimated coefficients indicate that the medium-high technology sectors negatively influence sales growth. This negative relationship holds for SMEs. The underlying rationale for this effect may rely on the fact that firms operating in these industries need significant funds to grow, when SMEs are financially constrained firms (Svetličič et al., 2007).

The results also indicate that being a public limited company has a significant and negative influence on sales growth, especially in SMEs. In this sense, our results coincide with those obtained by Calvo (2006), which also referred to Spanish companies. One possible reason for this result can be that, in SMEs, the amount of funds required to create a public limited company represents a higher cost compared to that of the large firms in relative terms, and therefore this cost hampers the growth possibilities of the former.

Finally, the lagged growth (L.GROWTH) factor that we have used to test the possible existence of serial correlation, does not show any influence on sales growth. This result would indicate that the growth in the previous year does not influence the growth in the current year in terms of sales. Similarly, firm age fails to be significant in the estimated models. This may be because as defined by the age variable, does not allow discrimination between very young companies and mature companies. Although 49.39% of the companies in the sample would have been established after 1986, this still does not allow differentiating between companies younger than 10 or five years since we are working with an age range that goes from one to 30 years.

2.5 Conclusions

In developed economies, innovative firms have become the cornerstone of public policies aimed at fostering sustained regional growth. Similarly, after the economic downturn of 2007, export activities have been stressed as a key vehicle to counterbalance the drop in the demand of domestic markets. Thus, the overall ambition of this chapter has been to advance the debate on how innovation and export strategies shape sales growth, conditioned by the firm size.

To do so, a sample of 3267 Spanish manufacturing firms over the period 2004–2014 have been analysed. After applying dynamic panel methodology and controlling for several factors, the key findings indicate that process innovation increases firm sales growth regardless of firm size, whereas innovation through patents enables sales growth only in large firms. In turn, exporting is positively associated with sales growth in SMEs. This evidence puts forward that future work on the growth-innovation relationship needs to simultaneously consider firm size, exports and the different types of innovation activities developed by the firm.

The key findings of the analysis have interesting managerial and policy implications. Firstly, overall sales growth benefits from process innovation, regardless of firm size. Process innovation tends to be more difficult to imitate than product innovation, providing companies with a sustainable strategy to grow (Fernández-López, Nogueira-Moreiras, Rodeiro-Pazos, & Rodríguez-Gulías, 2020). Therefore, firms should persist in implementing process innovation activities. This recommendation is in line with the arguments of Freeman, Clark, and Soete (1982), who note that, in challenging situations, such as the economic crises experienced by our sample companies over the period of analysis, firms become more risk-averse and need a whole system around them to be able to innovate. In these circumstances, they prioritise process rather than product innovation. Moreover, in downturns, cost-cutting processes are triggered by the need to adapt to the threats in the environment (González, 2018). Secondly, the considerable effort in terms of time and financial resource needed to create patents reduces the success of this innovation activity to the large firms. Therefore, from a micro-level perspective, we recommend patenting only if the firm expects high growth rates and has enough resources available. Thirdly, exporting is a successful strategy to foster sales growth in SMEs. Moreover, the estimate coefficients indicate that SMEs should prioritise exporting rather than process innovation.

From a policy point of view, governments must boost innovation, as well as increase export activities in order to foster regional growth and competitiveness in a sustainable way. Moreover, previous findings also stress where public interventions should put the emphasis. Large companies need to be supported with patent creation and SMEs in selling to international markets. Particularly, in the case of SMEs, export support programmes providing technical assistance that accompanies the firm through the different stages of the export process have proved to be effective (Garone, Bernini, Castillo, & Maffioli, 2017). Additionally, policymakers can apply some policies to improve the environment for the successful process innovation, such as tax incentives and support with tariff and no-tariff export barriers. With this support, SMEs can mitigate against their limited resources, insufficient managerial knowhow and liquidity constraints.

This research contributes to the literature along three dimensions. Firstly, it enriches the strand of the literature on the export and innovation activities and firm performance by putting the emphasis on the role played by firm size. To the date, sparse attention has been paid to the performance implications of the internationalisation strategy in the small firms (Bagheri et al., 2019) Secondly, the use of a wide set of measures of the firm's innovation activities helps understand which type of innovation has positive effects on firm sales growth according to firm size. Thirdly, the characteristics of Spain and the period of analysis allow the current study to provide useful suggestions for small and large firms that run business in a moderate innovator and exporting country and have to choose between growth-enhancing strategies due to financial constraints.

Finally, some limitations of this study that can open the door for further research are the availability of information, limited to ESEE. In particular, firm age was only measured by a dummy variable which prevents us from analysing the case of young companies. A continuous variable should be used in future research for a better understanding. Furthermore, we are not able to have a continuous variable for employees, 200 employees being the threshold of SMEs, which does not correspond exactly with the EU definition of SMEs. Finally, a vast literature on the topic has explored the joint effect of export and innovation activities on firm growth. Further research would benefit from considering this joint effect as well as the firm size simultaneously.

References

Aghion, P., & Howitt, P. (1992). A model of growth through creative destruction. *Econometrica, 60,* 323–351.

Arellano, M., & Bond, S. (1991). Some tests of specification for panel data: Monte Carlo evidence and an application to employment equations. *The Review of Economic Studies, 58*(2), 277–297.

Bagheri, M., Mitchelmore, S., Bamiatzi, V., & Nikolopoulos, K. (2019). Internationalization orientation in SMEs: The mediating role of technological innovation. *Journal of International Management, 25*(1), 121–139

Becchetti, L., & Trovato, G. (2002). The determinants of growth for small and medium sized firms: The role of the availability of external finance. *Small Business Economics, 19*(4), 291–306.

Bianchini, S., Pellegrino, G., & Tamagni, F. (2015). Innovation strategies and firm growth: New longitudinal evidence from Spanish firms. *DRUID Conference*. 15–17 June 2015, Rome.

Bottazzi, G., Dosi, G., Lippi, M., Pammolli, F , & Riccaboni, M. (2001). Innovation and corporate growth in the evolution of the drug industry. *International Journal of Industrial Organization, 19*, 1161–1187.

Calvo, J. (2006). Testing Gibrat's law for small, young and innovating firms. *Small Business Economics, 26*, 117–123.

Cassia, L., Colombelli, A., & Paleari, S. (2009). Firms' growth: Does the innovation system matter? *Structural Change and Economic Dynamics, 20*(3), 211–220.

Chen, X., Zou, H., & Wang, D. T. (2009). How do new ventures grow? Firm capabilities, growth strategies and performance. *International Journal of Research in Marketing, 26*(4), 294–303.

Coad, A. (2009). *The growth of firms: A survey of theories and empirical evidence*. Cheltenham, UK: Edward Elgar Publishing.

Coad, A., & Rao, R. (2008). Innovation and firm growth in high-tech sectors: A quantile regression approach. *Research Policy, 37*(4), 633–648.

Coad, A., Segarra, A., & Teruel, M. (2016). Innovation and firm growth: Does firm age play a role? *Research Policy, 45*(2), 387–400.

Colombelli, A., Haned, N., & Le Bas, C. (2013). On firm growth and innovation: Some new empirical perspectives using French CIS (1992–2004). *Structural Change and Economic Dynamics, 26*, 14–26.

Corsino, M. (2008). *Product innovation and growth: The case of integrated circuits*. Laboratory of Economics and Management, Sant'Anna School of Advanced Studies Working Paper Series.

Corsino, M., & Gabriele, R. (2010). Product innovation and firm growth: Evidence from the integrated circuits industry. *Industrial and Corporate Change, 20*, 29–56.

COTEC. (2017). *Informe COTEC*. Madrid: Fundación COTEC para la innovación tecnológica.

Cucculelli, M., & Ermini, B. (2012). New product introduction and product tenure: What effects on firm growth? *Research Policy, 41*(5), 808–821.

Czarnitzki, D., & Delanote, J. (2013). Young innovative companies: The new high-growth firms? *Industrial and Corporate Change, 22*(5), 1315–1340.
Demirel, P., & Mazzucato, M. (2012). Innovation and firm growth: Is R&D worth it? *Industry and Innovation, 19*(1), 45–62.
Di Cintio, M., Ghosh, S., & Grassia, E. (2017). Firm growth, R&D expenditures and exports: An empirical analysis of Italian SMEs. *Research Policy, 46*(4), 836–852.
Dones Tacero, M., Heredero de Pablos, M. I., & Ruesga Benito, S. M. (2017). Exports and employment in the Spanish economy: A repetitive pattern. *Investigación Económica, 76*(301), 137–169.
Du, J., & Temouri, Y. (2011, March 26–28). Internationalisation and high growth firms: The OECD experience. In *International Conference on Information Management, Technical Management and Intelligent Technology* (ICITI). Hong Kong.
Durán, J. J. (2014). La empresa internacional de origen español en la crisis in N. E. García. In S. M. Ruesga (Ed.), *¿Qué ha pasado con la economía española? La Gran Recesión 2.0 (2008–2013)* (pp. 187–206). Madrid: Pirámide.
Ericson, R., & Pakes, A. (1995). Markov-perfect industry dynamics: A framework for empirical work. *The Review of Economic Studies, 62*(1), 53–82.
Ettlie, J. E., Bridges, W. P., & O'Keefe, R. D. (1984). Organization strategy and structural differences for radical versus incremental innovation. *Management Science, 30,* 682–695.
European Commission. (2014). Investments for jobs and growth, promoting development and good governance in EU regions and cities. In *Sixth Report on Economic, Social and Territorial Cohesion*. Luxembourg: Publications Office of the European Union.
Eurostat. (2018). *Community Innovation Survey. Science and Technology, Enterprises by Main Types of Innovation, NACE Rev. 2 Activity and Size Class*. http://ec.europa.eu/eurostat/en/web/products-datasets/-/INN_CIS9_TYPE. Accessed 15 July 2018.
Falk, M. (2012). Quantile estimates of the impact of R&D intensity on firm performance. *Small Business Economics, 39*(1), 19–37.
Falk, M., & Hagsten, E. (2018). An exploration of growth in computer software micro firms. *Journal of Small Business & Entrepreneurship, 30*(3), 233–252.
Fernández-López, S., Nogueira-Moreiras, M. A., Rodeiro-Pazos, D., & Rodríguez-Gulías, M. J., (2020). Exports and firm growth: The moderating effect of innovation. *European Journal of International Management*. Paper in press. https://doi.org/10.1504/EJIM.2020.10025654.
Filatotchev, I., & Piesse, J. (2009). R&D, internationalization and growth of newly listed firms: European evidence. *Journal of International Business Studies, 40*(8), 1260–1276.

Freel, M. (2000). Do small innovating firms outperform non-innovators? *Small Business Economics, 14,* 195–210.

Freel, M., & Robson, P. (2004). Small firm innovation, growth and performance: Evidence from Scotland and northern England. *International Small Business Journal, 22*(6), 561–575.

Freeman, C., Clark, J., & Soete, L. (1982). *Unemployment and technical innovation: A study of long waves and economic development*. London: Burns & Oates.

Fuertes-Callén, Y., & Cuellar-Fernández, B. (2019). Inter-relationship between firm growth and profitability in a context of economic crisis. *Journal of Business Economics and Management, 20*(1), 86–106.

Garone, L. F., Bernini, F., Castillo, V., & Maffioli, A. (2017). *Supporting SMEs to export: The importance of the dynamics and sequence of the effects*. Lacer. Lacea. Org.

Geroski, P. (1995). What do we know about entry? *International Journal of Industrial Organization, 13*(4), 421–440.

Geroski, P. (1999). *The growth of firms in theory and in practice* (Centre for Economic and Policy Research, 2092). London: Centre for Economic and Policy Research.

Geroski, P. A., Machin, S. J., & Walters, C. F. (1997). Corporate growth and profitability. *The Journal of Industrial Economics, 45*(2), 171–189.

Gibrat, R. (1931). *Les inégalités économiques. Applications: aux inégalités des richesses, à la concentration des entreprises, aux populations des villes, aux statistiques des familles, etc. d'une loi nouvelle: la loi de l'effet proportionnel*. Paris: Librairie du Recueil Sirey.

González, J. S. (2018). Cost-cutting as an innovation driver among suppliers during an industry downturn. In T. Thune, O. A. Engen, & O. Wicken (Eds.), *Petroleum industry transformations* (pp. 70–83). New York: Routledge.

Grabowski, H., Vernon, J., & DiMasi, J. A. (2002). Returns on research and development for 1990s new drug introductions. *Pharmacoeconomics, 20*(3), 11–29.

Hall, B. H., Griliches, Z., & Hausman, J. A. (1984). Patents and R&D: Is there a lag? *International Economic Review, 27*(2), 265–283.

Hall, B. H., & Harhoff, D. (2012). Recent Research on the Economics of Patents. *Annual Review of Economics, 4*(1), 541–565.

Hernández, H., Grassano, N., Tübke, A., Potters, L., Amoroso, S., Dosso, M., ... Vezzani, A. (2018). *The 2016 EU Industrial R&D Investment Scoreboard (No. JRC108520)*, Joint Research Centre, Seville.

Hernandez, V., & Nieto, M. J. (2016). Inward-outward connections and their impact on firm growth. *International Business Review, 25*(1), 296–306.

Hölzl, W. (2009). Is the R&D behaviour of fast-growing SMEs different? Evidence from CIS III data for 16 countries. *Small Business Economy, 33*(1), 59–75.

Klette, T. J., & Griliches, Z. (2000). Empirical patterns of firm growth and R&D investment: A quality ladder model interpretation. *The Economic Journal, 110*(463), 363–387.

Lu, J. W., & Beamish, P. W. (2001). The internationalization and performance of SMEs. *Strategic Management Journal, 22*(6–7), 565–586.

Lu, J. W., & Beamish, P. W. (2006). SME internationalization and performance: Growth vs. profitability. *Journal of International Entrepreneurship, 4*(1), 27–48.

Lucas, R. E., Jr. (1978). On the size distribution of business firms. *The Bell Journal of Economics, 9*(2), 508–523.

Mazzucato, M., & Parris, S. (2015). High-growth firms in changing competitive environments: The US pharmaceutical industry (1963 to 2002). *Small Business Economics, 44*(1), 145–170.

Mora Sanguinetti, J., & Fuentes, A. (2012). *An analysis of productivity performance in Spain before and during the crisis: Exploring the role of institutions* (OECD Economics Department Working Paper, 973).

Na, K., & Kang, Y. H. (2019). Relations between innovation and firm performance of manufacturing firms in southeast asian emerging markets: Empirical evidence from Indonesia, Malaysia, and Vietnam. *Journal of Open Innovation: Technology, Market, and Complexity, 5*(4), 98.

Nogueira, M. A., Fernández-López, S., Rodríguez-Gulías, M. J., Vivel-Bua, M., & Rodeiro-Pazos, D. (2019). The hidden effect of innovation on the growth of Spanish firms. *International Journal of Entrepreneurship and Small Business, 37*(2), 167–189.

Pakes, A., & Ericson, R. (1998). Empirical implications of alternative models of firm dynamics. *Journal of Economic Theory, 79*(1), 1–45.

Pangarkar, N. (2008). Internationalization and performance of small and medium-sized enterprises. *Journal of World Business, 43*, 475–485.

Park, K., & Jang, S. S. (2010). Firm growth patterns: Examining the associations with firm size and internationalization. *International Journal of Hospitality Management, 29*(3), 368–377.

Penrose, E. T. (1959). *The theory of the growth of the firm*. New York: Sharpe.

Reçica, F., Hashi, I., Jackson, I., & Krasniqi, B. A. (2019). Innovation and the export performance of firms in transition economies: The relevance of the business environment and the stage of transition. *International Journal of Entrepreneurship and Small Business, 38*(4), 476–506.

Requena Silvente, F. (2005). Changing export status and firm performance: Evidence from UK small firms. *Applied Economics Letters, 12*(9), 567–571.

Robson, P. J., & Bennett, R. J. (2000). SME growth: The relationship with business advice and external collaboration. *Small Business Economics, 15*(3), 193–208.

Romano, L. (2019). Explaining growth differences across firms: The interplay between innovation and management practices. *Structural Change and Economic Dynamics, 49*, 130–145.

Roodman, D. (2006). *How to do xtabond2: An introduction to difference and system GMM in Stata* (Center for Global Development Working Paper, 103).

Roper, S. (1997). Product innovation and small business growth: A comparison of the strategies of German, UK and Irish companies. *Small Business Economics, 9*, 523–537.

Saridakis, G., Idris, B., Hansen, J. M., & Dana, L. P. (2019). SMEs' internationalisation: When does innovation matter? *Journal of Business Research, 96*, 250–263.

Segarra, A., & Teruel, M. (2014). High-growth firms and innovation: An empirical analysis for Spanish firms. *Small Business Economics, 43*(4), 805–821.

Shrader, R. C., Oviatt, B. M., & McDougall, P. P. (2000). How new ventures exploit trade-offs among international risk factors: Lessons for the accelerated internationalization of the 21st century. *Academy of Management Journal, 43*(6), 1227–1247.

Spescha, A., & Woerter, M. (2019). Innovation and firm growth over the business cycle. *Industry and Innovation, 26*(3), 321–347.

Svetličič, M., Jaklič, A., & Burger, A. (2007). Internationalization of small and medium-size enterprises from selected central European economies. *Eastern European Economics, 45*(4), 36–65.

Taylor, A., & Taylor, M. (2014). Factors influencing effective implementation of performance measurement systems in small and medium-sized enterprises and large firms: A perspective from Contingency Theory. *International Journal of Production Research, 52*(3), 847–866.

Variyam, J. N., & Kraybill, D. S. (1993). Small firms' choice of business strategies. *Southern Economic Journal, 60*(1), 136–145.

Wagner, J. (2007). Exports and productivity: A survey of the evidence from firm level data. *The World Economy, 30*(1), 60–82.

Wakelin, K. (2001). Productivity growth and R&D expenditure in UK manufacturing firms. *Research Policy, 30*, 1079–1090.

Windmeijer, F. (2005). A finite sample correction for the variance of linear efficient two-step GMM estimators. *Journal of Econometrics, 126*(1), 25–51.

CHAPTER 3

How Do Innovation, Technology, and Competitiveness Contribute to Business Growth

John McManus

3.1 Introduction

The late Professor Peter Drucker suggested there is only one valid definition of business purpose which is to create a customer and this is highly dependent on new innovation (Drucker, 1954). This statement is true today as it was sixty-five years ago and applies to both product and service industries. Post Drucker, other writers such as Kline and Rosenberg (1986), Bernstein and Singh (2006), Dereli (2015), and Moreira and Stramar (2015), have all put forward views on the importance of innovation in the support of marketing new products and developing new business.

Bernstein and Singh (2006) view the innovation process as a sequence of activities aimed at creation and implementation of innovation which needed to be managed and controlled. The "4Ps" model of innovation

J. McManus (✉)
Stoke-on-Trent, UK

J. J. M. Ferreira et al. (eds.), *Technological Innovation and International Competitiveness for Business Growth*, Palgrave Studies in Democracy, Innovation, and Entrepreneurship for Growth,
https://doi.org/10.1007/978-3-030-51995-7_3

developed by Tidd, Bessant, and Pavitt (2008) provides a useful framework, which consists of four forms of change: Product innovation regards new or changed products and services. Process innovation which reviews the way products and services are designed. Position innovation examines changes in consumer preferences in the way that products or services are introduced to the market. Paradigm innovation deals with the changes and formations upon which a business is built.

For many businesses, innovation has been a source of economic growth and competitive advantage (Botten & McManus 1999). Whilst innovation provides the means to commercialise on new products and services, many businesses are turning to new technology as a means to reduce costs and increase productivity. New and emerging technologies have significantly influenced the way business is conducted particularly in those sectors which are associated with e-commerce. New and emerging technologies have not only provided the means to competitive advantage but have also changed the way in which business is conducted and paid for.

As we approach the third decade of this century, innovation and technological developments have become the "*pathway to change*" and *w*hilst academics argue over the specifics of each subject most agree that both have had positive effect on economic growth, employment, and the prosperity for the majority of people (Maleyeff, 2011). The "***next section***", explores the contribution innovation makes to business and wider society by examining Schumpeter's classical vision of the entrepreneur and the role such entrepreneurs play in the innovation process by contrasting Schumpeter's views of business growth with those of contemporary management approaches to creating new business opportunities.

3.2 Innovation the Pathway to Change

Whilst the concept of innovation is not new, its impact on business and society is profound (Huang & Rice, 2012, p. 1). Consider for instance the way advances in bio-sciences or Internet-enabled technologies have changed many people's lives. There are many ways to describe innovation. At a basic level it is: turning an idea into a solution that adds value to the consumer and wider society. In many respects, innovation is about transformation and change (it's not about invention).

The economist Joseph Schumpeter theory on innovation provides a construct for analysing economic outcomes. Schumpeter argued that capitalism can only be understood as an evolutionary process of continuous innovation and creative destruction. In Schumpeter's account, it is the entrepreneur who creates innovation. In this context, entrepreneurship is an endogenous response to opportunities provided by investments in new knowledge. The Schumpeterian entrepreneur driven by competition to improve technology, finance, and organisation does more than any other individual to fuel the spirit of economic growth. Schumpeter developed a two-stage model: the first approximation and second approximation in order to explain his business cycle theory of innovation. The first approximation lays emphasis on the primary impact of innovatory ideas. This includes all those activities which reduce the overall cost of production such as the introduction of new methods of production, the introduction of new technology, and innovative methods of systematising the industry. The secondary approximation deals with the subsequent responses obtained from the application of the innovations. This includes all such activities which increase the demand for a product, the introduction of a new commodity, service, or the emergence or opening of a new market, finding new sources of raw material, or a new variety or a design of the product. Schumpeter's theory of innovation is widely acceptable in the modern economy and is used to establish likely fluctuations in economic activity.

It is not by accident that Schumpeterian ideas on innovation, entrepreneurship, and business strategy form the very heart of modern business. With hundreds of theories, business managers are often overwhelmed with advice and rhetoric on how to deal with the challenges they face, in large part because they sometimes have proven too difficult to formalise. Framing the challenges correctly is a critical key to understanding where the business is heading. Having a viable business model which incorporates innovation is essential to sustainable growth. Management which wishes to build an organisation that innovates consistently must provide to its workers: freedom, resources, diversity, support, encouragement, and challenge.

Successful innovation practice is based on organised and efficient management (Abidin, Mokhtar, & Yusoff, 2011; Botten & McManus, 1999; Chesbrough, 2006). What this means is taking a holistic approach to innovation which incorporates the many interrelated political, economic, social, and technological facets of the business and the markets it operates within. From a strategic perspective, the approach should be to push the boundaries of what is possible and provide employees and other stakeholders with an engaging environment, which is underpinned by knowledge, discipline, but also driven by consumer value for money. The greater the value, the more sustainable the innovation will be to a consumer. As Steve Jobs, (of Apple) put it, "to turn really interesting ideas and fledgling technologies into a company that can continue to innovate for years, it requires a lot of discipline". Ultimately, the way we think about innovation and business innovation is changing rapidly. A key measure of innovation is "time to market", which is driven by the firm's strategy and market conditions whether local, regional, or global. There is, however, a substantial difference in scale and investment needed to launch any new product or service in each of these markets.

The author Henry Chesbrough argued that companies should organise their innovation processes to become more open to external knowledge and ideas. He also suggested that companies let more of their internal ideas and knowledge flow outside when those ideas and knowledge are not being used within the company (Chesbrough, 2006, p. 21). On the face of it, Chesbrough logic seems reasonable, however, firms are generally in competition with one another and sharing intellectual property, knowledge, and ideas carries legal and commercial risks both for the provider and for the recipient. For some firms, a strategic discussion on sharing intellectual property might start by determining the extent to which open innovation overlaps with their core objectives and how any obstacles and commercial risks might be overcome.

The competitive link between innovation, technology, and business growth is the central theme of this "***next section***". Globalisation is the glue which binds these three subjects together. As Johnson, Scholes, and Whittington (2005, p. 291) point out "*the globalisation of markets and competition*" can be seen as both cause and consequence of the internationalisation of individual organisations.

3.3 The World of Globalisation

There are a considerable number of points of view regarding what is meant by globalisation. In the twenty-first century globalisation has become the catalyst for transformational change in organisations, markets, financial institutions, and consumer behaviour (Lewis & Moore, 2009). In this context, the analysis of contemporary globalisation processes points to changes in the way businesses interact with consumer markets.

Business sectors benefit from globalisation and competitive innovation through reduced costs of product development, process improvement, accelerating the time to market for new products, improving product quality, increasing access to consumer and supplier expertise, and enhancing image and reputation. Whilst globalisation offers clear advantages there are downsides too. For instance, the most important source of competitive advantage is knowledge (both internal and external).

According to many published international consumer reports, customers are taking a more active role in what is termed the co-creation process. For instance, Johannessen and Olsen (2010) discuss the connected customer, which is a consumer who increasingly expects tailor-made products and services based on individualised and immediate needs. To meet these requirements organisations have become more agile and investment driven with improved provider-to-user supply chains. Shifting the focus from a large or mass consumer market to a market of one may reduce the firm's focus at the expense of its broader consumer markets which in turn may have a negative effect on long-term profits and shareholder value.

Globalisation is often associated with the free movement of people, capital, and goods. Business growth is predicated on all three The availability of capital and human capital (people) in many ways determines how quickly a firm can enhance its position in the market place. The availability of skilled people is one of the main drivers for firms to enter new markets. Human capital has also been highlighted as being a factor in whether a business is entrepreneurial and innovative. Fritsch and Schindele (2011) argue that an educated workforce with a strong endowment of skills and wide availability of labour is positively related to the contribution of new businesses and to national and regional employment.

Globalisation has led many firms to refocus their strategies away from short-term profits to more long-term initiatives. Firm size is no longer a guarantee for success. In this context, Small Medium Enterprises (SMEs) today account for a significant proportion Gross Domestic Product (GDP) in many emerging economies. For example, SMEs in Southeast Asian are estimated to comprise over 90% of the total number of enterprises, and they contribute to around 40% of GDP. Similarly, in the United Kingdom SMEs account for 70% of employment (OECD, 2017, p. 6). The largest of the service industries in terms of the number of businesses are professional, scientific, and technical industries which account for one-sixth of businesses. Comparable statistics can also be found for the United States and some countries in Western Europe.

The global growth in SMEs is partly attributed to a mobile and educated workforce who does not see national boundaries as a barrier to progression. Many SMEs have seen location as a means of taking advantage of capital resources. For example, technology start-ups often cluster in similar locations such as Silicon Valley, California, USA. Clustering facilitates the exchange of personnel and diffusion of technology often creates new possibilities for efficiency gains. Importantly, these networks and the support systems they offer can help SMEs meet the challenges of globalisation.

Much of new business growth can be credited to Innovations in communication tools (e.g. Internet) which make it easier for small- and medium-sized firms to reach potential partners around the globe. As a result, SMEs have become more involved in international strategic alliances and joint ventures. Larger corporations are also partnering with smaller firms with technological advantages to economise on research and development, to minimise the lead times for new products, and serve new and emerging markets. Such benefits often outweigh the drawbacks which make alliances and joint ventures so attractive. Commercial risk means that one or both parties can ill afford to fail, once a contract is in place.

No firm has access to unlimited resources therefore management must use its resources to its best advantage. Focusing on where and what to invest in is a considerable challenge for management. Business growth is no longer predicated on cost advantage nor is it based on trying to replicate the competition's products. Instead, it is asserted on paying attention to the customer and to developing an equidistant view of who they are and what they want. Before all else, understanding and seeing your customer clearly is what matters for business growth. The strength of a global business is derived from its ability to understand local customers' needs, whilst at the same time, deploying global thinking to position resources and know-how on a global scale.

With more than half of the world's economies based on services (McManus, 2009) and the proliferation of new and emerging digital businesses, by and large, the majority of firms are increasingly reliant on information technology and information communication technologies. This "next section" explores the role of technology in business, specifically the role of information communication technologies (ICT) and their application to new and emerging business models such as those that link business directly to the consumer.

3.4 The Enabling World of Technology

As previously suggested within developed economies, the pursuit of business growth and the creation of new markets in the last three decades can largely be attributed to the growth in "new knowledge industries", especially those sectors related to the development and application of information and communication technology (ICT). ICT has overwhelmingly enabled many businesses to compete within different market sectors without paying huge entry costs at the same time reducing the marginal cost of doing business. Balancing the thrust of technology with market pull is a fundamental requirement for maintaining sustainable market advantage.

ICT firms are frequently associated with those that offer services which feed off creativity outputs from R&D and co-creation processes. Competition between ICT firms is on an international scale; therefore, the challenge is to find effective ways of recruiting talent and retaining it. Firms must continually invest substantially in continuing education and development if they wish to keep ahead of the competition and retain their employees.

ICT industries are frequently associated with those sectors that are heavily reliant on knowledge. A common characteristic of knowledge industries is the way they are structured, the formal command and control structures within hierarchical organisations to greater or lesser extent have been dismantled in favour flatter structures which enable one-to-one communication. In this context, the task of management is to do with enabling a working environment which channels effort into opportunities which directly contribute to the achievement of the firm's goals. In applying this process, management must take account of the preferred ways of working whilst providing a range of incentives to motivate the workforce.

As previously assumed, time is now a competitive weapon and the development of ICT technologies has enabled many firms to speed-up the transaction times between customer demand and firm supply. Integrated supply chains supported by technology systems such as Supply Chain Management (SCM), Decision Support Systems (DSS), and Enterprise Systems (ES) integration have all assisted in reducing operational costs.

The strategy towards computer-assisted technology and systems integration is no accident and firms wishing to do business have to integrate if they wish to share knowledge and information. Contemporary ICT systems have the means to capture, transmit, process, store, and retrieve information at significant speed and with great flexibility. In this sense, critical information between businesses can be forwarded to those who need or want the information within seconds.

ICT technologies (see definition), embrace technologies such as the Internet, and electronic interchange systems and platforms. These systems provide the means for products to be exchanged between businesses or sold directly to the final consumer, including increasingly products that can be packaged in digitised formats. The proliferations of Internet-based businesses have demonstrated significant growth in Business-to-Business (B2B), Business-to-Customer (B2C), and Cloud Computing applications. These new business applications are grounded in the way many online shopping and retail service providers undertake business transactions. The most noticeable impact here is on those firms whose business processes are concerned with the buying and selling of retail commodities such as Books, CDs, Games, Wine and spirits, and Toys.

The shift in momentum from B2B to B2C business models has afforded many Internet providers and suppliers to offer consumers attractive and competitive prices through discounts; enabled from lower costs of business administration. This consumer market, one with abundance of choice has forced many B2B firms to re-evaluate their offerings. In other words, cost and quality are no longer the main differentiators when it comes to selling goods and services. Firms such as Amazon, Alibaba, and eBay have expanded upon their success to become industry leaders in B2C provision.

An emerging technology of recent years Cloud Computing is rapidly gaining impetus. Cloud technology was described in a recent study as a significant disruptive technology, given its implications for markets, economies, and societies (Chaisiri, Lee, & Niyato, 2012; Manyika et al., 2013). McKinsey Global Institute has estimated that by 2025, cloud delivery of computing and Internet services would be a common phenomenon, with many organisational operations and processes being cloud-enabled. Although still in its formative years the term cloud computing is a popular business narrative for describing the way computing services are formulated for various business applications with minimal management effort or service provider interaction (Mell & Grance, 2011).

Many of the data-intensive applications are now deployed in the clouds. With growing demand for cloud services, its purpose is to ensure smooth interoperability between services providers regardless of the underlying infrastructure used. To take advantage of the cloud it is preferable to operate in communities where many firms associated with B2C have robust markets and predefined business objectives which satisfy this criterion. In the context of supply management and logistics, this means having the ability and potential to transform processes, customer relationships, and create added value. To illustrate the benefits of cloud computing, pharmaceutical giant Pfizer moved its supply chain operations into the cloud in 2012. Pfizer competes in two distinct market segments the patented and the generic drug markets. Whilst these are different consumer segments, both markets rely on supply chains which are optimal to their respective operating models for speed and agility. Pfizer's virtual cloud-based supply chain initiative required 500 of its suppliers to implement a cloud-based common information exchange framework on which each supplier was depicted as a node on this virtual supply chain. According to Pfizer's vice president, Jim Cafone, "moving to the cloud helped make the supply chain much faster when responding to unexpected events and everyday market pressures" (Taylor, 2012).

Cloud computing still faces some open challenges, but to provide better reliability, availability, cost efficiency, and quality of service, inter-cloud computing has already been envisioned. The next wave of business technology will likely use cloud technology to create and capture the value of big data and more diversified community of users participating in enabled cloud services. For instance, when customers use a particular travel site such as TripAdvisor, the site's platform can provide feedback on rates paid, journey length, and popularity of particular hotels, restaurants, and car-rental agencies all accessible from mobile apps.

Digitisation and connected intelligent systems are also making strides within commerce and industrial markets. Recent developments in both technologies have enabled firms such as General Electric (GE) to pair different technologies together to coin the term "digital twins" which in essence link the physical and digital worlds. In essence, the digital twin is an integration of technology, coupled with intelligent monitoring capabilities enabled through advance predictive algorithms (Pavlou & El Sawy,

2011). This method has been used to predict the future performance of assets through various simulating scenarios.

The meaning of competition is well documented within the literature on strategic management. David Teece for example highlights the need to identify specific capabilities which contribute to competitive advantage. The concept of dynamic capabilities, especially in terms of organisational knowledge processes, has become the predominant paradigm for the explanation of competitive advantages (Teece, 2014). The work by Michael Porter has become linked with the interpretation of different types of generic strategies (Porter, 1985). In this "*next section*", the meaning of competition will be explored together with why different strategies influence success or failure in the market place. The issue here lies in defining the market in which a firm competes in a way that gives economic importance to the firm.

3.5 The Meaning of Competitiveness

As technology, advances and the mix of capital and labour changes, national governments are asking questions about the future direction of their economies. Similarly, many firms are asking similar questions about how to compete in the digital age. Technological advances in the last decade have contributed to soaring world unemployment, advanced robotics, increasingly sophisticated algorithms, deep learning networks, exponential growth in computer processing power and bandwidth, and other technologies such as Artificial Intelligence and 3D Printing are all paving the way towards a highly automated society which may result in a whole generation of white collar jobs being superfluous.

Competing in the twenty-first century will be premised on a firm's ability to recruit talented human capital. Getting the right people into the organisation might become more important than capital. Teece (2014) argues the point that strategic capabilities linked to internal and external firm-specific competencies are essential to addressing changing market environments. Elements of Teece can be found in Schumpeter's teachings (1950). For many writers the fundamental question in the field of strategic management is how firms achieve and sustain competitive advantage. In the mid-1980s, Professor Michael Porter came up with a number of important ideas about how to run a business more efficiently and create a sustainable competitive advantage (Porter, 1985, 1990, 2001).

Porter's ideas were instrumental in changing the way firms viewed strategy and competition. Porter's principles on competitive advantage can be condensed into deciding where you want your business to go, and deciding how to get there. According to Porter, a firm's relative position within an industry is given by its choice of competitive advantage cost leadership versus differentiation and its options for competitive scope. Competitive scope distinguishes between firms targeting broad industry segments and firms focusing on a narrow segment. For a firm to be successful in its preferred business; competitive strategy must grow out of a sophisticated understanding of the rules of competition that determine an industry's attractiveness. Porter claims, the ultimate aim of competitive strategy is to cope with and, ideally, to change those rules in the firm's behaviour (1985, p. 4).

The publication of the article by Barney (1991) "*Firm resources and sustained competitive advantage*", argued that to have the potential to generate competitive advantage, a firm resource must have four attributes:

1. It must be valuable, in the sense that it exploits opportunities and/or neutralizes threats in a firm's environment.
2. It must be rare among a firm's current and potential competition.
3. It must be imperfectly imitable.
4. There cannot be strategically equivalent substitutes for this resource.

Elaborating a firm is said to have a competitive advantage when it is implementing a value-creating strategy which is not simultaneously being implemented by any current or potential competitors. Choosing a unique position is not enough to guarantee a sustainable advantage in the marketplace. A valuable position will attract imitation by incumbents, who are likely to copy it in a number of ways. For example:

- A competitor can reposition itself to match the superior performer. Apple, for instance, has been repositioning itself from away from its competitors who are cloning its technology and iPhone designs. Apple is increasing its investment in R&D and enforcing its IP licencing agreements as counter measures.
- A far more common type of imitation is straddling. The straddler seeks to match the benefits of a successful position whilst maintaining

its existing position. It grafts new features, services, or technologies onto the activities it already performs, again Apple's competitors such as Samsung and Huawei fall into this category.

This resource-based view is not without its critics. It has been criticised for showing evidence of circular reasoning in that one of its fundamental elements, value, can only be assessed in terms of a particular context. Whilst resources may lead to competitive advantage this in turn characterises relevant competitive structures, which in turn defines what is a valuable resource, and so on (Fahy, 2000).

When trying to determine the sources of competitive advantage in an industry, the firm should consider all the things which they may have in their favour, whether tangible or intangible assets. For a great many firms technology has been a game changer. Technology has opened up boundaries in terms of knowledge and resource sharing, to the extent that businesses have become increasingly adept at locating technology applications and assets around the world to give them an advantage in the marketplace. However, acquiring technological know-how may be difficult to acquire or even trade. For instance, transfer of knowledge within a firm tends to be easier than across markets. Sometimes firms choose not to patent technology discoveries, even when patents can be obtained. One reason is that they are required to register their findings at the patents office. Through registering, they reveal their knowledge and this is not always strategic or advantageous.

Large multinational corporations such as Exxon Mobil, Google, GE, Microsoft, Proctor & Gamble, and the Ford Motor Company often have business models which offer them advantages in the market place, such as distinct supply chains, Patents, or unique competencies which cannot be copied or exploited (Iyer & Davenport, 2008). One of the central tenants of competitive strategy is that of having unique competencies that affords your business some level of competitive advantage. Core competencies are sources of competitive advantage, are generally unique to the firm, and are deeply embedded in its DNA or patterns of behaviour. For example, knowledge and skills that take time and learning to evolve are not easily sold, exchanged, or imitated. They may however be shared through collaborative projects or joint R&D (Botten & McManus, 1999, p. 98). Collaboration is seen by many CEOs as the new way to create growth and increase shareholder value.

As the requirement for business to cooperate more closely continues to grow, who better to learn about collaboration from than people who rely on sharing resources across the globe to create new business opportunities. Prahalad and Hamel (1990) have argued that shared core competencies are the bases on which to build collaborative strategies. The authors suggest that competence has three different dimensions, functionality, market access, and product integrity plus the understanding that a core competency can be contained in any one of these dimensions. A point worth noting is core competence does not diminish with use (Prahalad & Hamel, 1990). In contrast to physical assets, which do deteriorate over time, competencies are enhanced as they are applied and shared. However, competencies still need to be nurtured and protected; knowledge fades if it is not used (De Pablos, 2006).

Whilst firm strategy, is the basic approach towards achieving its competitive objectives. It is the careful, deliberate, and systematic approach to consumers and the market together with the quality of executive decision-making which influences the growth of the firm and subsequent profits. In this "final section" an exploration of the forces which drive business growth is considered. Attention will be given to the size of the firm (large SMEs), technology, and capital integration and how transaction in business influences business costs.

3.6 The Case for Business Growth

As markets change, so does the relationship between business and consumers, in ways which have significant implications for future business growth and profits. If we accept Peter Drucker (1954) hypothesis that there is only one valid definition of business purpose which is to create a customer. Any business enterprise then has two and only two functions marketing and innovation. The general ethos of this hypothesis requires that all innovations be thought of as intended to acquire and retain customers in short, to make the firm profitable and competitive.

There is considerable agreement between government policy makers and academics that the last two decades of the twenty-first century have been characterized by far-reaching, or even radical, change in the sphere of work, employment, and competition. In the discourse of current and future business growth, a number of related elements can be examined. These include:

- The growth in SMEs.
- The availability of capital.
- The reduction in transaction costs.

Access to new and emerging technologies has given rise to the expansion of SMEs in all sectors of business. As previously noted SMEs now contribute more to national GDP and by explanation collectively employ a considerable number of specialists and highly skilled workers. In high technology sectors such as aerospace, defence, and Bio-pharmaceutical, large companies work with innovative SMEs to test new research and technologies in real-world applications. These collaborations help pull innovations through to market and drive growth across large and small companies.

The agility and flexibility, which SMEs are striving for, is in fact resulting in a business reorientation, where complex and noncomplex tasks are performed by more university graduates for corresponding rewards. SMEs account for a high percentage of manufacturing firms in many OECD countries and provide at least half of OECD manufacturing employment. Smaller firms are increasingly present in technology-intensive industries such as information and communications technology (ICT) and biotechnology (OECD, 2017, p. 7).

The emphasis on European universities to recruit individuals into STEM subjects as given rise to an upsurge in **science, technology, and engineering-related businesses within many OECD countries**. Long-term employment trends suggest a considerable process of diffusion is taking place within many sectors of industry. OECD also highlights the importance of technology for business growth. It is therefore essential that businesses are given the right technological support, tools, and guidance to enable them to embrace any new opportunities to maximise their growth potential.

Where a firm is experiencing growth the financing of its expansion is highly dependent on the amount of cash flowing through it at any one time. All firms use cash, cash is used to buy materials, pay salaries, administration, selling, and distribution expenses. Sales from goods and services eventually find their way into the working capital cycle. Working capital is used in the day-to-day business operations, and is calculated as the current assets (which include cash and cash equivalents, marketable securities, accounts receivable, inventory, prepaid expenses, and other liquid assets) minus the current liabilities (which are obligations which appear on a company's balance sheet and include short-term debt, accounts payable, accrued liabilities, and other similar debts).

A key point to note is that firms can decrease their financing costs and raise the funds available for expansion projects or R&D by minimising the amount of investment tied up in current assets. In many ways, the determents of working capital are governed by the type of industry a firm operates within. For manufacturing firms, the production process has a lot of impact on the working capital requirement. The manufacturing cycle comprises of the purchase and the use of raw materials and the production of finished goods. The longer the manufacturing cycle, the larger will be the firm's working capital requirements. Alternatively, if a manufacturing company experiences stagnant growth it becomes difficult for the company to take advantage of new opportunities, develop new products, or adapt to alteration of production techniques needed when new opportunities arise.

There are considerable risks to firms if working capital is mismanaged (Dobbins & Witt, 1988, p. 34). For example:

- If the company carries too great a quantity or variety of finished goods, then these must be financed at the cost of other regular expenses.
- If a company slows down the collection of cash from its customers, then this can result in cash shortages.
- Even if the company has enough assets to pay its creditors, if the money is not at hand, the company might have to sell its assets or even declare bankruptcy to cover its debts.

As noted the availability of capital is essential to the operational activities within business. It is useful to make the distinction between "fixed capital" and "capital investment". Fixed capital is made up of several elements: buildings, equipment, vehicles, tooling, etc.; and it is likely that these fractions of capital do not play a uniform role in the formation of business activities. Capital investment is the cash provided to a company to further its business objectives. Growth in business cannot be achieved without investment. The individuals at the centre of business investment decisions are generally the Finance Director and Divisional Managers.

These are the ones that make the case for investment within the business and direct it, including where it is done and how it is used to drive business growth and success.

Understanding how individual managers make investment decisions, and which aspects of the current business environment to encourage or discourage further in is crucial not only to meeting growth and profitability targets but to realising the potential benefits of doing so in terms of innovation, skills, and better outcomes for long-term business growth and survival of the firm. Whilst survival in business is paramount and relies on the cooperation of many stakeholders, it should be noted that the enthusiasm and drive for investment and innovation demonstrated by one organisation may not be matched by another. Where business growth is reliant on partnerships with SMEs this can sometimes lead to delays in decision-making or delivery of initiatives, unhelpful management practices, and potentially conflicting priorities.

All investments involve risk and judgement. A disciplined approach helps management to make rational decisions based on the probable impact of an investment on the future of the business. For many firms, especially SMEs, the natural response is to reject high-risk business opportunities or to be reluctant to invest or adopt new opportunities. For new start-ups, we know that only a small percentage succeed, and therefore, growth is linked to high risk, loss of firm value, and wastage of resources that in the end might ruin the firm's competitive advantage.

Business growth is premised on transaction between buyers and sellers, the more we sell the more revenue a firm receives. Whenever exchange takes place, we refer to an economic transaction. Since we are all customers (buyers) and require goods and services of others, a vast network of exchange is necessary to allocate the available goods and services. The accomplishment of transaction is achieved through the economic system by means of coordination. This coordination of exchange takes place either across markets or within organisations. At any one time, there are any such number of exchanges for goods and services. At its basic level, the price system is the coordinating device within markets. Within organisations, the price system is replaced by authority as a coordinating mechanism.

3.6.1 Business-Enabled Transactions

In business economics, the cost of doing business includes the cost of market transactions and the cost of internal transactions. The dominant method of economic organisation in markets is the price system. If information or knowledge were perfect and individuals, perfectly candid, organising interdependencies between individuals would be costless; in other words, transaction costs would be zero (Williamson, 1975). In the real world, however, this is rarely the case.

Transaction costs cover many elements; these include both direct and indirect costs of doing business. Firms invariably attempt to transact business at the lowest possible cost the market will tolerate. In practice, these costs are likely to vary across activities, across time periods, across countries, and across firms, based on the available information upon which the transaction is made.

Some transaction costs might prove wasteful and deserve elimination. Therefore, any reduction of transaction costs between businesses is highly desirable (Williamson, 1979, p. 234). The goal of reducing or eliminating transaction costs has strongly influenced both strategy and management decision-making in many organisations. For instance, when Internet service providers calculate transaction costs, they have to factor in countless items of expenditure along with the actual number of transactions. When there are fewer transactions, the cost per transaction is higher. On the other hand, transactions arriving in high quantities can overwhelm operational personnel and distributors. In an e-commerce business, the transaction cost is the same across the board, whether one order or thousands are received. An e-commerce business is also able to reduce labour and other costs in areas, such as document preparation, invoice reconciliation, mail preparation, telephone calling, data entry, and overtime and management expenses. Hence, innovation and technology transfer in service provision will generally benefit both the provider and consumer. Allowing the organisation to invest in new business opportunities and affording the business the chance to reduce product and service costs. As a final thought on transaction cost, in attempting to keep the transaction costs stable, the costs of transferring information or knowledge within the firm should be lower, the smaller if the distance between the firm's own market and the target market is preferable (Ghoshal & Moran, 1996).

3.7 Conclusion

For businesses to grow they require new customers and investment in Innovation. Such investment is generated from sales revenue in the form of retained earnings or from external sources such as loans. For many firms, innovation is the pathway to competitive advantage and the means by which growth is achieved whilst delivering important benefits to shareholders and the wider stakeholder community.

The way firms think about innovation is dependent on the nature of the industry or business sector they operate within. How we perceive and measure innovation is a major consideration for funding. A measure of innovation is "time to market", which is driven by the organisation's commitment to R&D and the market conditions they operate in whether local, regional, or global. In global markets where differential conditions apply and where such differentials drive profitability or where products may be easily replicated "time" becomes a competitive goal which can hinder the firm's creative abilities. The availability of human capital (people) in many ways determines how quickly a firm can enhance its position in the market place. Firms which adopt a resource-based view often have a better chance of succeeding in the market place than those that do not.

Authors such as Barney (1991), Botten and McManus (1999), and Fritsch and Schindele (2011), all have the same opinion that competing is to some degree premised on a firm's ability to recruit talented people and retain them. Getting the right people into the organisation has become more important than capital investment; skills associated with technology, interpersonal team work, creative thinking, and decision-making are critical for competitive performance. Contemporary business leaders tend to emphasise the development of these types of skills. Clearly, proficiency in soft skills is transferrable in many organisations. Technology has opened up boundaries in terms of knowledge and resource sharing, to the extent that organisations have become increasingly adept at relocating people and physical assets around the world to give them an advantage in the marketplace.

As markets change, so does the relationship between business and consumers, in ways which have significant implications for future growth and profits. Growth in business cannot be achieved without some element of risk. All business transactions carry an element of risk; to both buyer and seller. For instance, organisations that compete in "export markets" are more prone to transaction risk due to currency fluctuations. Whilst investment in transaction-specific assets improves the efficiency of trading in the short term in the longer-term they expose the firm to debt and hinder profitability.

This chapter is by no means a complete survey of the literature on the approach to technology or innovation-driven business growth. Rather it attempts to demonstrate how management theory can provide a unifying concept to explain the most common forms of strategy taken by firms to take advantage of emerging opportunities in the market place. In considering further research, the author suggests that the unified approach to technology, innovation, and strategy is promising both in terms of future research potential and as an aid to management endeavouring to gain competitive advantage in increasingly demanding business environments.

References

Abidin, S. Z., Mokhtar, S. S., & Yusoff, R. Z. (2011). Systematic analysis of innovation studies: A proposed framework on relationship between innovation process and firms performance. *The Asian Journal of Technology Management, 4*(2), 65–83.

Barney, J. B. (1991). Firm resources and sustained competitive advantage. *Journal of Management, 17*(1), 99–120.

Bernstein, B., & Singh, P. J. (2006). An integrated innovation process model based on practices of Australian biotechnology firms. *Technovation, 26*(5), 561–572.

Botten, N., & McManus, J. (1999). *Competitive strategies for service organisations*. West Lafayette: Ichor Business Books, USA.

Chaisiri, S., Lee, B. S., & Niyato, D. (2012). Optimization of resource provisioning cost in cloud computing. *IEEE Transactions on Services Computing, 5*(2), 164–177.

Chesbrough, H. (2006). *Open Business Models: How to Thrive in the New Innovation Landscape*, Harvard Business Press: Boston, MA.

De Pablos, P. O. (2006). Transnational corporations and strategic challenges: An analysis of knowledge flows and competitive advantage. *The Learning Organization, 13*(6), 544–559.

Dereli, D. D. (2015). Innovation management in global competition and competitive advantage. *Procedia-Social and Behavioural Sciences, 195*, 1365–1370.

Dobbins, W., & Witt, S. F. (1988). *Practical financial management*. Oxford, UK: Basil Blackwell.

Drucker, P. (1954). *The practice of management*. London-Heinemann, UK: Harper and Row.

Fahy, J. (2000). The resource-based view of the firm: Some stumbling-blocks on the road to understanding sustainable competitive advantage. *Journal of European Industrial Training, 24*(2), 94–104.

Fritsch, M., & Schindele, Y. (2011). The contribution of new businesses to regional employment: An empirical analysis. *Economic Geography, 87*(2), 153–180.

Ghoshal, S., & Moran, P. (1996). Bad for practice: A critique of transaction costs theory. *Academy of Management Review, 21,* 13–47.

Huang, F., & Rice, J. (2012). Openness in product and process innovation. *International Journal of Innovation Management, 16*(4), 1–24.

Iyer, B., & Davenport, T. H. (2008). Reverse engineering Google's innovation machine. *Harvard Business Review, 86,* 58–68.

Johannessen, J. A., & Olsen, B. (2010). The future of value creation and innovations: Aspects of a theory of value creation and innovation in a global knowledge economy. *International Journal of Information Management, 30,* 502–511.

Johnson, G., Scholes, K., & Whittington, R. (2005). *Exploring corporate strategy* (7th ed.). Harlow, Essex: Prentice Hall.

Kline, S. J., & Rosenberg, N. (1986). *An overview of innovation: The positive sum strategy*. Washington, DC: National Academic Press.

Lewis, D., & Moore, K. (2009). *The origins of globalization*. London: Routledge.

Maleyeff, J. (2011). Factors impacting innovation in new service offerings. *Journal of Service Science and Management, 4,* 111–117.

Manyika, J., Chui, M., Bughin, J., Dobbs, R., Bisson, P., & Marrs, A. (2013). *Disruptive technologies: Advances that will transform life, business, and the global economy*. New York, USA: McKinsey Global Institute.

McManus, J. (2009). The service economy. *Journal Management Services, 53*(2), 16–20.

Mell, P., & Grance, T. (2011). *The NIST definition of cloud computing*. National Institute Standards and Technology, Special Publication 800-145, Gaithersburg, USA.

Moreira, É. T., & Stramar, A. R. (2015). Modelo holístico da gestão da inovação com ênfase na cooperação, flexibilidade e adaptação. *Review of Administration and Innovation, 11*(4), 193.

OECD Publication. (2017). Enhancing the contribution of SMEs in a global and digitalised economy. *Report from OECD*, Paris, 2, rue André-Pascal, 75775 Paris Cedex 16.

Pavlou, P. A., & El Sawy, O. A. (2011). Understanding the elusive black box of dynamic capabilities. *Decision Sciences, 42*(1), 239–273.

Porter, M. E. (1985). *Competitive advantage*. New York, USA: The Free Press.

Porter, M. E. (1990). *The competitive advantage of nations*. London: Macmillan Press.

Porter, M. E. (2001). Strategy and the Internet. *Harvard Business Review, 79*(3), 62–78.

Prahalad, C. K., & Hamel, G. (1990, May–June). The core competences of the corporation. *Harvard Business Review, 68*(3), 79–91.

Schumpeter, J. A. (1950). *Capitalism, socialism and democracy* (3rd ed.). London: Allen and Unwin.

Taylor, P. (2012, September 11). Pfizer moves supply chain to cloud. *Financial Times Online*. Accessed 20 Sept 2019.

Teece, D. J. (2014). A dynamic capabilities-based entrepreneurial theory of the multinational enterprise. *Journal of International Business Studies, 45*(1), 8–37.

Tidd, J., Bessant, J., & Pavitt, K. (2008). *Innovation management:* Gestão da inovação (3rd ed.). Porto Alegre: Bookman Publication.

Williamson, O. E. (1975). *Markets and hierarchies: Analysis and antitrust implications*. New York: Free Press.

Williamson, O. E. (1979). Transaction cost economics: The governance of contractual relations. *The Journal of Law and Economics, 22*(2), 233–261.

CHAPTER 4

International Growth and Social Media Competitiveness of Small Software Firms

Matti Saari, Minnie Kontkanen, Ahmad Arslan, and Pia Hurmelinna-Laukkanen

4.1 Introduction

International growth of firms is an important topic in management and strategy research domains (e.g., D'Angelo & Presutti, 2019; Ng & Hamilton, 2016; Yli-Renko, Autio, & Tontti, 2002). International

M. Saari · M. Kontkanen
School of Marketing & Communications, University of Vaasa, Vaasa, Finland
e-mail: matti.saari@univaasa.fi

M. Kontkanen
e-mail: minnie.kontkanen@univaasa.fi

A. Arslan (✉) · P. Hurmelinna-Laukkanen
Department of Marketing, Management & IB, Oulu Business School, University of Oulu, Oulu, Finland
e-mail: ahmad.arslan@oulu.fi

P. Hurmelinna-Laukkanen
e-mail: pia.hurmelinna-laukkanen@oulu.fi

J. J. M. Ferreira et al. (eds.), *Technological Innovation and International Competitiveness for Business Growth*, Palgrave Studies in Democracy, Innovation, and Entrepreneurship for Growth,
https://doi.org/10.1007/978-3-030-51995-7_4

growth has been studied significantly using a range of theoretical lenses and empirical analysis techniques (e.g., D'Angelo & Presutti, 2019; Del Giudice, Arslan, Scuotto, & Caputo, 2019; Etemad, 2018). Most of the prior studies have focused on identifying the growth patterns and strategies for small firms in terms of used operation modes, location choices, and development of networks among others (e.g., Jin, Chung, Yang, & Jeong, 2018; Sepulveda & Gabrielsson, 2013). Some studies have specifically highlighted the difference in international growth strategies and patterns of small (and medium-sized) firms compared to large firms (Nummela, 2010).

So far, prior studies have contributed to existing knowledge by identifying several critical elements that generally influence international growth in a small firm context. It has been argued that small firms tend to lack physical, financial and human resources, but at the same time, they have intangible resources as an important source of competitiveness: In the context of international operations of small-sized firms, intangible resources have been found to play a major role in their strategies and success (e.g., Del Giudice et al., 2017; Radulovich, Javalgi, & Scherer, 2018). However, intangible resources come in different forms, and not all of them have received equal attention in the existing literature. Therefore, the roles and implications of such resources are not always as clear—especially with regard to international growth.

Among those intangibles that have really surfaced relatively recently, social media has been noted to help small firms in dealing with an increasingly competitive and uncertain business world (Benitez, Castillo, Llorens, & Braojos, 2018; Alarcón-del-Amo, Rialp-Criado & Rialp-Criado, 2018). Research on social media has proliferated in recent years, which is in line with its growing usage and impact on every aspect of life (Kapoor et al., 2018; Sloan & Quan-Haase, 2017). Existing research shows that social media is used to find and establish business relationships, increase sales, and improve brand visibility and awareness (Hurmelinna-Laukkanen, Haapanen, & Holma, 2020). However, a review of extant literature reveals that role of social media competitiveness in the specific context of international growth of small and medium-sized enterprises (SMEs) is a rather limited—even if it has been increasingly gaining researchers' attention in recent years (e.g., Dabić et al., 2020; Hurmelinna-Laukkanen et al., 2020; Moen, Rialp, & Rialp, 2020; Pergelova, Manolova, Simeonova-Ganeva, & Yordanova, 2019; Alarcón-del-Amo et al., 2018). Thus, there is a need to increase understanding of how social media as a tool could become a source of competitiveness and enhance SMEs' international growth. This argument forms the research question of the study.

We contribute to extant international growth and social media literatures by addressing and analyzing social media competitiveness as a driver of international growth for small firms. We focus on information technology (IT) sector in Finland and conduct case studies in two Finnish firms specializing in different software systems. IT sector has been considered to be one of the most dynamic business sectors (Akhtar, Khan, Tarba, & Jayawickrama, 2018), and a field where social media has been found to play an increasingly important role in both operations and strategies (Del Giudice et al., 2019). Moreover, social media usage in both personal and organizational contexts have been found to be notably high in Nordic countries, including Finland (Ammirato et al., 2019; Koiranen, Keipi, Koivula, & Räsänen, 2020), which makes our research setting a relevant context for identifying central factors and aspects. Furthermore, the focus on single industry is expected to help in terms of issues of generalization, even if qualitative study is not typically widely generalizable; we suggest that the observed issues may be found in other organizations in this industry.

The rest of the chapter is organized as follows. The next section presents a literature review. This is followed by the discussion on research methodology. After that, case firms are introduced, and study findings are presented. The chapter concludes with the presentation of implications, limitations, and future research directions.

4.2 Literature Review

4.2.1 Drivers of International Growth

Firm growth is an intensively researched area. Prior studies have found several factors at different levels, ranging from industry and firm-specific factors to managerial factors, which influence the organizational growth (e.g., Demir, Wennberg, & McKelvie, 2017; Weinzimmer, 2000). Although firm growth has been extensively researched, it has been argued that studies focusing on firm growth in specifically in international markets are rather limited (D'Angelo & Presutti, 2019; Del Giudice et al., 2019). It is a well-established fact that internationalizing firms suffer from liability of foreignness (e.g., Arslan, 2012; Zaheer & Mosakowski, 1997).

In addition to this, small and relatively young firms quite often experience the liabilities of smallness and newness, suffering from the limited access to relevant resources (Zahra, 2005) which limit possibilities to internationalize and innovate simultaneously (Lecerf, 2012). Despite the changes in the business environments brought by issues such as digitalization, earlier theorizations, that the balanced use of resources is critical in firm expansion (Penrose, 1959), seem to hold. For small and young firms, it may create extra layer of challenges in their attempts to achieve growth in international markets. Rugman and Verbeke (2002) argue that especially managerial constraints set limits to growth, and that learning is an important element in the growth process. For high-tech firms that usually operate in competitive and uncertain markets characterized by technological volatility, growth challenges can be even higher (Evers & Andersson, 2019). However, operating in such environments may also be positive in terms of international growth if the changes in the environment create opportunities leading to growth (Wiklund, Patzelt, & Shepherd, 2009).

In this context, prior studies have stressed the importance of knowledge and technology-related factors. For example increased knowledge intensity resulting in knowledge as a source of competitive advantage (Autio, Sapienza, & Almeida, 2000; Yli-Renko et al., 2002), and the possession of technological knowledge, measured by integrative patent base, for instance (Ji, Axinn, & Garcia de Campos, 2018) have been found to have positive effects on international growth. The important role of knowledge in international growth is explained by the fact that firms relying on knowledge as a source of competitive advantage focus more on developing learning skills needed in new environments (Autio et al., 2000). Therefore, access to knowledge and information can be a highly important issue for SMEs pursuing growth.

Further on, international growth has also been associated with networks and relationships (see e.g., Fernhaber & Li, 2013; Shneor et al., 2016). Access to networks has been argued to influence the possibility to acquire external resources and act as a source of information on foreign markets (Cannone & Ughetto, 2014; Ojala, Evers, & Rialp, 2018; Ryan, Evers, Smith, & Andersson, 2019, Sekliuckiene, Vaitkiene, & Vainauskiene, 2018), which can be considered important for smaller firms that may not hold resources of their own. The study by Yli-Renko et al. (2002) found that external social capital accumulated through management contacts and customer involvement has a positive influence on international growth. Ji et al. (2018) found that especially domestic alliances, compensating for limited resources and enhancing learning, moderated positively the effect of technological knowledge on increasing high-commitment international growth. Moreover, Del Giudice et al. (2019) found that cooperation supported international growth through technological and knowledge spillovers. Hence, the role of networks specifically in high-tech firms' context seems to be more pronounced in terms of indirect influence through learning and knowledge.

Moreover, firm-level factors like entrepreneurial orientation and learning orientation (D'Angelo & Presutti, 2019), firm age (Autio et al., 2000; Puig, Gonzalez-Loureiro, & Ghauri, 2018; Saarenketo, Puumalainen, Kuivalainen, & Kylaheiko, 2009) and ability to build on economies of scale and scope (Saarenketo et al., 2009) have been found to positively influence the international growth. The positive influences of economies of scope support the idea that a firm that builds on synergies and systemics can benefit from optimizing factor costs in different markets and leverages existing knowledge in new markets (Saarenketo et al., 2009). Flexibility as a key feature of organizational culture has also been found to positively influence international growth (Hansen & Hamilton, 2011). However, organizational barriers such as lack of clear internal organization as well as leadership skills, can potentially have negative influences on international growth (Rastrollo-Horrillo & Martín-Armario, 2019).

Although the positive direct effects of managerial experiences and attitudes on firm growth have been verified (see e.g., review by Demir et al., 2017), the managerial factors contributing to international growth have been rather limitedly researched (exception of this see e.g., D'Angelo & Presutti, 2019). However, there are conceptual studies arguing that managerial level factors influence indirectly on international growth (Sapienza, Autio, George, & Zahra, 2006; Weerawardena, Mort, Liesch, & Knight, 2007). The indirect effect of managerial level factors on international growth is supported by D'Angelo & Presutti, (2019) in high-tech firm context. They found that founder/CEO's previous entrepreneurial and industry-specific experience moderates positively the influence of entrepreneurial and learning orientation on international growth. Managerial factors are seen more as enablers for firm growth, providing access to networks based on prior achievements, increasing possibilities to identify opportunities (Sapienza et al., 2006) and to develop dynamic capabilities (Weerawardena et al., 2007). In such situations, it is possible that highly experienced managers can steer even small firms with limited resources toward growth in international markets if the resources can be extended with cost-efficient means (e.g., Hurmelinna-Laukkanen et al., 2020).

4.2.2 Social Media Competitiveness and International Growth

Based on the discussion above, many of the factors found to drive international growth of high-tech firms are the ones that small and young firms tend to lack. Therefore, small and relatively young firms need to find ways to overcome their relative disadvantages in order to grow in international markets. One option is to build competitive advantage by utilizing the technological developments related to digitalization to overcome these disadvantages. In fact, the potential of social media in improving organization competitiveness (Kwayu, Lal, & Abubakare, 2018) and internationalization performance has been acknowledged by the scholars (Alarcón-del-Amo et al., 2018). However, there still is lack of empirical evidence on how the use of social media contributes to international growth (for exceptions on this see Hurmelinna-Laukkanen et al., 2020; Mathews, Bianchi, Perks, Healy, & Wickramasekera, 2016). It has been argued that social media can be an important tool of interactive communication and a source of information, which can help firms to identify market opportunities and speed up their internationalization (Hurmelinna-Laukkanen et al., 2020; Restrepo, 2013). In similar vein, the same mechanisms may facilitate growth. The study by Glavas, Mathew, and Russell-Bennet (2019) is among the first ones to have specifically explored the ways of acquiring information and knowledge through internet in relation to internationalization. Even though the focus in their study was broadly on internet-enabled technology, the identification of four types of internet-enabled experiences increases the understanding of how both incrementally and non-incrementally internationalizing firms use internet to generate knowledge. The findings of Glavas et al. (2019) indicate that incrementally internationalizing firms are using internet to collect explicit and factual information to get support for already existing knowledge. However, for firms following non-incremental path, the internet becomes a source of both explicit and tacit information with the so-called functional and immersive internet-enabled experiences dominating internationalization. In other words, instead of just using technological platforms as a source of information, which may support internationalization, internet technology is integrated strategically to the infrastructure and operations of the firm to generate possibilities for learning and facilitating international growth.

Mathews et al. (2016) offer further support for the role of internet-related technology for international growth. They found that internet marketing capabilities have positive impact both on the information availability and developing international network capabilities (Mathews et al., 2016), which points toward opportunities for learning to be present as a result. Similarly, and more explicitly in the realm of our study, findings by Scarmozzino, Corvello, and Grimaldi (2017) show that in high-tech context, social media (and specifically professional social networking sites) can facilitate entrepreneurial learning. Sigfusson and Chetty (2013) found that international software entrepreneurs benefitted from active use of social media (e.g., LinkedIn) by connecting with potential partners to explore and exploit opportunities in relation to getting access to local networks and acquiring important resources and capabilities. Enhancement of online business networking has been found to lead to search and exploitation of new business opportunities abroad as well as to improved business internationalization effectiveness for European SMEs (e.g., Vătămănescu, Andrei, Nicolescu, Pînzaru, & Zbuchea, 2017). Furthermore, because each SME's social media network is inimitable, Sigfusson and Chetty (2013) argue that the effective use of social media can bring competitive advantage for internationalization.

In light of these arguments, social media may be viewed be a valuable resource that allows SMEs to have unique assets, overcome the disadvantages related to lack of financial resources, and increase their visibility to ease entering new markets and growing in them (e.g., Bocconcelli, Cioppi, & Pagano, 2017). Mollá-Descals, Gomez-Borja, Lorenzo-Romero, and Mondéjar-Jiménez (2010) argue that the use of Web 2.0 and social media tools in retailing have notable potential in terms of achieving increased demand and internationalization over the internet. These ideas are supported by findings of Restrepo (2013) who investigated the usefulness of social media in the internationalization of Columbian SMEs. The relative affordability and wide coverage of social media for marketing purposes (Zahoor & Qureshi, 2017; Zolkepli & Kamarulzaman, 2015) can potentially enhance international growth of SMEs. Possibilities to interact with their customers and other stakeholders, as well as engaging efficiently (Bochenek & Blili, 2014; Okazaki & Taylor, 2013) can further positively influence international growth potential of SMEs. Moreover, possibilities for SMEs to enhance their image through co-branding strategies, or to support marketing strategies of international partners using social media (Restrepo, 2013) can also potentially enhance their international growth.

However, at the same time there are limitations and challenges associated with social media. Studying the connection between social media and internationalization, Hurmelinna-Laukkanen et al. (2020) highlighted the inherent uncontrollability of social media. Social media leaves it quite open how and when different stakeholders communicate about the firm and its offerings—the SME has little control over these issues (Kannan, 2017), especially as they have limited resources to do so. Therefore, more empirical insights are needed to understand how and to what extent social media competitiveness can drive international growth.

4.3 Research Methodology

A multiple case study method was selected for this study due to the explanatory nature of the research question. We chose to examine two firms and their international growth closely. Such focus allowed us to go deeper into the cases, while at the same time finding differences and similarities in them. Eisenhardt (1989) suggests that multiple case study enables studying patterns that are common to the cases and theory under investigation. In addition, the case study method also makes it possible to explain the significance and cause-and-effect relationships of the examined phenomena (Yin, 1994).

4.3.1 Case Selection

The cases were selected from the Finnish Software Entrepreneurs Association member list. The Finnish Software Entrepreneurs Association is a non-aligned association for professional and entrepreneurial software business executives. The association supports Finnish software firms in their trajectories and develops the software industry in Finland. Finland was chosen as the country of origin due to its small and open economy with a very limited domestic market. Due to its small domestic market, international growth is generally a common growth strategy for Finnish software firms. Software sector was chosen (especially software as a service), since these firms are high technology firms and they are familiar with new digital tools and platforms such as social media (e.g., Ammirato et al., 2019). The case firms were selected for this study for theoretical reasons as advised in the study of Eisenhardt (1989) instead of random sampling. The selection criteria for the firms were following: First, firms had to meet European Commission's definition of small and medium-sized enterprises: an SME is a firm employs fewer than 250 employees and annual turnover not exceeding EUR 50 million. As an alternative for net sales it is possible to determine the balance sheet, where sheet total may not exceed EUR 43 million (European Commission, 2003). Second, the firms needed to be involved in exporting (international growth) for at least one year, and they should be present on at least two social media platforms as well as have vivid international activities on these platforms. Two software firms meeting these criteria were selected for this study. These firms were contacted by telephone to identify an appropriate key informant for the research. In this study, key informants were owner–managers or CEOs, since they had the best knowledge of their firm's environment, strategy, and performance.

4.3.2 *Data Collection*

Semi-structured interviews were chosen as the main data collection approach because they provide reliable and comparable qualitative data for the study. The interview is a flexible data collection tool, and it involves direct linguistic interaction between the interviewer and the interviewee (Saunders, Lewis, & Thornhill, 2009; Yin, 1994). It allows to guide and control data collection as well as offers possibilities to gain in-depth information and understand motives behind the answers (Eriksson & Kovalainen, 2008). We also observed social media platforms that case firms use for the purpose of data triangulation. Primary data was collected in two interview rounds. The first interview round was undertaken in May 2018 followed by the second one in January 2020, thereby adding temporal depth into data collection and subsequent analyzes. Interviews were conducted according to the themed interview framework. Themes for the interview framework were developed in two phases. First, the initial themes for an interview guide were developed based on an in-depth literature review on social media and internationalization of firms. Due to the lack of earlier investigations of the role of social media in internationalization of SMEs, the relevance of the interview themes was tested with two case firms. These initial interviews gave the necessary data to develop more focused themes for actual interviews. All themes were developed by following the guidelines of Yin (1994), trying to make the questions

Table 4.1 Interviews details

Firm/location	*Interviewee*	*Date*	*Time*	*Duration*	*Language*
Firm A/Finland	Co-Founder	14.5.2018	13.00–14.05	65 min.	English
		17.1.2020	12.00–12.45	45 min.	
Firm B/Finland	CEO	22.5.2018	12.00–12.45	45 min.	English
		20.1.2020	14.00–14.43	43 min.	

as nonleading as possible. This allowed the interviewees to give genuine answers to the themes during the interviews (Table 4.1).

4.3.3 Data Analysis

Data analysis was conducted in line with the recommendations of Yin (1994) and Miles and Huberman (1994) to identify similarities and differences in the cases. The data analysis included within-case and cross-case displays to find specific themes and patterns in the data (Miles & Huberman, 1994). We used integrated comparative and within-case analysis (Welch et al., 2011). When identifying patterns, we discussed differences and similarities between the cases and the literature (Eisenhardt, 1989). The interviews were digitally recorded, carefully listened to, and transcribed to verbatim with the help of a word processor. A second listening was arranged to ensure correspondence between the recorded and transcribed data.

4.4 Description of Case Firms

4.4.1 Firm A

Firm A is a Finnish cloud technology firm founded in 2014. The "software as a service" (SaaS) solution includes metadata-driven contract management, all-digital board portal, virtual data rooms (VDR) and secure e-signatures. The firm has customers in 41 countries and is owned by leading Finnish and international lawyers and other private investors. Firm is also financed by the Finnish Funding Agency for Technology and Innovation, which has funded famous ventures such as Supercell, Rovio, and F-Secure. Firm A has offices in Helsinki, Finland, and Palo Alto, the United States.

4.4.2 *Firm B*

Firm B is a SaaS price monitoring service for retail and e-commerce firms of all sizes. The product collects accurate information on market pricing, which helps in analysis and margin optimization to its customers. Technologically advanced price monitoring enables to combine internal data with online data collected into the solution. Firm B was founded in 2015 and is based in Helsinki, Finland (Tables 4.2 and 4.3).

4.5 Findings

Interviews supported the notion of importance of social media competitiveness for small software firms in their international growth. Both case firms use social media for various purposes to accelerate their international growth. The co-founder of the firm A state:

> *In our business, you don't exist, if you are not in social media. So, we are using social media a lot and various purposes. In fact, social media platforms are the foundation of our communication marketing efforts. We use social media, for example, to generate leads and build awareness globally. With social media you can reach a larger target audience faster than traditional sales and marketing – and it is also low-cost channel.*

In line with this, the CEO of firm B argues that social media platforms like Facebook and LinkedIn have been very useful for them. The competition in the international environment is fierce and social media provide tools for be competitive, especially in terms of visibility and market presence.

Table 4.2 Case firms' overview

Firms	*Founded*	*Products/services*	*Number of personnel*	*Social media usage in international environment/years*
Firm A	2014	Contract management system	5 (Platform development/administration outsourced)	4 years
Firm B	2015	Price monitoring service for retail and ecommerce firms	13	3 years

Table 4.3 Key figures of the case firms

Firm A	*Year 2018*	*Year 2019*	*Annual growth (%)*
Number of countries	20	41	102
Number of customers (firms)	182	350	92
Number of employees	3	5	66
Turnover	80,000 €	160,000 €	100
Exports	32,000 €	112,000 €	225
Firm B			
Number of countries	3	7	133
Number of customers (firms)	33	36	9.09
Number of employees	7	13	85.71
Turnover	264,000	450,000	70.45
Exports	44,880	49,500	10.29

For example, the use of social media has increased awareness about the firm and boosted their leads and sales. Based on interviews, we present findings related to learning, marketing, and communication, recruiting and networking and support, research and development functions in context of international growth of both case firms as follows.

4.5.1 *Learning, Marketing, and Communication*

4.5.1.1 Learning

Both managers emphasized the importance of learning during international growth. Social media platforms have been agile and valuable tools for the case firms when gathering information about market trends, target markets, countries, competitors and customers' needs and preferences. The data collected through social media has been combined with the information from other channels, which, in turn, has contributed to the accumulation of new knowledge assets. This is in line with the research conducted by Scarmozzino et al. (2017), who state that social media platforms (e.g., LinkedIn) can facilitate entrepreneurial learning in high-tech context. Moreover, social media can be effective tool when identifying opportunities abroad. Sigfusson and Chetty (2013) argue that software international entrepreneurs may benefit from active use of social media by connecting with potential partners to explore and exploit opportunities. Since social media enables interaction with customers and partners globally, and the information flows rapidly through platforms, the case firms have been able to identify growth opportunities more effectively and efficiently. A Co-founder of the firm A explains this:

> *Fast development of business environment has brought more challenges for us. We think that continuous learning is the only way to create sustainable business. Through social media, we have learned important things about our customers and their needs. In addition, social media has also accelerated access to information about foreign markets.*

Firm B has used social media as a low-threshold market research tool to find potential customer groups and markets abroad. With the information gained through social media platforms (e.g. Twitter, LinkedIn, Facebook and discussion forums), they have been able to identify markets and customers relevant to them. This information has helped them to allocate resources in the right place, which in turn has accelerated internationalization and international growth, as explained by CEO of firm B:

> *According to our experiences, social media is fast and the agile way to identify markets and customers abroad. With social media, we have learned valuable things about customers and target countries. For example, through various social media communities we have learned how customers behave in certain markets.*
>
> Firm B, CEO

4.5.1.2 Marketing and Communication

Social media can be used in marketing activities to disseminate information about the company and its products and to attract potential international clients (Restrepo, 2013). In addition, social media offers information about market trends, competitors, and consumer's needs and preferences (Maltby, 2012; Zhang & Vos, 2014). The findings of our study reveal that both case firms have been using social media actively in marketing and communication activities to disseminate information about the firm and its products and services. The firms communicate and interact with their users and partners in various platforms. Most used platforms in international context are Instagram, LinkedIn, Facebook, YouTube, and Twitter. According to the interviewees, these platforms provide wide reach and good access to their customers and partners. In addition, since our case firms are also challenged by limited resources and capabilities (e.g., financial and technological) like other SMEs, social media has been an important tool allowing firms to increase their visibility and credibility globally. The CEO of firm B explains that social media is a good and cost-effective way for engaging and interacting with customers globally.

> *We have noticed that social media is important in terms of creditability and trust. For example, in last two years we have been more active in social media and received positive feedback from our customers. Interaction on social media has increased creditability and trust between our firm and customers.*
>
> Firm B, CEO

According to the co-founder of the firm A, in recent years, social media firms (e.g., Facebook and Instagram) have developed algorithms to the point where it is impossible to get organic growth without paid advertising. Organic growth here refers growth through the users following a social media channel, while "paid advertising" is purchased from a platform provider and is then targeted to the users. In organic growth, the firm does not have to pay anything. As the result of the development of algorithms, firm A has significantly invested in paid advertising on social media and through that gained international growth. However, the CEO of firm B has a different view. He explains that it is true that organic reach and growth on social media have been on decline over the years, but you can still gain organic growth at certain level. This growth may actually be more desirable and easier to manage than an uncontrollable increase in market visibility. There are a couple of key issues in organic growth. First, one needs to understand how algorithms work. For example, Facebook and Instagram have revealed the main factors that determine the posts a user sees on the feed. Based on these main factors you can modify your content and gain organic results. Another way is to test new social media platforms (e.g., TikTok and Steemit) and interact with users more by focusing on the quality of the posts rather than the quantity. That is, with some technological understanding, SMEs can enhance their use of social media.

4.5.2 *Recruiting and Networking*

4.5.2.1 *Recruiting*

Apart from learning from and affecting external stakeholders, social media helps in international growth by offering new ways to identify and attract personnel with capabilities and knowledge needed in growing firms. Kazienko, Szozda, Filipowski, and Blysz (2013) and Crowne, Goeke, and Shoemaker (2015) argue that social media platforms (e.g., LinkedIn, Facebook, and Google+) can be useful tools when attracting new employees and capture the targeted market of those who are the most valuable. Firm B has used Facebook and LinkedIn when recruiting new employees to the firm. According to CEO of the firm, LinkedIn is more focused on the professional career building, while Facebook includes conversations that are more informal. Moreover, Facebook usually reaches more people than LinkedIn. However, both platforms have been useful for recruitment for firm B. In addition, the CEO argues that social media is a very low-cost tool when recruiting. Basically, you do not need to pay anything to get the word out in relevant arena of discussion. In social media, one can find passionate and talented people relatively easily. Also, evaluation is easier when one can view a person's complete work and education history. This is specifically highlighted by the CEO of firm B:

> *Facebook and LinkedIn have been very useful tools when we have recruited new employees. Facebook is not so "official" and it reaches people extensively, while LinkedIn is more focused in professionals. Anyway, we have good experiences with both of them.*
>
> Firm B, CEO

Firm A has not used social media platforms in recruiting. One reason for this may be that they have not recruited much and have limited number of personnel currently. However, the co-founder of the firm explains that in the near future, they plan to recruit several employees, and LinkedIn and Facebook will be used in this process.

4.5.2.2 Networking

In addition to finding new additions to a company, social medial can also, extend the relevant resource base of the firm beyond the organizational boundaries. Social media platforms are networks by their nature. Seroka-Stolka and Tomski (2015) argue that social media networks can be seen as a powerful way of enabling firms to reach their international contacts and to gather the information efficiently. Likewise, social media allows SMEs to reach larger audiences also by using contacts of other companies and by building on their reach (Bochenek & Blili, 2014; Okazaki & Taylor, 2013). Both of the case firms use social media for networking with partners and customers. Firm A uses Facebook, Twitter, and LinkedIn while firm B uses Facebook, Instagram, LinkedIn, and Twitter. The CEO of firm B explains that networking in social media is important since social networking makes relationships more personal also between organizations, not just the focal firm and its (potential) customers. It is a two-way online channel where you have an opportunity to build international contacts fast. Sigfusson and Chetty (2013) emphasize that firms use social networking sites since online tools make it easier for them to manage a large number of relationships. The co-founder of the firm A states that especially LinkedIn has been an effective tool for them when building professional contacts and networks. Since SMEs usually do not have large budgets, they cannot afford to arrange large international meetings or attend seminars. Helping to overcome these challenges, social media platforms have been an easy and inexpensive solution for international networking. In this concern, firm A founder says that

> *We do not have the resources to organize big events or attend international seminars. Instead, we have created international contacts and networks in Facebook and LinkedIn.*
>
> Firm A, Co-Founder

4.5.3 Support, Research, and Development

4.5.3.1 Support

Firms are increasingly providing customer support through social media, helping customers on a real-time basis (Gunarathne, Rui, & Seidmann, 2018). Both interviewees argue that social media platforms are effective tools for customer and partner support in international context. The co-founder of firm A explains that first you must identify the channels where the audience spends their time, and then start to use them actively. For example, Firm B has created "how-to"-videos on YouTube, and they have best practices blog and other educational content that they share on Facebook. They also use chatbots. According to the interviewed co-founder, chatbots are a good way to offer basic social customer service. They give customers the information they want immediately, without involving customer service people. Moreover, chatbots can save time and money, provide greater partner and customer satisfaction, and cut down errors. However, chatbots work only for easy and simple questions. When you have more complicated questions, you need to use other channels.

> *YouTube has been an important platform to us. We have been able to provide various product related instruction videos to our partners and customers globally. We have noticed that by providing clear and informative product related videos on social media, customers and partners are more engaged to our products and services.*
>
> Firm B, Co-Founder

The CEO of firm B argues that for them, it is very important to provide high-quality partner and customer support. High-quality support is a factor that makes them stand out from competitors and that allows building competitive advantage in international markets. The CEO continues that social media platforms are good for providing support since they are low cost, effective, and fast. They have mainly used Facebook and YouTube. According to the CEO, Facebook is fast and mobile, which makes it a great tool for customer interactions and a valuable platform for customer care. Moreover, it is easy to share various instructions and guides on Facebook and get instant feedback. In YouTube, the firm provides various product-related instructions, for example user guides and product updates.

> *Of course social is not only tool we are using for support -however, it is very important.*
>
> Firm B, CEO

4.5.3.2 Research and Development

Social media platforms enable various users both inside and outside the company to collaboratively develop and manage products and services

(Maltby, 2012). For example, social media tools like shared collaboration spaces have been found to positively affect generation of new concepts and management evaluation (Marion, Barczak, & Hultink, 2014). According to the co-founder of the firm A, various social media platforms have been effective tools when the firm has been developing products and services. Since social media is fast and the reach is wide, they have received a large amount of feedback from their customers. The information gained through feedback in social media, has enabled rapid and agile development of services and products. This is in line with the study by Maltby (2012), who found that entrepreneurs use forum-enabled interactions to develop their products to meet the specific needs and requirements of users. The co-founder of firm A emphasizes that social media has been an excellent way to attract customers to co-create. Through social media, the firm has been able to genuinely interact and collaborate with their customers and partners using chatbots and Facebook. The CEO of firm B explains that their aim is to engage customers in the product development, and that social media is an effective place for that.

4.5.4 *Social Media's Role in International Growth of Case Firms*

Table 4.4 offers an overview of social media channels and their usage in international environment for the two case firms.

Tables 4.5 and 4.6 present the overall findings from both case firms linked to the international growth aspect, highlighting an important role of social media competitiveness. Finally, Table 4.7 offers a summary of study findings by highlighting the key aspects and their impacts.

4.6 Conclusions

Our findings are in line with many of the arguments presented in prior studies on similar topics, but also deviate from them by taking the discussion explicitly to the context of international growth of small-sized firms and by providing more nuanced insights. Most research on social media has been linked to marketing related activities (e.g., Hurmelinna-Laukkanen et al., 2020), which only forms a part of international growth. Nevertheless, these aspects came up quite strongly also in our examination. We found that internet marketing capability (that is, active use of internet applications for different marketing-related functions; Mathews

Table 4.4 An overview of social media channels and their usage in case firms

Firm	*Firm blog*	*Facebook*	*Twitter*	*YouTube*	*Instagram*	*LinkedIn*	*SlideShare*
A	Information about the firm/its services	Marketing/communication tool	Marketing/communication tool	Marketing/communication tool	–	Marketing/communication tool	Marketing tool
B	General information about the firm	Marketing/communication tool	Marketing/communication tool	Product support tool, Marketing/communication tool	Marketing/communication tool	Recruiting tool, Marketing/communication tool	Marketing tool

Table 4.5 Firm A

Business activity	*Social media platform*	*Function*	*International growth*
Sales, marketing and communication	Firm blog, Facebook, Slideshare, Twitter, YouTube	Brand exposure Market research tool: - targeting foreign markets/countries - targeting foreign partners/customers Learning Lead generation Trust building between firm and its stakeholders	Increased brand exposure, reduced marketing costs Access to the information about markets/countries Access to the information about potential partners and customers Increased lead generation globally Increased trust and creditability Opportunity recognition abroad
Research and development Innovations	Facebook, Discussion forums and communities	Further development of products and services Market insights Competitor monitoring	User interaction (discussion, feedbacks, comments, etc.) on platforms allows rapid and agile development of products and services (e.g. taking account country or market characteristics, customer behavior)
Partner and customer support	Facebook, Twitter, discussion forums, YouTube	Firm-partner-customer Interaction/feedbacks Online/additional instructions Real-time and personalized support	Increased partner/customer experience Increased partner/customer retention and loyalty →sustainable business Reduced support costs
Human resources, networking	LinkedIn, Facebook	Networking and relationships building and maintenance	Increased networking globally

Table 4.6 Firm B

Business activity	*Social media platform*	*Function*	*International growth*
Sales, marketing and communication	Firm blog, Facebook, Instagram, Twitter, YouTube	Brand exposure Market research tool: • Targeting foreign markets/countries • Targeting foreign partners/customers Learning, Lead generation Trust building between firm and its stakeholders	Increased brand exposure, reduced marketing costs, Access to the information about markets/countries Access to the information about potential partners and customers Increased lead generation globally Increased trust and creditability Opportunity recognition abroad
Research and development Innovations	Facebook, discussion forums and communities	Further development of products and services New ideas captured from the communities	User interaction (discussion, feedbacks, comments, etc.) on platforms allows rapid and agile development of products and services (e.g. taking account country or market characteristics, customer behavior)
Partner and customer support	Facebook, Twitter, discussion forums, YouTube	Firm-partner-customer Interaction/feedbacks Online/additional instructions	Increased partner/customer experience Increased partner/customer retention and loyalty, → sustainable business → competitive advantage, Reduced support costs
Human resources	LinkedIn, Facebook	Networking and relationships maintenance, Recruitment	Increased networking globally Reduced recruitment costs

Table 4.7 Social media usage and their impact on case firms' international growth

Organizational function	*Social media platform*	*Benefits in international growth context*	*Firm A*	*Firm B*
Sales and marketing	Blogs, Facebook, Instagram, Slideshare, Twitter, YouTube	Reduced marketing costs Increased brand exposure Lead generation Increased targeted traffic Brand reputation management	+++ +++ ++ + –	+++ +++ ++ ++ –
Innovations Research and development	Facebook, Discussion forums and communities	Further development of products and services Market insights New ideas captured from communities Competitor monitoring	++ +++ ++ ++	++ +++ + –
Partner and customer support	Facebook, Chats, Twitter, Discussion forums, YouTube	Better partner/customer Interaction > feedbacks Online instructions Reduced support costs Real-time and personalized support Increased partner/customer experience Increased partner/customer retention and loyalty	+++ ++ ++ ++ +++ +	+++ ++ + + +++ ++
Human resources	LinkedIn, Facebook	Networking Facilitated recruitment Reduced recruitment costs	+++ – –	+++ +++ +

+++ Significant impact; ++ Medium impact; + Low impact; – No impact or no experience

et al., 2016) to be notably visible in our findings. Both firms were active on social media platforms like Facebook, Instagram, Twitter, YouTube, and others showing their internet marketing capabilities in marketing communication and market research. The case firms even went further in this respect, and as highlighted in Table 4.7, specific marketing functions like brand exposure or lead generation were linked to specific social media platforms. This can be viewed as strength of internet marketing capabilities. Besides these aspects, the role of social media in branding along with reaching and engaging with a wide array of customers globally (e.g., Gao, Tate, Zhang, Chen, & Liang, 2018; Okazaki & Taylor, 2013) also received support in our findings. Furthermore, similarly to Bochenek and Blili (2014), both case firms used social media as an efficient interaction channel improving the customer engagement.

Moreover, the argument presented in some recent studies that social media is an important source of information for internationalization (Glavas et al., 2019) comes up also in our findings. In line with Restrepo (2013) and Vătămănescu et al. (2017), we found that research and development activity can be facilitated in the wake of identification of market opportunities and new customers, and customer feedback. These outcomes of using social media as a source of information can be highly relevant for international growth. Relatedly, we found support for the argument presented by Scarmozzino et al. (2017) that social media activity on professional networking sites like LinkedIn facilitates entrepreneurial learning. Matching with potential partners and enhanced networking have been found as important elements of social media competitiveness in international growth context (Sigfusson & Chetty, 2013; Vătămănescu et al., 2017). Likewise, acquiring the needed talent to enable and maintain growth can be done via social media, as the recruiting of committed and skillful employees can be promoted relying on digital means. This indicates that social media use can connect to the human resource management functions of growing SMEs in the international context.

Our findings also highlighted some additional aspects and factors not as explicitly covered in prior studies related to the role of social media in internationalization. In general, utilizing multiple social media platforms broadly for the benefit of different functions at the firm seemed to contribute to international growth. Specifically, case firms were able to build on the synergies and systemics which have been claimed to contribute to international growth in general (see Saarenketo et al., 2009). This gives further support for the important role of social media as a tool for enabling agile operations in international markets and supporting the flexible firm culture, which Hansen and Hamilton (2011) argued to be a key feature of growth-oriented firms. An interesting notion also is, that the use of social media may be linked to the type of growth. Although our empirical evidence is admittedly limited in examining this idea in full, the findings suggest that firms approach growth through social media in different ways, for example, by relying on organic growth or then being more proactive and aggressive in terms of promotion. This can be a highly relevant topic to be studied later, especially in the light of findings that suggest uncontrollability of social media to be sometimes a counterproductive issue for SMEs (see Hurmelinna-Laukkanen et al., 2020).

4.7 Implications, Limitations, and Future Research Directions

Our study offers both theoretical and managerial implications based on the findings presented above. First, at the more general level of discussion, the current chapter highlighted and certified the important role of social media competitiveness for international growth of small-sized firms. Second, a key theoretical implication relates to specific organizational functions that have been linked to different social media platforms in context of international growth of the case firms. This aspect is important for theory development on the role of social media in internationalization context, especially because marketing aspects have been highlighted so far perhaps to a greater extent than the other elements. Specific organizational functions like sales and marketing, research and development, partner and customer support, and human resource management all have different and important roles during international growth. The current chapter has built bases for specific research on this topic rather than merely relying on general discussion on social media competitiveness or managerial capabilities.

For small firms' managers especially operating in high-tech sectors like software industry, there are several implications in this chapter. First, recognizing the specific organizational functions, and considering social media use for each of them separately is important. An analytical approach making a distinction between the outcomes of social media use for specific functions can help the managers to measure the social media competitiveness in a relatively concrete manner. For example, as suggested above, issues like increased lead generation globally, or brand and opportunity recognition aboard, can be used as benchmarks for measuring social media competitiveness for international growth in sales, marketing, and communication. Furthermore, country-specific interactive inputs can be used to measure social media competitiveness in relation to R&D function. Finally, increased global networking being manifested by more partnerships (or high-quality partnerships) as well as ease of hiring new staff can be used to measure human resources and support functions. At the same time, recognizing the risks and uncontrollability can be enhanced.

Our study has limitations like any other academic study. First, we focus only on social media competitiveness in context of international growth. The role and perception of social media competitiveness in this specific context can have some potential differences compared to other organizational contexts. However, as it is an emerging field, our chapter does offer some useful insights, which we believe are applicable to multiple organizational settings including international growth. Another limitation is that the empirical part is based on two case firms operating in software sector and having their origins in a single country. Hence, the findings cannot be generalized widely. However, software sector has been referred to be rather universal with similarities in operations of firms operating in different countries (e.g., Band, 2019). Therefore, we believe that our findings are useful for managers of such firms. Future research can also benefit from our study by taking it as a stepping-stone to build on, and specifically analyze social media competitiveness of firms operating in other similar high-tech industries to see if the findings match ours or not. The hints of potentially relevant questions regarding the limits to the usefulness of social media also are relevant in pointing direction to future research. It might be particularly interesting to examine, to what extent and under which conditions social media is relevant for different functions when international growth is pursued. Moreover, future studies can also try to see if specific industrial or national contexts result in some peculiar differences or not. Such research will be useful as it will contribute to the emerging debate on globalization in context of social media.

References

Akhtar, P., Khan, Z., Tarba, S., & Jayawickrama, U. (2018). The Internet of Things, dynamic data and information processing capabilities, and operational agility. *Technological Forecasting and Social Change, 136*, 307–316.

Alarcón-del-Amo, M., Rialp-Criado, A., & Rialp-Criado, J. (2018). Examining the impact of managerial involvement with social media on exporting firm performance. *International Business Review, 27*(2), 355–366.

Ammirato, S., Felicetti, A. M., Della Gala, M., Aramo-Immonen, H., Jussila, J. J., & Kärkkäinen, H. (2019). The use of social media for knowledge acquisition and dissemination in B2B companies: An empirical study of Finnish technology industries. *Knowledge Management Research & Practice, 17*(1), 52–69.

Arslan, A. (2012). Impacts of institutional pressures and the strength of market supporting institutions in the host country on the ownership strategy of multinational enterprises: Theoretical discussion and propositions. *Journal of Management and Governance, 16*(1), 107–124.

Autio, E., Sapienza, H. J., & Almeida, J. G. (2000). Effects of age at entry, knowledge intensity, and imitability on international growth. *Academy of Management Journal, 43*(5), 909–924.

Band, J. (2019). *Interfaces on trial: Intellectual property and interoperability in the global software industry*. Abingdon, Oxon: Routledge.

Benitez, J., Castillo, A., Llorens, J., & Braojos, J. (2018). IT-enabled knowledge ambidexterity and innovation performance in small US firms: The moderator role of social media capability. *Information & Management, 55*(1), 131–143.

Bocconcelli, R., Cioppi, M., & Pagano, A. (2017). Social media as a resource in SMEs' sales process. *Journal of Business & Industrial Marketing, 32*(5), 693–709.

Bochenek, L. M., & Blili, S. (2014). Social media champions—Drivers and sophistication process of social media strategic management. In M. R. Oliva-Lujan & T. Bondarouk (Eds.), *Social media in strategic management*. Advanced series in management (Vol. 11). Emerald: Bingley.

Cannone, G., & Ughetto, E. (2014). Born globals: A cross-country survey on high-tech start-ups. *International Business Review, 23*(1), 272–283.

Crowne, K. A., Goeke, R. J., & Shoemaker, M. (2015). Enhancing international assignees' performance with online social networks. *Journal of Global Mobility, 3*(4), 397–417.

D'Angelo, A., & Presutti, M. (2019). SMEs international growth: The moderating role of experience on entrepreneurial and learning orientations. *International Business Review, 28*(3), 613–624.

Dabić, M., Maley, J., Dana, L. P., Novak, I., Pellegrini, M. M., & Caputo, A. (2020). Pathways of SME internationalization: A bibliometric and systematic review. *Small Business Economics, 55*(3), 705–725.

Del Giudice, M., Arslan, A., Scuotto, V., & Caputo, F. (2017). Influences of cognitive dimensions on the collaborative entry mode choice of small- and medium-sized enterprises. *International Marketing Review, 34*(5), 652–673.

Del Giudice, M., Scuotto, V., Garcia-Perez, A., & Petruzzelli, A. M. (2019). Shifting Wealth II in Chinese economy: The effect of the horizontal technology spillover for SMEs for international growth. *Technological Forecasting and Social Change, 145,* 307–316.

Demir, R., Wennberg, R., & McKelvie, A. (2017). The strategic management of high growth firms: A review and theoretical conceptualization. *Long Range Planning, 50*(4), 431–456.

Eisenhardt, K. M. (1989). Building theories from case study research. *Academy of Management Review, 14*(4), 532–550.

Eriksson, P., & Kovalainen, A. (2008). *Qualitative methods in business research.* London: Sage.

Etemad, H. (2018). Growth and learning mechanisms in the evolving multilayered and multidimensional view of international entrepreneurship. *Journal of International Entrepreneurship, 16*(1), 1–11.

European Commission. (2003). Commission recommendations of 06/05/2003 concerning the definition of micro, small and medium-sized enterprises. Brussels.

Evers, N., & Andersson, S. (2019). Predictive and effectual decision-making in high-tech international new ventures—A matter of sequential ambidexterity. *International Business Review*. Available online at: https://doi.org/10.1016/j.ibusrev.2019.101655.

Fernhaber, S. A., & Li, D. (2013). International exposure through network relationships: Implications for new venture internationalization. *Journal of Business Venturing, 28*(2), 316–334.

Gao, H., Tate, M., Zhang, H., Chen, S., & Liang, B. (2018). Social media ties strategy in international branding: An application of resource-based theory. *Journal of International Marketing, 26*(3), 45–69.

Glavas, C., Mathew, S., & Russell-Bennet, R. (2019). Knowledge acquisition via internet-enabled platforms Examining incrementally and nonincrementally internationalizing SMEs. *International Marketing Review, 36*(1), 74–107.

Gunarathne, P., Rui, H., & Seidmann, A. (2018). When social media delivers customer service: Differential customer treatment in the airline industry. *MIS Quarterly, 42*(2), 489–520.

Hansen, B., & Hamilton, T. (2011). Factors distinguishing small firm growers and non-growers. *International Small Business Journal, 29*(3), 278–294.

Hurmelinna-Laukkanen, P., Haapanen, L., & Holma, S. (2020). Social media and small entrepreneurial firms' internationalization. In L. Schjoedt et al. (Eds.), *Understanding Social Media and Entrepreneurship*. Cham: Springer. pp. 141–168.

Ji, F. X., Axinn, C. N., & Garcia de Campos, L. A. (2018). Exploring high-commitment international growth of high-technology new ventures: The contingent model of formal alliance. *International Studies of Management & Organization, 48,* 204–220.

Jin, B., Chung, J., Yang, H., & Jeong, S. W. (2018). Entry market choices and post-entry growth patterns among born globals in consumer goods sectors. *International Marketing Review, 35*(6), 958–980.

Kannan, P. K. (2017). Digital marketing: A framework, review and research agenda. *International Journal of Research in Marketing, 34*(1), 22–45.

Kapoor, K. K., Tamilmani, K., Rana, N. P., Patil, P., Dwivedi, Y. K., & Nerur, S. (2018). Advances in social media research: Past, present and future. *Information Systems Frontiers, 20*(3), 531–558.

Kazienko, P., Szozda, P., Filipowski, T., & Blysz, W. (2013). New business client acquisition using social networking sites. *Electronic Markets, 23,* 93–103.

Koiranen, I., Keipi, T., Koivula, A., & Räsänen, P. (2020). Changing patterns of social media use? A population-level study of Finland. *Universal Access in the Information Society, 19,* 603–617.

Kwayu, S., Lal, B., & Abubakare, M. (2018). Enhancing organizational competitiveness via social media—A strategy as practice perspective. *Information Systems Frontiers, 20*(3), 439–456.

Lecerf, M.-A. (2012). Internationalization and innovation: The effects of a strategy mix on the economic performance of French SMEs. *International Business Research, 5*(6), 2–13.

Maltby, T. (2012). Using social media to accelerate the internationalization of startups from inception. *Technology Innovation Management Review, 2*(10), 22–26.

Marion, T. J., Barczak, G., & Hultink, E. J. (2014). Do social media tools impact the development phase? An exploratory study. *Journal of Product Innovation Management, 31*(1), 18–29.

Mathews, S., Bianchi, C., Perks, K. J., Healy, M., & Wickramasekera, R. (2016). Internet marketing capabilities and international market growth. *International Business Review, 25*(4), 820–830.

Miles, M. B., & Huberman, A. M. (1994). *Qualitative data analysis: An expanded sourcebook.* Thousand Oaks, CA: Sage.

Moen, Ø., Rialp, A., & Rialp, J. (2020). Examining the importance of social media and other emerging ICTs in far distance internationalisation: The case of a Western exporter entering China. In *International business and emerging economy firms* (pp. 221–251). Cham: Palgrave Macmillan.

Mollá-Descals, A., Gómez-Borja, M.-A., Lorenzo-Romero, C., & Mondéjar-Jiménez, J.-A. (2010). Application of social web tools to the internationalization of retail companies. *Journal of Business Case Studies, 6*(7), 31–35 (Spanish Edition).

Ng, P. Y., & Hamilton, R. T. (2016). Experiences of high-growth technology firms in Malaysia and New Zealand. *Technology Analysis & Strategic Management, 28*(8), 901–915.

Nummela, N. (2010). *International growth of small and medium enterprises*. Abingdon, Oxon: Routledge.

Ojala, A., Evers, N., & Rialp, A. (2018). Extending the international new venture phenomenon to digital platform providers: A longitudinal case study. *Journal of World Business, 53*(5), 725–739.

Okazaki, S., & Taylor, C. R. (2013). Social media and international advertising: Theoretical challenges and future directions. *International Marketing Review, 30*(1), 56–71.

Penrose, E. (1959). *The theory of the growth of the firm*. Oxford: Blackwell.

Pergelova, A., Manolova, T., Simeonova-Ganeva, R., & Yordanova, D. (2019). Democratizing entrepreneurship? Digital technologies and the internationalization of female-led SMEs. *Journal of Small Business Management, 57*(1), 14–39.

Puig, F., Gonzalez-Loureiro, M., & Ghauri, P. (2018). Running faster and jumping higher? Survival and growth in international manufacturing new ventures. *International Small Business Journal, 36*(7), 829–850.

Radulovich, L., Javalgi, R. R. G., & Scherer, R. F. (2018). Intangible resources influencing the international performance of professional service SMEs in an emerging market: Evidence from India. *International Marketing Review, 35*(1), 113–135.

Rastrollo-Horrillo, M., & Martín-Armario, J. (2019). Organisational barriers to nascent born-global growth: Learning from the inside. *Journal of International Entrepreneurship, 17*, 454–473.

Restrepo, M. M. T. (2013). Exploring the usefulness of social media in the internationalisation process of SMEs. *Escenarios. Empresa y Territorio No. 2*. Available online at: http://revistas.esumer.edu.co/index.php/escenarios/article/viewFile/35/35.

Rialp-Criado, A., & Rialp-Criado, J. (2018). Examining the impact of managerial involvement with social media on exporting firm performance. *International Business Review, 27*(2), 355–366.

Rugman, A. M., & Verbeke, A. (2002). Edith Penrose's contribution to the resource-based view of strategic management. *Strategic Management Journal, 23*(8), 769–780.

Ryan, P., Evers, N., Smith, A., & Andersson, S. (2019). Local horizontal network membership for accelerated global market reach. *International Marketing Review, 36*(1), 6–30.

Saarenketo, S., Puumalainen, K., Kuivalainen, O., & Kylaheiko, K. (2009). A knowledge-based view of growth in new ventures. *European Business Review, 21*(6), 531–546.

Sapienza, H. J., Autio, E., George, G., & Zahra, S. A. (2006). A capabilities perspective on the effects of early internationalization on firm survival and growth. *Academy of Management Review, 31*(4), 914–933.

Saunders, M., Lewis, P., & Thornhill, A. (2009). *Research methods for business students* (5th ed.). Essex, England: Pearson Education Limited.

Scarmozzino, E., Corvello, V., & Grimaldi, M. (2017). Entrepreneurial learning through online social networking in high-tech startups. *International Journal of Entrepreneurial Behavior & Research, 23*(3), 406–425.

Sekliuckiene, J., Vaitkiene, R., & Vainauskiene, V. (2018). Organisational learning in startup development and international growth. *Entrepreneurial Business and Economics Review, 6*(4), 125–144.

Sepulveda, F., & Gabrielsson, M. (2013). Network development and firm growth: A resource-based study of B2B Born Globals. *Industrial Marketing Management, 42*(5), 792–804.

Seroka-Stolka, O., & Tomski, P. (2015). Internet social media and international entrepreneurial intentions. In *The 2015 WEI International Academic Conference Proceedings*. Vienna, Austria. Available online at: https://www.westeastinstitute.com/wp-content/uploads/2015/04/Oksana-Seroka-Stolka-and-Piotr-Tomski.pdf.

Shneor, R., Jenssen, J. I., Vissak, T., Torkkeli, L., Kuivalainen, O., Saarenketo, S., & Puumalainen, K. (2016). Network competence in Finnish SMEs: Implications for growth. *Baltic Journal of Management, 11*(2), 207–230.

Sigfusson, T., & Chetty, S. (2013). Building international entrepreneurial virtual networks in cyberspace. *Journal of World Business, 48*, 260–270.

Sloan, L., & Quan-Haase, A. (2017). *The SAGE handbook of social media research methods*. Thousand Oaks, CA: Sage.

Vătămănescu, E.-M., Andrei, A. G., Nicolescu, L., Pînzaru, F., & Zbuchea, A. (2017). The influence of competitiveness on SMEs internationalization effectiveness: Online versus offline business networking. *Information Systems Management, 34*(3), 205–219.

Weerawardena, J., Mort, G. S., Liesch, P. W., & Knight, G. (2007). Conceptualizing accelerated internationalization in the born global firm: A dynamic capabilities perspective. *Journal of World Business, 42*(3), 294–306.

Weinzimmer, L. G. (2000). A replication and extension of organizational growth determinants. *Journal of Business Research, 48*(1), 35–41.

Welch, C., Piekkari, R., Plakoyiannaki, E., & Paavilainen-Mäntymäki, E. (2011). Theorising from case studies: Towards a pluralist future for international business research. *Journal of International Business Studies, 42*(5), 740–762.

Wiklund, J., Patzelt, H., & Shepherd, D. A. (2009). Building an integrative model of small business growth. *Small Business Economics, 32*(4), 351–374.

Yin, R. K. (1994). *Case study research: Design and methods*. Newbury Park, CA: Sage.

Yli-Renko, H., Autio, E., & Tontti, V. (2002). Social capital, knowledge, and the international growth of technology-based new firms. *International Business Review, 11,* 279–304.

Zaheer, S., & Mosakowski, E. (1997). The dynamics of the liability of foreignness: A global study of survival in financial services. *Strategic Management Journal, 18,* 439–464.

Zahoor, S. Z., & Qureshi, I. H. (2017). Social media marketing and brand equity: A literature review. *IUP Journal of Marketing Management, 16*(1), 47.

Zahra, S. A. (2005). A theory of international new ventures: A decade of research. *Journal of International Business Studies, 36,* 20–28.

Zhang, B., & Vos, M. (2014). Social media monitoring: Aims methods, and challenges for international companies. *Corporate Communications: An International Journal, 19*(4), 371–383.

Zolkepli, I. A., & Kamarulzaman, Y. (2015). Social media adoption: The role of media needs and innovation characteristics. *Computers in Human Behavior, 43,* 189–209.

PART II

Dynamics of International Business Competitiveness

CHAPTER 5

The Impact of Innovation and Entrepreneurship on Competitiveness

Cristina I. Fernandes, Pedro Mota Veiga, João J. M. Ferreira, Sérgio J. Teixeira, and Hussain G. Rammal

5.1 Introduction

The notion of competitiveness has been of central importance in the strategic management literature (Hu and Trivedi, 2020; Klein, Dooley, Lapierre, Pitura, & Adduono, 2020; Martin, Raj, Javalgi, & Ciravegna, 2020; Michael, Reisinger, & Hayes, 2019; Teixeira, Lopes Casteleiro,

C. I. Fernandes (✉) · J. J. M. Ferreira
Department of Management and Economics & NECE Research Unit in Business Sciences, University of Beira Interior, Covilhã, Portugal
e-mail: cristina.isabel.fernandes@ubi.pt

J. J. M. Ferreira
e-mail: jjmf@ubi.pt

P. M. Veiga
Escola Superior de Educação de Viseu - Instituto Politécnico de Viseu e Universidade Católica Portuguesa & NECE-Research Unit, Covilhã, Portugal
e-mail: motaveiga@curva-de-gauss.pt

J. J. M. Ferreira et al. (eds.), *Technological Innovation and International Competitiveness for Business Growth*, Palgrave Studies in Democracy, Innovation, and Entrepreneurship for Growth,
https://doi.org/10.1007/978-3-030-51995-7_5

Rodrigues, & Guerra, 2018) and has experienced an increased profile since the 1980s (Chursin & Makarov, 2015; Clark et al., 1988; Rugman, 1987; Tyson, 1990). Even though the concept of competitiveness has been deployed with increasing frequency, it remains both relatively complex and controversial (Aiginger & Vogel, 2015; Antonio et al., 2020; Klein et al., 2020; Nenem, Graham, & Dennis, 2020) with researchers defining competitiveness broadly in accordance with their own respective points of view and scientific fields (Delbari, Ng, Aziz, & Ho, 2015; Lei, Yao, & Zhang, 2020).

A White Paper released by the National Commission on Entrepreneurship (NCOE, 2001) contends that innovation constitutes the greatest contribution made by entrepreneurship at the local level. Since the 1980s, there has been an evolution in the traditional and linear model of innovation in order to incorporate more dynamic and interactive visibility (Kline & Rosenberg, 1986; Lentz & Mortensen, 2016; Li, 2017; Raposo, Ferreira, & Fernandes, 2014; Von Hippel, 1988). Currently, innovation receives widespread recognition as one of the main drivers of economic growth in what is termed as the "age of knowledge" (Aiginger & Vogel, 2015; Bush & Starkie, 2014; Chan & Quah, 2012; Stough, 2003). Therefore, within the scope of the increasingly competitive global business environment, innovation has steadily become a critical factor to companies striving to attain dominant positions (Cheng, Lai, & Wu, 2010) and to revitalize their competencies (Hu & Hsu, 2008; Kaminski, de Oliveira, & Lopes, 2008). Thus, there is the perception of innovation being one of the main means of adapting to increasingly dynamic surrounding environments (Doloreux & Melancon, 2008; Hua & Wemmerlov, 2006; Roberts & Amit, 2003). According to Wood (2005), research findings on regional innovation only echo the national

S. J. Teixeira
Higher Institute of Administration and Languages, Research Centre—ISAL, Funchal, Portugal
e-mail: sergio.teixeira@isal.pt

NECE—Research Unit in Business Sciences, Funchal, Portugal

H. G. Rammal
UTS Business School, University of Technology Sydney, Sydney, Australia
e-mail: hussain.rammal@uts.edu.au

studies in attributing primacy to regional competitiveness as an oriented process and technologically driven by innovation (Chen et al., 2018; Huggins & Williams, 2011). Nevertheless, this recognition has now extended to stressing the importance of the innovation taking place inside institutions to this same regional development and competitiveness (Den Hertog, 2002; Gupta, Malhotra, Czinkota, & Foroudi, 2015; Luh, Jiang, & Huang, 2016; Wood, 2005). Despite those who defend that innovation is fundamental to the performance and competitiveness of companies, the literature does not provide any consensus as to the best means to evaluate this (Akman, Okay, & Okay, 2013; Drazin & Schoonhoven, 1996; Gupta et al., 2015; Kodama, 2006, 2009; Tushman & O'Reilly, 1997).

Innovation has been approached from different perspectives that are based on the objects they focus on, their concepts, strategic considerations, methodologies, and models for measuring and analysing innovation. Various researchers have displayed a particular interest in emphasizing the characteristics of companies and the factors that drive them to innovate (Hwang, 2004; Lemon & Sahota, 2004; Tidd & Bessant, 2009). In regional terms, competitiveness gets determined by the productivity with which the region deploys both its human and natural resources and its capital (Li, Ku, Liu, & Zhou, 2020; Martin et al., 2020; Porter, 1990, 1998; Porter & Ketels, 2003). There are also empirical findings that indicate how the number of patents registered provides a fairly reliable measure of ongoing innovative activities (Acs, Anselin, & Varga, 2002; Furman, Porter, & Stern, 2002; Jonker et al., 2017; Teixeira et al., 2018), in conjunction with the registration of brands (Greenhalgh & Rogers, 2012; Mendonça, Pereira, & Godinho, 2004). Hence, our research seeks to address the gap in the literature concerning the measurement of innovation and entrepreneurship, and its influence over competitiveness. Through enabling evaluation of the impact of innovation and entrepreneurship on competitiveness, we seek to contribute by advancing the literature in this research field.

5.2 Literature Review

The effective implementation of innovation has gained increasing recognition as the foundation for the building of sustainable competitive advantage, and, thus, boosting the performance of organisations (Abbas,

Avdic, Xiaobao, Hasan, & Ming, 2018; Koc & Ceylan, 2007; Przychodzen, Przychodzen, & Lerner, 2016; Razumova, Ibáñez, & Palmer, 2015; Zhang et al., 2017).

The specific social, cultural, economic, and political environment are together framing the context for any innovation combine to take on a systemic character (Liu, 2018; Zheng & Wong, 2010). Edquist (1997) defines innovation as the interaction of the complexes of factors or components that mutually work together to condition and contract other complexes, with each facet retaining their well-defined functions. According to Lundvall (1992), an innovation system features inputs and relationships that interact in the production, dissemination, and application of new economic knowledge. This approach serves as the foundation for the exploration of regional innovation systems (Cooke, 1998; Cooke, Uranga, & Etxebarria, 1997; Fukugawa, 2016; Galindo, Vaz, & Nijkamp, 2011; García-Rodríguez, Gil-Soto, Ruiz-Rosa, & Gutiérrez-Taño, 2017). In addition to agglomeration and competitiveness, innovation represents one of the most important aspects underlying economic growth in the current knowledge era (Huang et al., 2020; Stough, 2003).

Porter and Stern (2001) explain that the vitality of innovation depends on the *capacity for national innovation*. This capacity above all conveys the potential for each country, in political and economic terms, to produce flows of commercially relevant innovation.

According to Drucker (1985), innovation provides a specific tool for entrepreneurs to endow resources with a new capacity for generating wealth. Therefore, innovative companies correspondingly tend to turn in better economic and financial performances than their non-innovative peers (Batle, Orfila-Sintes, & Moon, 2018; Belitz & Lejpras, 2016; Ferreira, Marques, & Fernandes, 2010; Jonker et al., 2017; Marques, Garry, Covelo, Braga, & Braga, 2011). Innovation is fundamental not only to the survival of any sector of the economy but also to prevail in an increasingly globalised world.

In the global business context, innovation is often linked to knowledge-intensive technologies and inventions. Hence, the emphasis on protecting this knowledge and technology by patenting around the world. While the research on innovation in small-and-medium-enterprises has primarily been on firms in the United States (Pérez & Rose, 2010), there is a growing interest in the role the regional dynamics play in the innovation of European entrepreneurial firms (Nicolini & Resmini, 2011; Petrakos, Skayannis, Papdoulis, & Anastasiou, 2011).

For international entrepreneurial and born global firms, the speed of internationalisation and transfer of knowledge across national borders is of critical importance and provides them with a competitive advantage (Hilmersson, Jansson, & Sandberg, 2011). However, the local institutional environment, the competition landscape, knowledge absorption capacity, and consumer perception and behaviour vary across regions and require firms to adapt their business activities. Despite the claim that business is global, many studies argue that multinational enterprises (MNEs) are, in fact, regional in their focus (Verbeke & Kano, 2016). Countries within regional markets like Europe have lower psychic, geographic, and institutional distances, and European entrepreneurial firms have the opportunity to increase their consumer base without significant changes to the way their products and/or services are offered.

Innovation enables companies to respond to diversified and constantly changing demand and enables improvements to be made to the different domains and activities ongoing in a particular society (Cooke, Heidenreich, & Braczyk, 2004; Fundeanu, 2015; Gomezelj Omerzel & Smolčić Jurdana, 2016; Grillo, Ferreira, Marques, & Ferreira, 2018; Meissner & Shmatko, 2017). Thus, innovation gets perceived as a motor of progress through enhancing both competitiveness and economic development (Cibinskiene & Navickas, 2011; Del Giudice, Carayannis, & Maggioni, 2017; Johansson, Karlsson, & Stough, 2001; Kolehmainen et al., 2016; Romer, 1994).

Since innovation has also been proven to be a complex process, small- and medium-sized companies encounter obstacles to innovation and may only be able to engage in innovation through cooperation with other firms optimising the utilisation of their own internal knowledge in combination with the specific competencies of their partners (Muller & Zenker, 2001). Kleinknecht (1989) identifies the following as obstacles to innovation: (i) scarce financial capital resources; (ii) lack of qualifications in terms of management; and (iii) difficulties in obtaining the technological information and know-how necessary to innovate.

The growing recourse to information flows, and their applications represent an essential dimension to establishing the organisational capacities that lead to the emergence of the fundamental foundations for organisational success (Cohendet & Steinmueller, 2000; Long, Looijen, & Blok, 2018; Ramos, Man, Mustafa, & Ng, 2014; Segarra-Ciprés, Roca-Puig, & Bou-Llusar, 2014). In turn, Bughin and Jacques (1994) affirm that the major obstacle to innovation does not derive from companies appearing to suffer from “myopia” but rather due to the fundamental incapacity of companies to adopt that which they designate “key management principles. In an increasingly competitive environment, innovation amounts to a critical factor for any company seeking dominant and competitive market positions as well as boosting their profitability levels (Hu & Hsu, 2008; Jonker et al., 2017; Kaminski et al., 2008; Nas & Kalaycioglu, 2016; Nuruzzaman, Singh, & Pattnaik, 2019).

5.3 Methodology

5.3.1 Data and Measures

The data used in this study were collected from the Eurostat Regional Statistics and refer to the 276 Nomenclature of Territorial Units for Statistics 2 regions (NUTS2) in the Member States of the European Union, and all available data were used (2005–2012). The NUTS classification is a hierarchical system that divides up the EU economic territory for the purpose of collecting, developing, and harmonising European regional statistics. The socio-economic analysis of the region is divided into NUT 1, which covers major socio-economic regions; NUTS2, which looks at the basic regions for the application of the relevant regional policies and NUTS3, which includes small regions for specific diagnoses (Eurostat, 2020).

5.3.2 Dependent Variable

In regional terms, competitiveness gets determined by the productivity with which the region applies both its human and natural resources and its capital (Garreton, 2017; Porter, 1990, 1998; Porter & Ketels, 2003; Rutkauskas, 2008). This study, thus, applies the labour productivity ratio stemming from the regional Gross Added Value versus the number of workers in the region as its variable for measuring competitiveness.

5.3.3 Predictor Variables

5.3.3.1 Innovation

There is empirical evidence suggesting that the number of patents registered provides a fairly robust measurement of the ongoing innovative activities (Acs et al., 2002; Allen, Berg, Markey-Towler, Novak, & Potts,

2020; Cacciolatti, Rosli, Ruiz-Alba, & Chang, 2020; Croes & Kubickova, 2013; Furman et al., 2002; Mendola & Volo, 2017; Stern, Porter, & Furman, 2000) and isolating mechanisms, such as patents helping sustain higher returns achieved from a new product innovation (Lawson, Samson, & Roden, 2012). Within this scope, one of the variables applied to measure innovation incorporates the annual number of patent requests by region per million of active inhabitants.

The registration of brands represents another indicator serving to capture relevant aspects of innovation and industrial dynamics (Aristei, Vecchi, & Venturini, 2016; Greenhalgh & Rogers, 2012; Huang, Yang, & Wong, 2016; Kamaruzzaman, Lou, Zainon, Mohamed Zaid, & Wong, 2016; Mendonça et al., 2004; Przychodzen et al., 2016), and like in patents, brands are an isolation mechanism which helps sustain high returns from a new product innovation (Lawson et al., 2012; Missimer, Robèrt, & Broman, 2017; Trachuk & Linder, 2018) and is associated with marketing innovation (Gupta et al., 2015). Thus, we correspondingly make recourse to the number of annual brand registrations per region and per million of active inhabitants to evaluate innovation.

5.3.3.2 Entrepreneurship

The measurement of regional entrepreneurship encapsulates the number of new firms being established and launched (Audretsch, Dohse, & Niebuhr, 2010; Cucculelli & Goffi, 2013; Elia, Margherita, & Passiante, 2020; Jonker et al., 2017; Khan, 2018; Lee, Florida, & Ács, 2004; Mahn, Kim, & Bae, 2020; Mei, Zhan, Fong, Liang, & Ma, 2016; Uyarra, Zabala-Iturriagagoitia, Flanagan, & Magro, 2020), and this study correspondingly applies the company birth rate ratio deriving from the new company launches against the number of active companies in business in each region.

The contribution of new companies to the generation of employment involves specific dynamics in keeping with how some companies generate a large number of new jobs in comparison with their peer companies (Decker, Haltiwanger, Jarmin, & Miranda, 2014; Henrekson & Johansson, 2010; Neutzling, dos Santos, de Barcellos, & Land, 2015). Thus, in order to measure the generation of employment by new companies, we study the average number of employees at new firms and businesses. Table 5.1 presents a summary of the range of variables applied in this study.

Table 5.1 Analytical variables applied

Variable	*Units*
Yearly competitiveness (COMP)	Thousands of euros
Patent applications to the EPO by priority year (PAT)	Number per million of active population
Community Trademarks applications by priority year (MARK)	Number per million of active population
Firms birth rate by year (BIRTH)	As a percentage of total firms
Persons employed in the population of new firms (EMPL)	Number of persons per new firm

5.3.4 Data Analysis

The econometric analysis applied to evaluate the influence of the variables portraying innovation and entrepreneurship incorporates panel-based regression models. The data correspond to a non-balanced panel given that not all of the values are available for all of the variables throughout the eight years under analysis for every one of the 276 NUTS2 regions. The effects on the competitiveness of the variables alluding to entrepreneurship and innovation not only impacts on one specific year but also carry over into the following years and, hence, requires the estimation of dynamic panels. The traditional means of estimating panel data, such as grouped OLS, fixed effects or random effects, return estimates with biased and inconsistent parameters, when applied to models incorporating dynamic panels and this study, therefore, made recourse to the generalised method of moments (GMM) estimator methodology by Arellano-Bover/Blundell-Bond (Arellano & Bover, 1995; Blundell & Bond, 1998) given that this acts to eliminate the aforementioned biases and inconsistencies in the estimates. The econometric models calculated were the following:

$$COMP_{i,t} = \alpha_0 + \alpha_1 COMP_{i,t-1} + \alpha_2 PAT_{i,t} + \alpha_3 PAT_{i,t-1} + \alpha_4 MARK_{i,t} + \alpha_5 MARK_{i,t-1}$$

$$COMP_{i,t} = \alpha_0 + \alpha_1 COMP_{i,t-1} + \alpha_2 BIRTH_{i,t} + \alpha_3 BIRTH_{i,t-1} + \alpha_4 EMPL_{i,t} + \alpha_5 EMPL_{i,t-1}$$

$$\begin{aligned} COMP_{i,t} = {} & \alpha_0 + \alpha_1 COMP_{i,t-1} + \alpha_2 PAT_{i,t} + \alpha_3 PAT_{i,t-1} + \alpha_4 MARK_{i,t} \\ & + \alpha_5 MARK_{i,t-1} + \alpha_6 BIRTH_{i,t} + \alpha_7 BIRTH_{i,t-1} \\ & + \alpha_8 EMPL_{i,t} + \alpha_9 EMPL_{i,t-1} \end{aligned}$$

i—region, t—year

The first estimate contains the objective of evaluating the way in which innovation impacts on competitiveness. The second model, in turn, aims to ascertain the effect of entrepreneurship on competitiveness while the third analyses the simultaneous impact of innovation and entrepreneurship on competitiveness. Several local, industry, and firm variables were not considered since competitiveness as an independent variable at the previous moment is not necessary to insert any other control variables. The data obtained were processed by STATA version 12.0 software (StataCorp LP, Texas, USA).

5.4 Results

5.4.1 Descriptive Statistics

Table 5.2 presents the descriptive statistics and the correlation coefficients for the variables applied by the econometric model. We would observe that average annual regional labour productivity stood at 452,500 euros, with an average annual level of 154.24 patents registered per million of active workers while there was an average total of 215.42 brands registered per million employees in each region. The average regional rate of new companies stood at 13.95% per year and with each new company, on average, generating 0.61 new companies.

Table 5.2 Correlation matrix for variables used in the empirical analyses

	Mean	*SD*	*1*	*2*	*3*	*4*	*5*
1 – COMP	46.25	20.22	1	–	–	–	–
2 – PAT	154.24	193.12	0.604**	1	–	–	–
3 - MARK	215.42	181.42	0.597**	0.564**	1	–	–
4 - BIRTH	13.95	4.79	−0.188**	−0.238**	−0.152**	1	–
5 - EMPL	0.61	0.47	−0.531**	−0.228**	−0.131**	−0.237**	1

$^{*}p < 0.05$; $^{**}p < 0.01$

5.4.2 *Modelling*

Table 5.3 presents the results of the estimated models. In terms of patents, the findings point to current patents generating a statistically positive effect on competitiveness (Model 1: $\beta = 0.01$; $p< 0.01$; Model 3: $\beta = 0.01$; $p <0.01$). Regarding brands, we observe a statistically positive effect on current competitiveness (Model 1: $\beta = 0.02$; $p< 0.01$; Model 3: $\beta = 0.01$; $p< 0.01$) and in the following year (Model 1: $\beta = 0.02$; $p <0.01$; Model 3: $\beta = 0.01$; $p< 0.01$). We thus conclude that innovation generates a positive impact on competitiveness. As regards entrepreneurship, we find that there is a statistically significant negative effect of the average of employees at new companies and their competitiveness in the following year (Model 2: $\beta = 1.85$; $p< 0.05$; Model 3: $\beta = -1.54$; $p< 0.01$). These results demonstrate that the variables portraying regional innovation have a positive effect on regional competitiveness and that regional entrepreneurship negatively predicts this competitiveness. As regards entrepreneurship, we verify this holds an eventual effect on the competitiveness of developing or growing countries. In these countries, the rate of new company births is extremely high even while this does not provide for sustainable entrepreneurship and hence the failure rate also proves disproportionately high and hence inflicting a negative impact on competitiveness (Efrat, Hughes, Nemkova, Souchon, & Sy-Changco, 2018; Luh et al., 2016; Stanickova, 2015; Zhao, Pan, & Chen, 2018).

Table 5.3 Econometric models: regression coefficients (standard error)

	Model 1	*Model 2*	*Model 3*
Constant	18.28 (4.82)**	8.7 (3.32)*	16.48 (3.64)**
$COMP_{t-1}$	0.36 (0.11)**	0.90 (0.04)**	0.58 (0.06)**
PAT_t	0.01 (0.00)*	–	0.01 (0.00)**
PAT_{t-1}	0.01 (0.01)	–	0.01 (0.01)
$MARK_t$	0.02 (0.00)**	–	0.01 (0.00)**
$MARK_{t-1}$	0.02 (0.00)**	–	0.01 (0.00)**
$BIRTH_t$	–	−0.09 (0.07)	−0.15 (0.10)
$BIRTH_{t-1}$	–	−0.04 (0.06)	−0.07 (0.12)
$EMPL_t$	–	−1.09 (0.64)	−1.00 (0.60)
$EMPL_{t-1}$	–	−1.85 (0.85)*	−1.54 (0.75)*
N	961	961	961
Wald Chi-Squared	77.39**	90.44**	376.46**

*$p < 0.05$; **$p < 0.01$

5.5 Final Considerations

The concept of business competitiveness interrelates with the concept of competitive advantage that encapsulates the existence of a position of superiority in relation to competitors engaged in the same sector (Atherton, 2013; Feenstra, 2014; Sölvell, 2015; Wong, 2017). This superiority, in turn, is divided into two basic types; a lower cost base than the rivals, or the capacity to differentiate and determine a higher price in excess of the extra cost incurred in making that differentiation (Bhabra & Hossain, 2018; Ma, Huang, Lin, & Yang, 2019; Porter, 1990). Our research study sought to display the impact that entrepreneurship and innovation wield over competitiveness. We find that while innovation generates a positive impact, entrepreneurship returns a negative influence on competitiveness. Thus, we may conclude that public support measures for entrepreneurship are not proving especially efficient since this is not generating a positive impact on competitiveness. Furthermore, a large number of new companies are being launched; however, there is also a high rate of business failure, indicating the presence of unsustainable entrepreneurship in the region.

Thus, our contributions to the academic field are the conclusions in terms of the impact of innovation and entrepreneurship on competitiveness as well as how specific variables account for the greatest contributions towards competitiveness. This also provides a practical input into decision-making and effective policies able to foster sustainable entrepreneurship able in turn to nurture competitiveness in keeping with that theoretically defended. One limitation of the study is that a cost-oriented variable is used as a measure of competitiveness. For the future lines of research, we would propose a deeper study of the factors that leave the entrepreneurship construct weak and are responsible for the failure of entrepreneurship to make any contribution towards competitiveness. This might furthermore enable the finding of solutions to invert this conclusion. Studies with other variables related to competitiveness that do not only focus on costs, such as the attraction of Foreign Direct Investment or the variation of productivity, should also be carried out.

Acknowledgements The authors would like to thank of NECE—Research Unit in Business Sciences funded by the Multiannual Funding Programme of R&D Centres of FCT—Fundação para a Ciência e a Tecnologia, under the project "UID/GES/04630/2020".

References

Abbas, A., Avdic, A., Xiaobao, P., Hasan, M. M., & Ming, W. (2018). University-government collaboration for the generation and commercialization of new knowledge for use in industry. *Journal of Innovation & Knowledge, 2017*. Available at: https://doi.org/10.1016/J.JIK.2018.03.002.

Acs, Z. J., Anselin, L., & Varga, A. (2002). Patents and innovation counts as measures of regional production of new knowledge. *Research Policy, 31*(7), 1069–1085.

Aiginger, K., & Vogel, J. (2015). Competitiveness: From a misleading concept to a strategy supporting beyond GDP goals. *Competitiveness Review, 25*(5), 497–523.

Akman, U., Okay, E., & Okay, N. (2013). Current snapshot of the Turkish ESCO market. *Energy Policy, 60*, 106–115.

Allen, D. W. E., Berg, C., Markey-Towler, B., Novak, M., & Potts, J. (2020). Blockchain and the evolution of institutional technologies: Implications for innovation policy. *Research Policy, 49*(1), 103865.

Antonio, J., Fernández, S., Serdeira, P., María, J., Martín, M., Antonio, J., & Martín, R. (2020). Determinants of tourism destination competitiveness in the countries most visited by international tourists: Proposal of a synthetic index. *Tourism Management Perspectives, 33*(September 2019), 100582, Elsevier.

Arellano, M., & Bover, O. (1995). Another look at the instrumental variable estimation of error-components models. *Journal of Econometrics, 68*(1), 29–51.

Aristei, D., Vecchi, M., & Venturini, F. (2016). University and inter-firm R&D collaborations: Propensity and intensity of cooperation in Europe. *Journal of Technology Transfer, 41*(4), 841–871, Springer US.

Atherton, A. (2013). Organisational 'know-where' and 'know-when': Re-framing configurations and distributions of knowledge in organisations. *Knowledge Management Research and Practice, 11*(4), 410–421.

Audretsch, D. B., Dohse, D., & Niebuhr, A. (2010). Cultural diversity and entrepreneurship: A regional analysis for Germany. *Annals of Regional Science, 45*(1, SI), 55–85.

Batle, J., Orfila-Sintes, F., & Moon, C. J. (2018). Environmental management best practices: Towards social innovation. *International Journal of Hospitality Management, 69*(October 2017), 14–20.

Belitz, H., & Lejpras, A. (2016). Financing patterns of R&D in small and medium-sized enterprises and the perception of innovation barriers in Germany. *Science and Public Policy, 43*(2), 245–261.

Bhabra, H. S., & Hossain, A. T. (2018). Does location influence executive compensation? Evidence from Canadian SMEs. *Journal of Management and Governance, 22*(1), 89–109, Springer US.

Blundell, R., & Bond, S. (1998). Initial conditions and moment restrictions in dynamic panel data models. *Journal of Econometrics, 87*(1), 115–143.

Bughin, J., & Jacques, J. M. (1994). Managerial efficiency and the Schumpeterian link between size, market structure and innovation revisited. *Research Policy, 23,* 653–659.

Bush, H., & Starkie, D. (2014). Competitive drivers towards improved airport/airline relationships. *Journal of Air Transport Management, 41,* 45–49.

Cacciolatti, L., Rosli, A., Ruiz-alba, J. L., & Chang, J. (2020). Strategic alliances and firm performance in startups with a social mission. *Journal of Business Research, 106*(August 2019), 106–117.

Chan, J. K. L., & Quah, W. B. (2012). Start-up factors for small and medium-sized accommodation businesses in Sabah, Malaysia: Push and pull factors. *Asia Pacific Journal of Tourism Research, 17*(1), 49–62.

Chen, J., Yin, X., & Mei, L. (2018). Holistic innovation: An emerging innovation paradigm. *International Journal of Innovation Studies, 2*(1), 1–13, Elsevier.

Cheng, C., Lai, M., & Wu, W. (2010). Exploring the impact of innovation strategy on R&D employees job satisfaction: A mathematical model and empirical research. *Technovation, 30,* 459–470.

Chursin, A., & Makarov, Y. (2015). *Management of competitiveness Theory and practice* (A. Chursin & Y. Makarov, Eds.). Cham: Springer International Publishing Switzerland.

Cibinskiene, A., & Navickas, V. (2011). Impact of products and services prices of infrastructural natural monopolies on the factors of national competitiveness. *Economics and Management, 16*(May), 144–151.

Clark, J. E., Brown, G. E., Sprehe, J. T., Weingarten, F. W., McClure, C. R., Bement, A. L., & Lahoud, J. J. A. (1988). Federal information—Foundation for national competitiveness. *Government Information Quarterly, 5*(4), 353–368.

Cohendet, P., & Steinmueller, W. E. (2000). The codification of knowledge: A conceptual and empirical exploration. *Industrial and Corporate Change, 2,* 195–209.

Cooke, P. (1998). Origins of the concept. In H.-J. Braczyk, P. Cooke, & M. Heidenreich (Eds.), *Regional innovation systems—The role of governance in a globalized world* (pp. 2–25). London: UCL Press.

Cooke, P., Heidenreich, M., & Braczyk, H.-J. (Eds.). (2004). *Regional systems of innovation.* London: Routledge.

Cooke, P., Uranga, M., & Etxebarria, G. (1997). Regional innovation systems: Institutional and organizational dimensions. *Research Policy, 26*(4–5), 475–491.

Croes, R., & Kubickova, M. (2013). From potential to ability to compete: Towards a performance-based tourism competitiveness index. *Journal of Destination Marketing and Management, 2*(3). Available at: https://doi.org/10.1016/j.jdmm.2013.07.002.

Cucculelli, M., & Goffi, G. (2013). Does sustainability enhance tourism destination competitiveness? Evidence from Italian destinations of excellence. *Journal of Cleaner Production, 111,* 370–382.

Decker, R., Haltiwanger, J., Jarmin, R., & Miranda, J. (2014). The role of entrepreneurship in US job creation and economic dynamism. *Journal of Economic Perspectives, 28*(3), 3–24.

Del Giudice, M., Carayannis, E. G., & Maggioni, V. (2017). Global knowledge intensive enterprises and international technology transfer: Emerging perspectives from a quadruple helix environment. *Journal of Technology Transfer, 42*(2), 229–235.

Delbari, S. A., Ng, S. I., Aziz, Y. A., & Ho, J. A. (2015). Measuring the influence and impact of competitiveness research: A web of science approach. *Scientometrics, 105*(2), 773–788.

Den Hertog, P. (2002). Co-producers of innovation: In the role of knowledge-intensive business services in innovation. In J. Gadrey & F. Gallouj (Eds.), *Productivity, innovation and knowledge in services: New economic and socio-economic approaches* (pp. 223–255). Cheltenham, UK and Northampton, MA: Edward Elgar.

Doloreux, D., & Melancon, Y. (2008). On the dynamics of innovation in Quebec's coastal maritime industry. *Technovation, 28,* 231–243.

Drazin, R., & Schoonhoven, C. B. (1996). Community, population, and organization effects on innovation: A multilevel perspective. *Academy of Management Journal, 39*(5), 1065–1083.

Drucker, P. (1985). *Innovation and entrepreneurship—Practice and principals.* New York: Harper & Row.

Edquist, C. (1997). Systems of innovation approaches—Their emergence and characteristics (Chapter One). In C. Edquist (Ed.), *Systems of innovation: Technologies, institutions and organizations* (pp. 1–35). London: Pinter.

Efrat, K., Hughes, P., Nemkova, E., Souchon, A. L., & Sy-Changco, J. (2018). Leveraging of dynamic export capabilities for competitive advantage and performance consequences: Evidence from China. *Journal of Business Research, 84*(August 2017), 114–124.

Elia, G., Margherita, A., & Passiante, G. (2020). Technological forecasting & social change digital entrepreneurship ecosystem: How digital technologies and collective intelligence are reshaping the entrepreneurial process. *Technological Forecasting and Social Change, 150*(September 2019), 119791.

Eurostat. (2020). *NUTS—Nomenclature of Territorial Units for Statistics, Background.* https://ec.europa.eu/eurostat/web/nuts/background.

Feenstra, R. (2014). Restoring the product variety and pro-competitive gains from trade with heterogeneous firms and bounded productivity. *Journal of International Economics, 110,* 16–27.

Ferreira, J., Marques, C., & Fernandes, C. (2010). Decision-making for location of new knowledge intensive businesses on ICT sector: Portuguese evidences. *International Journal of E-Entrepreneurship and Innovation, 1*(1), 60–82.

Fukugawa, N. (2016). Knowledge creation and dissemination by Kosetsushi in sectoral innovation systems: Insights from patent data. *Scientometrics, 109*(3), 2303–2327.

Fundeanu, D. D. (2015). Innovative regional cluster, model of tourism development. *Procedia Economics and Finance, 23*(October 2014), 744–749.

Furman, J. L., Porter, M. E., & Stern, S. (2002). The determinants of national innovative capacity. *Research Policy, 31*(2002), 899–933.

Galindo, P. V., Vaz, Td N, & Nijkamp, P. (2011). Institutional capacity to dynamically innovate: An application to the Portuguese case. *Technological Forecasting and Social Change, 78*(1), 3–12.

García-Rodríguez, F. J., Gil-Soto, E., Ruiz-Rosa, I., & Gutiérrez-Taño, D. (2017). Entrepreneurial potential in less innovative regions: The impact of social and cultural environment. *European Journal of Management and Business Economics, 26*(2), 163–179.

Garreton, M. (2017). City profile: Actually, existing neoliberalism in Greater Santiago. *Cities, 65,* 32–50.

Gomezelj Omerzel, D., & Smolčić Jurdana, D. (2016). The influence of intellectual capital on innovativeness and growth in tourism SMEs: Empirical evidence from Slovenia and Croatia. *Economic Research-Ekonomska Istraživanja, 29*(1), 1075–1090.

Greenhalgh, C., & Rogers, M. (2012). Trade marks and performance in UK firms: Evidence of Schumpeterian competition through innovation. *Australian Economic Review, 45*(1), 50–76.

Grillo, C., Ferreira, F. A. F., Marques, C. S. E., & Ferreira, J. (2018). A knowledge-based innovation assessment system for small- and medium-sized enterprises: Adding value with cognitive mapping and MCDA. *Journal of Knowledge Management, 22*(3), 696–718. JKM-08-2017-0332.

Gupta, S., Malhotra, N. K., Czinkota, M., & Foroudi, P. (2016). Marketing innovation: A consequence of competitiveness. *Journal of Business Research, 69*(12), 5671–5681.

Henrekson, M., & Johansson, D. (2010). Gazelles as job creators: A survey and interpretation of the evidence. *Small Business Economics, 35*(2), 227–244.

Hilmersson, M., Jansson, H., & Sandberg, S. (2011). Experiential knowledge profiles of internationalising SMEs—The ability to sustain market positions in the new turbulent era of global business. In A. Verbeke, A. T T. Lehmann,

& R. Van Tulder (Eds.), *Entrepreneurship in the global firm* (pp. 77–96). Bingley: Emerald.

Hu, F., & Trivedi, R. H. (2020). Mapping hotel brand positioning and competitive landscapes by text-mining user-generated content. *International Journal of Hospitality Management, 84*(May 2019), 102317, Elsevier.

Hu, J., & Hsu, Y. (2008). The more interactive, the more innovative? A case study of South Korean cellular phone manufacturers. *Technovation, 28,* 75–87.

Hua, S., & Wemmerlov, U. (2006). Product change intensity, product advantage, and market performance: An empirical investigation of the PC industry. *Journal of Product Innovation Management, 23,* 316–329.

Huang, Y.-C., Yang, M.-L., & Wong, Y.-J. (2016). The effect of internal factors and family influence on firms' adoption of green product innovation. *Management Research Review, 39*(10), 1167–1198.

Huang, Z., Sidhu, H. S., Towers, I. N., Jovanoski, Z., Watt, S., & Gubernov, V. V. (2020). Properties of nonadiabatic combustion waves in competitive exothermic reactions. *Applied Mathematical Modelling, 77,* 1216–1228.

Huggins, R., & Williams, N. (2011). Entrepreneurship and regional competitiveness: The role and progression of policy. *Entrepreneurship & Regional Development, 23*(9–10), 907–932.

Hwang, A. (2004). Integrating technology marketing and management innovation. *Research Technology Management, 47*(4), 27–31.

Johansson, B., Karlsson, C., & Stough, R. (2001). *Theories of endogenous regional growth, lessons for regional policies*. Berlin: Springer.

Jonker, J., Ageron, B., Gunasekaran, A., Spalanzani, A., Roy, R., Walker, H., Jones, N., et al. (2017). Re-thinking project initiation and project management by considering principles of sustainable development, edited by R. B. Zakaria, M. I. Mohamad, M.M.T.S.B.H.M.S.F.B.Y.A.B.M. *Journal of Cleaner Production, 18*(1), 2928–2932.

Kamaruzzaman, S. N., Lou, E. C. W., Zainon, N., Mohamed Zaid, N. S., & Wong, P. F. (2016). Environmental assessment schemes for non-domestic building refurbishment in the Malaysian context. *Ecological Indicators, 69,* 548–558, Elsevier B.V.

Kaminski, P., de Oliveira, A., & Lopes, T. M. (2008). Knowledge transfer in product development processes: A case study in small and medium enterprises (SMEs) of the metal mechanic sector from São Paulo, Brazil. *Technovation, 28,* 29–36.

Khan, E. A. (2018). The voice of informal entrepreneurs: Resources and capabilities perspective. *Journal of Developmental Entrepreneurship, 23*(3). Available at: https://doi.org/10.1142/S1084946718500152.

Klein, R. G., Dooley, D., Lapierre, K., Pitura, V. A., & Adduono, D. (2020). Trait perfectionism and competitiveness: Conceptual similarities and differences in a lab-based competitive task. *Personality and Individual Differences, Pergamon, 153,* 109610.

Kleinknecht, A. (1989). *Firm size and innovation: Observations in dutch manufacturing industries* (Vol. 53). Amsterdam: SEO (reprint).

Kline, S. J., & Rosenberg, N. (1986). An overview of innovation. In R. Laudau & N. Rosenberg (Eds.), *The positive sum strategy: Harnessing technology for economic growth* (pp. 275–306). Washington, DC: National Academy Press.

Koc, T., & Ceylan, C. (2007). Factors impacting the innovative capacity in large-scale companies. *Technovation, 27,* 105–114.

Kodama, M. (2006). Knowledge based view of corporate strategy. *Technovation, 26*(12), 1390–1406.

Kodama, M. (2009). *Innovation networks in knowledge—Based firms—Developing ICT—Based integrative competences*. Cheltenham: Edward Elgar.

Kolehmainen, J., Irvine, J., Stewart, L., Karacsonyi, Z., Szabó, T., Alarinta, J., & Norberg, A. (2016). Quadruple helix, innovation and the knowledge-based development: Lessons from remote, rural and less-favoured regions. *Journal of the Knowledge Economy, 7*(1), 23–42.

Lawson, B., Samson, D., & Roden, S. (2012). Appropriating the value from innovation: Inimitability and the effectiveness of isolating mechanisms. *R&D Management, 42*(5), 420–434.

Lee, S. Y., Florida, R., & Ács, Z. (2004). Creativity and entrepreneurship: A regional analysis of new firm formation. *Regional Studies, 38*(8), 879–891.

Lei, H., Yao, X., & Zhang, J. (2020). The competitiveness of provincial electric power supply in China: Based on a bottom-up perspective. *Electrical Power and Energy Systems, 116*(July 2019), 105557.

Lemon, M., & Sahota, P. (2004). Organizational culture as a knowledge repository for increased innovative capacity. *Technovation, 24,* 483–498.

Lentz, R., & Mortensen, D. T. (2016). Optimal growth through product innovation. *Review of Economic Dynamics, 19,* 4–19.

Li, J., Ku, Y., Liu, C., & Zhou, Y. (2020). Dual credit policy: Promoting new energy vehicles with battery recycling in a competitive environment? *Journal of Cleaner Production, 243,* 118456.

Li, W. (2017). Can intellectual property rights protection and governmental R&D investment promote Chinese enterprises' R&D investment? *Knowledge Management Research & Practice, 15*(4), 551–559.

Liu, C. H. S. (2018). Examining social capital, organizational learning and knowledge transfer in cultural and creative industries of practice. *Tourism Management, 64,* 258–270.

Long, T. B., Looijen, A., & Blok, V. (2018). Critical success factors for the transition to business models for sustainability in the food and beverage industry in the Netherlands. *Journal of Cleaner Production, 175,* 82–95.

Luh, Y. H., Jiang, W. J., & Huang, S. C. (2016). Trade-related spillovers and industrial competitiveness: Exploring the linkages for OECD countries. *Economic Modelling, 54,* 309–325.

Lundvall, B. A. (1992). *National systems of innovation: Towards a theory of innovation and interactive learning*. London: Pinter Publishers.

Ma, M., Huang, J., Lin, S., & Yang, S. (2019). From finance to marketing: Initial public offering ownership overhang and marketing in the hospitality industry. *International Journal of Hospitality Management, 76*(March 2018), 71–82.

Mahn, J., Kim, J., & Bae, J. (2020). Founder CEOs and innovation: Evidence from CEO sudden deaths in public firms. *Research Policy, 49*(1), 103862.

Marques, C., Garry, C., Covelo, S., Braga, A., & Braga, B. (2011). Innovation and the performance of Portuguese businesses: A 'SURE' approach. *International Journal of Management and Enterprise Development, 10*(2–3), 114–128.

Martin, S. L., Raj, R., Javalgi, G., & Ciravegna, L. (2020). Marketing capabilities and international new venture performance: The mediation role of marketing communication and the moderation effect of technological turbulence. *Journal of Business Research, 107*(September 2019), 25–37.

Mei, H., Zhan, Z., Fong, P. S. W., Liang, T., & Ma, Z. (2016). Planned behaviour of tourism students' entrepreneurial intentions in China. *Applied Economics, 48*(13), 1240–1254.

Meissner, D., & Shmatko, N. (2017). 'Keep open': The potential of gatekeepers for the aligning universities to the new Knowledge Triangle. *Technological Forecasting and Social Change, 123,* 191–198.

Mendola, D., & Volo, S. (2017). Building composite indicators in tourism studies: Measurements and applications in tourism destination competitiveness. *Tourism Management, 59,* 541–553.

Mendonça, S., Pereira, T. S., & Godinho, M. M. (2004). Trademarks as an indicator of innovation and industrial change. *Research Policy, 33*(9), 1385–1404.

Michael, N., Reisinger, Y., & Hayes, J. P. (2019). The UAE's tourism competitiveness: A business perspective. *Tourism Management Perspectives, 30,* 53–64.

Missimer, M., Robèrt, K.-H., & Broman, G. (2017). A strategic approach to social sustainability—Part 2: A principle-based definition. *Journal of Cleaner Production, 140,* 42–52.

Muller, E., & Zenker, A. (2001). Business services as actors of knowledge transformation: The role of KIBS in regional and national innovation systems. *Research Policy, 30*(9), 1501–1516.

Nas, T. I., & Kalaycioglu, O. (2016). The effects of the board composition, board size and CEO duality on export performance evidence from Turkey. *Management Research Review, 39*(11), 1374–1409.

NCOE. (2001). *Embracing innovation: Entrepreneurship and American economic growth* (National Commission on Entrepreneurship White Paper), pp. 1–11.

Nenem, S., Graham, A., & Dennis, N. (2020). Annals of Tourism Research Airline schedule and network competitiveness: A consumer-centric approach for business travel. *Annals of Tourism Research, 80*(October 2018), 102822, Elsevier.

Neutzling, D. M., dos Santos, M. S., de Barcellos, M. D., & Land, A. L. (2015). Value creation from internationalization of sugar cane by-products: A multi-stakeholder view of artisanal cachaça production. *Review of Business Management, 17*(55), 890–910.

Nicolini, M., & Resmini, L. (2011). Productivity spillovers, regional spillovers and the role of by multinational enterprises in the new EU members states. In K. Kourtit, P. Nijkamp, & R. R. Stough (Eds.), *Drivers of innovation, entrepreneurship and regional dynamics* (pp. 105–120). Heidelberg: Springer.

Nuruzzaman, N., Singh, D., & Pattnaik, C. (2019). Competing to be innovative: Foreign competition and imitative innovation of emerging economy firms. *International Business Review, 28*(5). Available at: https://doi.org/10.1016/j.ibusrev.2018.03.005.

Pérez, P. F., & Rose, M. B. (2010). Introduction: Innovation and entrepreneurial networks in Europe. In P. F. Pérez & M. B. Rose (Eds.), *Innovation and entrepreneurial networks in Europe* (pp. 1–13). New York: Routledge.

Petrakos, G., Skayannis, P., Papdoulis, A., & Anastasiou, G. (2011). Entrepreneurship, innovation and regional development: A Southern European perspective. In K. Kourtit, P. Nijkamp, & R. R. Stough (Eds.), *Drivers of innovation, entrepreneurship and regional dynamics* (pp. 81–104). Heidelberg: Springer.

Porter, M. E. (1990). The competitive advantage of nations. *Harvard Business Review, 68*(2), 73–93.

Porter, M. E. (1998). Clusters and the new economics of competition. *Harvard Business Review*, No. November–December, pp. 77–90.

Porter, M. E., & Ketels, C. H. M. (2003). *UK competitiveness: Moving to the next stage* (DTI Economics Paper, No. May 2003).

Porter, M. E., & Stern, S. (2001). Innovation: Location matters. *MIT Sloan Management Review, 42*(4, Summer), 28–36.

Przychodzen, W., Przychodzen, J., & Lerner, D. A. (2016). Critical factors for transforming creativity into sustainability. *Journal of Cleaner Production, 135*, 1514–1523.

Ramos, H. M., Man, T. W. Y., Mustafa, M., & Ng, Z. Z. (2014). Psychological ownership in small family firms: Family and non-family employees' work attitudes and behaviours. *Journal of Family Business Strategy, 5*(3, SI), 300–311.

Raposo, M. L., Ferreira, J. J. M., & Fernandes, C. I. (2014). Local and cross-border SME cooperation: Effects on innovation and performance. *Revista Europea de Dirección y Economía de La Empresa, 23*(4), 157–165.

Razumova, M., Ibáñez, J. L., & Palmer, J. R. M. (2015). Drivers of environmental innovation in Majorcan hotels. *Journal of Sustainable Tourism, 23*(10), 1529–1549.

Roberts, P., & Amit, R. (2003). The dynamics of innovative activity and competitive advantage: The case of Australian retail banking, 1981 to 1995. *Organization Science, 14*(2), 107–122.

Romer, P. M. (1994). The origins of endogenous growth. *Journal of Economic Perspectives, 8*(1), 2–22.

Rugman, A. M. (1987). Strategies for national competitiveness. *Long Range Planning, 20*(3), 92–97. https://doi.org/10.1016/0024-6301(87)90076-8.

Rutkauskas, A. V. (2008). On the sustainability of regional competitiveness development considering risk. *Technological and Economic Development of Economy, 14*(1), 89–99.

Segarra-Ciprés, M., Roca-Puig, V., & Bou-Llusar, J. C. (2014). External knowledge acquisition and innovation output: An analysis of the moderating effect of internal knowledge transfer. *Knowledge Management Research & Practice, 12*(2), 203–214.

Sölvell, Ö. (2015). The competitive advantage of nations book 25 years—Opening up new perspectives on competitiveness. *Competitiveness Review, 25*(5), 471–481.

Stanickova, M. (2015). Classifying the EU competitiveness factors using multivariate statistical methods. *Procedia Economics and Finance, 23*(October 2014), 313–320.

Stern, S., Porter, M. E., & Furman, J. L. (2000). *The determinants of national innovative capacity, No. w7876*. National Bureau of Economic Research.

Stough, R. (2003). Strategic management of places and policy. *Annals of Regional Science, 37*(1), 179–201.

Teixeira, S. J., Lopes Casteleiro, C. M., Rodrigues, R., & Guerra, M. (2018). Entrepreneurial intentions and entrepreneurship in European countries. *International Journal of Innovation Science, 10*(1), 22–42.

Tidd, J., & Bessant, J. (2009). Managing innovation—Integrating technological. In *Market and organizational change*. Chichester, England: Wiley.

Trachuk, A., & Linder, N. (2018). Learning-by-exporting effects on innovative performance: Empiric study results. *Knowledge Management Research & Practice, 16*(2), 220–234.

Tushman, M., & O'Reilly, C. (1997). *Winning through innovation: A practical guide to leading organizational change and renewal III*. Boston: Harvard Business School Press.

Tyson, L. D. (1990). Why a national competitiveness policy is needed? *International Journal of Technology Management, 5*(3), 245–257.

Uyarra, E., Zabala-Iturriagagoitia, J. M., Flanagan, K., & Magro, E. (2020). Public procurement, innovation and industrial policy: Rationales, roles, capabilities and implementation. *Research Policy, 49*(1), 103844.

Verbeke, A., & Kano, L. (2016). An *internalization theory* perspective on the global and regional strategies of multinational enterprises. *Journal of World Business, 51*(1), 83–92.

Von Hippel, E. (1988). *The sources of innovation*. New York: Oxford University Press.

Wong, P. P. W. (2017). Competitiveness of Malaysian destinations and its influence on destination loyalty. *Anatolia, 28*(2), 250–262.

Wood, P. (2005). A service-informed approach to regional innovation – or adaptation? *Service Industries Journal, 25*(4), 429–445. https://doi.org/10.1080/02642060500092063.

Zhang, X., Meng, Y., Chen, H., Yu, J., Sun, Y., De Pablos, P. C., & He, J. W. (2017). A bibliometric analysis of digital innovation from 1998 to 2016. *Journal of Management Science and Engineering, 2*(2), 95–115.

Zhao, X., Pan, W., & Chen, L. (2018). Disentangling the relationships between business model innovation for low or zero carbon buildings and its influencing factors using structural equation modelling. *Journal of Cleaner Production, 178*, 154–165.

Zheng, V., & Wong, S.-L. (2010). The mystery of capital: Eurasian entrepreneurs' socio-cultural strategies for commercial success in early 20(th)-century Hong Kong. *Asian Studies Review, 34*(4), 467–487.

CHAPTER 6

Internal Barriers for the Brazilian Economy to Achieve External Competitiveness

Arilda Teixeira, Silveli Cristo-Andrade, and Emerson Wagner Mainardes

6.1 Introduction

Attention to technical progress is justified by its relationship with growth that leads to the convergence of income and product per capita between countries. It is the context presented by the precursors of endogenous growth models (Barro & Sala-i-Martin, 1992; Lucas, 1988; Romer, 1986, 1987; Solow, 1956) to identify the determinants of convergence to a

A. Teixeira (✉) · S. Cristo-Andrade · E. W. Mainardes
Fucape Business School, Vitoria, ES, Brazil
e-mail: arilda@fucape.br

S. Cristo-Andrade
e-mail: silveli@fucape.br

E. W. Mainardes
e-mail: emerson@fucape.br

J. J. M. Ferreira et al. (eds.), *Technological Innovation and International Competitiveness for Business Growth*, Palgrave Studies in Democracy, Innovation, and Entrepreneurship for Growth,
https://doi.org/10.1007/978-3-030-51995-7_6

worldwide growth pattern, assuming that a country's macroeconomic environment is a reflection of its microeconomic decisions (Fagerberg, 2000).

Structural change is a process dependent on the choice that is made to achieve it; the ability of economic agents to improve it; and the intensity with which it is disseminated in the economy. Its continuity depends on the innovative capacity and allocation of resources by Human Capital (HC) (Acemoglu, Akcigit, Alp, Bloom, & Kerr, 2013; Aghion & Jaravel, 2015; Hechman & Jacobs, 2010). More efficient countries in this allocation have better results in the pace and direction of growth (Barro, 1996; Fagerberg, 2000; Romer, 1986, 1987). Learning by doing induces the adoption of new technologies—vectors that spread knowledge spillover (Buera & Kaboski, 2012; Fagerberg, 2000; Herrendorf, Rogerson, & Valentinyi, 2014; Romano & Traú, 2017)—that disseminate structural change, which sustains long-term growth.

As this process depends on the quality of the HC, the growth with technical progress depends on the teaching structure (Barro, 1996; Barro & Sala-i-Martin, 2004; Becker, 1964; Grossman & Helpman, 1995; Hall & Jones, 1999; Lucas, 1988; Mankiw, Romer, & Weil, 1992; North, 1994; OECD, 2016; Saviotti, Pyka, & Jun, 2016; WEF, 2015). Consequently, the competitiveness of an economy is the result of the productivity of its productive structure. The more competitive, the greater the ability to raise and sustain future income growth (WEF, 2008, 2018).

The fourth industrial revolution (4IR) ongoing reiterates the need for HC qualification and institutional enforcement—institutions, infrastructure, and cognitive ability—to sustain and raise long-term incomes (GCR, 2018). According to the Global Competitiveness Report (GCR) (2018) the governments of Singapore, Luxembourg, and the United States are best prepared for the 4IR economy; and those from Brazil, Greece, and Venezuela are the least prepared.

This debate is in the literature. As for Takashi (2019) who compared structural changes in Latin American and East Asian economies after their industrialization, in which the first stagnated in the 1980s and continues on a trajectory of low labor productivity; and the second accelerated and sustained technological advancement, productivity, and competitiveness.

Mijiyawa (2017) analyzed drivers for the development of the manufacturing industry in 53 African countries. It was identified that, the curve that describes the relation between percentage participation of the manufacturing industry in the GDP and in the GDP per capita has U shape; the increase in the exchange rate stimulates the production of this industry; market size has a positive relationship with the percentage share of industry in GDP; structural change brought about by industrialization is not guaranteed in these countries.

Herrendorf et al. (2014) considered that the structural change that the US underwent is explained by its ability to reallocate activities between sectors of the economy. Analogously Buera and Kaboski (2012) discussed the structural change with sectorial reallocation, through the interaction between firm size and the market. They identified that the pattern of change in the industry sector is different from that of the services sector. In the industry, technological advancement increases market share; in service, it can increase or decrease.

Badriah, Alisjahbana, Wibowo, and Hadiyanto (2019) analyzed the reallocation of labor (from agriculture to industry) during the process of structural change in Indonesia. They compared the advance in productivity in the manufacturing industry in relation to those brought about by structural changes. They identified that the changes in the labor reallocation process that occurred during the change reduced the pace of growth in labor productivity.

Dekle and Vandenbroucke (2012) addressed the structural change in China's agricultural companies. They pointed out that the increase in productivity was due to the reallocation of resources from agriculture to the industrial sector; reducing government intervention in the economy; and reducing inefficiency.

Romano and Traú (2017) discussed the structural changes arising from the internationalization of markets. They considered that the structural change process imposed by this market profile changed both the concentration of the industry sector, regarding the domestic structure of economies. However, the speed with which structural change occurs depends on the domestic capacity to process it.

Fagerberg (2000) focused on the impact of structural change and sector specialization on increasing productivity in the industry sector. Studied a sample of 39 countries, in the 1973–1990 period. Their results suggested that the structural change cannot be guaranteed to increase productivity; but countries that strive to achieve technical progress increase their productivity.

Autor and Salomons (2018) dealt with the replacement of labor by machine during the structural change processes. They admitted that technology can increase Total Factor Productivity and replace labor. However, there is some possibility of reallocating this workforce between industries.

Calcagnini, Grombini, and Travaglini (2018) used an endogenous growth model to describe the conflicting relationship between labor market regulation, innovation, and investment in Italy, Germany, and France. Regulation of the labor market increases the cost of firms. Consequently, it reduces their investments. However, it also encourages them to invest, innovate, produce, because this tripod will allow them to achieve productivity that will give them competitiveness in the market.

D'Agostino and Scarlato (2019) interpreted the relationship between institutions, innovation, and economic growth in European countries, through the evolutionary approach to economic growth. They assumed that knowledge externalities could compensate for institutional difficulties in accessing knowledge. Their results suggested that, in situations where institutions fulfilled their roles, equal opportunities for innovation were guaranteed, and there was a subsequent increase in the growth rate of GDP per capita.

Brixy (2014) estimated the impact that the number of start-ups, and their survival rates, have on the productivity total factor (PTF) and employment in the region where they are. The study was done with start-ups from West and East Germany. However, it failed to show the expected impact because it differs according to the region.

Herrendorf and Todd (2018) studied a group of 13 countries—developed and developing—and identified that agriculture has lower returns than other sectors, and that has fewer skilled workers. Their results pointed to two factors that hinder structural change: the unobserved characteristics of the workforce; and differences in human capital intensity between sectors.

The work by Syverson (2011) analyzed previous research that addressed productivity differences between sectors of the economy. He identified that the determinants are several and depend on the management practice. Suggested that future research brings these answers.

In analyzing food retail productivity in developing countries Lagakos (2016) pointed out that managers deliberately choose technologies that result in low labor productivity. In addition, being low-income countries, consumption of durable goods is limited. This demand profile limits the growth and diversification of supply. Thus, a possible increase in the productivity of food retail does not mean an increase in well-being.

Blandin and Peterman (2019) associated the accumulation of human capital with the tax charged on their income. The research aimed to identify the level of taxation that does not compromise the role of Human Capital (HC) in the trajectory for structural change. They considered that this taxation depends on how human capital is accumulated (learning-by-doing, learning-or-doing, or exogenous accumulation).

Kogan, Papanikolaou, Seru, and Stoffman (2017) identified through a sample of US firm patents obtained between 1926 and 2010, that the technological innovations of these companies stimulated economic growth and the Total Productivity of the Factors (TPF).

From the debate exposed above, it can be admitted that most of the determinants and aggravating factors of endogenous growth are already addressed in the literature. However, no comparative statistics were made for the Brazilian economy, in relation to those of its peers, supported by the fundamentals of endogenous growth, and described by the parameters of the Global Competitiveness Report and the Doing Business. This particularity deserves to be presented because such statistics ratify the foundations of the endogenous growth theory. For this reason, this chapter aimed to present and interpret the statistics of the performance of the Brazilian economy compared to those of the BRICS countries, Latin America, and Asia.

The relevance of this line of approach is that it puts face-to-face performance indicators for economies at the same stage of development that, in theory, should present equivalent performance indicators. The comparison that will be made in this chapter is an opportunity to reinforce that economic performance is the result of efficient resource allocation. Therefore, equivalent economies with different performances are explained by the criteria of their choices. *Coeteris paribus*, not a fatality.

The text is distributed in three parts. The first is this introduction with the contextualization of the debate on technical progress and sustained growth; the second, brings the historiography of the Brazilian technological gap to signal the elements that led its economy to the stagnation in which it finds itself; the third presents the graphs and tables that compare the performance of the economies. And in the fourth section, we make the final remarks.

6.2 Historiography of Brazilian Technological Gap

Until the twentieth century, the greatest structural change in the Brazilian economy took place with industrialization in the 1950s. Between 1956 and 1980, real GDP multiplied by 15; GDP per capita for 5; the volume of investment as a proportion of GDP remained between 22 and 24%; and the exported quantum grew at an average rate of 6% a.a.—the average growth rate of world exports was 5.1% (Fritsch & Franco, 1991; Fritsch, 1992; Werneck, 1988).

As their inward-oriented industrialization model followed the postulates of the Dependency Theory (Prebisch, 1962, 1973), it was autarchic and led by the state. A choice that left it out of the competition between markets; and induced economic agents to underestimate the role of allocative efficiency to sustain structural change (Fishlow, 1972; Fritsch, 1992; Fritsch & Franco, 1991). Its choice hindered the advancement of technical progress, withdrew its capacity for external insertion, and prevented its industrial park from advancing in technology-intensive products. It ran out in the early 1980s when the growth rate of exports dropped to 20% from what it had been between 1960 and 1970; technology-intensive products accounted for only 10% of these exports; and imports were predominantly of technology-intensive goods. It had no breath to keep up with ongoing technological, managerial, and organizational innovations (Erber, 2000; Fischer, 1996; Suzigan, 2003; Thomas and Grindle, 1992). In the early 1990s, the structure of its manufacturing industry remained insufficient for the intense technological standard of knowledge (Figueiredo & Nakabashi, 2016).

The Development Agenda of the first half of the 1990s aimed at reversing the setback with market-oriented reforms, but it was not enough (Bonelli, 2015). What was accomplished was the restoration of currency stability and the restructuring of the financial system. The Tax Reform proposal did not materialize until 2016; and the post-privatization regulatory framework was also not enough—sector specificities were disregarded, making room for Regulatory Agencies to be captured by regulated agents (Nunes, 2003; Pacheco, 2006).

During this period the educational policy deteriorated to such an extent that in 2017 the average years of education for Brazilians was 12 years; only 15.3% of the population old enough to have completed higher education completed it; 26.8% of the population old enough to have completed high school completed it; and 8.5% of those who are old enough to have finished elementary school completed it—Fig. 6.1. In 2015 Brazil occupied 96th place in the ranking of the Program for International Student Assessment (PISA) out of a total of 200 countries (IE, 2018).

The by-product of this reality is the concentration of income and labou with low productivity (Souza, Ribeiro, & Carvalhães, 2010). The teaching structure in Brazil is a machine to produce social inequality (IBGE/SIS, 2018). The country has higher rates of employability and wage return for those who complete higher education than that of the 36 OECD member countries and its 10 partner countries. The wages of those with higher education is 2.5 times that of those who only finished high school; the OECD average is 1.6 times. This places it as one of the most unequal countries in the world (Hasenbalg 2003; IBGE/SIS, 2018; IBGE/PNAD, 2018; OECD, 2018).

This scenario confirms the role of government institutions and policies to create an economic environment conducive to the increase in

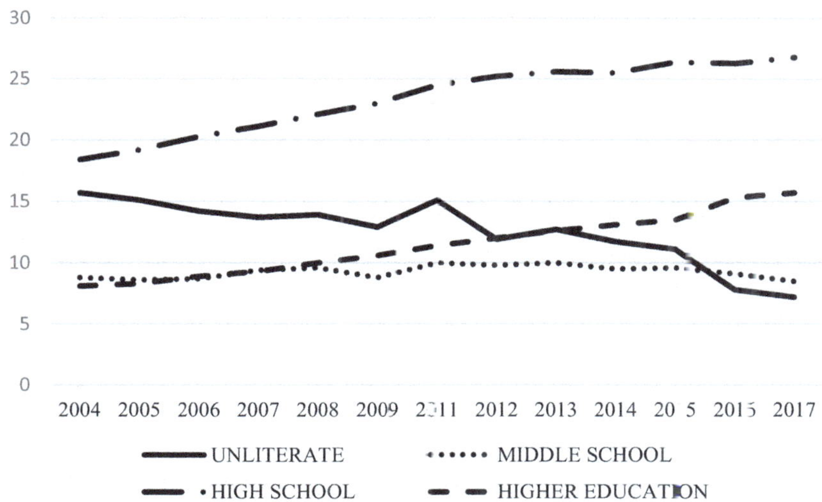

Fig. 6.1 Brazil: % people aged 25 or over by level of education (*Source* Brazilian Institute of Geographic Statistic (IBGE)—Synthesis Social Indicators, 2004–2018. Obs.: Annual publication except census years. So, there is no data for 2010)

Total Productivity Factor (TPF), able to boost the catch-up process (Figueiredo & Nakabashi, 2016; Hall & Jones, 1999; Kehoe, Costa, & Raveendranathan, 2016).

As the quality of the labor market is directly related to labor productivity, schooling statistics—Fig. 6.1—suggest that education in Brazil is an obstacle to the growth of its GDP per capita (Cavalcante & De Negri, 2014). Moreover, because it is the result of the adopted teaching policy, it is the choice of the State; that because it is wrong, it blocks technological advances in the country (WEO, 2018).

In the first two decades of the 2000s, its economy remained excluded from the global production chain due to the low dynamism of its capital accumulation process and its low productivity (Bonelli, 2015; Cavalcante, Jacinto, & De Negri, 2015; Messa, 2015). Between 1992 and 2007, the TPF grew only 11.3%, and the human capital of the workforce remained stationary (Barbosa Filho, Pessoa, & Veloso, 2010).

The macroeconomic environment is another impediment to technological advancement. It sustained monetary and fiscal instability from industrialization to the first half of the 1990s. In 1994, currency stability was restored and the Inflation Targets Regime was adopted to implement monetary policy. However, fiscal irresponsibility in the public sector remained—even after the Fiscal Responsibility Law was passed in 1998. Public debt went from 55.6% of GDP in 2006 to 77.2% in 2018 (*Banco Central do Brasil*, 2018). The resulting increase in the need for public sector financing has reduced the availability of resources for investments in infrastructure and R&D projects.

This record has led to uncertainty, legal uncertainty, and deterioration of the business environment. It led to persistent declines in the growth rate of GDP per capita—from 4.5% a.a. between 1950 and 1980 to 0.7% a.a. between 1980 and 2016 (De Negri, Araujo, & Bacelette, 2018). Internal barriers to the external competitiveness of the Brazilian economy.

6.3 Performance Statistics

Sanctioning the hypothesis of endogenous growth theory, Brazil's growth trajectory has been on a slowdown since the 1970s—Fig. 6.2—suggesting the misalignment of its development model with the sustainability of long-term growth rates.

In addition to low schooling—Fig. 6.1—Brazil has the most closed economy, among the BRICS, among its Latin American peers, and among

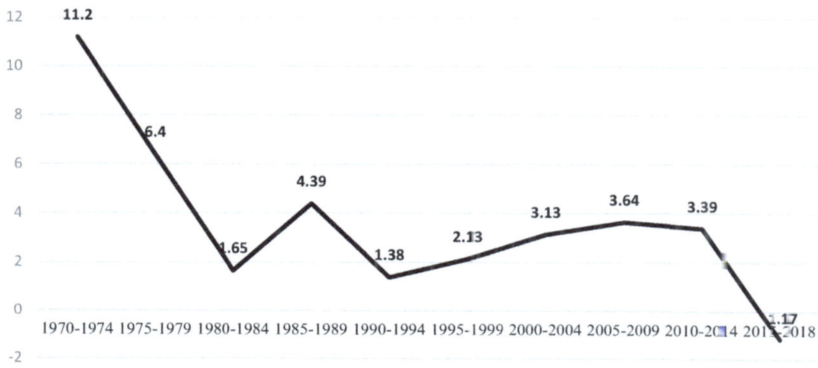

Fig. 6.2 Brazil GDP (1970–2018): real growth rate—period average (*Source* Brazilian Institute of Geographic Statistic (IBGE/NSA)/National System Account (SCN) [2018])

developing countries—Figs. 6.3 and 6.4. This profile explains its difficulty for external insertion, and why its participation in world trade has stagnated at 1.2% for 40 years (UNCTAD, 2018). Brazil is also the country with the lowest investment volume as a proportion of GDP—in addition to having decreasing rates in these investments—Fig. 6.5.

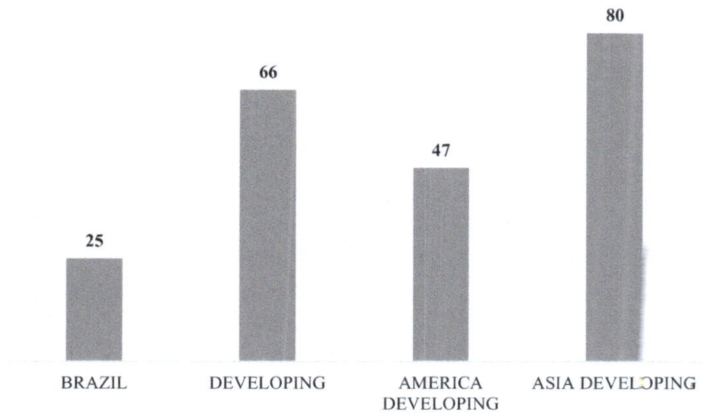

Fig. 6.3 Countries degree of openness (*Source* UNCTAD: country profile)

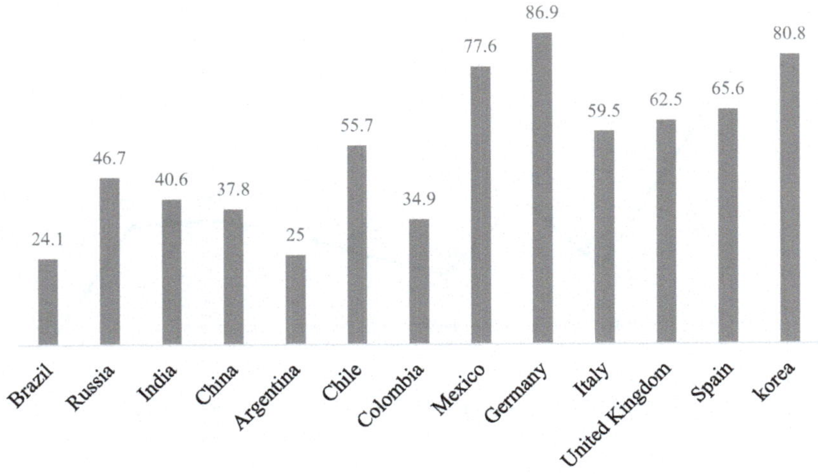

Fig. 6.4 Trade chain 2017—% GDP (*Source* UNCTAD: country profile)

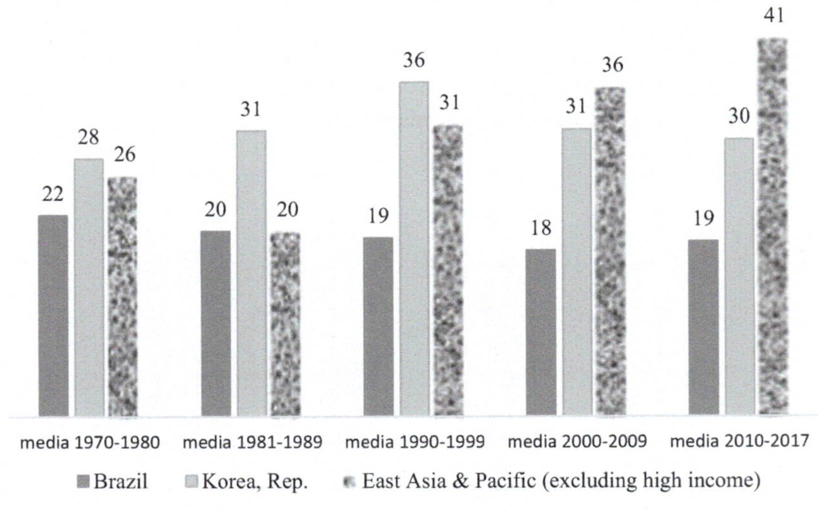

Fig. 6.5 GFCF % GDP: Brazil, Korea, and East Asia (*Source* World Bank)

Between 1970 and 1980 Gross Fixed Capital Formation (GFCF) as a percentage of GDP it was 22%; dropped to 20% in the 1980s; and reached 19% in 2010. While Korea and East Asia supported investments of around 30%—Fig. 6.5.

The overlap of, low education, closed economy, and low investment volume, resulted in technological gap and low potential for innovation. Between 2005–2015 the share of ICT Goods in total exports from Brazil was 0.45%; in Korea it was 22%; and in China 27% (UNCTAD, 2018).

These statistics suggest that its development model took away the opportunity for the learning curve that leads to innovation to occur. Innovation rates in the manufacturing industry between 1998 and 2014 confirm this. Its average percentage of innovation remained stagnant at 35%—Fig. 6.6. But, product innovation and, mainly, in R&D, fell 50% in relation to what was in the 1998–2000 biennium—Fig. 6.7.

Koeller (2017) pointed out that, in the period 2012–2014, the innovation rate of Brazilian companies was 39%, which places Brazil in 15th position among 32 of the Community Innovation Survey (CIS). However, this rate is below the European Union average, and is lower than that of leading countries in innovative activities. Furthermore, it is still very concentrated in machinery and equipment at the expense of R&D expenses (Koeller, 2017).

The low volume of investment also explains part of this result. Between 1955 and 1980, Brazil had an investment volume equivalent to that of East Asia, and higher than that of Korea and China. From the 1980s, this trajectory reversed, reaching the twenty-first century with the lowest

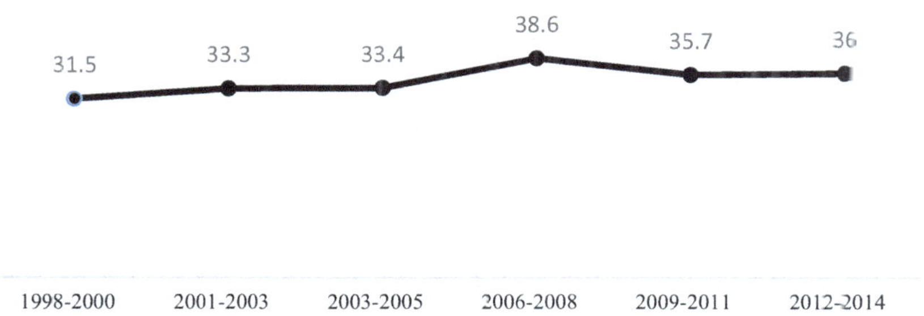

Fig. 6.6 % manufacturing industry innovation (*Source* Brazilian Institute of Geographic Statistic (IBGE/PINTEC)—Business Demography 2019—PINTEC 2000, 2003, 2005, 2008, 2011, 2014)

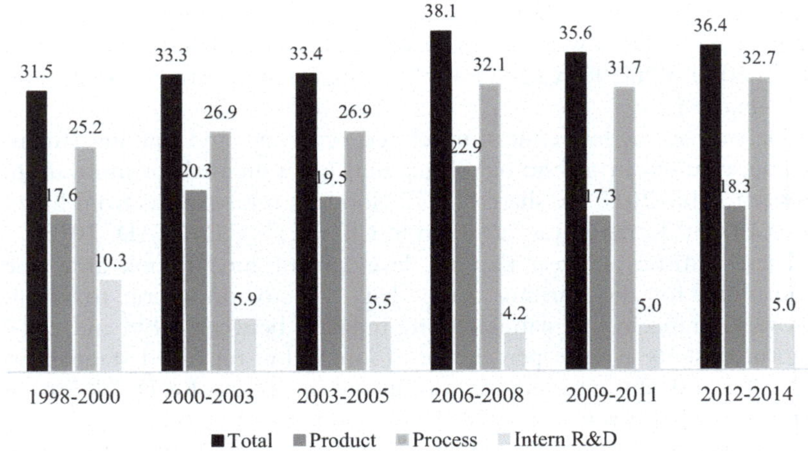

Fig. 6.7 % innovation and R&D in manufacturing companies (*Source* Brazilian Institute of Geographic Statistic (IBGE/PINTEC)—Business Demography 2018—PINTEC 2000, 2003, 2005, 2008, 2011, 2014)

volume of investment in proportion to GDP, in relation to these two Asian countries—Fig. 6.8.

It should be noted that the Brazilian investment pattern is equivalent to that of its Latin American peers—Fig. 6.9—which reinforces the hypothesis that Brazil's shortfall is structural, a legacy of its industrialization model, reproduced in other countries in the region (Kaufman & Stalling, 1991; Dornbusch & Edwards, 1991).

6.3.1 *Brazil Competitiveness According to Global Competitiveness Report (GCR)*

This item describes the competitiveness of the Brazilian economy through the Global Competitiveness Index indicators (GCI 4.0), of the GCR. It starts with the position in the general ranking, and then on the pillars of competitiveness GCR. Brazil's position initially improved; but it deteriorated from 2014—Fig. 6.10.

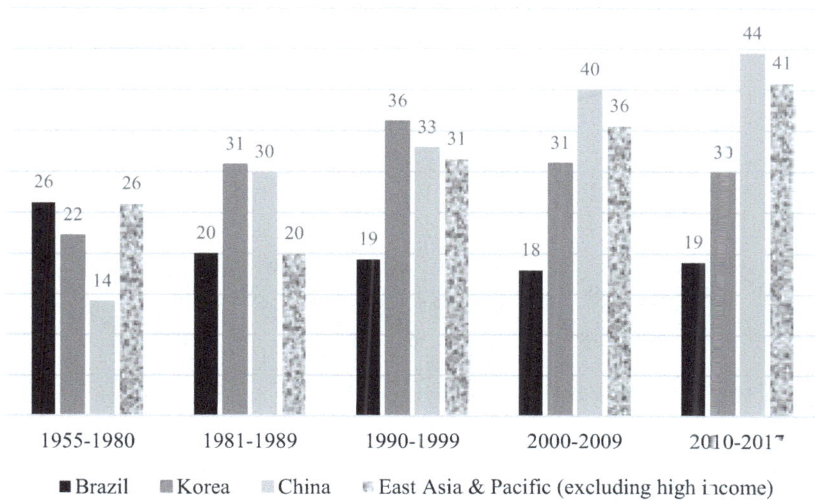

Fig. 6.8 Brazil, Korea, China and East Asia: media GFCF %PIB (*Source* World Bank)

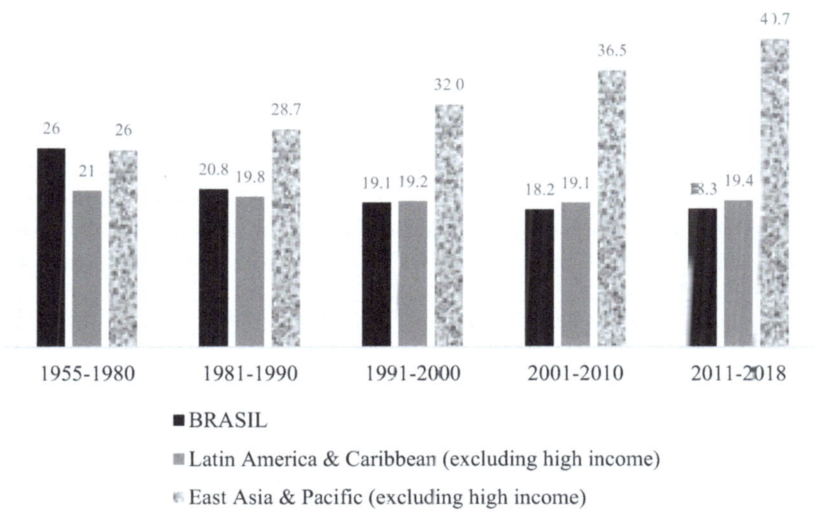

Fig. 6.9 Brazil, Latin America, and East Asia—GFCF %GDP: period average (*Source* World Bank)

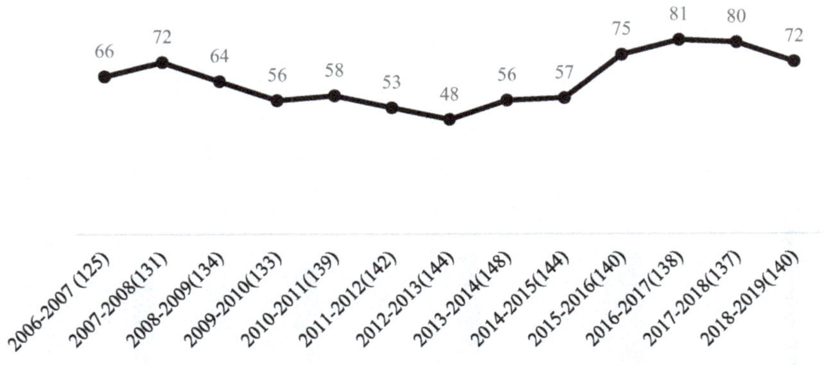

Fig. 6.10 Brazil: Global Competitiveness Report ranking position (*Source* Global Competitiveness Report)

6.3.2 Competitiveness According to the GCI 4.0 Pillars

Figure 6.11 confirms China's leadership in competitiveness in the BRICS group in all pillars. And Brazil and South Africa as the least competitive. Given the history described in the Brazilian economy, this result is not surprising. However, it surprises Russia to have more qualified human capital and less capacity for innovation than China.

The low competitiveness of the Brazilian economy can be explained by the obstacles it offers to those who want to do business in their market. According to Doing Business criteria, Brazil occupies the last positions in its ranking in most processes to start a business. Despite improving minority investor protection, contract enforcement, and insolvency resolution, there are still more obstacles than facilities for negotiating in Brazil—Fig. 6.12.

It is worth remembering that these aspects treated by Doing Business are related to the institutional apparatus of the economic environment, which is a key element in creating a favorable business environment (GCR, 2018). Therefore, they influence a country's competitiveness.

Thus, the statistics in Fig. 6.12 call attention to how institutional obstacles can hinder the long-term growth path of the Brazilian economy. They distort the dynamics of allocative efficiency; that blocks productivity; that reduces competitiveness; that prevents the advance of technical progress; that separates the economy from world trends. Persisting in this

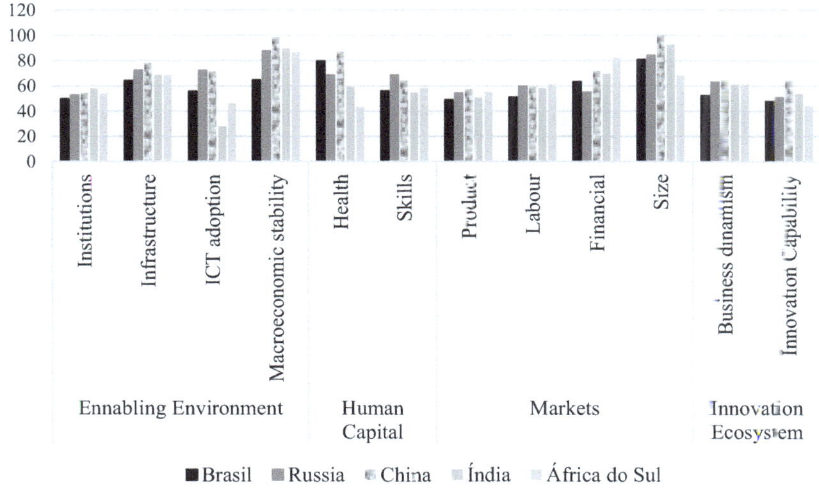

Fig. 6.11 BRICS on the pillars of competitiveness (*Source* Global Competitiveness Report, 2018. Obs.: Score from 0 to 100 [zero is worse; 100 is the best])

direction, the Brazilian economy will not develop technology to live up to the pattern of competition and competition that 4RI is bringing.

6.4 Conclusions

The purpose of this chapter was to present and interpret the statistics of the performance of the Brazilian economy compared to those of the BRICS countries, Latin America, and Asia. We pointed out the obstacles for the Brazilian economy to enter the growth path with structural change imposed by the 4th Industrial Revolution in progress. According to competitiveness indicators, productive activity based on products and intense processes in materials still predominates, while the new paradigm works with knowledge-intensive products and processes. In addition, it persists with policies that lead to inequality and income concentration—that abort the process of human capital formation—and underestimate the role of institutions as enforcement to ensure legal certainty and predictability in their market.

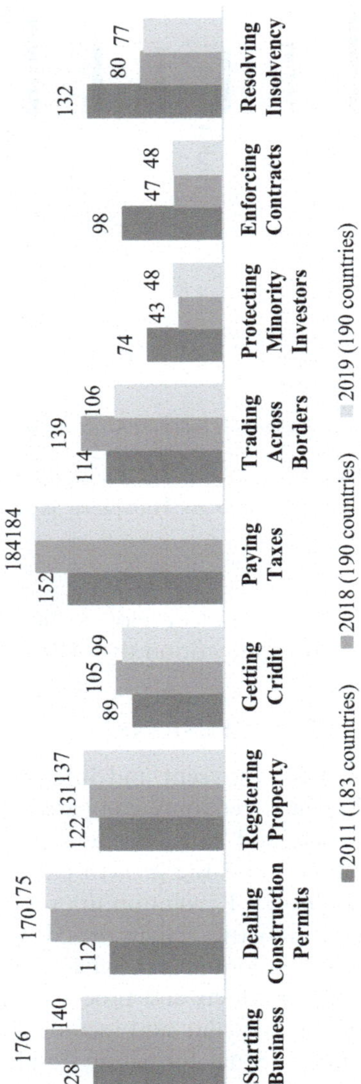

Fig. 6.12 Brazil position in the Doing Business ranking by business regulation area (*Source* World Bank-Doing Business, 2018)

The Brazilian economy has internal barriers to achieving technical progress. To break them, one needs to change their market culture that is refractory to knowledge, planning, accountability, and social equity. The ongoing industrial revolution changed the context in which the capitalist system operates. Therefore, capitalists need to change the parameters of decision and performance so that the economy can stay on the path of sustained growth. This change, for Brazil, involves admitting the delay and working to overcome it, technically and institutionally. However, statistics suggest that the country is not yet aligned with the 4RI paradigm. It has not yet constituted an innovative ecosystem that guarantees it a long-term growth path for its economy. A position that represents a risk that it will remain underdeveloped and, above all, unable to keep up with the world economy.

The limitation of this study was that it did not approach developing countries on all continents to offer a complete picture of the inefficiency focuses. We suggest that future research completes the analysis started here.

References

Acemoglu, D., Akcigit, U., Alp, H., Bloom, N., & Kerr, W. (2013, April). *Innovation, reallocation and growth* (NBER Working Paper No.18993).

Aghion, P., & Jaravel, X. (2015, March). Knowledge spillovers, innovation and growth. *Economic Journal, 125*(583), 533–573. Available on: https://doi.org/10.1111/ecoj.12199.

Autor, D., & Salomons, A. (2018). *Is automation labor-displacing? productivity growth, employment, and the labor share* (NBER Working Paper No. 24871). Available on: https://www.nber.org/papers/w24871.pdf.

Badriah, L. S., Alisjahbana, A. S., Wibowo, K., et al. (2019). Labor productivity growth in the industrial sector of Indonesia: Structural bonus or structural burden. *Malaysian Journal of Economic Studies, 56*(1), 139–159. ISSN: 1511-4554.

Banco Central do Brasil. (2018). *Evolução da Dívida Pública – Tabelas Adicionais*. Available on: https://www.bcb.gov.br/estatisticas/tabelasespeciais.

Barbosa Filho, F. H., Pessoa, S. A., & Veloso, F. A. (2010). Evolução da Produtividade Total dos Fatores na Economia Brasileira com Ênfase no Capital Humano – 1992–2007. *Revista Brasileira de Economia*, Rio de Janeiro, v.64 n.2/ pp. 91–113, Abr-Jun.

Barro, R. J. (1996). *Determinants of economic growth: A cross-country empirical study*. Cambridge, MA and London: MIT Press.

Barro, R. J., & Sala-i-Martin, X. (1992). Convergence. *Journal of Political Economy, 100*(April), 223–251.

Barro, R. J., & Sala-i-Martin, X. (2004). *Economic growth* (2nd ed.). Cambridge, MA: MIT Press.

Becker, G. (1964). *Human capital: A theoretical and empirical analysis with special reference to education*. New York: Columbia Press.

Blandin, A., & Peterman, W. (2019, October). The importance of how human capital is accumulated. *European Economic Review, 119,* 482–508.

Bonelli, R. (2015). *Labor productivity in Brazil during the 1990s* (Discussion Paper 117). Brasília: IPEA. Available on: http://www.ipea.gov.br/portal/images/stories/PDFs/TDs/ingles/dp_117.pdf.

Brixy, U. (2014). The significance of entry and exit for regional productivity growth. *Regional Studies, 48*(6), 1051–1070. Available on: https://doi.org/10.1080/00343404.2014.895804.

Buera, F. J., & Kaboski, J. P. (2012). Scale and the origin of structural change. *Journal of Economic Theory, 147*(2), 684–712. Available on: https://doi.org/10.1016/j.jet.2010.11.007.

Calcagnini, G., Grombini, G., & Travalini, G. (2018). A Schumpeterian model of investment an innovation with labor market regulation. *Economics of Innovation and Technology, 27*(7), 628–651. Available on: https://doi.org/10.1080/10438599.2018.1389107.

Cavalcante, L. R., & De Negri, F. (2014). Evolução Recente dos Indicadores de Produtividade no Brasil. In F. De Negri & L. R. Cavalcante (Orgs.), *Produtividade no Brasil – Desempenho e Determinantes*. Brasília: IPEA.

Cavalcante, L. R., Jacinto, P. A., & De Negri, F. (2015). P&D, Inovação e Produtividade na Indústria Brasileira. In *Produtividade no Brasil – Desempenho e Determinantes* (Vol. 2). Brasília: ABDI: IPEA. Available on: http://www.ipea.gov.br/portal/images/stories/PDFs/livros/livros/150831_livro_produtividade_v2.pdf.

d'Agostino, G., & Scarlato, M. (2019). Knowledge externalities, innovation and growth in European countries: The role of institutions. *Economics of Innovation and New Technology, 28*(1), 82–99. Available on: https://doi.org/10.1080/10438599.2018.1429536.

De Negri, J. A., Araujo, B. C., & Bacelette, R. (Orgs.). (2018). *Desafios da Nação – Artigos de Apoio* (Vol. 1, pp. 702p.). Brasilia: IPEA. Available on: http://www.ipea.gov.br/portal/images/stories/PDFs/livros/livros/livro_produtividade_no_brasil.pdf.

Dekle, R., & Vandenbroucke, G. (2012). A quantitative analysis of China's structural transformation. *Journal of Economic Dynamics and Control, 36*(1), 119–135. Available on: https://doi.org/10.1016/j.jedc.2011.07.004.

Dornbusch, R., & Edwards, S. (1991). The macroeconomics of populism. In R. Dornbusch & S. Edwards (Eds.), *The macroeconomics of populism in Latin America*. Chicago and London: The University of Chicago Press.

Erber, F. S. (2000). *Brazilian development in the nineties—Myths, circles and structures*. Rio de Janeiro: IE/UFRJ. Texto em PDF.

Fagerberg, J. (2000, December). Technological progress, structural change and productivity growth: A comparative study. *Structural Change or Economic Dynamics, 11*(4), 393–411.

Figueiredo, L., & Nakabashi, L. (2016, May–August). The relative importance of total factor productivity and factor of production in income per worker: Evidence from Brazilian states. *EconomiA, 17*(2), 159–175. Available on: https://doi.org/10.1016/j.econ.2016.03.005.

Fischer, S. (1996). Lessons from East Asia and Pacific. *Brookings Papers on Economic Activity, 1996*(2), 345–350. Available on: https://www.jstor.org/stable/i343498.

Fishlow, A. (1972, March). Brazilian size distribution of income. *American Economic Review, 62*(1/2, 1), 391–402.

Fritsch, W. (1992). Foreign direct investment and patterns of trade and industrialization in developing countries: Notes with reference to the Brazilian experience. In G. K. Helleiner (Ed.), *Trade policy, industrialization and development: A reconsideration*. Oxford: Clarendon Press.

Fritsch, W., & Franco, G. (1991). *Trade policy issues in Brazil in the 1990s*. Texto para Discussão 268. Rio de Janeiro: PUC. Available on: https://www.econstor.eu/bitstream/10419/186514/1/td268.pdf.

Grossman, G., & Helpman, E. (1995). *Innovation and growth in the global economy*. Cambridge, MA: MIT Press.

Hall, R. E., & Jones, C. I. (1999, February). Why do some countries produce so much more output per worker than others? *The Quarterly Journal of Economics, 114*(1), 83–116. Available on: https://doi.org/10.1162/003355399555954.

Hasenbalg, C. (2003). A Transição da Escola ao Mercado de Trabalho. In C. Hasenbalg, & N. do Silva (Orgs.), *Origens e destinos: desigualdades sociais ao longo da vida*. Rio de Janeiro: Top Books.

Hechman, J. J., & Jacobs, B. (2010). *Policies to create and destroy human capital in Europe* (NBER Working Paper 15742). Available on: http://www.nber.org/papers/w15742.

Herrendorf, B., Rogerson, R., & Valentinyi, A. (2014). Growth and structural transformation. *Handbook of Economic Growth, 2*, 855–941. Available on: https://doi.org/10.1016/B978-0-444-53540-5.00006-9.

Herrendorf, B., & Todd, S. (2018). Wages, human capital, and barriers to structural transformation. *American Journal: Macroeconomics, 10*(2), 1–23. https://doi.org/10.1257/mac.20160236.

IBGE/PINTEC. (2018). Brazilian Institute of Geographic Statistic-Bussiness Demography. *Pesquisa de Inovação.* Available on: https://www.ibge.gov.br/estatisticas/multidominio/ciencia-tecnologia-e-inovacao/9141-pesquisa-de-inovação.html?=&=series-historicas.

IBGE/PNAD. (2018). Instituto Brasileiro de Geografia e Estatística. *Indicadores IBGE: Pesquisa Nacional por Amostra de Domicílios.* Available on: https://biblioteca.ibge.gov.br/visualizaco/periodicos/3086/pnacm_2018_dez.pdf.

IBGE/PNAD/SCN10 Anual. (2018). PIB - preços de mercado - var. real anual. Instituto Brasileiro de Geografia e Estatística, Sistema de Contas Nacionais (IBGE/SCN Anual).

IBGE/SIS. (2018). Instituto Brasileiro de Geografia e Estatística. Síntese de Indicadores Sociais de 2017. Publicado em 2018. Available on: https://biblioteca.ibge.gov.br/visualização/livros/liv101629.pdf.

IE—International Education Data Base. (2015, 2018). *World Best Education Systems, 2015–2018.*

Kaufman, R. R., & Stallings, B. (1991). The political economy of Latin American populism. In R. Dornbusch & S. Edwards (Eds.), *The macroeconomics of populism in Latin America.* Chicago and London: The University of Chicago Press.

Kehoe, T. J., Costa, D., & Raveendranathan, G. (2016). *The stages of economic growth revisited: Part 1: A general framework and taking off into growth* (Economic Policy Paper 16-5). Federal Reserve Bank of Minneapolis.

Klauss, S. (2018). *Global Competitiveness Report* (Ed.). World Economic Forum.

Koeller, P. (2017). Dinâmica da Inovação no Brasil em Contraposição a Países Selecionados. *Radar n.51.* Available on: http://repositorio.ipea.gov.br/handle/11058/7955.

Kogan, L., Papanikolaou, D., Seru, A., et al. (2017, May). Technological innovation resource allocation, and growth. *The Quarterly Journal of Economics, 132*(2), 665–712. Available on: https://doi.org/10.1093/qje/qjw040.

Lagakos, D. (2016). Explain cross-country productivity differences in retail trade. *Journal of Political Economy, 124*(2), 579–620. Available on: https://doi.org/10.1086/684718.

Lucas, R. (1988, July). On the mechanics of economic development. *Journal of Monetary Economics, 22*(1), 3–42.

Mankiw, N. G., Romer, D., & Weil, D. N. (1992). A contritubion to the empirics of economic growth. *Quarterly Journal of Economics, 107*(2), 407–437.

Messa, A. (2015). Determinantes da Produtividade na Indústria Brasileira. In F. De Negri & L. R. Cavalcante (Orgs.), *Produtividade no Brasil – Desempenho e Determinantes* (Vol. 2). Brasília: IPEA. Available on: http://www.ipea.gov.br/portal/images/stories/PDFs/livros/livros/150831_livro_produtividade_v2.pdf.

Mijiyawa, A. G. (2017, November). Drivers of structural transformation: The case of the manufacturing sector in Africa. *World Development, 99*, 141–159. Available on: https://doi.org/10.1016/j.worlddev.2017.07.007.

North, D. (1994). Economic performance through time. *American Economic Review, 84*(3), 359–368.

Nunes, E. (2003). Agências Regulatórias: gênese, contexto, perspectivas e controle. *Revista do Direito Público e Econômico*, Editora Forum, Belo Horizonte, ano 1, no.2, abr/mai/jun.

OECD. (2016, June 1–2). *The productivity-inclusiveness nexus: Meeting at the OECD Council at Ministerial Level*, Paris.

OECD. (2018). *Indicators: Education at a Glance*. OECD, 2018, 458p. Available on: https://www.oecd-ilibrary.org/education/education-at-a-glance-2018eaf-2018-en.

Pacheco, R. S. (2006). Regulação no Brasil desenho das agências e formas de controle. *Revista Brasileira de Administração Pública, 40*(4), 523–544.

Prebisch, R. (1962). O desenvolvimento Econômico da América Latina e Alguns de seus Problemas Principais. CEPAL, *Boletín Económico de América Latina, vol VII, nº1*, Santiago do Chile, 1962. Publicação das Nações Unidas nº de venda: 62.II.G.1. In: Cinquentas anos do Pensamento da CEPAL. Rio de Janeiro: Record/CEPAL 2000, v.1, pp. 69–136. Available on: https://repositorio.cepal.org/bitstream/handle/11362/1611/003_pt.pdf?sequence=1&isAllowed=y.

Prebisch, R. (1973). *Problemas Teóricos y práticos del crescimento econômico*. Santiago do Chile, CEPAL, 1973. Originalmente publicado em 1952 como documento da CEPAL, com a sigla E/CN.12/221. IN: Cinquentas anos do Pensamento da CEPAL. Rio de Janeiro: Record/CEPAL 2000, v.1, pp. 181–215. Available on: https://repositorio.cepal.org/handle/11362/2958.

Romano, L., & Traú, F. (2017). The nature of industrial development and the speed of structural change. *Structural Change and Economics Dynamics, 42*, 26–37. Available on: https://doi.org/10.1016/j.strueco.2017.05.003.

Romer, P. (1986, October). Increasing returns and long run growth. *Journal of Political Economy, 94*(5), 1002–1037.

Romer, P. (1987). Growth based on increasing returns due to specialization. *American Economic Review, 77*(2), 56–62.

Saviotti, P. P., Pyka, A., & Jun, B. (2016, September). Education, structural change and economic development. *Structural Change and Economic Dynamics, 38*, 55–68. Available on: https://doi.org/10.1016/j.strueco.2016.04.002.

Solow, R. M. (1956). A contribution to the theory of economic growth. *Quarterly Journal of Economics, 70*(1), 65–94.

Souza, F. P., Ribeiro, C. A. C., & Carvalhães, S. F. (2010). Desigualdade de Oportunidades no Brasil: considerações sobre classe, educação e raça. *Revista Brasileira de Ciências Sociais*. São Paulo: ANPOCS, v.25, n.73.

Suzigan, W. (1995). Estratégia industrial e desenvolvimento econômico: uma agenda política e de política econômica. *Indicadores Econômicos FEE*. Porto Alegre: Fundação de Economia e Estatística, v.23, n.1, p. 108, maio.

Suzigan, W. (2003). El rumbo de las reformas. Hacia uma nueva agenda para América Latina. *Revista da CEPAL*.

Syverson, C. (2011). What determines productivity? *Journal of Economic Literature, 49*(2), 326–365. https://doi.org/10.1257/jel.49.2.326.

Takashi, M. (2019). Per capita output convergence across Asian countries: Evidence from covariate unit root test with an endogenous structural break. *Economic Modelling, 82,* 99–118.

Thomas, J. W., & Grindle, M. (1992, September). Public choice and policy change: The political economy of reform in developing countries. *American Political Science Review, 86*(3), 827–829.

UNCTAD. (2018). *UnctadStat: Country profile 2018*. Available on: http://unctadstat.unctad.org.

Werneck, R. F. (1988). *A longa Transição dos Anos 80*. Rio de Janeiro: Revista da ANBID, março.

World Bank. *Atlas of Sustainable Development Goals (2018)*. World Development Indicators.

World Bank-Doing Business. (2018). *Reforming to Create Jobs*. Available on: https://eproofing.springer.com/books_v3/mainpage.php?token=dioXb48VtcWR_0d-un29aoZiCpQq83bP_yrlZ3Ytwq7Dd-3lM-lBCnOldFqiUm3Q.

World Economic Forum (WEF). (2015). *The Global Competitiviness Report 2015–2016*. Bridging the Skills and Innovation Gap to Boost Productivity in Latin America. Insight Report prepared in collaboration with Deloitte. Geneva.

World Economic Forum (WEF). (2018). *The Global Competitiveness Report*.

World Economic Forum (WEF). *The Global Competitiveness Report 2008–2009*.

World Economic Outlook (WEO). (2018). *Data Base*, April Editon. Available on: www.imf.org/weo.

CHAPTER 7

Social Sustainability on Competitiveness in the Tourism Industry: Toward New Approach?

José Manuel Guaita Martínez, José María Martín Martín, Domingo Enrique Ribeiro Soriano, and José Antonio Salinas Fernández

7.1 Introduction

The activities included within the so-called tourism sector have played an important role in economic and social development around the world (Martín, Salinas, & Rodríguez, 2019). Many regions in developed as

J. M. Guaita Martínez (✉)
Universitat Politècnica de València, Valencia, Spain

J. M. Martín Martín
International University of La Rioja, Logroño, Spain
e-mail: josemaria.martin@unir.net

D. E. Ribeiro Soriano
University of Valencia, Valencia, Spain
e-mail: domingo.ribeiro@uv.es

J. J. M. Ferreira et al. (eds.), *Technological Innovation and International Competitiveness for Business Growth*, Palgrave Studies in Democracy Innovation, and Entrepreneurship for Growth,
https://doi.org/10.1007/978-3-030-51995-7_7

well as in developing countries have made this industry the main pillar of their development strategy, thus being responsible for a large part of the creation of employment and wealth (Guaita, Martín, Salinas, & Mogorrón-Guerrero, 2019). In fact, in some countries, tourism has reached an important level similar to that of other sectors that had traditionally been the driving force behind their development model (Mendola & Volo, 2017; UNWTO, 2018). Forecasts only confirm this reality: tourism will be one of the fastest growing activities at the international level (Gómez-Vega & Picazo-Tadeo, 2019), and it will play an increasingly important role in the economic growth and social development of a large group of developing countries (Joshi, Poudyal, & Larson, 2017). In developed countries, the growing tourist activity continues to provide wealth and employment in a situation where jobs are being lost as a result of deindustrialization, the relocation of activities, and the decrease in competitiveness of the agricultural sector (Martín, Salinas, Rodríguez, & Jiménez, 2017). Therefore, the benefits of this activity extend to countries and regions of diverse profiles in the process of development or in productive reconversion. This sector is one whose capacity to promote growth and generate employment is beyond any doubt (Gómez & Barrón, 2019).

Notwithstanding the above and bearing in mind the prominent role of the tourism industry in the process of economic recovery after the crisis that began in 2007, a growing feeling of rejection toward tourism has emerged in many countries, the so-called "tourism-phobia" (Martín, Guaita, & Salinas, 2018). This is accounted for by the fact that, in addition to the positive benefits mentioned above associated with the generation of employment and wealth, tourism generates other less positive interactions. The development of the tourist activity and, above all, the continuous growth of the flows of visitors, derives in environmental, socio-cultural, and economic changes in the environment in which the activity takes place (Lee, 2013). These changes, some of which are beneficial and others not so much, undoubtedly affect the lives of the citizens of the destination. The support of the host community will be conditioned by the type of changes that are generated, the way in which they evolve, and the perception that the local population has of them. It is precisely

---

J. A. Salinas Fernández
University of Granada, Granada, Spain
e-mail: jasalinas@ugr.es

the support of the local population and its participation in the process of tourism development that are key factors in ensuring the success and sustainability of the tourism industry in any destination (Gursoy, Chi, & Dyer, 2010).

If the above is assumed to be true, it is taken for granted that the success of a destination, its long-term sustainability, and, therefore, its competitiveness are conditioned by the social support of the activity, which, in turn, derives from the impacts it causes on local communities. The conceptualization and measurement of competitiveness in the tourism sector has generated controversy and lack of agreement as a consequence of the complexity of the concept and the heterogeneous dimensions that integrate it (Abreu-Novais, Ruhanen, & Arcodia, 2018; Salinas, Serdeira, Martín, & Rodríguez, 2020). In this chapter, we reflect on the importance of considering social sustainability as part of the concept of tourism competitiveness, something that has often been overlooked. What is more, social sustainability is not recognized explicitly and with sufficient emphasis as a determining factor for the long-term sustainability of destinations. The World Tourism Organization encapsulates tourism sustainability in seven dimensions: tourism seasonality, leakages, employment, tourism as a contributor to nature conservation, community and destination economic benefits, tourism and poverty alleviation, and competitiveness of tourism businesses (Qiu, Fan, Lyu, Lin, & Jenkins, 2018). In this classification, the social perspective is associated only with factors related to the generation of wealth and employment for local communities. This results in an incomplete picture that leaves out the real complexity of the social interactions between tourism and the local communities. The analysis and discussion of the social perspective of tourism competitiveness is limited in academic literature as well.

Specifically, through a review of the academic literature, this chapter tries to answer the following two research questions:

RQ1: Is social sustainability part of the analysis of tourism competitiveness?

RQ2: What is the importance of social sustainability for tourist destinations?

The following sections will detail the effects that tourism activity generates on local communities. We will reflect on how these effects influence citizen support for tourism development, and how this lack of support can condition the success of the destination. In addition, the way in which different approaches to measuring competitiveness have addressed the social perspective will be presented. Doing so will provide a comprehensive overview of the problem of social sustainability, which can undermine the competitiveness of certain tourist destinations and limit their success if ignored from the public agenda.

7.2 Challenges Arising from the Growth of Tourist Activity

The above-mentioned feeling of rejection toward the tourist activity has not been fully explained. This type of rejection may result from a large increase in the number of tourists arriving at certain destinations, the development of new models of tourism organization, and the lack of public planning and regulation (Martín, Ostos, & Salinas, 2019). The situation in some European cities is complicated and the outlook is not positive at all. Such is the case of Barcelona, Berlin, London, Amsterdam, Venice, Rome, or Florence. In Barcelona, which ranks third in Europe in terms of tourist attraction, 59.9% of citizens believe that the city has reached its limit in terms of carrying capacity (Ayuntamiento de Barcelona, 2018), a percentage that five years earlier stood at 25%. In Venice, the pressure exerted by tourism is so intense that the term "Venice Syndrome" had to be coined. This term refers to the depopulation of the center of tourist destinations and an increase in the price of housing, phenomena developed in parallel with overtourism (Milano, 2017). The previous cases represent two examples out of many that could be discussed. This is the outcome of decades of pro-growth strategies being pushed by the public sector, which have been reinforced by the consolidation of low-cost airlines and the expansion of new collaborative economy models (Dredge, Gyimóthy, Birkbak, Jensen, & Madsen, 2016; Martín, 2019; Martín, Rodríguez, Zermeño, & Salinas, 2018).

It is difficult to determine accurately the volume of tourists arriving at the main tourist destinations, as official statistics tend to collect only data on tourists staying in hotels. This complicates the monitoring of the problem and its diagnosis since tourists staying in unregulated establishments, tourist apartments, or the homes of friends or relatives are not accounted for (Martín, Rodríguez, et al., 2018). This unaccounted number of visitors, besides being large, is growing faster than that associated with the traditional supply of accommodation. For example, in the city of Madrid, there are 85,000 available hotel bed places for use (Instituto Nacional de Estadística, 2018), while the estimation referring to tourist housing reaches 25,000 bed places just by including the Airbnb database (Datahippo, 2019). These new types of accommodation have introduced tourist activity in residential buildings, bringing social impacts to the homes of local residents. This is the reason that the social impacts associated with tourist apartments require special attention.

Even though there are reported benefits for residents associated with the new means of tourist housing intermediation, there is great concern on the part of academics, policymakers, residents, and entrepreneurs (Dredge & Gyimóthy, 2015). It is relatively easy to take up entrepreneurial initiatives within the framework of collaborative economy (Nadler, 2014). In addition, these activities can raise residents' incomes, but they can also deteriorate the working conditions of the residents when they are solely dependent on said activities (Lyons & Wearing, 2015; Schor & Fitzmaurice, 2015). Other negative impacts associated with these platforms refer to issues such as the increase of residential housing prices, evictions of long-stay tenants, and even shortages of residential housing in tourist areas (Edelman & Geradin, 2015), disturbances and noise in residential buildings, loss of local cohesion (Dredge et al., 2016), increased traffic, appropriation of public spaces or overcrowding. In addition to the effects on local communities, other impacts on society as a whole have been described, such as tax evasion or unfair competition (Lyons & Wearing, 2015). This creates a challenge for the public sector, whose response is still at a very early stage, since the legislation has yet to match the severity of the problem and is also very heterogeneous between cities (Martín et al., 2019).

The growth of tourism and the development of new forms of interaction with the locals have altered their perception of the impacts. This perception is of great importance, as it conditions social support for the tourist activity, which is a key factor for the tourism industry (Deery, Jago, & Fredline, 2012). Locals' negative attitude toward tourism can condition the sustainability of tourist destinations and, thus, their competitiveness (Diedrich & García, 2009). This derives from the fact that this industry depends on the hospitality of the residents and the involvement of tourists in the activities carried out in the destination (Gursoy, Jurowski, & Uysal, 2002). Therefore, a social conception leading to hostile behavior toward tourists can become a limiting factor in the competitiveness of the destination, just as the opposite attitude would reinforce it, as tourists tend to visit places where they feel welcome (Yoon, Gursoy, & Chen, 1999). For tourists, it is really important the way in which they are treated by the locals and if they do not feel accepted, they will look for other destinations to visit (Diedrich & García, 2009).

Both researchers and policymakers have acknowledged the need to integrate the local perspective into the planning of tourist destinations (Liu, Sheldon, & Var, 1987). The sustainable development of tourist destinations could be more successful if the local community was given access to decision-making processes so that they could express their needs, desires, fears, and objectives (Marien & Pizan, 2005). It is essential to monitor the opinions of the residents and incorporate them into the development process of the tourism project. In addition to having a clear positive impact on the communities, this will help public or private planners to manage the negative factors associated with the project and the way in which they are perceived by the residents (Dyer, Gursoy, Sharma, & Carter, 2007). Gathering the opinions of the local residents will allow the most positive aspects of the project to be reinforced, and together with it, positive attitudes, which will give the tourist destination greater viability in the long term (Vargas, Oom, Da Costa, & Albino, 2015).

7.3 Social Sustainability as a Necessary Condition for Tourism Growth

The development of tourism does not take place in isolation but is included in an environmental, economic, and social context. Each destination has a particular set of characteristics and needs that differentiate it from others. Interactions between tourists and locals have always taken place. At present, as a consequence of the new models of tourist organization, interaction with residential areas is becoming more intense, which makes it necessary to pay more attention to models of tourism development. Social sustainability should not be taken as an excuse to hinder a potentially beneficial activity for its development. Instead of sacrificing this potential source of development, imaginative and ambitious solutions capable of preserving the social sustainability of tourism should be promoted (Seraphin, Sheeran, & Pilato, 2018).

The relationship established between tourists and the social context in which the activity takes place is not always desirable. This relationship will depend on the type of interactions generated, their nature, and intensity. Such interactions are complex, and the materialization in concrete effects on the environment is carried out by means of the so-called "tourism impacts" (Huei-Wen & Huei-Fu, 2016), which can be either negative or positive. The initial studies on the effects of tourist activity on the environments in which it takes place focused on the analysis of economic impacts, particularly studying the positive ones and, thus, ignoring all the negative interactions generated. Among the positive impacts are the creation of companies, the generation of employment, the improvement of the quality of life of residents, the preservation of local identity, the creation of new infrastructures, interaction with other cultures, or the promotion of historical or natural resources (Andereck & Nyaupane, 2011; Andereck, Valentine, Knopf, & Vogt, 2005; Keogh, 1989; Martín, Guaita, et al., 2018; Milano, 2017). On the other hand, negative impacts are classified into the following categories: economic, socio-cultural, and ecological. The impacts that are ultimately brought about on a territory and the degree of intensity of these will depend on the destination itself, its context, the model of organization, the type of visitor, and the activities carried out (Martín, Guaita, et al., 2018). The main negative impacts that have been described in the scholarly literature are the following: an increase in prices, overcrowding of infrastructures and public spaces, noise and insecurity, substitution of local businesses for others more tourist-oriented, more waste production, alteration of traditional lifestyles, overuse of resources, greater consumption of alcohol and drugs, and environmental deterioration, among others (Almeida, Peláez, Balbuena, & Cortés, 2016).

Some authors focus especially on social impacts, as they directly affect the lives of citizens and, therefore, influence their attitude toward tourism to a greater extent (Cohen, 1984). Planning efforts, both public and private, should therefore prioritize limiting negative impacts and maximizing noneconomic social benefits in order to increase the residents' commitment to tourism development (Lin, Chen, & Filieri, 2017; Martín, Jiménez, & Molina, 2014; Sharpley, 1994). Social impacts can in turn be divided into two groups, socio-cultural impacts and socio-economic impacts. The first category includes impacts such as the disappearance of traditional lifestyles, disturbances and nuisances, cultural degradation, and the development of undesirable activities, among others.

The second category includes impacts related to the increase in the standard of living, changes in the economic system, the decrease in the quality of employment and low salaries, the increase in the value of properties, and the rise in rental prices, among others. The assessment of social impacts is more complex than that of economic impacts since it involves subjective variables associated with the quantification of costs and benefits (Butler, 1980). Such an evaluation is personal and its result will depend on the interaction that each citizen has with the tourist activity itself. In other words, the result will be based on a comparison of the benefits and costs associated with the development of tourism and the effect these have on their lives.

Taking the above into account, the type of impacts generated is just as important in shaping the opinion of residents as the process by which their attitude is shaped. Several theories have been expressed in the academic literature that try to explain the process by which residents' attitudes are shaped. For instance, Doxey (1975) put forward an index describing the intensity of local discontent at the increase of tourist activity. This index goes through the following stages as the tourist activity grows: euphoria, apathy, annoyance, and antagonism. Upchurch and Teivane (2000) also link the degree of support of citizens to the level of development of the activity, which translates into an increase in the pressure exerted on the destination. This model is related to the theory of the destination life cycle proposed by Butler (Butler, 1980), under whose model the following phases or types of attitude are defined: exploration, involvement, development, consolidation, stagnation, and decline or renewal (Gjerald, 2005). Ap and Crompton (1993) have, too, proposed a scale that shows the types of attitude toward tourism linked as well to the degree of development of the destination: embracement, tolerance, adjustment, and withdrawal.

As stated earlier, the connection between the increase in activity and the rejection of the locals is a recurring idea. That is, as tourist activity increases, the impacts become more evident (Gjerald, 2005). For this reason, it is a great challenge to promote the growth of a destination while at the same time guaranteeing its social sustainability. This will be possible as long as the types of impacts generated on each stakeholder are known so that they can be minimized (Gogonea, Baltalunga, Nedelcu, & Dumitrescu, 2017). Positive impacts will increase citizens' commitment to tourist development, while negative impacts will reduce its support (Sharpley, 2014). Some factors may condition the attitude of residents toward certain impacts. These factors include the socio-economic and ethnic characteristics of the visitor, the type of activities carried out, the average length of stay, the potential damage to the local culture, the characteristics of the local community (political ideology, religion, etc.), the importance of tourism within the local economic system, the dependence on this activity, the economic situation of the region, the way in which the space is used, and, of course, the number of visitors (Butler, 1974). Examples of theories that try to explain the way in which citizens construct their opinion include: the Theory of Reasoned Action (Dyer et al., 2007), the Social Representation Theory (Andriotis & Vaughan, 2003), Fishbein and Ajzen's theory (Fishbein & Ajzen, 1975), Butler's model of Intercultural Perception (Colantonio & Potter, 2006), the Social Carrying Capacity Theory (Saveriades, 2000), or Doxey's Irridex (Holden, 2006). Among the proposed alternatives, the Social Exchange Theory (SET) is the most widespread at present. It claims that in order to determine the degree of support for tourist activity, citizens make a comparison of the costs and benefits that said activity has for their lives, whose result is a specific mindset (Ap, 1992).

The above includes the description of factors that interfere with the assessment of the impacts and how the increase in the number of arrivals triggers different stages in the attitude-shaping process of the local population. There remains the need to reflect on the processes according to which citizens shape their opinion. Understanding how citizens shape their opinions on the effect of tourism on their lives is of paramount importance. The way in which citizens perceive impacts and form an opinion will condition their attitude toward this activity and, thus, their commitment to support it (Nicholas, Thapa, & Ko, 2009; Park, Lee, Choi, & Yoon, 2012; Peric, Durkin, & Wise, 2016; Telfer & Sharpley, 2008). The process by which citizens shape their attitude has been approached through various theoretical frameworks. An example of these frameworks would be the stakeholder theory (Peric et al., 2016), although there are more advanced and precise alternatives. Cost-benefit analysis has usually been used to explain the way in which citizens form their opinion of tourism. Presumably, such an opinion arises from a comparison between the benefits associated with tourism and the costs that it generates (Lee, 2013). This methodology, however, poses a basic problem, namely that it labels each type of impact in advance as a benefit or as a cost, which may lead to a bias in the evaluations (Gursoy et al., 2010). This methodology has evolved and become known as "domain related costs-benefits." It also begins with the pre-categorization of impacts as benefit or cost, but it also classifies them into three areas (economic, socio-cultural, and environmental). These two methodologies suggest an association between the benefits of tourism and the degree of support, and between the costs and the degree of rejection (Dyer et al., 2007; Jurowski, Uysal, & Williams, 1997). In no case is the citizen offered the possibility of classifying each impact as cost or benefit according to their own criteria (Andereck & Nyaupane, 2011). The methodologies described have been overtaken by the application of non-forced approaches. Under these frameworks, citizens are offered the possibility of deciding whether an impact is positive or negative according to their criteria, as well as the level of intensity associated with them (Andereck & Nyaupane, 2011; Cohen, 1984). To this end, the impacts must be presented in a neutral manner.

7.4 Approaches to the Extended Concept of Tourism Competitiveness

Analyses focused on the sustainable development of the tourism sector often overlook the social perspective, even when its importance is evident. On a positive note, this social perspective is becoming more and more accredited (Rodríguez, Martín, & Salinas, 2017; Rodríguez, Aguilera, Martín, & Salinas, 2018). The World Commission on Environment and Development (WCED) defines Sustainable Development (SD) as follows "development that meets the needs of the present without compromising the ability of future generations to meet their own needs" (WCED, 1987, p. 43). This approach was taken into account in the development of policies issued in the United Nations (UN) conference on Environment and Development in Rio de Janeiro in 1992, as well as in the subsequent conferences on sustainability organized within the framework of the United Nations (2004).

In the tourism industry, when talking about sustainable development and competitiveness, improving the quality of life of the residents should be a primary goal, since sustainability itself depends on them. To this end, it is necessary to maximize the economic benefits of the locals while respecting both the environment and the hosting community (Bramwell & Lane, 1993; Hall & Lew, 1998; McIntyre, 1993; Park & Yoon, 2009; Park, Yoon, Lee, 2008; Stabler, 1997). In tourism, as in many other sectors, economic growth has been given priority over social issues. The extended vision discussed in this chapter suggests that tourism development must be economically competitive but at the same time environmentally and socially viable (Puczkó & Rátz, 2000). As stated above, the locals' support for tourism and their involvement in it are essential to ensure the sustainability of this industry and its competitiveness (Gursoy et al., 2010). This support depends on how the activity is perceived, which makes it essential to know and understand the point of view of the locals in relation to the type of impacts generated. This will allow for effective strategies capable of guaranteeing local support (Prayag, Hosany, Nunkoo, & Alders, 2013), which will undoubtedly increase the competitiveness of the destination.

Including the social perspective in the analysis of the competitiveness of a destination is not frequent, something that should be corrected. Below is a review of the elements that are usually taken into account in competitiveness analysis. It highlights how an important aspect such as social sustainability is left out of most analyses. The analysis of the literature set out below can be synthesized through a conceptual model that considers the following pillars of tourism competitiveness: primary and secondary resources, management and planning systems, economic sustainability, environmental sustainability, social sustainability, and demand-related factors.

The very concept of tourism competitiveness leads to a great deal of confusion and controversy, since in addition to the complexity of this concept, its measurement includes dimensions of a different nature (Abreu-Novais et al., 2018). In fact, although the concept of competitiveness has been widely studied, there are no generally accepted definitions (Mazanec, Wöber, & Zins, 2007). According to Crouch and Ritchie (1999), two problems arise in the definition of competitiveness: how to approach the comparative advantages and which concepts should be taken into account. Difficulties in defining competitiveness derive from its own complexity and the lack of consensus to identify, measure, and aggregate the different dimensions that should be considered part of it (Abreu-Novais, Ruhanen, & Arcodia, 2015). In addition, the dimensions used in the estimation of competitiveness are not fixed and the way in which they are measured and analyzed is very heterogeneous, which leads to a major problem (Dwyer & Kim, 2003). In the scholarly literature it is possible to find numerous studies pointing out various factors involved in the competitiveness of tourist destinations, but there is little work focused on pointing out those that are most important (Crouch, 2011).

Numerous studies (Crouch & Ritchie, 1994, 1995, 1999, 2005; Ritchie & Crouch, 1993, 2000, 2003, 2010) have proposed the creation of competitiveness models based on "the national diamond model" developed by Porter (1990). This is based on a set of variables determined by CEOs of organizations located in tourist destinations. These models compare the advantages of resource allocation available at each tourist destination to the competitive advantages, defined as the resources made available by each destination to contribute to growth and development of tourism (Guaita, Martín, & Salinas, 2020). Ritchie and Crouch (2003, 2010) identify four groups of factors: "core resources and attractors" that correspond to the key elements that visitors consider when selecting a destination; "supporting factors and resources," which are the factors on which the tourist activity is based (services, infrastructures, lodging, accessibility, among others); "destination policy, planning and development" which govern the type of tourism development that drives a destination, and a fourth group; "destination management" which depends on the individual and collective actions that drive a destination. Finally, there are "qualifying and amplifying determinants," which increase or limit the competitiveness of the destination. Other relevant works, such as those developed by Dwyer and Kim (2003) and Dwyer, Mellor, Livaic, Edwards, and Kim (2004) have defined large groups of indicators (Created Resources, Endowed Resources, Demand Factors, Market Performance Indicators, Supporting Factors, Destination Management, and Situational Conditions). These groups of factors contain most of the dimensions and variables identified by Crouch and Ritchie's development model, as well as the main elements identified by Buhalis (2000), Hassan (2000), and Mihalic (2000). Usually, this type of study has been developed by means of the construction of synthetic indicators based on the aggregation of simple indicators, which in many cases have little to say about the competitiveness of a destination (Croes & Kubickova, 2013). Such indicators are somewhat convenient in the interpretation of the data, as they yield only one value (Croes, 2011), which may, however, lead to public policy decisions based on overly simplistic criteria. The OECD reports claim that there is no perfect indicator and consider the improvement of measurement systems to be a major challenge. One of the most widespread indicators of tourism competitiveness is the one proposed by the World Economic Forum (2007, 2008, 2009, 2011, 2013, 2015, 2017). This indicator, known as The Travel & Tourism Competitiveness Report (TTCR), produces a ranking based on the information provided by 90 variables structured in 4 sub-indexes (T&T policy and enabling conditions, enabling environment, natural and cultural resources, and infrastructure). The aforementioned models do not explicitly consider the social perspective and, therefore, do not include social sustainability as a key element, even though they enjoy great importance and are widely accepted in the measurement of tourism competitiveness. The methodology employed in this type of indicator encompasses entire nations, and therefore, it is only obvious that this particular indicator pays little attention to the social perspective considering how complex it would be to take into account the opinion of every citizen in a given tourist destination. The 2017 edition (WEF, 2017), specifically points out the importance of promoting a more inclusive and sustainable development, capable of respecting the environment and at the same time preserving the local communities that depend on tourism. However, this preservation places more emphasis on the economic aspect than on the social or cultural one.

A variant of the type of analysis described above would be the one that incorporates the results of opinion studies. Dwyer, Livaic, and Mellor (2003) and Dwyer et al. (2004) pointed out the significance of having the opinions of tourists and entrepreneurs of the tourism sector to determine the relative importance of the indicators used to assess competitiveness. But nothing is said about the relevance of taking the locals' opinions into account. The model of competitiveness proposed by Heath (2003) points out that one of the components that conditions competitiveness is the relations established between stakeholders and the creation of partnerships between them. Nevertheless, this model does not address the importance of social sustainability from the perspective of the local people. Fortunately, the social perspective is increasingly being taken into account in the conceptualization of tourism competitiveness. For example, Ritchie and Crouch (2003) point out that the competitiveness of a destination is the "ability to increase tourism expenditure, to increasingly attract visitors while providing them with satisfying, memorable experiences and to do so in a profitable way, while enhancing the well-being of destination residents and preserving the natural capital of the destination for future generations." The definition of tourism competitiveness provided by Dupeyras and MacCallum (2013) is a very close one "the ability of the place to optimize its attractiveness for residents and non-residents, to deliver quality, innovative, and attractive tourism services to consumers and to gain market shares on the domestic and global market places, while ensuring that the available resources supporting tourism are used efficiently and in a sustainable way." According to Abreu-Novais et al. (2018), competitiveness is concerned with three main aims: improving the attractiveness of a destination and the satisfaction it brings, the well-being of the local population, and sustainability. In this case, social and environmental sustainability are set apart. Some authors relate economic and social sustainability, as they argue that competitiveness must help to achieve economic goals that increase the income of citizens while improving their well-being, yet they are not mutually exclusive (Bahar & Kozak, 2007; Bordas, 2001; Buhalis, 2000; Crouch & Ritchie, 1999; Dwyer & Kim, 2003; Dwyer et al., 2004; Ritchie & Crouch, 2003). The examples here described point to a growing awareness of the importance of social sustainability in the analysis of a destination's competitiveness, although it does not seem to be enough.

The following table summarizes the main competitiveness factors highlighted in the academic literature. Other factors related to social sustainability that should be incorporated have also been presented, taking into account the literature on social sustainability in tourist destinations (Table 7.1).

Considering the above, it is recommended to include in the analyses on tourism competitiveness and in the planning of destinations, the social perspective and the opinions and concerns of the residents. This will help strengthen the competitiveness of the destination and allow long-term business growth. It is also recommended to expand research on how to incorporate this social perspective in the models of analysis of competitiveness and social viability of business projects within the tourism sector.

7.5 Conclusions

Tourist activity has usually been referred to as a "smoke-free" industry, meaning that the negative effects derived from it become less evident. Moreover, these effects have been expressed or highlighted in a more comprehensive way with regard to environmental sustainability. In environmentally sensitive destinations, it is gradually being assimilated that current tourism development should not jeopardize the use of resources in the future. However, there has not been the same level of awareness regarding the social degradation of tourist environments and the impact on the lives of residents. The problem has become evident when after decades of pro-growth policies serious problems have appeared in tourist

Table 7.1 Factors related to tourism competitiveness

Factors identified in the academic literature	*Authors who have pointed out these factors*
Core resources and attractors	Ritchie and Crouch (2003, 2010)
Services, infrastructures, lodging, accessibility	
Destination policy, planning, and development	
Destination management	Ritchie and Crouch (2003, 2010), Dwyer and Kim (2003), and Dwyer et al. (2004)
Created resources	Dwyer and Kim (2003), and Dwyer et al. (2004)
Endowed resources	
Demand factors	
Market performance indicators	
Supporting factors	
Situational conditions	
Natural and cultural resources	World Economic Forum (2007, 2008, 2009, 2011, 2013, 2015, 2017)
Opinions of tourists and entrepreneurs	Dwyer et al. (2003, 2004)
Tourism expenditure	Ritchie and Crouch (2003)
Scarcely developed factors in academic literature	
Citizen support	Abreu-Novais et al. (2018), and Martín (2019)
Life cost increase	Crouch and Ritchie (1999)
Social and cultural impacts	Guaita et al. (2020), Abreu-Novais et al (2018), and Salinas et al. (2020)
Increase congestion public spaces	Ritchie and Crouch (2003), Dwyer et al. (2004), and Martín (2019)
Population decline	Martín (2019), and Bahar and Kozak (2007)

cities. There has been a growing feeling of rejection toward tourism on the part of the locals, even though when this activity is a cornerstone of the development of these communities.

Tourism competitiveness has traditionally been associated with an increase in the number of visitors. Therefore, the most successful competitiveness policies have resulted in the saturation of some destinations, which from a social point of view has generated numerous interferences in the life of the locals that in many cases have not made up for the economic gains. This has generated the aforementioned feeling of rejection toward tourism, which endangers the support of citizens for this activity, and with it, the very viability of the destination in the future.

Therefore, policies aimed at improving competitiveness and, in general, the development plans of tourist destinations should assume a joint understanding of economic, social, and environmental sustainability. This understanding is not widely represented in the most widespread tourism competitiveness assessment systems. Although the importance of the social perspective is recognized in many cases, it is not correctly integrated into the measurements. This is due partly to the complexity of constructing synthetic indicators which, in addition to incorporating information referring to quantitative variables, also include information representative of the local perspective.

The definition of sustainability proposed by the United Nations (1987) indicates that this concept stands for the ability of productive activities to meet current needs without compromising future possibilities. This expression, understood in a broad sense, should also consider the social perspective, since it jeopardizes the future development of the tourist activity as much as the environmental one. More specifically, The World Tourism Organization points out that sustainable tourism models must meet the needs of both the current tourists and the host destination while protecting the resources on which these activities are based, so as to ensure future opportunities (World Tourism Organization, 1993). In this definition, issued decades ago, the social perspective appears more clearly, although it has not been adequately reflected in public policies or private development projects.

Taking up the research questions presented in the introduction section, it is possible to point out that social sustainability is not part of the vast majority of models of tourism competitiveness analysis. With regard to the second question, the importance of social sustainability for the development and consolidation of tourist destinations is beyond doubt. Both statements, based on the bibliographic analysis carried out, make up the main contribution of this work, and allow two clear recommendations to be issued. In order to guarantee the sustainability of tourist destinations and their business growth, greater attention must be paid to social sustainability from the public and business spheres. The models of tourism competitiveness analysis should be expanded to include the social perspective, something that is not straightforward. Specifically, research should deepen the statistical systems for measuring tourism competitiveness. New methodologies should be proposed capable of incorporating information on the social impacts associated with an uncontrolled tourism activity.

This represents a great challenge, as it is not a simple task to incorporate the opinion of the residents in the competitiveness measurement systems.

References

Abreu-Novais, M., Ruhanen, L., & Arcodia, C. (2015). Destination competitiveness: What we know, what we know but shouldn't and what we don't know but should. *Current Issues in Tourism, 19*(6), 1–21.

Abreu-Novais, M., Ruhanen, L., & Arcodia, C. (2018). Destination competitiveness: A phenomenographic study. *Tourism Management, 64*, 324–334.

Almeida, F., Peláez, M. A., Balbuena, A., & Cortés, R. (2016). Residents' perceptions of tourism development in Benalmadena (Spain). *Tourism Management, 54*, 259–274.

Andereck, K. L., & Nyaupane, G. P. (2011). Exploring the nature of tourism and quality of life perceptions among residents. *Journal of Travel Research, 50*, 248–260.

Andereck, K. L., Valentine, K. M., Knopf, R. C., & Vogt, C. A. (2005). Residents' perceptions of community tourism impacts. *Annals of Tourism Research, 32*, 1056–1076.

Andriotis, K., & Vaughan, R. D. (2003). Urban residents' attitudes toward tourism development: The case of Crete. *Journal of Travel Research, 42*, 172–185.

Ap, J. (1992). Residents' perceptions on tourism impacts. *Annals of Tourism Research, 19*, 665–690.

Ap, J., & Crompton, J. L. (1993). Residents' strategies for responding to tourism impacts. *Journal of Travel Research, 32*, 47–50.

Ayuntamiento de Barcelona. (2018). *Tourism activity report of Barcelona*. Barcelona, Spain: Ayuntamiento de Barcelona.

Bahar, O., & Kozak, M. (2007). Advancing destination competitiveness research: Comparison between tourists and service providers. *Journal of Travel & Tourism Marketing, 22*(2), 61–71.

Bordas, E. (2001). Improving public–private sectors cooperation in tourism: A new paradigm for destinations. *Tourism Review, 56*(3/4), 38–41.

Bramwell, B., & Lane, B. (1993). Sustainable tourism: An evolving global approach. *Journal of Sustainable Tourism, 1*(1), 1–5.

Buhalis, D. (2000). Marketing the competitive destination in the future. *Tourism Management, 21*(1), 97–116.

Butler, R. W. (1974). Social implications of tourism development *Annals Tourism Research, 2*, 100–111.

Butler, R. W. (1980). The concept of a tourist area cycle of evolution: Implications for management and resources. *Canadian Geographer/Le Géographe Canadien, 25*, 5–12.

Cohen, E. (1984). The sociology of tourism: Approaches, issues, and findings. *Annual Review of Sociology, 10,* 373–392.

Colantonio, A., & Potter, R. B. (2006). *Urban tourism and development in the socialist state: Havana during the 'special period'*. La Habana, Cuba: Ashgate.

Croes, R. (2011). Measuring and explaining competitiveness in the context of small island destinations. *Journal of Travel Research, 50*(4), 431–442.

Croes, R., & Kubickova, M. (2013). From potential to ability to compete: Towards a performance based tourism competitiveness index. *Journal of Destination Marketing and Management, 2*(3), 146–154.

Crouch, G. I. (2011). Destination competitiveness: An analysis of determinant attributes. *Journal of Travel Research, 50*(1), 27–45.

Crouch, G. I., & Ritchie, J. R. B. (1994). Destination competitive—Exploring foundations for a long-term research programme. In *Proceedings of the Administrative Sciences Association of Canada 1994 Annual Conference* (pp. 79–88). Halifax, Nova Scotia.

Crouch, G. I., & Ritchie, J. R. B. (1995, July 13–16). Destination competitiveness and the role of the tourism enterprise. In *Proceedings of the Fourth Annual Business Congress* (pp. 43–48). Istanbul, Turkey.

Crouch, G. I., & Ritchie, J. R. B. (1999). Tourism, competitiveness, and societal prosperity. *Journal of Business Research, 44,* 137–152.

Crouch, G. I., & Ritchie, J. R. B. (2005). Application of the analytic hierarchy process to tourism choice and decision making: A review and illustration applied to destination competitiveness. *Tourism Analysis, 10*(1), 17–25.

Datahippo. (2019). https://datahippo.org/es/. Accessed 30 Sept 2018.

Deery, M., Jago, L., & Fredline, L. (2012). Rethinking social impacts of tourism research: A new research agenda. *Tourism Management, 33,* 64–73.

Diedrich, A., & García, E. (2009). Local perceptions of tourism as indicators of destination decline. *Tourism Management, 30,* 512–521.

Doxey, G. V. (1975). Leisure, tourism and Canada's aging population tourism in Canada: Selected issues and options. *Western Geographical Series, 21,* 57–72.

Dredge, D., & Gyimóthy, S. (2015). The collaborative economy and tourism: Critical perspectives, questionable claims and silenced voices. *Tourism Recreation Research, 40,* 286–302.

Dredge, D., Gyimóthy, S., Birkbak, A., Jensen T. E., Madsen, A. K. (2016). *The impact of regulatory approaches targeting collaborative economy in the tourism accommodation sector: Barcelona, Berlin, Amsterdam and Paris*. Impulse Paper N. 9 Prepared for the European Commission DG GROWTH. Copenhagen, Denmark: Aalborg University.

Dupeyras, A., & MacCallum, N. (2013). *Indicators for measuring competitiveness in tourism: A guidance document* (OECD Tourism Papers, 2013/02). Paris, France: OECD Publishing. http://dx.doi.org/10.1787/5k47t9q2t923-en.

Dwyer, L., & Kim, C. (2003). Destination competitiveness: Determinants and indicators. *Current Issues in Tourism, 6*(5), 369–414.

Dwyer, L., Livaic, Z., & Mellor, R. (2003). Competitiveness of Australia as a tourist destination. *Journal of Hospitality and Tourism Management, 10*(1), 60–78.

Dwyer, L., Mellor, R., Livaic, Z., Edwards, D., & Kim, C. (2004). Attributes of destination competitiveness: A factor analysis. *Tourism Analysis, 9*(1), 91–101.

Dyer, P., Gursoy, D., Sharma, B., & Carter, J. (2007). Structural modeling of resident perceptions of tourism and associated development on the Sunshine Coast, Australia. *Tourism Management, 28*, 409–422.

Edelman, B. G., & Geradin, D. (2015). *Efficiencies and regulatory shortcuts: How should we regulate companies like Airbnb and Uber?* (Harvard Business School Working Paper, 16-026).

Fishbein, M., & Ajzen, I. (1975). *Belief, attitude, intention, and behavior*. Reading, PA, USA: Addison-Wesley.

Gjerald, O. (2005). Sociocultural impacts of tourism: A case study from Norway. *Journal of Tourism Cultural Change, 3*, 36–58.

Gogonea, R. M., Baltalunga, A. A., Nedelcu, A., & Dumitrescu, D. (2017). Sustainable tourism aims to channel tourism to the advantage of all stakeholders—Destination places and communities, tourists and all the associated activities and services. Tourism pressure at the regional level in the context of sustainable development in Romania. *Sustainability, 9*, 698.

Gómez, C. S., & Barrón, K. S. (2019). Impacts of tourism and the generation of employment in Mexico. *Journal of Tourism Analysis: Revista de Análisis Turístico, 26*(2), 94–114.

Gómez-Vega, M., & Picazo-Tadeo, A. (2019). Ranking world tourist destinations with a composite indicator of competitiveness: To weigh or not to weigh? *Tourism Management, 72*, 281–291.

Guaita, J. M., Martín, J. M., Salinas, J. A. (2020). Innovation in the measurement of tourism competitiveness. In M. A. Galindo-Martín, M. T. Mendez-Picazo, M. S. Castaño-Martínez (Eds.), *Analyzing the relationship between innovation, value creation, and entrepreneurship* (pp. 268–288). Hershey, USA: IGI Global. https://doi.org/10.4018/978-1-7998-1169-5.ch013.

Guaita, J. M., Martín, J. M., Salinas, J. A., Mogorrón-Guerrero, H. (2019). An analysis of the stability of rural tourism as a desired condition for sustainable tourism. *Journal of Business Research, 100*, 165–174.

Gursoy, D., Chi, C. G., & Dyer, P. (2010). Locals' attitudes toward mass and alternative tourism: The case of Sunshine Coast, Australia. *Journal of Travel Research, 49*(3), 381–394.

Gursoy, D., Jurowski, C., & Uysal, M. (2002). Resident attitudes: A structural modeling approach. *Annals of Tourism Research, 29*, 79–105.

Hall, C. M., & Lew, A. A. (1998). The geography of sustainable tourism development: introduction. In C. M. Hall & A. A. Lew (Eds.), *Sustainable tourism: Geographical perspectives* (pp. 1–24). New York, USA: Addison Wesley Longman.

Hassan, S. (2000). Determinants of market competitiveness in an environmentally sustainable tourism industry. *Journal of Travel Research, 38*(3), 239–245.

Heath, E. (2003). Towards a model to enhance destination competitiveness: A southern african perspective. *Journal of Hospitality & Tourism Research, 10*(2), 124–141.

Holden, A. (2006). *Tourism studies and the social sciences*. New York, USA: Routledge.

Huei-Wen, L., & Huei-Fu, L. (2016). Valuing residents' perceptions of sport tourism development in Taiwan's North Coast and Guanyinshan National Scenic Area, Asia. *Pacific Journal Tourism Research, 21,* 398–424.

Instituto Nacional de Estadística. (2018). *Encuesta de ocupación en Alojamientos Turísticos*. Madrid, Spain: INE.

Joshi, O., Poudyal, N. C., & Larson, L. C. (2017). The influence of sociopolitical, natural, and cultural factors on international tourism growth: A cross-country panel analysis. *Environment, Development and Sustainability, 19*(3), 825–838.

Jurowski, C., Uysal, M., & Williams, D. R. (1997). A theoretical analysis of host community resident reactions to tourism. *Journal of Travel Research, 36,* 3–11.

Keogh, B. (1989). Social impact. In G. Wall (Ed.), *Outdoor recreation in Canada* (pp. 233–275). Toronto, Canada: Wiley.

Lee, T. H. (2013). Influence analysis of community resident support for sustainable tourism development. *Tourism Management, 34,* 37–46.

Lin, Z., Chen, Y., & Filieri, R. (2017). Resident-tourist value co-creation: The role of residents' perceived tourism impacts and life satisfaction. *Tourism Management, 61,* 436–442.

Liu, J., Sheldon, P. J., & Var, T. (1987). Resident perception of the environmental impacts of tourism. *Annals of Tourism Research, 14,* 17–37.

Lyons, K., & Wearing, S. (2015). *The sharing economy issues, impacts, and regulatory responses in the context of the NSW visitor economy*. Sydney, Australia: NSW Business Chamber.

Marien, C., & Pizan, A. (2005). Implementing sustainable tourism development through citizen participation in the planning process. In S. Wahab & J. J. Pigram (Eds.), *Tourism, development and growth: The challenge of sustainability*. London, UK: Routledge.

Martín, J. M. (2019). Impacts of the tourist activity and citizens' evaluation about the necessity for resting periods. In. M. A. Camilleri (Ed.),

Strategic perspectives in destination marketing (pp. 81–112). Hershey, USA: IGI Global.

Martín, J. M., Guaita, J. A., & Salinas, J. A. (2018). An analysis of the factors behind the citizen's attitude of rejection towards tourism in a context of overtourism and economic dependence on this activity. *Sustainability, 10*(8), 2851.

Martín, J. M., Jiménez, J. D., & Molina, V. (2014). Impacts of seasonality on environmental sustainability in the tourism sector based on destination type: An application to Spain's Andalusia region. *Tourism Economics, 20*(1), 123–142.

Martín, J. M., Ostos, M. S., & Salinas, J. A. (2019). Why regulation is needed in emerging markets in the tourism sector. *The American Journal of Economics and Sociology, 78*(1), 225–254.

Martín, J. M., Rodríguez, J. A., Zermeño, K., & Salinas, J. A. (2018). Effects of vacation rental websites on the concentration of tourists—Potential environmental impacts: An application to the Balearic Islands in Spain. *International Journal of Environmental Research and Public Health, 15*(2), 347.

Martín, J. M., Salinas, J. A., & Rodríguez, J. A. (2019). Comprehensive evaluation of the tourism seasonality using a synthetic DP2 indicator. *Tourism Geographies, 21*(2), 284–305.

Martín, J. M., Salinas, J. A., Rodríguez, J. A., & Jiménez, J. D. (2017). Assessment of the tourism's potential as a sustainable development instrument in terms of annual stability: Application to Spanish rural destinations in process of consolidation. *Sustainability, 9*(10), 1692.

Mazanec, J. A., Wöber, K., & Zins, A. H. (2007). Tourism destination competitiveness: From definition to explanation? *Journal of Travel Research, 46*, 86–95.

McIntyre, G. (1993). *Sustainable tourism development: Guide for local planners*. Madrid, Spain: World Tourism Organization.

Mendola, D., & Volo, S. (2017). Building composite indicators in tourism studies: Measurements and applications in tourism destination competitiveness. *Tourism Management, 59*, 541–553.

Mihalic, T. (2000). Environmental management of a tourist destination: A factor of tourism competitiveness. *Tourism Management, 21*(1), 65–78.

Milano, C. (2017). *Overtourism and Tourismphobia: Global trends and local contexts*. Ostelea School of Tourism & Hospitality. Available online http://www.aept.org/archivos/files/ostelea_informe_overtourism_y_turismofobia.pdf. Accessed 18 May 2018.

Nadler, S. N. (2014). *The sharing economy: What is it and where is it going?*. Cambridge, MA, USA: Massachusetts Institute of Technology.

Nicholas, L. N., Thapa, B., & Ko, Y. J. (2009). Residents' perspectives of a World Heritage Site: The Pitons Management Area, St. Lucia. *Annals of Tourism Research, 36,* 390–412.

Park, D. B., Lee, K. W., Choi, H. S., & Yoon, Y. (2012). Factors influencing social capital in rural tourism communities in South Korea. *Tourism Management, 33,* 1511–1520.

Park, D., & Yoon, Y. (2009). Segmentation by motivation in rural tourism: A Korean case study. *Tourism Management, 30,* 99–108.

Park, D., Yoon, Y., & Lee, M. (2008). Rural community development and policy challenges in South Korea. *Journal of the Economic Geographical Society of Korea, 11*(4), 600–617.

Peric, M., Durkin, J., & Wise, N. (2016). Leveraging small-scale sport events: Challenges of organising, delivering and managing sustainable outcomes in rural communities, the case of Gorski Kotar, Croatia. *Sustainability, 8,* 1337.

Porter, M. E. (1990). *The competitive advantage of nations*. New York, USA: The Free Press.

Prayag, G., Hosany, S., Nunkoo, R., & Alders, T. (2013). London residents' support for the 2012 Olympic Games: the mediating effect of overall attitude. *Tourism Management, 36,* 629–640.

Puczkó, L., & Rátz, T. (2000). Tourist and resident perceptions of the physical impacts of tourism at Lake Balaton, Hungary: Issues for sustainable tourism management. *Journal of Sustainable Tourism, 8,* 458–478.

Qiu, H., Fan, D. X. F., Lyu, J., Lin, P. M. C., & Jenkins, C. L. (2018). Analyzing the economic sustainability of tourism development: Evidence from Hong Kong. *Journal of Hospitality & Tourism Research, 43*(2), 226–248.

Ritchie, J. R. B., & Crouch, G. (1993, October 17–23). Competitiveness in international tourism: A framework for understanding and analysis. In *Proceedings of the 43rd Congress of Association Internationale d'Experts Scientifique de Tourisme*. San Carlos de Bariloche, Argentina.

Ritchie, J. R. B., & Crouch, G. (2000). The competitive destination: A sustainability perspective. *Tourism Management, 21*(1), 1–7.

Ritchie, J. R. B., & Crouch, G. (2003). *The competitive destination: A sustainable tourism perspective*. Wallingford, UK: CABI Publishing.

Ritchie, J. R. B., & Crouch, G. (2010). A model of destination competitiveness/sustainability: Brazilian perspectives. *Revista de Administración Pública, 44*(5), 1049–1066.

Rodríguez, J. A., Aguilera, J. D., Martín, J. M., & Salinas, J. A. (2018). Crisis in the Horn of Africa: Measurement of progress towards millennium development goals. *Social Indicators Research, 135*(2), 499–514.

Rodríguez, J. A., Martín, J. M., & Salinas, J. A. (2017). Assessing MDG 6 in Sub-Saharan Africa: A territorial analysis using a synthetic indicator. *Revista de Economía Mundial, 47,* 203–221.

Salinas, J. A., Serdeira, P., Martín, J. M., & Rodríguez, J. A. (2020). Determinants of tourism destination competitiveness in the countries most visited by international tourists: Proposal of a synthetic index. *Tourism Management Perspectives, 33,* 100582.

Saveriades, S. (2000). Establishing the social tourism carrying capacity for the tourist resorts of the east coast of the Republic of Cyprus. *Tourism Management, 21,* 147–156.

Schor, J. B., & Fitzmaurice, C. (2015). Collaborating and connecting: The emergence of the sharing economy. In L. Reisch & J. Thogersen (Eds.), *Handbook of research on sustainable consumption* (pp. 410–425). Cheltenham, UK: Edward Elgar.

Seraphin, H. S., Sheeran, P., & Pilato, M. (2018). Over-tourism and the fall of Venice as a destination. *Journal Destination Marketing Management, 9,* 374–376.

Sharpley, R. (1994). *Tourism, tourists and society.* Huntingdon, UK: ELM Publishers.

Sharpley, R. (2014). Host perceptions of tourism: A review of the research. *Tourism Management, 42,* 37–49.

Stabler, M. J. (Ed.). (1997). *Tourism and sustainability: Principles to practice.* New York, USA: Cab International.

Telfer, D. J., & Sharpley, R. (2008). *Tourism and development in the developing world.* Abingdon, UK: Routledge.

United Nations. (1987). *Informe de la Comisión Mundial sobre el Medio Ambiente y el Desarrollo.* New York, USA: United Nations.

United Nations. (2004). *Indicators of sustainable development for tourism destinations.* Madrid, Spain: United Nations.

UNWTO. (2018). *UNWTO annual report 2017.* Madrid. Spain: UNWTO.

Upchurch, R. S., & Teivane, U. (2000). Resident perceptions of tourism development in Riga, Latvia. *Tourism Management, 21,* 499–507.

Vargas, A., Oom, P., Da Costa, J., & Albino, S. (2015). Residents' attitude and level of destination development: An international comparison. *Tourism Management, 48*(3), 199–210.

WCED. (1987). *Our common future (Report of the World Commission on Environment and Development).* Oxford and New York, USA: Oxford University Press.

WEF. (2007). *The travel & tourism competitiveness report 2007: Furthering the process of economic development.* Geneva. Dataset extracted from: http://reports.weforum.org/travel-and-tourism-competitiveness-report-2017/downloads/.

WEF. (2008). *The travel & tourism competitiveness report 2008: Balancing economic development and environmental sustainability.* Geneva. Dataset extracted from: http://reports.weforum.org/travel-and-tourism-competitiveness-report-2017/downloads/.

WEF. (2009). *The travel & tourism competitiveness report 2009: Managing in a time of turbulence*. Geneva. Dataset extracted from: http://reports.weforum.org/travel-and-tourism-competitiveness-report-2017/downloads/.

WEF. (2011). *The travel & tourism competitiveness report 2011: Beyond the downturn*. Geneva. Dataset extracted from: http://reports.weforum.org/travel-and-tourism-competitiveness-report-2017/downloads/.

WEF. (2013). *The travel & tourism competitiveness report 2013: Reducing barriers to economic growth and job creation*. Geneva. Dataset extracted from: http://reports.weforum.org/travel-and-tourism-competitiveness-report-2017/downloads/.

WEF. (2015). *The travel & tourism competitiveness report 2015: Growth through Shocks*. Geneva. Dataset extracted from: http://reports.weforum.org/travel-and-tourism-competitiveness-report-2017/downloads/.

WEF. (2017). *The travel & tourism competitiveness report 2017: Paving the way for a more sustainable and inclusive future*. Geneva. Dataset extracted from: http://reports.weforum.org/travel-and-tourism-competitiveness-report-2017/downloads/.

WTO. (1993). *Tourism report year 2000 and beyond qualitative aspects*. Madrid, Spain: World Tourism Organization.

Yoon, Y., Gursoy, D., & Chen, J. S. (1999). An investigation of the relationship between tourism impacts and host communities' characteristics. *Journal of Tourism and Hospitality Research, 10*(1), 29–44.

PART III

Refining the Technological Innovation and Business Growth Link

CHAPTER 8

Reframing Technological Innovation Capabilities: Empirical Evidence and a Framework for Study

Minna Saunila, Vanessa Pertuz, and Adith Pérez

8.1 Introduction

Gaining competitiveness requires departing from the existing knowledge base. Recent studies have suggested that a firm's technological innovation capabilities must support strategic expertise at all levels of the firm in order to promote competitiveness (e.g., Joo, Seo, & Min, 2018; Shafia, Shavvalpour, Hosseini, & Hosseini, 2016; Yu, Zhang, Lin, & Wu, 2017).

M. Saunila (✉)
School of Engineering Science, LUT University, Lahti, Finland
e-mail: minna.saunila@lut.fi

V. Pertuz · A. Pérez
University of Santander, Valledupar, Colombia
e-mail: van.pertuz@mail.udes.edu.co

A. Pérez
e-mail: adi.perez@mail.udes.edu.co

J. J. M. Ferreira et al. (eds.), *Technological Innovation and International Competitiveness for Business Growth*, Palgrave Studies in Democracy, Innovation, and Entrepreneurship for Growth,
https://doi.org/10.1007/978-3-030-51995-7_8

The ability to control and improve firm competitiveness is the result of fully realizing these capabilities (Mortazavi Ravari, Mehrabanfar, Banaitis, & Banaitienė, 2016; Saunila & Ukko, 2012). Traditionally, technological innovation capabilities are defined as a varied number of firm features that enhance and support the firm's technological innovation strategies (Burgelman, Maidique, & Wheelwright, 2004). These capabilities allow firms to adapt to rapidly changing environments, enhancing their competitiveness (Mortazavi Ravari et al., 2016). Thus, technological innovation capabilities are formed when a firm has strategic expertise and practices aimed at more competitive technologies and processes.

Prior studies on technological innovation capabilities have concentrated on firm-level capabilities for innovation, including resource capability, R&D capability, learning capability, manufacturing capability, organizational capability, financial capability, marketing capability, and strategic planning capability (Chen, Wang, & Huang, 2019; Shafia et al., 2016; Wang & Zhang, 2018). This literature also discusses the role of distinct external and internal resources in these capabilities' development. Other studies only focus on a specific type of innovation, such as product or process innovation (e.g., Burgelman & Siegel, 2007), instead of generic technological innovation capabilities. Thus, the existing literature does not adequately represent all of the distinct perspectives and levels of the phenomenon needed to understand the relationship between technological innovation capabilities and a firm's competitiveness, which includes more than just product competitiveness. The micro-foundations of this topic especially require further research. This chapter builds on prior research by defining technological innovation capabilities at both the individual and firm levels and clarifying their relationship to firm competitiveness. Departing from the previous studies that concentrated primarily on determinants (e.g., Lau & Lo, 2019; Liu and Jiang, 2016) or implications (e.g., Camisón & Villar-López, 2014; Joo et al., 2018; Yam, Lo, Tang, & Lau, 2011) of technological innovation capabilities, this study contributes to the research by integrating several different level capabilities within a unifying framework in SME context.

First, we present a conceptual framework that illustrates the dimensions required for building competitiveness through technological innovation capabilities. We argue that this framework needs to be reflected in certain dimensions of both human behavior and firm capabilities.

Second, the framework is tested with empirical data. The research question is as follows: How do technological innovation capabilities generate competitiveness?

The chapter is structured as follows. First, prior research on technological innovation capabilities is presented as the foundation for the conceptual framework. The empirical case and methodology are also described. Next, the results are presented to connect the conceptual framework to empirical data. This section is followed by the conclusions, implications for research and practice, explanations of the study limitations, and suggestions for further studies.

8.2 Defining Technological Innovation Capabilities

8.2.1 Definition

The success of a firm's innovation system and performance is dependent on its different innovation capabilities (e.g., Aljanabi, 2017; Razavi, Nargesi, Hajihoseini, & Akbari, 2016; Siallagan, Silaban, & Ali, 2019; Yam et al., 2011). Indeed, technological innovation capability is one of the most fundamental areas of study in the field of technological innovation management (Mortazavi Ravari et al., 2016). In this regard, the authors Razavi et al. (2016) draw attention to research related to technological innovation capability that has been carried out in manufacturing firms in order to develop a framework describing the relevance of these capacities and their economic outcomes.

The evolution of the concept of technological innovation capability began with the asset approach (Liu & Jiang, 2016; Rahim & Zainuddin, 2017). Liu and Jiang (2016) claim that the authors Adler and Shenhar (1990) first discussed technological innovation capabilities, defining it in four dimensions: technological assets, organizational assets, external assets, and projects. In accordance with Razavi et al. (2016), Lall (1992) was the first to present a framework for technological innovation capabilities, classifying them in three categories: investment capacity, production capacity, and link capacity. Later, Christensen (1995) categorized technological innovation capabilities into four classes: scientific research assets, process innovation assets, product innovation assets, and aesthetic design assets (Liu & Jiang, 2016; Razavi et al., 2016).

The second step in the evolution of technological innovation capabilities was the process approach. Chiesa, Coughlan, and Voss (1996) developed a model to check a firm's capacity for technological innovation using process assessment and performance examination (Razavi et al., 2016). Later, the framework proposed by Chiesa and Manzini (1998) incorporated additional significant elements to support technological innovation, such as learning, organization, and strategic planning (Liu & Jiang, 2016). Next, Burgelman et al. (2004) proposed a five-dimensional framework integrating technological innovation capabilities: availability and resources allocation, ability to understand innovative competition strategies and industrial evolution, ability to understand technological developments, strategic management capacity, and structural and cultural context (Razavi et al., 2016).

More recently, the functional approach of innovation capabilities has gained prominence. Yam et al. (2004) propose a seven-dimensional framework related to the technological innovation capacity of firms: learning capacity, R&D capacity, resource allocation capacity, production capacity, marketing capacity, organizational capacity, and strategic planning capacity. This framework proposed by Yam et al. (2004) includes both the capacity perspective and the performance perspective (Liu & Jiang, 2016). This definition from Yam et al. (2004) has been widely used in the subsequent literature on technological innovation capabilities (Chen et al., 2019; Lin, 2014; Rahim & Zainuddin, 2017; Razavi et al., 2016; Shafia et al., 2016; Strand, Wiig, Torheim, Solli-SÆther, & Nesset, 2017; Yam et al., 2011).

Other literature categorizes the capacity for technological innovation into two fields: innovations in products and processes (Aljanabi, 2017; Camisón & Villar-López, 2014; Purwanto & Raihan, 2016; Razavi et al., 2016; Razavi, Talebpour, Azimzadeh, & Mohammadkazemi, 2019; Shafia et al., 2016; Yu et al., 2017). Additional literature uses patent analysis to present an approximation of technological innovation capabilities (Fan, Liu, & Zhu, 2017; Qiu & Yang, 2018). Also, the study of Fan et al. (2017) proposes three dimensions of technological innovation capabilities: relative growth rate, relative patent position, and revealed technological advantage.

Regarding the above approaches, it is important to note that there is no consensus in the literature on the definition of technological innovation capabilities, since the concept covers a great diversity of resources, making it complex and multidisciplinary (Chen et al., 2019; Ince, Imamoglu, &

Turkcan, 2016; Razavi et al., 2016). Thus, technological innovation capabilities are a multidimensional concept (Chen et al., 2019; Ince et al., 2016; Razavi et al., 2016; Shafia et al., 2016; Strand et al., 2017; Yu et al., 2017) that has been analyzed using different models (Razavi et al., 2016), including resource-based view (e.g., Aljanabi, 2017; Camisón & Villar-López, 2014; Joo et al., 2018; Lin, 2014; Rahim & Zainuddin, 2017; Razavi et al., 2016), distinctive skill, dynamic capability (e.g., Shafia et al., 2016), and knowledge-based view (e.g., Yu et al., 2017).

Building on the work of the previously mentioned authors, we propose that technological innovation capabilities can be defined as a set of advantages generated from the integral characteristics of firms (Lin, 2014) or a series of management activities (Bao & Chen, 2019) facilitating technological innovation strategies. These capabilities allow firms to respond to the needs of a changing and competitive market (Ince et al., 2016; Mortazavi Ravari et al., 2016; Rahim & Zainuddin, 2017; Shafia et al., 2016; Siallagan et al., 2019), create value for the customer (Joo et al., 2018), generate an innovative culture (Rahim & Zainuddin, 2017), and use new knowledge to drive growth (Siallagan et al., 2019).

Moreover, there is a growing trend of research in the literature analyzing the effects of technological innovation capabilities on a firm's competitive advantages and performance (Rahim & Zainuddin, 2017). Previous studies reveal that technological innovation capabilities generate greater competitiveness in firms (Aljanabi, 2017; Camisón & Villar-López, 2014; Chen et al., 2019; Joo et al., 2018; Ince et al., 2016; Liu and Jiang, 2016; Mortazavi Ravari et al., 2016; Purwanto & Raihan, 2016; Rahim & Zainuddin, 2017; Razavi et al., 2016, Shafia et al., 2016; Siallagan et al., 2019; Strand et al., 2017; Yam et al., 2011).

8.2.2 Driving Forces and Barriers

Resource configuration and firm characteristics can expand or restrict the development of technological innovation capabilities. A review of studies related to this subject shows that driving forces and barriers emerge at the individual and firm levels. First, research related to the effects of knowledge, skills, experience, creativity, leadership, and motivational techniques at the individual level of technological innovation capabilities will be analyzed. Second, organizational learning, absorption capacity, innovation strategy, business cooperation, and organizational factors will be analyzed as key factors affecting technological innovation capacity.

8.2.2.1 Individual Level

From an individual perspective, human capital has a significant effect on the technological innovation capabilities of a firm (Razavi et al., 2019). Therefore, it is essential to promote knowledge, skills, expertise, experience, creativity, leadership, and motivation in the firm's human talent to generate effective innovation processes (Dasgupta, Gupta, & Sahay, 2011; Razavi et al., 2019). In this context, incentive and reward schemes are important mechanisms to get employees to share knowledge with each other and value teamwork (Dasgupta et al., 2011).

Likewise, firms must promote learning processes at the individual level to develop technological innovation capabilities (Lau & Lo, 2019; Liu & Jiang, 2016; Yu et al., 2017). In this sense, firms must effectively manage tacit knowledge and individual empirical knowledge (Dasgupta et al., 2011; Liu and Jiang, 2016). Firms must also cultivate the organizational conditions necessary for developing learning processes at the individual level (acquisition, assimilation, transformation, and exploitation), considering these processes improve the innovative performance of firms and promote the consolidation of technological innovation capabilities (Lau & Lo, 2019). Because training and staff development programs are among the most effective mechanisms to generate technological innovation capabilities (Dasgupta et al., 2011), they are essential to achieving these ends.

8.2.2.2 Firm Level

First, much of the academic literature analyzes the relationship between organizational factors and the development of technological innovation capabilities. A firm's environment and work culture must be conducive to open communication and learning in order to encourage the development of technological innovation capabilities (Dasgupta et al., 2011). Furthermore, firm innovation must support these goals (Camisón & Villar-López, 2014) through flexible organizational structures openly communicating with one another and quickly responding to innovations (Dasgupta et al., 2011). Therefore, a highly centralized administrative structure making decisions with full autonomy under a rigid and conservative leadership is a barrier to the development of technological innovation capabilities in firms (Dasgupta et al., 2011). In contrast, implementing information technologies and systems contributes to the development of technological innovation capabilities and the successful performance of projects (Yang & Huang, 2016).

Second, the literature shows that organizational learning is an important mechanism for developing and increasing technological innovation capabilities (Aljanabi, 2017; Dasgupta et al., 2011; Ince et al., 2016; Yu et al., 2017). Beyond its role in technological innovation (Yu et al., 2017), organizational knowledge can also help develop other intangible resources for the firm (Aljanabi, 2017). In addition, knowledge absorption capacity has a positive impact on technological innovation capabilities and innovative performance because it enables the transfer of knowledge necessary for the development of firm processes (Dasgupta et al., 2011; Ince et al., 2016; Lau & Lo, 2019; Wu & Wang, 2018; Yam et al., 2011).

Third, the literature discusses cooperation and collaboration as important factors for the development of technological innovation capabilities (Ince et al., 2016; Wu & Wang, 2018; Yam et al., 2011). Thus, in their interaction with the environment, firms acquire new knowledge to improve all of their capabilities (Ince et al., 2016; Yam et al., 2011). Firms can accomplish this goal through partnerships or research and development processes within the framework of open innovation (Wu & Wang, 2018). They can also achieve these ends through formal and informal networks of internal and external knowledge (Dasgupta et al. 2011; Yam et al., 2011).

Fourth, the literature discusses why an innovation strategy and the resources associated with it are important to the development of a firm's technological innovation capabilities (Dasgupta et al., 2011; Liu & Jiang, 2016; Wang & Zhang, 2018). On this topic, Dasgupta et al. (2011) state that successful management of technological innovation requires effective resource allocation to achieve technological change. As a result, firms should align their organizational factors and innovation strategies to favor innovation capabilities and competitive advantages.

Finally, the literature uses the model proposed by Yam et al. (2004) to highlight the capabilities that significantly promote the development of technological innovation. On this topic, the works of Yam et al. (2011) and Razavi et al. (2016) emphasize the importance of learning ability. Some studies also discuss the effect of marketing capacity on technological innovation (Razavi et al., 2016; Strand et al., 2017). In addition, Razavi et al. (2016) describe the importance of R&D capacity and resource allocation, and Strand et al. (2017) endorse organizational and production capacity in the development of technological innovation capabilities.

8.3 The Conceptual Framework and Its Propositions

A conceptual framework (Fig. 8.1) was constructed based on the previously reviewed research. The goal was to present an overall framework of technological innovation capabilities. Thus, the framework did not take into account individual firm characteristics such as size or industry. Instead, the framework focused on the role of industry attributes, which are connected to the turbulence of the market or technology, including its overall competitive intensity. These industry attributes include changes and trends occurring in the industry. In determining the technological innovation capabilities important to a firm, the framework also prioritizes the focus of operation inside the firm. This concept includes the internal territory or function of the firm. The role of these issues is discussed later in this section. First, the conceptual framework and its propositions will be explained.

Traditionally, technological innovation capabilities are defined as a varied number of firm features that enhance and support the firm's technological innovation strategies (Burgelman et al., 2004). In this paradigm, technological innovation capabilities are shaped by expertise and practices that contribute to developing more competitive technologies and processes. Prior research divides technological innovation capabilities in multiple ways, but several individual-level and firm-level factors can be identified. For example, Lall (1992) considers skills and knowledge to be the crucial technological innovation capabilities. Guan and Ma (2003) refer to technological innovation capabilities as a special asset of a firm, incorporating product, process, technology, organization, knowledge, and experience. Firm-level technological innovation capabilities also include resource capability, R&D capability, marketing capability, financial capability, manufacturing capability, organizing capability, and strategic planning capability (Chen et al., 2019; Shafia et al., 2016; Wang & Zhang, 2018) among others. Based on these studies, the impacts of human experience, skills, and values on technological innovation should be highlighted, as should the impacts of firm-level technological innovation capabilities. The joint interaction between these two types of capabilities shapes the overall technological innovation capabilities of the firm. Thus, the first proposition focuses on the multilevel nature of technological innovation capabilities.

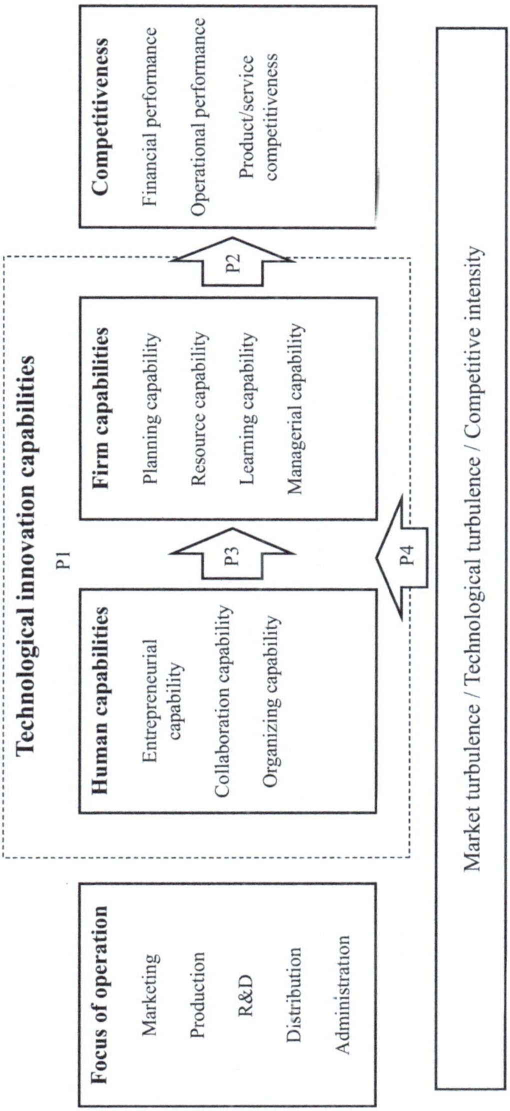

Fig. 8.1 The implications of technological innovation capabilities: the conceptual framework (*Source* Figueiredo and Ferreira [2019])

P1. Technological innovation capability is impacted by individual-level and firm-level capabilities.

Recent studies have suggested that a firm's technological innovation capabilities depend on strategic expertise that has the potential to affect its competitiveness (e.g., Chen et al., 2019; Joo et al., 2018; Shafia et al., 2016; Yu et al., 2017). Firm competitiveness can be described as the ability of a firm to successfully design, generate, and launch products in comparison to its competitors (D'Cruz & Rugman, 1992). Human resources, strategic management, technology management, and operations management are all involved in gaining competitiveness (Ajitabh & Momaya, 2004). All of these processes drive technological innovation capabilities, both at the individual level (e.g., Liu & Jiang, 2016; Razavi et al., 2019; Yu et al., 2017) and the firm level (e.g., Camisón & Villar-López, 2014; Dasgupta et al., 2011). Thus, technological innovation capabilities determine the progress and competitive ability of a firm. Only with robust technological innovation capabilities can firms gain a competitive advantage and improve their competitiveness. For these reasons, we propose that:

P2. Technological innovation capabilities drive competitiveness.

The prior argument is that firm-level competitiveness is shaped by a set of complex capabilities. Previous research shows that both individual-level and firm-level capabilities are crucial to competitiveness. The first of these characteristic refers to the capability of the humans to create, diffuse, and use innovations that provide value to the firm, ultimately contributing to the firm's human knowledge. Since human knowledge is considered to be one of the firm's unique resources (Wernerfelt, 1984; Wright, Dunford, & Snell, 2001), related capabilities can enhance the firm's unique firm-level capabilities and consequently increase the chances of gaining a competitive advantage (Joo et al., 2018; Shafia et al., 2016; Yu et al., 2017). Individual-level capabilities affect both the types and levels of the firm's capabilities. One can assume that firms possessing a high level of human knowledge in technological innovation are more likely to adjust their firm-level capabilities in relation to the operating environment and obtain favorable responses from the market. Those favorable responses can be turned into higher levels of competitiveness. This paradigm highlights the twofold role of firm-level capabilities: as a factor shaped by individual-level capabilities and as a crucial determinant of competitiveness. As a result, the third proposition relates both individual-level and firm-level capabilities to the establishment of competitiveness.

P3. Individual-level capabilities influence competitiveness by facilitating the exploration of firm-level capabilities.

A firm's technological innovation capabilities may depend on certain contextual factors. There is evidence that innovation capability may differ based on the focus of the operation, for example in terms of what unit the individuals work for (Saunila, Mäkimattila, & Salminen, 2014) or the position of individuals (Saunila, 2017). Thus, different operations will require different experience and skills. These factors are preconditions that need to be taken into account when enhancing innovation capability, especially in situations where they will be difficult to change.

The external environment also shapes firm composition and operation (Li & Liu, 2014; Quinton et al., 2018; Shafia et al., 2016). In other words, the environmental features of a firm influence the relationship between its technological innovation capabilities and competitiveness. As the external environment is impacted by diverse types of turbulence and competition, utilizing technological innovation capabilities can help manage such conditions. Under conditions of high turbulence and competition, customer demands will vary (Jaworski & Kohli, 1993). As a result, a firm that does not develop its technological innovation capabilities is likely to lose customers to competitors, which in turn will lower the firm's competitiveness. Thus, a firm must evaluate its external environment and develop technological innovation capabilities to maintain its competitiveness. The discussion above suggests that:

P4. Technological turbulence, market turbulence, and competitive intensity affect the extent to which individual-level and firm-level capabilities drive competitiveness.

8.4 Case Study

A case study was used as the basis for this research. Following a process described by Yin (1994), the aim was to examine a contemporary phenomenon in its real-life context by using single-case design. This strategy was chosen for the rich insights it made possible. The empirical evidence concerned a case study of a media firm in southern Finland. The firm has a number of business units with independent and common functions. For example, the firm manages printed newspapers, online news, and radio. Its support units include printing, distribution, IT, and administration. The firm is also part of a larger corporation, and the number of employees vary depending on the situation since a large portion of them

Table 8.1 Interviews

Interviewee	*Position*	*Interview duration*	*Form of data*	*Analysis*
1	Innovation manager	35 min.	Recorded and transcribed	Qualitative content analysis
2	Product manager	62 min.	Recorded and transcribed	Qualitative content analysis
3	Sales manager	40 min.	Recorded and transcribed	Qualitative content analysis
4	Production manager	60 min.	Recorded and transcribed	Qualitative content analysis
5	Web producer	60 min.	Recorded and transcribed	Qualitative content analysis
6	Production manager	47 min.	Recorded and transcribed	Qualitative content analysis

work part-time. Like its competitors, the firm faces common challenges in a changing business environment due to the rise of online media. Cutting costs is not the solution for its long-term competitiveness.

The data consisted of semi-structured personal interviews with six interviewees (see Table 8.1 for further information). Each interviewee was selected based on their roles and responsibilities in the firm. Leadership or hands-on experience with innovation development was necessary for each interviewee. Interview questions were defined in advance, but the interviews followed an informal procedure that allowed complementary questions from the interviewers. In addition to the recorded and transcribed interview data, notes, and observations during the interview were used for analysis. The interviews covered the current situations and challenges related to innovation projects, the implementation of innovations to solve these challenges, and the outcomes to be achieved. A qualitative content analysis was used to investigate the firm's technological innovation capabilities in light of the conceptual framework presented in the previous section.

8.5 Results—Application of the Framework

In this section, empirical evidence from the case study is provided. The results are provided at three levels described in the conceptual framework: Individual-level capabilities, Firm-level capabilities, and Competitiveness.

The following sections discuss and elaborate upon these findings The key results are summarized in Table 8.2.

8.5.1 Individual-Level Capabilities

The case study evidence reveals that a firm must balance strict practices and policies with opportunities for innovation. The interviewees confirmed that both characteristics are necessary in the work environment to facilitate technological innovation. In particular, the case study evidence supports the point that individuals' personalities and approaches toward innovation are foundational to the successful utilization of individual-level capabilities. Employees whose work is entrepreneurial and regenerative are especially essential for developing technological innovation. The interviewees also stated that open communication between employees encourages them to participate in innovation activities and helps them recognize their role in innovation. Individuals with this type of entrepreneurial capability are the key to technological innovation The interviewees stated:

> *Through that kind of free ideation, we can kind of create something new for that activity. (Interviewee 2)*

> *... the group structure, some combination just doesn't work. There has to be a little forward-looking and outward-locking activity, not that its purpose is just to frustrate everyone. (Interviewee 6)*

> *And if they [employees] doesn't have that activity, if their bosses don't have that activity, then the whole process leaks out. This is not a one person thing. (Interviewee 1)*

This type of human collaboration can motivate employees to generate technological innovation through innovative action. The case study evidence supports the view that opportunities for employees to collaborate among different departments and with people of different skills and personalities are important to technological innovation. Acquiring knowledge and ideas from outside the firm is also important in developing technological innovation. This external collaboration can occur through interactions with customers, suppliers, and competitors. Thus, collaboration capability is essential to technological innovation.

Table 8.2 Summary of the case study

Proposition	*Case evidence*
P1. Technological innovation capability is impacted by individual-level and firm-level capabilities	Technological innovation capabilities are determined by several individual-level and firm-level capabilities The actions towards technological innovation capability development should be developed in parallel at the individual and firm levels in order to gain positive effects
P2. Technological innovation capabilities drive competitiveness	Technological innovation capabilities possess the potential to reduce costs and enhance profitability Increasing sales of existing services and creating sales from novel services were potential factors in reaching targets Technological innovation capabilities development could also result in negative consequences, such as extra costs
P3. Individual-level capabilities influence competitiveness by facilitating the exploration of firm-level capabilities	*Individual-level capabilities* Entrepreneurial capability helps build dialogue over the development of technological innovation Organizing capability assists in balancing the different needs for the distinct development phases of technological innovation Collaboration capability can motivate employees to generate technological innovation through innovative action *Firm-level capabilities* Planning capability establishes limits on the technological innovation activities through multiple phases and threshold points before being commercialized Resource capability facilitates technological innovations as they do not succeed by accident and without sufficient resources throughout the innovation development process Learning capability allows for both radical and incremental innovations to emerge when learning is supported throughout the firm Managerial capability increases cooperation among employees and involvement in innovation development through successful management initiatives

(continued)

Table 8.2 (continued)

Proposition	*Case evidence*
P4. Technological turbulence, market turbulence, and competitive intensity affect the extent to which individual-level and firm-level capabilities drive competitiveness	Variety in a firm's capabilities is necessary for technological innovation development since contexts and markets change External environment turbulence requires a balance between tight practices and policies and employees' freedom to be creative External environment turbulence generates puzzles in technological innovation development due to distinct requirements in exploitation and exploration Technological innovation capabilities may also assist in adjusting to the rapidly changing business environment

The interviewees also stated that changing even one person in the innovation development group opened possibilities for very different outcomes. As a result, it is clear that human knowledge determines the outcomes of innovation activities. More employees were involved in the development of technological innovation than in the core innovation development group. Thus, an ability to motivate others to participate in innovation activities, provide ideas, and drive the overall development was highlighted. Technological innovation requires a firm to possess organizing capability, as different phases of the innovation process can create different needs. These ideas were discussed by the interviewees in the following quotes:

> *You should guide it [innovation activities] through the actions and shape the initiatives and measures accordingly. (Interviewee 4)*

> *I think it has clarified [the innovation activities] that idea has an owner, who takes care of the fact that it's going forward. And then if that single person is named for it, who's responsible for producing a product for it within a certain timeframe, I think it has clarified quite a bit of the job. (Interviewee 2)*

8.5.2 *Firm-Level Capabilities*

The case study showed that competitiveness cannot be determined simply by paying attention to individual-level capabilities. In addition, competitiveness requires firm-level capabilities such as learning, resources, planning, and management. There were multiple activities in the case study related to firm-level capabilities. Firm-level capabilities also represent better processes for doing something, otherwise known as planning capability. A firm's planning capability includes the boundaries it puts around technological innovation activities. For example, the case study firm developed a procedure through which innovations were developed toward commercial ends. This focus reduced the amount of unsuccessful innovations in the market and the time spent on the development of innovations. Interviewee 1 made the following point:

> *If you do not have a clear pattern, a frame to carry them on [innovation activities], then the result would be worse. (Interviewee 1)*

Among the interviewees, goal orientation was emphasized, because prosperous results, such as novel products or services, do not transform into commercial ends overnight. They are developed through several distinct phases before being commercialized and distributed. In addition, careful planning of technological innovation imperatives reduces the need to cease the development of promising ideas, especially when support and resources have been provided to those ideas over a long period of time. This type of resource capability is important, as technological innovations do not succeed by accident and without sufficient resources throughout the innovation development process. Interviewees stated the following:

> *Do we have the resources, do we have the right people to do things, do we have time to do it by a certain deadline, who will commit to it... after figuring these out, we will start getting our projects through. (Interviewee 4)*

> *Our group [innovation development group] is still going. One big challenge is to give people enough time to do these things. (Interviewee 1)*

Another firm-level responsibility is to support learning aimed at innovation development. Initial ideas from individuals or groups of employees were provided to an innovation development group. The group was responsible for providing an initial assessment of the idea's suitability and, if appropriate, advancing the idea further. Feedback was provided to the individual or group, who were sometimes allowed to present a revised version of the concept. This type of learning capability has allowed both radical and incremental innovations to emerge. Learning capabilities within the firm, especially when supported by digital systems, was a key ingredient in technological innovation development. Interviewees revealed the following:

> *I do not believe that we have been able to unravel this very far, because the presence of an outsider in a way then completely dismantles our internal order of command. (Interviewee 4)*

> *The benefit of that [external input] is that you get comments, with a little bit of new perspectives, ways of looking things, something like that. (Interviewee 5)*

> *It's not enough that those members of the management team know, you need to know that at grassroots level. (Interviewee 2)*

Management support was one of the most crucial aspects of technological innovation development. While reflecting on managerial capability, interviewees discussed the importance of the working climate and enhanced functioning of operational processes. Increased collaboration and involvement in innovation development was seen as the result of successful management initiatives. In the case study, decision-making responsibilities were spread throughout the firm, creating obstacles for moving innovations forward. This problem was overcome by forming an innovation management group who offered support for idea developments and simplified the interactions between strategic management and everyday innovation activities. This approach was also seen as a way to align strategic innovations. The interviewees supported the innovation management group's role in furthering innovation processes and saw it as a proper protectant against issues between managerial capability and technological innovation. On this topic, the interviewees stated the following:

> *What role anyone has in it [innovation activities], where they can find support and where they can put ideas, who decides what and who implements it. Clarifying these things in this organization and giving instructions, that's*

> *one big, very important thing. And the way that these things are carried forward and how they are being coordinated, they are a big deal. (Interviewee 1)*

> *First you have to let people talk and think, let them innovate more on that, to give employees the feeling that, hey, "I have an influence on this." I think it develops that sense of being together, I can influence things. (Interviewee 4)*

8.5.3 *Competitiveness*

After analyzing the case study, it has become clear that technological innovation capabilities possess the potential to reduce a firm's costs and enhance its profitability. Technological innovation seems to be a major factor in improving sales. According to the above interviews, increasing sales of existing services and creating new sales from novel services are both important for reaching a firm's targets. Systematic technological innovation development enables these possibilities for additional business.

Despite these positives, the interviewees did point out some negatives as well. One interviewee stated the following:

> *...from a sales point of view, then it's too soon. In a way, what is the time window for innovation that we do, so it feels like we're too short-term all the time, we can't see over a sufficient time. (Interviewee 3)*

Other interviewees pointed out that the development of technological innovation capabilities could result in negative consequences, such as extra costs. For these reasons, the majority of the interviewees emphasized that capabilities development should be systematic: the procedures toward capability development should be developed in parallel at the individual-level and firm-level in order to generate positive results.

8.6 Conclusions

This study contributes to technological innovation management research by emphasizing the essential capabilities of technological innovation and their role in building competitive advantages. Although not exhaustive, the literature review offered an extensive basis for constructing a conceptual framework for technological innovation capabilities. The framework was then examined in the context of SMEs to understand the interplay between technological innovation capabilities and competitiveness. The following processes were discussed: the formation of technological innovation capabilities, and the establishment of competitiveness through technological innovation capabilities. In this chapter, we established that individual-level capabilities are essential determinants for realizing firm-level capabilities in technological innovation actions. Further, the external environment plays a role in shaping the relationship between a firm's technological innovation capabilities and firm competitiveness.

8.6.1 *Theoretical Implications*

In regards to theory, this chapter offers multiple implications for further studies on the technological innovation management research of SMEs. First, by exploring the role that technological innovation capabilities play in developing competitiveness, this study contributes to prior research by proposing that technological innovation capabilities enable individual firms to build competitive advantages by developing their individual-level and firm-level capabilities. Of the individual-level capabilities affecting a firm's technological innovation capabilities, entrepreneurial, organizing, and collaboration capabilities seem to determine the extent to which individuals contribute to technological innovation. In addition, firms need to motivate employees by providing necessary planning, resource, learning, and managerial capabilities for technological innovation development.

Few studies besides this one have explored multilevel technological innovation capabilities as a contingency. Prior studies concentrated primarily on determinants (e.g., Lau & Lo, 2019; Liu & Jiang, 2016) or implications (e.g., Camisón & Villar-López, 2014; Joo et al., 2018; Yam et al., 2011) of technological innovation capabilities without taking into account the micro-foundations of the phenomena. This study's results indicate that the contingency role of technological innovation capabilities determines the extent to which SMEs attain a competitive advantage.

Finally, this study enriches the literature by integrating several different level capabilities within a unifying framework in SME context. Regarding the conceptual framework, the case study evidence highlights the importance of developing both individual-level and firm-level technological innovation capabilities in order to establish and maintain a competitive advantage. The propositions and conceptual framework for technological innovation capabilities detailed in this chapter open up possibilities for further research.

8.6.2 *Managerial Implications*

From a practical point of view, these conclusions about the interplay between firm competitiveness and technological innovation capabilities at the individual and firm levels offer insights regarding how the managers of SMEs can promote technological innovation to attain competitive advantages. Specifically, managers must strive to develop individual-level and firm-level technological innovation capabilities in conjunction with each other to make their firms more competitive. Individual-level capabilities can assist firms in accessing new knowledge and capabilities related to new technologies, and firm-level capabilities can cultivate processes aimed at improving their competitiveness. Thus, individual-level and firm-level technological innovation capabilities cannot be viewed as separate activities. Instead, they should be pursued simultaneously, with consideration given to the conditions of the external environment. Furthermore, the essential capabilities that shape technological innovation capabilities in SMEs identified in this chapter must be known to policymakers before they choose an innovation policy.

8.6.3 *Limitations and Further Research Directions*

The study has two main limitations. The first limitation is the conceptual focus of the chapter. The research builds on one case and, although the results support the conceptual framework and its propositions, more research on the conceptual framework is necessary to strengthen and expand the theoretical conclusions. The second limitation is the chapter's focus on intra-organizational capabilities. Few firms operate alone, and innovation is increasingly created in collaboration with several firms. Thus, extending the research focus to inter-organizational relationships would be valuable. While none of the elements and capabilities recognized in the framework are truly new, they have never been explored in an SME setting or the media business context before, and this focus is the novelty of this study. Further studies on technological innovation capabilities will only add to this chapter's conclusions on the interplay between different level capabilities, as well as their drivers and barriers.

References

Adler, P., & Shenhar, A. (1990). Adapting your technological base: The organizational challenge. *Sloan Management Review, 25*, 25–37.

Ajitabh, A., & Momaya, K. (2004). Competitiveness of firms: Review of theory, frameworks and models. *Singapore Management Review, 26*(1), 45–61.

Aljanabi, A. R. A. (2017). The mediating role of absorptive capacity on the relationship between entrepreneurial orientation and technological innovation capabilities. *International Journal of Entrepreneurial Behaviour and Research, 24*(4), 818–841.

Bao, Z., & Chen, L. (2019). Construction of evaluation index system of technological innovation capability of Smes in manufacturing industry based on AHP method. In *IOP Conference Series: Materials Science and Engineering*, 612(3).

Burgelman, R., Maidique, M. A., & Wheelwright, S. C. (2004). *Strategic management of technology and innovation*. New York: McGraw-Hill.

Burgelman, R. A., & Siegel, R. E. (2007). Defining the minimum winning game in high-technology ventures. *California Management Review, 49*(3), 6–26.

Camisón, C., & Villar-López, A. (2014). Organizational innovation as an enabler of technological innovation capabilities and firm performance. *Journal of Business Research, 67*(1), 2891–2902.

Chen, Q., Wang, C. H., & Huang, S. Z. (2019). Effects of organizational innovation and technological innovation capabilities on firm performance: evidence from firms in China's Pearl River Delta. *Asia Pacific Business Review, 26*(1), 1–25.

Chiesa, V., Coughlan, P., & Voss, C. A. (1996). Development of a technical innovation audit. *Journal of Product Innovation Management, 13*(2), 105–136.

Chiesa, V., & Manzini, R. (1998). Profiting from the virtual organization of technological innovation: Suggestions from an empirical study. *International Journal of Technology Management, 15*(1–2), 109–123.

Christensen, J. F. (1995). Asset profiles for technological innovation. *Research Policy, 24*(5), 727–745.

D'Cruz, J., & Rugman, A. (1992). *New concepts for Canadian competitiveness*. Canada: Kodak.

Dasgupta, M., Gupta, R. K., & Sahay, A. (2011). Linking technological innovation, technology strategy and organizational factors: A review. *Global Business Review, 12*(2), 257–277.

Fan, X., Liu, W., & Zhu, G. (2017). Scientific linkage and technological innovation capabilities: International comparisons of patenting in the solar energy industry. *Scientometrics, 111*(1), 117–138.

Guan, J., & Ma, N. (2003). Innovative capability and export performance of Chinese firms. *Technovation, 23*(9), 737–747.

Ince, H., Imamoglu, S. Z., & Turkcan, H. (2016). The effect of technological innovation capabilities and absorptive capacity on firm innovativeness: A conceptual framework. *Procedia—Social and Behavioral Sciences, 235*(October), 764–770.

Jaworski, B. J., & Kohli, A. K. (1993). Market orientation: Antecedents and consequences. *Journal of Marketing, 57*(3), 53–70.

Joo, H. Y., Seo, Y. W., & Min, H. (2018). Examining the effects of government intervention on the firm's environmental and technological innovation capabilities and export performance. *International Journal of Production Research, 56*(18), 6090–6111.

Lall, S. (1992). Technological capabilities and industrialization. *World Development, 20*(2), 165–186.

Lau, A. K. W., & Lo, W. (2019). Absorptive capacity, technological innovation capability and innovation performance: An empirical study in Hong Kong. *International Journal of Technology Management, 80*(1–2), 107–148.

Li, D. Y., & Liu, J. (2014). Dynamic capabilities, environmental dynamism, and competitive advantage: Evidence from China. *Journal of Business Research, 67*(1), 2793–2799.

Lin, H. F. (2014). The impact of socialization mechanisms and technological innovation capabilities on partnership quality and supply chain integration. *Information Systems and E-Business Management, 12*(2), 285–306.

Liu, L., & Jiang, Z. (2016). Influence of technological innovation capabilities on product competitiveness. *Industrial Management and Data Systems, 116*(5), 883–892.

Mortazavi Ravari, S. S., Mehrabanfar, E., Banaitis, A., & Banaitienė, N. (2016). Framework for assessing technological innovation capability in research and technology organizations. *Journal of Business Economics and Management, 17*(6), 825–847.

Purwanto, U. S., & Raihan, A. (2016). The relationship between of manufacturing flexibility, innovation capability, and operational performance in Indonesian manufacturing SMEs. *IOP Conference Series: Materials Science and Engineering, 114*(1), 012074.

Qiu, H. H., & Yang, J. (2018). An assessment of technological innovation capabilities of carbon capture and storage technology based on patent analysis: A comparative study between China and the United States. *Sustainability (Switzerland), 10,* 1–20.

Quinton, S., Canhoto, A., Molinillo, S., Pera, R., & Budhathoki, T. (2018). Conceptualising a digital orientation: Antecedents of supporting SME performance in the digital economy. *Journal of Strategic Marketing, 26*(5), 427–439.

Rahim, F. b. T., & Zainuddin, Y. b. (2017). Moderating effect of environmental turbulence on firm's technological innovation capabilities (TIC) and business performance in the automotive industry in Malaysia: A conceptual framework. In Malaysia Automotive Institute (MAI) (Ed.), *MATEC Web of Conferences 90* (Vol. 01009). Malaysia.

Razavi, S. M. H., Nargesi, G. R., Hajihoseini, H., & Akbari, M. (2016). The impact of technological innovation capabilities on competitive performance of Iranian ICT firms. *Iranian Journal of Management Studies, 9*(4), 855–882.

Razavi, S. M. J., Talebpour, M., Azimzadeh, S. M., & Mohammadkazemi, R. (2019). Enhancing technological innovation capabilities: The role of human capital in Iranian sports manufacturing companies. *Annals of Applied Sport Science, 7*(3), 31–40.

Saunila, M. (2017). Innovation capability in achieving higher performance: Perspectives of management and employees. *Technology Analysis & Strategic Management, 29*(8), 903–916.

Saunila, M., Mäkimattila, M., & Salminen, J. (2014). Matrix structure for supporting organizational innovation capability. *International Journal of Business Innovation and Research, 8*(1), 20–35.

Saunila, M., & Ukko, J. (2012). A conceptual framework for the measurement of innovation capability and its effects. *Baltic Journal of Management, 7*(4), 355–375.

Shafia, M. A., Shavvalpour, S., Hosseini, M., & Hosseini, R. (2016). Mediating effect of technological innovation capabilities between dynamic capabilities and competitiveness of research and technology organisations. *Technology Analysis & Strategic Management, 28*(7), 811–826.

Siallagan, S., Silaban, R., & Ali, A. Y. (2019). Academic review on literatures pertaining to the definitions of technological innovation capabilities in the new millennium. *IOP Conference Series: Materials Science and Engineering, 505*(1), 012132.

Strand, Ø., Wiig, M., Torheim, T., Solli-SÆther, H., & Nesset, E. (2017). Technological innovation capability and interaction effect in a Scandinavian industry cluster. *International Journal of Innovation Management, 21*(5), 1–22.

Wang, W., & Zhang, C. (2018). Evaluation of relative technological innovation capability: Model and case study for China's coal mine. *Resources Policy, 58,* 144–149.

Wernerfelt, B. (1984). A resource-based view of the firm. *Strategic Management Journal, 5*(2), 171–180.

Wright, P. M., Dunford, B. B., & Snell, S. A. (2001). Human resources and the resource based view of the firm. *Journal of Management, 27*(6), 701–721.

Wu, Q., & Wang, W. (2018). Dynamic growth of technological innovation capability of manufacturing enterprises from the perspective of open innovation on evaluation. In *5th International Conference on Industrial Economics System and Industrial Security Engineering*, IEIS 2018—Proceeding.

Yam, R., Guan, J., Pun, K., & Tang, E. (2004). An audit of technological innovation capabilities in Chinese firms: Some empirical findings in Beijing, China. *Research Policy, 33*(8), 1123–1140.

Yam, R. C. M., Lo, W., Tang, E. P. Y., & Lau, A. K. W. (2011). Analysis of sources of innovation, technological innovation capabilities, and performance: An empirical study of Hong Kong manufacturing industries. *Research Policy, 40*(3), 391–402.

Yang, L. R., & Huang, C. F. (2016). Information platform to improve technological innovation capabilities: Role of cloud platform. *Journal of Civil Engineering and Management, 22*(7), 936–943.

Yin, R. K. (1994). *Case study research*. Thousands Oaks, CA: Sage.

Yu, C., Zhang, Z., Lin, C., & Wu, Y. (2017). Knowledge creation process and sustainable competitive advantage: The role of technological innovation capabilities. *Sustainability, 9*(12), 2280.

CHAPTER 9

Service Business Growth: "A Spinner Innovation Model Approach"

Ronnie Figueiredo and Bouchaib Bahli

9.1 Introduction

Globally, economic transformation and reindustrialization constantly change the geographical landscape of knowledge and technology-intensive industries (KTI), and the role of KTI agglomeration in city innovation is becoming increasingly decisive (Qi, Liu, Qi, & Liu, 2019). In general, research and development (R&D) service firms make significant contributions to innovation in other businesses (Li, Gagliardi, &

R. Figueiredo (✉)
Business School (FCES), Universidade Europeia (UE) & NECE-UBI, Lisbon, Portugal
e-mail: ronnie.figueiredo@universidadeeuropeia.pt

B. Bahli
Information Technology and Management, Ryerson University, Toronto, ON, Canada
e-mail: bahli@ryerson.ca

J. J. M. Ferreira et al. (eds.), *Technological Innovation and International Competitiveness for Business Growth*, Palgrave Studies in Democracy, Innovation, and Entrepreneurship for Growth,
https://doi.org/10.1007/978-3-030-51995-7_9

Miles, 2019) supported by firms that interact with universities for technological competence building or to gain access to cutting-edge scientific knowledge and technologies (Chung & Tseng, 2019).

Hrivnák, Melichová, Fáziková, and Roháčiková (2019) studied how graduates rollout by universities and knowledge spill-overs on basis of interpersonal relationships between entrepreneurs and senior academic researchers determines the emergence of knowledge-intensive ventures in Slovakia; meanwhile, we distinguish between total number of knowledge-intensive firms (KIF), knowledge-intensive manufacturing ventures (KIM), knowledge intensive business services (KIBS), and knowledge-intensive services (KIS).

Knowledge intensive business services (KIBS) are special for they rely on knowledge exchange between service providers and consumers; thus, intensive cooperation between the two parties is essential at all stages (Vinogradov, Shadrina, & Doroshenko, 2018). According to Doloreux, Shearmur, and Rodriguez (2018), KIBS' information value obtained from clients and suppliers and from generally available sources (including investors, conferences, and internet) have a higher propensity to innovate.

Despite evidence that KIBS firms do not typically consider formal appropriability mechanisms, such as patents, to be central mechanisms for capturing value from innovation, Miozzo, Desyllas, Lee, and Miles (2016) indicate that they are nevertheless important for their innovation collaboration.

Knowledge Intensive Business Services (KIBS) have been actively changing business knowledge because they are considered as a production factor and are becoming increasingly pronounced and applied by different organizations and science areas (Kekezi & Klaesson, 2019).

In this context, we can observe a different approach for KIBS application to understand the service business growth according to the Spinner Innovation Model. Our main goal is to compare studies indexed in journals in two different countries, Brazil and Canada, using the three Spinner Innovation Model, Figueiredo & Ferreira (2019) dimensions: 'knowledge creation, knowledge transfer, and innovation' to identify the main topics associated with the model.

The investigate issue is: *How many scientific studies in different areas are being conducted on the three pillars of the Spinner Innovation Model based on KIBS?*

The proposed methodology is based on a systematic literature review collected from Scopus database.

The remaining of this chapter is organized as follows: Sect. 9.2 presents the context of KIBS in the service sector and the Spinner Innovation Model (2019), Sect. 9.3 describes the methodology used, Sect. 9.4 presents the results and conclusions, and the discussion is presented in Sect. 9.5.

9.2 KIBS in the Service Sector and the Spinner Innovation Model Approach

The key role of knowledge intensive business services (KIBS) in economic growth has received in the past years much attention in the literature due to the increasing importance of knowledge as a production input. KIBS include consultancies, R&D firms, and IT firms, and their main function is to provide their clients with knowledge. Thus, they depend on face-to-face interactions with their clients and are often observed to be highly clustered in larger markets. Simultaneously, KIBS exhibit high rates of innovation themselves (Kekezi & Klaesson, 2019). In the manufacturing sectors, KIBS firms seek to reduce involuntary leakages or transfers of knowledge in the process of innovation collaboration. However, in the case of KIBS firms, where joint knowledge creation with clients is the norm, regular conflict over ownership of the jointly developed knowledge assets may take place (Miozzo et al., 2016).

Yet it remains unclear whether selecting target sectors may contribute to the overall economic growth, let alone which sectors should receive most attention from policymakers (Brenner, Capasso, Duschl, Frenken, & Treibich, 2018). Some firms have become innovation pioneers in specialized areas. However, the degree of openness varies among these firms. Smaller firms or firms facing fiercer competition tend to be less open. The access to external knowledge is sometimes constrained by insufficient resources or limited by the high risk of knowledge leaking. By contrast, larger firms with sufficient resources are more willing and able to source external knowledge via collaborations, partnerships, and outsourcing (Li et al., 2019).

The current work on innovation demonstrates that it relies on internal resources including, but not limited to, internal R&D and on interactions with heterogeneous economic players and resources outside the firms' boundaries (Doloreux et al., 2018). Relationships between internal and external capabilities depend on the quality of the partners interested in the co-creation process. In general, they can be small companies or even large corporates, provided they are aligned with the same goal and innovate with knowledge-intensive services (Figueiredo, Neto, Quelhas, & Ferreira, 2017). KIBS may be hired by another organization to create and transfer knowledge-intensive services to develop the service sector (Figueiredo, Quelhas, Neto, & Ferreira, 2019).

The Spinner Innovation Model, developed by Figueiredo and Ferreira (2019), dynamically presents three dimensions: knowledge creation, knowledge transfer, and innovation. It is similar to the three interaction axes of a fidget spinner with KIBS being at the center for economic development. The dimensions of propensity to innovation based on the model of Figueiredo and Ferreira (2019) are presented in (Fig. 9.1).

The proposed model revolves around KIBS which comprises of firms that provide knowledge-intensive services in the service sector and aim to create or transfer knowledge to companies in other sectors, either through a professional or a technological approach, generating innovation and consequently increasing competitiveness. The assessment of KIBS' prediction of propensity to innovate in the service sector refers to the

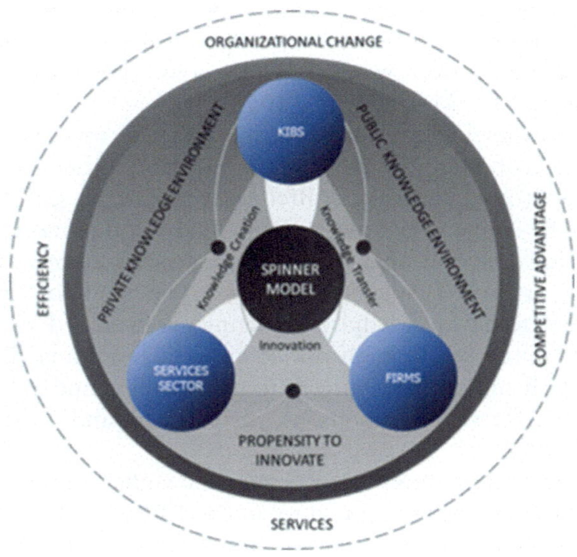

Fig. 9.1 Dimensions of service innovation based on The Spinner Innovation Model of Figueiredo and Ferreira (2019)

relationship between KIBS and the service sector, where KIBS' dynamic factors, such as knowledge creation and transfer, are associated with the demands of service providing firms served by KIBS. We understand that the integration of knowledge and its transfer can foster a firm's sustainable competitive advantage through innovation generated by the intensive use of knowledge.

This approach takes place within the public domain through the interaction with KIBS' private environment. Thereby, the relationship promotes organizational change when one of the companies served by KIBS exhibits an increase in sustainable competitiveness due to the efficient use of knowledge. Efficiency was measured by knowledge creation and transfer, and its relationship with the firm's innovation. The measurement of the dynamics of KIBS' innovative capacity was done among the private knowledge environment, where KIBS originates, and the public knowledge environment of the firms served by KIBS through the provision of knowledge-intensive services, called the organizational change environment.

The Spinner Innovation Model approach is based on the perspective of KIBS as a promoter of relationships with firms (service providing sector) aiming at the creation of new knowledge, transfer of knowledge, innovation, and economic development. Innovation is perceived as the result of the innovative capacity, created through the interaction of private and public knowledge, for the delivery of knowledge-intensive solutions based on professional or technological intelligence in a spinner of "dynamic interaction."

Since the significance of mature knowledge in fostering the economy has increased, KIBS play a key role in this process. The speed of organizational changes, the efficiency of deliveries to customers, and the quality of the provided services compose the firms' differentials in the service sector. In the current economic scenario, the challenge is to converge efforts rapidly in order to improve innovation systems through the creation and transfer of knowledge and achieving the necessary competitive advantage for the globalization of their services.

9.3 Methodology

The investigation was performed through a systematic literature review according to the methodology of Lim, Davis, Tang, Shannon, and Bonfield (2019), Palmatier, Houston, and Hulland (2018), and Dolati

Neghabadi, Evrard Samuel, and Espinouse (2019). Similar bibliometric studies can be observed in (Cadarette et al., 2017; Cullen, 2017; Sherman et al., 2013; Yergens, Tam-Tham, & Minty, 2016; Zaharia et al., 2016). We carried out an in-depth content review to identify key studies related to the proposed research.

9.3.1 Data Collection

The data used were collected and compiled through the Scopus online database which contains thousands of academic publications and bibliographic information. They were considered by year of publication and grouped into six clusters of terms according to the three dimensions of the Spinner Innovation Model (2019): D1–D1.1, Knowledge Creation ("Canada"), D1.2, Knowledge Creation ("Brazil"), D2–D2.1, Knowledge Transfer ("Canada"), D2.2, Knowledge Transfer ("Brazil"), D3–D3.1, Innovation ("Canada"), and D3.2, Innovation ("Brazil"), including untitled, abstract, or keyword (topic) papers in English.

9.3.2 Analysis

All data were analyzed using the VOS Viewer (Version 1.6.13) and Microsoft Excel. To perform the analysis according to the above three dimensions, six clusters were considered corresponding to the number of papers identified—(Fig. 9.2).

9.4 Results

9.4.1 Knowledge Creation in Canada: Cluster 1—N (106)

In the past two decades, a range of new information and communication technologies, Web 2.0, has fundamentally altered the nature of community building, collaboration, and organization at the economic and social levels (Fig. 9.3). Online communities (OC) give rise to tacit knowledge flows among participants. The crucial condition for these flows is not the advent of novel, digital technology, but the technology's domestication by humanity and the sociality it affords instead (Faraj, von Krogh, Monteiro, & Lakhani, 2016). Since being identified as a concept for understanding knowledge sharing, management, and creation, communities of practice (CoPs) have become increasingly popular within the health sector. The

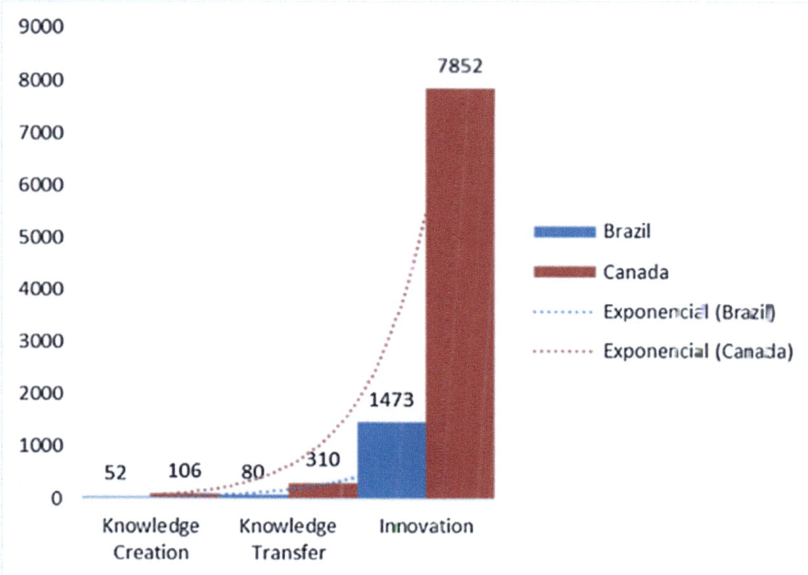

Fig. 9.2 Number of clusters and articles

Fig. 9.3 Authors' network of 106 publications and their clusters

CoP concept has been used in the business sector for over 20 years, but the use of CoPs in the health sector has been limited in comparison. The structure of CoP groups varied greatly, ranging from voluntary informal networks to work-supported formal education sessions, and from apprentice training to multidisciplinary, multisite project teams (Li et al., 2009). Collective knowledge as a social value may arise in cooperation among actors whose individual expertise is limited. The process of knowledge creation requires meaningful, logically coordinated interactions, which represent a challenging problem to physics and social dynamics modeling. By combining two-scale dynamics model with empirical data analysis from a well-known Questions & Answers system Mathematics, the process occurs as a collective phenomenon in an enlarged network (of actors and their artifacts) where the cognitive recognition interactions are properly encoded (Dankulov, Melnik, & Tadi, 2015). Generating a common understanding of knowledge translation among stakeholders is a key factor for increasing the use of research evidence in practice. Holt et al. (2018) developed a better understanding of knowledge translation in youth sport by providing a framework and guidelines for facilitating knowledge translation. Collaborative approaches are being promoted as inclusive forums for bringing state and non-state interests together to solve complex environmental problems. Networks have been recognized through previous research as important ways to involve stakeholders in such forums with members participating in knowledge creation and sharing as part of deliberative processes (Simpson & de Loë, 2017).

In general, studies on knowledge creation in Canada address the following topics: Online Communities (OC), Communities of Practice (CoPs), Collective Knowledge, Knowledge Translation, Collaborative Approaches, and Networking.

9.4.2 Knowledge Creation in Brazil: Cluster 2—N (52)

Binotto, Nakayama, and Siqueira (2013) analyze case studies of farmers in Brazil and Australia using various data types, including documents related to farm producers, on-site observations, questionnaires, semi-structured interviews, and focus groups (Fig. 9.4). It was found that in a property where people sought to socialize, question, and innovate constantly, there was more space to create tacit knowledge and transform it to explicit knowledge. Leadership plays an important role in creating value, innovation, and setting strategies of management and implementation of knowledge. In the context of leadership, there is the question of ethics and authenticity, especially due to scandals involving senior leaders of some organizations lately. Consequently, the study reveals that ethics and authenticity in relationships may favor knowledge creation and sharing

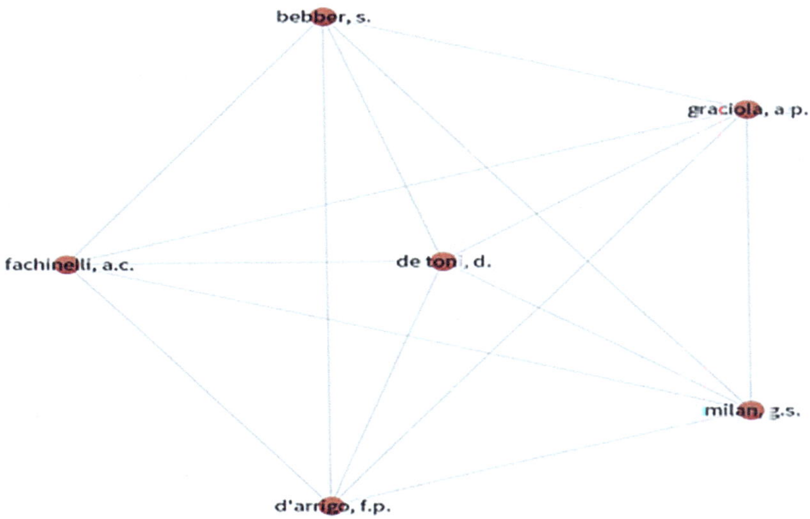

Fig. 9.4 Authors' network of 52 publications and their clusters

(Besen, Tecchio, & Fialho, 2017). The key to understanding successes and failures in knowledge creation (KC) by academic innovation teams in a scenario of university–industry relations is to identify and evaluate preconditions needed for efforts to flourish (Vick & Nagano, 2018). In the context of the relationship between the practices of eco-innovation and knowledge management, the emphasis is on the development of tools for environmental design, since they represent a way of integrating knowledge resources into the process of product development, according to Nagano, Vick, and Madeira (2017). A large number of recent studies show that sustainable innovation requires specific and new dynamic capabilities related to a new form of collaboration with suppliers, customers, research institutes, and other relevant partners. These sources and external knowledge and competences require new skills in managing relationships and knowledge integration. Júnior, Faccin, Martins, and Balestrin (2019) identify how knowledge-based dynamic capabilities (KBDCs) influence the process of developing sustainable innovations. Organizations are increasingly awakening to the need to manage organizational knowledge. On the other hand, the explosion of internet-facing systems and adoption of information technologies by organizations and governments encourage the development of a scenario where the knowledge of a tool that solves a certain problem is becoming important. Schmitz, Macedo, and Hatakeyama (2015) examined how this tool can contribute to the process of knowledge generation.

In general, studies on knowledge creation in Brazil address the following topics: Socialization, Leadership, University–Industry, Design Tools, Sustainable Innovation, and Workflow Tool.

9.4.3 Knowledge Transfer in Canada: Cluster 3—N (310)

Outdoor workers have a higher risk of skin cancers and heat stress (Fig. 9.5). Workplaces need solutions relevant to their needs that are proven to be effective in the real world and tested in workplace settings. Haynes et al. (2018) examine a workplace-based knowledge transfer and an exchange intervention project called Sun Safety at Work, Canada. It becomes critical for healthcare organizations to develop strategies that aim to design new work practices and to manage knowledge. The introduction of learning organizations is viewed as a promising choice for better knowledge management and continuing professional development

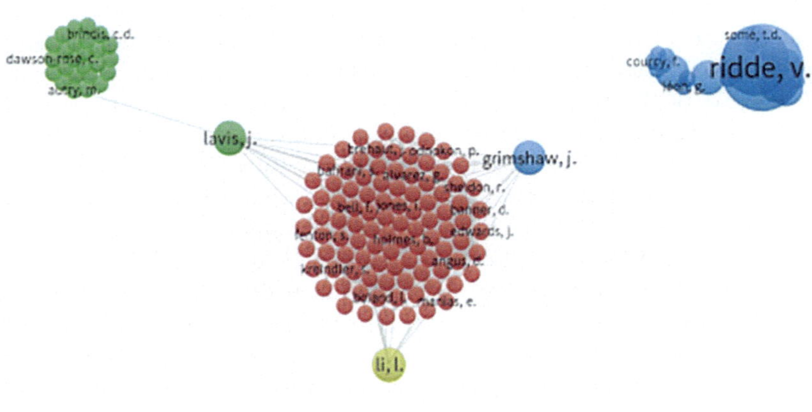

Fig. 9.5 Authors' network of 310 publications and their clusters

in healthcare. Gagnon et al. (2015) analyze the effects of a learning organization on nurses' continuing professional development, knowledge management, and retention in health and social services centers in Quebec, Canada. Jack, Brooks, Furgal, and Dobbins (2010) explored the perceptions of 28 environmental health researchers, senior external decision-makers, and decision-makers working within Aboriginal communities about factors influencing knowledge transfer and exchange, beliefs about research evidence and traditional knowledge, and the preferred communication channels for disseminating and receiving evidence.

Scientific knowledge can help develop interventions that improve public health. Dagenais et al. (2013) describe the status of research on knowledge transfer strategies in the field of complex social interventions in public health and identify priorities for future research in this field. Health research is conducted with the expectation that it advances knowledge and eventually translates into improved health systems and population health. However, research findings are often caught in the know-do gap: they are neither acted upon in a timely manner nor applied at all. Integrated knowledge translation (IKT) is advanced as a mean to increase the relevance, applicability, and impact of research. With IKT, knowledge users work with researchers throughout the research process, starting with the identification of the research question. Graham et al. (2018) present a protocol for a program of research testing the assumption of engaging users of research in phases of its production leads. Schomaker and Zaheer (2014) proposed a model on the effects of language on knowledge transfer to geographically dispersed operations. Rather than focusing on the distance between two language groups, they looked at the commonalities between their languages, introducing the construct of linguistic relevance as a way to measure the overlap in the structural features of the dominant languages used among firms and their overseas manufacturing operations.

In general, studies on knowledge transfer in Canada address the following topics: Cross-Knowledge, Learning Organization, Communities, Scientific Knowledge, Integrated Knowledge Translation (IKT), and Model.

9.4.4 Knowledge Transfer in Brazil: Cluster 4—N (80)

Frank, Ayala, Corso, and Ribeiro (2018) describe the relationship between the main factors influencing knowledge transfer (KT) among new product development (NPD) teams (Fig. 9.6). The relationships of 15 main factors can be used for practical assessments or for future theoretical studies. The literature on knowledge transfer has a privilege of a one-dimensional perspective in the analysis of factors that influence this process. In order to analyze the influence of these factors on the knowledge transfer process, de Castro, Diniz, Duarte, Dressler, and de Carvalho (2013) conducted a qualitative case study at Embrapa Corn and Sorghum. Results indicate that relational context factors, such as low connection and integration between organizations (source and recipient), and organizational context factors, such as low absorptive capacity of the recipient and low motivation (learn and teach) of the two parties (source

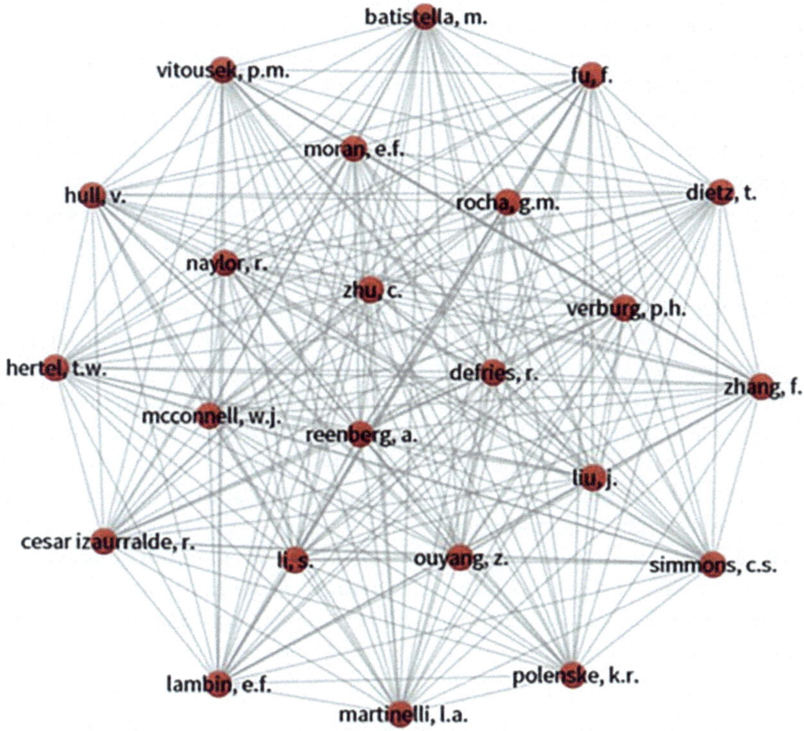

Fig. 9.6 Authors' network of 80 publications and their clusters

and recipient), adversely affect the process of knowledge transfer. To evaluate the knowledge transfer process, involving the Brazilian subsidiary, the American headquarters, and the French subsidiary of a multinational paper sector organization were seeking to identify the elements of success and the adopted transfer model. That was the study of Cunha and Ferreira (2011) where they describe the transfer success factors as the adequate selection of the coordinators and participants of the teams involved. Mussi, Angeloni, and Faraco (2014) identify four main pillars of the conception of digital social networks in the context of the technology park (Florianopolis, Brazilian state of Santa Catarina): types of knowledge, transmitters and receivers of knowledge, context for knowledge transfer, and the nature of the knowledge transfer. Redaelli, Paiva, and Teixeira (2015) explore the relationship between knowledge transfer from the manufacturer to the distributor. The research question is related to knowledge transfer from the manufacturer to the distributor and the potential improvement in the performance of the latter. This issue is important for companies that are expanding their markets. Several studies about knowledge transfer in multinational corporations have found that the process is influenced by factors such as absorptive capacity, tacit knowledge, and power relations, all of which impact knowledge sharing strategies among corporate headquarters and foreign subsidiaries. A multiple case study of Brazilian subsidiaries of three multinational corporations using in-depth interviews and based on a conceptual model consisting of four propositions was conducted by Schreiber, Junior, Vargas, and Maçada (2011) to identify factors linked to the knowledge transfer process and to assess their influence on that transfer.

In general, studies on knowledge transfer in Brazil address the following topics: Model, Analysis of Factors, Digital Social Networks, Performance, Knowledge Sharing, and Strategies

9.4.5 Innovation in Canada: Cluster 5—N (7852)

Doloreux et al. (2018) analyze the effect of internal R&D and external sources of information on the innovation performance of Knowledge Intensive Business Services (KIBS) (Fig. 9.7). The results indicate that KIBS innovation is positively connected to market-related information sources (but not to research and academic sources), KIBS innovation is positively associated with the performance of R&D, and there are no synergies associated with the combined performance of R&D and

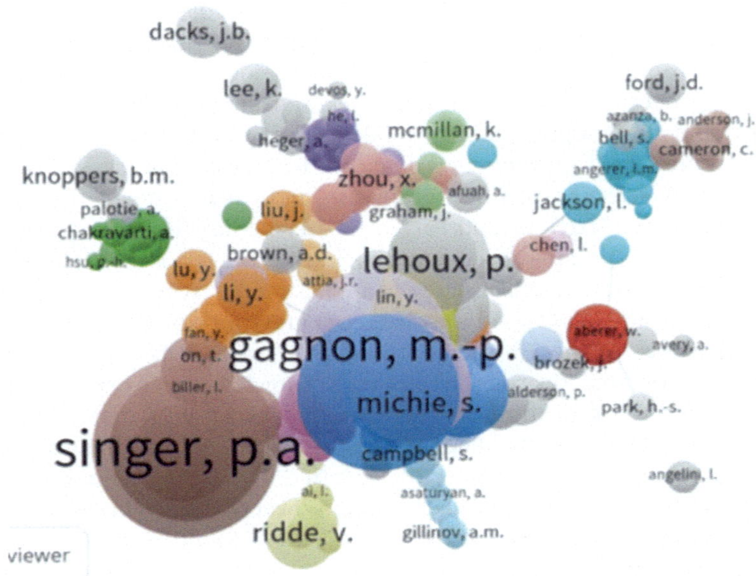

Fig. 9.7 Authors' network of 7852 publications and their clusters

external information gathering (their effects are independent and additive). Grünewälder (2015) developed a new typology that will help advance knowledge of metrics and facilitate their use in machine learning regression algorithms. The Mental Health Commission of Canada worked collaboratively with stakeholders to create a new framework for a federal mental health strategy. Park, Lencucha, Mattingly, Zafran, and Kirmayer (2015) explored the decision-making process among those who contributed to Canada's first federal mental health policy and those implementing this policy in the clinical setting. Health technology assessment (HTA) has to innovate to best support changing health system environments and to help provide access to valuable innovation under fiscal constraint. Early and ongoing multi-stakeholder engagement and revisiting approaches to valuing innovation are required. For Husereau, Henshall, Sampietro-Colom, and Thomas (2016) questions remain as to the most appropriate role of HTA bodies. Changing HTA paradigms extend HTA's traditional remit from being responsive to decision-makers' demands to being more proactive and considering the whole system's value. Gehman and Soublière (2017) identified the concept of cultural entrepreneurship. Over the past several decades, cultural entrepreneurship has emerged as a vibrant and fertile scholarly domain. This field has shifted from a focus on making culture to deploying culture. Mental illnesses are on the rise on campuses worldwide. There is a need for a scalable and economically sound innovation to address these mental health challenges. El Morr, Maule, Ashfaq, Ritvo, and Ahmad (2019) explored university students' needs and concerns in relation to an online mental health virtual community. The analysis informed design features for a mindfulness virtual community. Rémillard (2017) studied the asymptotic behavior of the sequential empirical process and the sequential empirical copula process, both constructed from residuals of multivariate stochastic volatility models. Applications for the detection of structural changes and specification tests of the distribution of innovations are discussed.

In general, studies on Innovation in Canada address the following topics: R&D, Machine Learning Regression Algorithms, Decision-Making, Innovation System Value, Cultural Entrepreneurship, Mindfulness Virtual Community, and Stochastic Volatility Matrices

9.4.6 Innovation in Brazil: Cluster 6—N (1473)

Emerging technologies are playing a major role in the generation of new approaches to assess the safety of both foods and drugs. However, the integration of emerging technologies in the regulatory decision-making process requires rigorous assessment and consensus among international partners and research communities. Based on this context, challenges and issues were discussed in the context of developing an international consensus for objective criteria in the development, application, and review of emerging technologies. The need for advanced approaches to allow for faster, less expensive, and more predictive methodologies was elaborated by Slikker et al. (2018). Gadelha, Nascimento, Braga, and Cesário (2018) articulate contemporary themes of the development agenda as global phenomena that affect the dissemination and direction of health technical progress; thus, subjecting the sustainability of the Unified Health System (SUS). Oliveira, Malvezzi, Gigante, Soeiro, and Campos (2018) developed research about the application of the Paideia Matrix Support activities in the Brazilian National Health System's medical residency programs. Mixed-methods participatory research was conducted in a municipality outside the capital of the state of São Paulo, Brazil, using the following strategies: exploratory questionnaire, participant observation, and focus groups applied to "matrix inducers" (preceptors and interns) and "matrix appliers" (health center local teams). Collaborative networks are of great value for science and technology (S&T) institutions as a way of sharing, generating, and disseminating new knowledge that could ultimately lead to innovations. Driven by the need to assess the contribution and effectiveness of these networks in informing S&T management, Fonseca, Da Silva, De Araújo, Sampaio, and Moraes (2017) explored the evolution and dynamics of tuberculosis scientific networks involving the Oswaldo Cruz Foundation (Fiocruz). Krassioukov et al. (2018) estimated gains in health utility of two different catheter features and a support service related to urinary catheters used for intermittent catheterization. Participants valued all three improvements in catheter design. Public policy planning associated with the management of the Science, Technology, and Innovation is decisive to improve public health. Feltrin, Guilam, Barral-Netto, Lima, and Moraes (2018) analyzed the dynamics of knowledge production in the context of program implementation. The combination of IoT and mobility promises to open a new frontier of innovations in smart environments, through the advent of the Internet of Moving Things (IoMT) paradigm. Da Silva and Venâncio Neto (2019) propose the Resilient MultiUser Session Control (ReMUSiC) framework which deploys emerging "softwarization" and "cloudification" technologies to afford flexible, optimized, and self-organized control plane perspectives.

In general, studies on Innovation in Brazil address the following topics: Emerging Technologies, Sustainable, Support Activities, Collaborative Networks, Design, Dynamics of Knowledge Production, and Internet of Moving Things (IoMT)

9.5 Conclusion and Discussion

As shown in Fig. 9.8 and Table 9.1, the results presented about the association with the Spinner Innovation Model (2019) demonstrates it as another important resource to analyze the propensity for innovation by companies in the knowledge-intensive services sector.

Moreover, the association of the model with international literature on service innovation reinforces the three main dimensions: knowledge creation, knowledge transfer, and innovation. We realize from research

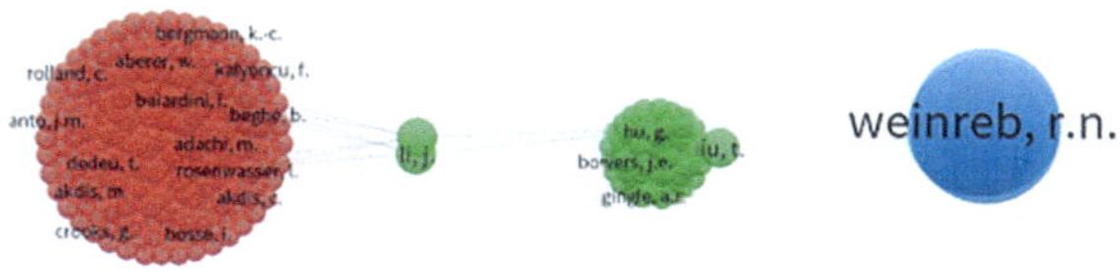

Fig. 9.8 Authors' network of 1473 publications and their clusters

Table 9.1 Clusters and approaches

N°	*Cluster*	*Approach*
1	Knowledge creation in Canada	Online Communities (OC), Communities of Practice (CoPs), Collective Knowledge, Knowledge Translation, Collaborative Approaches, and Networking
2	Knowledge creation in Brazil	Socialization, Leadership, University-Industry, Design Tools, Sustainable Innovation, and Workflow Tool
3	Knowledge transfer in Canada	Cross-Knowledge, Learning Organization, Communities, Scientific Knowledge, Integrated Knowledge Translation (IKT), and Model
4	Knowledge transfer in Brazil	Model, Analysis of Factors, Digital Social Networks, Performance, Knowledge Sharing, and Strategies
5	Innovation in Canada	R&D, Machine Learning Regression Algorithms, Decision Making, Innovation System Value, Cultural Entrepreneurship, Mindfulness Virtual Community, and Stochastic Volatility Matrices
6	Innovation in Brazil	Emerging Technologies, Sustainable, Support Activities, Collaborative Networks, Design, Dynamics of Knowledge Production and Internet of Moving Things (IoMT)

associated with the Spinner Innovation Model that knowledge creation, knowledge transfer, and innovation are relevant topics in the work agendas of scientific researchers. Overall, the main studies presented have shown that most of the contributions are focused on health and

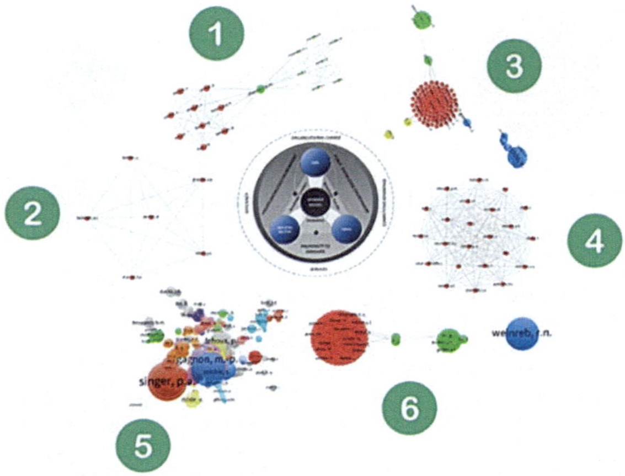

Fig. 9.9 Dimensions of service innovation based on The Spinner Innovation Model of Figueiredo and Ferreira (2019) in association with the 6 clusters

technology. In Brazil, the three themes covered are focused on social approach, while in Canada, on technological approaches.

This study sought to relate studies carried out broadly in various areas of science with the three dimensions of the Spinner Innovation Model. The intention was to demonstrate how many studies in various areas are being conducted based on the three pillars of the Spinner Innovation Model and for the purpose of further association in future studies (Fig. 9.9).

9.6 Implications

As a model, the "Spinner" can be used as a reference to understand how to combine different dimensions and approaches to promote the process for creating and transfer knowledge and innovation in the services sector. Another option is used to support other scientific areas, e.g., medicine, technology, industry, retail.... In general, according to the market needs, all organizations can use the Spinner Innovation Model as a reference to make your business grow, special in the service business.

9.7 Limitations and Future Research

The results can't be generalized because they are susceptible using only two different countries, Canada and Brazil. The approach of Spinner Innovation Model based on KIBS used three variables, as knowledge creation, knowledge transfer, and innovation. In general, other studies can add more variables or change to get new results. Any comparison with other sectors can be established using the Spinner Innovation Model as a reference. As an example, a comparison with the numbers of studies in Brazil and Canada and GDP (Gross Domestic Product) can be observed.

References

Besen, F., Tecchio, E., & Fialho, F. A. P. (2017). Liderança autêntica e a gestão do conhecimento TT—Authentic leadership and knowledge management. *Gestão & Produção, 24*(1), 2–14. https://doi.org/10.1590/0104-530x898-13.

Binotto, E., Nakayama, M. K., & Siqueira, E. S. (2013). A criação de conhecimento para a gestão de propriedades rurais no brasil e na austrália. *Revista de Economia e Sociologia Rural, 51*(4), 681–697. https://doi.org/10.1590/S0103-20032013000400004.

Brenner, T., Capasso, M., Duschl, M., Frenken, K., & Treibich, T. (2018). Causal relations between knowledge-intensive business services and regional employment growth. *Regional Studies, 52*(2), 172–183. https://doi.org/10.1080/00343404.2016.1265104.

Cadarette, S. M., Ban, J. K., Consiglio, G. P., Black, C. D., Dubins, D., Marin, A., & Tadrous, M. (2017). Diffusion of innovations model helps interpret the comparative uptake of two methodological innovations: Co-authorship network analysis and recommendations for the integration of novel methods in practice. *Journal of Clinical Epidemiology, 84*, 150–160.

Chung, T. A., & Tseng, C. Y. (2019). The knowledge intensity and the economic performance in Taiwan's knowledge intensity business services. *Economic Research-Ekonomska Istrazivanja, 32*(1), 797–811. https://doi.org/10.1080/1331677X.2019.1583586.

Cullen, J. (2017). Circular economy: Theoretical benchmark or perpetual motion machine?.

Cunha, A. J. M., & Ferreira, M. A. T. (2011). Knowledge transfer in multinational companies: Case study in the paper industry [Transferência de conhecimento em empresas multinacionais estudo de caso na indústria de papel]. *Perspectivas Em Ciencia Da Informacao, 16*, 95–118.

Retrieved from http://www.scopus.com/inward/record.url?eid=2-s2.0-84858011924&partnerID=40&md5=28f7d9aca984af7ea5c96f6f3347e24b.

Da Silva, H. W., & Venâncio Neto, A. J. (2019). Resilient multiuser session control in softwarized fog-supported internet of moving thing systems. *Sensors (Switzerland), 19*(12), 1–29. https://doi.org/10.3390/s19122766.

Dagenais, C., Malo, M., Robert, É., Ouimet, M., Berthelette, D., & Ridde, V. (2013). Knowledge transfer on complex social interventions in public health: A scoping study. *PLoS One*, *8*(12), e80233. https://doi.org/10.1371/journal.pone.0080233.

Dankulov, M. M., Melnik, R., & Tadi, B. (2015). The dynamics of meaningful social interactions and the emergence of collective knowledge. *Scientific Reports, 5,* 1–10. https://doi.org/10.1038/srep12197.

de Castro, J. M., Diniz, D. M., Duarte, R. G., Dressler, M., & de Carvalho, R. B. (2013). Fatores determinantes em processos de transferência de conhecimentos: Um estudo de caso na Embrapa Milho e Sorgo e firmas licenciadas. *Revista de Administracao Publica, 47*(5), 1283–1306. https://doi.org/10.1590/S0034-76122013000500010.

de Oliveira, J. M., Malvezzi, E., Gigante, R. L., Soeiro, E., & Campos, G. W. de S. (2018). Inovação na formação médica: Apoio matricial em programas de residência. *Interface: Communication, Health, Education, 22*(64), 211–222. https://doi.org/10.1590/1807-57622016.0758.

Dolati Neghabadi, P., Evrard Samuel, K., & Espinouse, M. L. (2019). Systematic literature review on city logistics: Overview, classification and analysis. *International Journal of Production Research, 57*(3), 865–887.

Doloreux, D., Shearmur, R., & Rodriguez, M. (2018). Internal R&D and external information in knowledge-intensive business service innovation: Complements, substitutes or independent? *Technological and Economic Development of Economy, 24*(6), 2255–2276. https://doi.org/10.3846/tede.2018.5694.

El Morr, C., Maule, C., Ashfaq, I., Ritvo, P., & Ahmad, F. (2019). Design of a mindfulness virtual community: A focus-group analysis. *Health Informatics Journal*. https://doi.org/10.1177/1460458219884840.

Faraj, S., von Krogh, G., Monteiro, E., & Lakhani, K. R. (2016). Online community as space for knowledge flows. *Information Systems Research, 27*(4), 668–684. https://doi.org/10.1287/isre.2016.0682.

Feltrin, R. B., Guilam, M. C. R., Barral-Netto, M., Lima, N. T., & Moraes, M. O. (2018). For socially engaged science: The dynamics of knowledge production in the Fiocruz graduate program in the framework of the "Brazil without extreme poverty plan". *PLoS One, 13*(10), 1–15. https://doi.org/10.1371/journal.pone.0204232.

Figueiredo, R., & de Matos Ferreira, J. J. (2019). Spinner Model: Prediction of propensity to innovate based on Knowledge-Intensive Business Services. *J Knowl Econ*. https://doi.org/10.1007/s13132-019-00607-2.

Figueiredo, R., & Ferreira, J. (2019). Spinner Innovation Model: Prediction of propensity to innovate based on KIBS. *Journal of the Knowledge Economy*, 1–20. https://doi.org/10.1007/s13132-019-00607-2.

Figueiredo, R., Neto, J. V., Quelhas, O. L. G., & Ferreira, J. J. M. (2017). Knowledge intensive business services (KIBS): Bibliometric analysis and their different behaviors in the scientific literature. *Revista de Administração e Inovação, 14*(3), 216–222.

Figueiredo, R., Quelhas, O., Neto, J. V., & Ferreira, J. J. (2019). The role of knowledge intensive business services in economic development: A bibliometric analysis from Bradford, Lotka and Zipf laws. *Gestao e Producao, 26*(4), 1–12. https://doi.org/10.1590/0104-530X4356-19.

Fonseca, B. D. P. F. E., Da Silva, M. V. P., De Araújo, K. M., Sampaio, R. B., & Moraes, M. O. (2017). Network analysis for science and technology management: Evidence from tuberculosis research in Fiocruz, Brazil. *PLoS One, 12*(8), 1–17. https://doi.org/10.1371/journal.pone.0181870.

Frank, A. G., Ayala, N. F., Corso, M., & Ribeiro, J. L. D. (2018). A relationship model for factors influencing knowledge transfer between NPD teams. *Producao, 28,* e20180055. https://doi.org/10.1590/0103-6513.20180055.

Gadelha, C. A. G., de Nascimento, M. A. C., da Braga, P. S. C., & Cesario, B. B. (2018). Global technological transformations and asymmetries: Development strategy and structural challenges for the unified health system. *Ciencia e Saude Coletiva, 23*(7), 2119–2132. https://doi.org/10.1590/1413-812320 18237.09452018.

Gagnon, M. P., Payne-Gagnon, J., Fortin, J. P., Paré, G., Côté, J., & Courcy, F. (2015). A learning organization in the service of knowledge management among nurses: A case study. *International Journal of Information Management, 35*(5), 636–642. https://doi.org/10.1016/j.ijinfomgt.2015.05.001.

Gehman, J., & Soublière, J. F. (2017). Cultural entrepreneurship: From making culture to cultural making. *Innovation: Management, Policy and Practice, 19*(1), 61–73. https://doi.org/10.1080/14479338.2016.1268521.

Graham, I. D., Kothari, A., McCutcheon, C., Alvarez, G., Banner, D., Botti, M., … Tetroe, J. (2018). Moving knowledge into action for more effective practice, programmes and policy: Protocol for a research programme on integrated knowledge translation. *Implementation Science, 13*(1), 1–15. https://doi.org/10.1186/s13012-017-0700-y.

Grünewälder, S. (2015). *Machine learning: What is machine learning?, 14*(113), 13–21.

Haynes, E., Kramer, D. M., Strahlendorf, P., Holness, D. L., Kushner, R., & Tenkate, T. (2018). A cross-Canada knowledge transfer and exchange workplace intervention targeting the adoption of sun safety programs and practices: Sun safety at work Canada. *Safety Science, 102*(May 2017), 238–250. https://doi.org/10.1016/j.ssci.2017.10.013.

Holt, N. L., Camiré, M., Tamminen, K. A., Pankow, K., Pynn, S. R., Strachan, L., … Fraser-Thomas, J. (2018). PYDSportNET: A knowledge translation project bridging gaps between research and practice in youth sport. *Journal of Sport Psychology in Action, 9*(2), 132–146. https://doi.org/10.1080/21520704.2017.1388893.

Hrivnák, M., Melichová, K., Fáziková, M., & Roháčiková, O. (2019). University graduates, knowledge spill-overs and localization of knowledge intensive ventures-case of post-socialistic country. *Entrepreneurship and Sustainability Issues, 7*(1), 146–165. https://doi.org/10.9770/jesi.2019.7.1(12).

Husereau, D., Henshall, C., Sampietro-Colom, L., & Thomas, S. (2016). Changing health technology assessment paradigms? *International Journal of Technology Assessment in Health Care, 32*(4), 191–199. https://doi.org/10.1017/S0266462316000386.

Jack, S. M., Brooks, S., Furgal, C. M., & Dobbins, M. (2010). Knowledge transfer and exchange processes for environmental health issues in Canadian Aboriginal communities. *International Journal of Environmental Research and Public Health, 7*(2), 651–674. https://doi.org/10.3390/ijerph7020651.

Júnior, N. B., Faccin, K., Martins, B. V., & Balestrin, A. (2019). Knowledge-based dynamic capabilities for sustainable innovation: The case of the green plastic project. *Sustainability (Switzerland), 11*(8), 21–26. https://doi.org/10.3390/su11082392.

Kekezi, O., & Klaesson, J. (2019). Agglomeration and innovation of knowledge intensive business services. *Industry and Innovation, 27*(5), 538–561. https://doi.org/10.1080/13662716.2019.1573660.

Krassioukov, A., Igawa, Y., Averbeck, M. A., Madersbacher, H., Lloyd, A. J., Bøgelund, M., & Thiruchelvam, N. (2018). Gains in health utility associated with urinary catheter innovations. *Medical Devices: Evidence and Research, 11*, 345–351. https://doi.org/10.2147/MDER.S165778.

Li, L. C., Grimshaw, J. M., Nielsen, C., Judd, M., Coyte, P. C., & Graham, I. D. (2009). Use of communities of practice in business and health care sectors: A systematic review. *Implementation Science, 4*(1), 1–9. https://doi.org/10.1186/1748-5908-4-27.

Li, X., Gagliardi, D., & Miles, I. (2019). Innovation in R&D service firms: Evidence from the UK. *Technology Analysis & Strategic Management, 31*(6), 732–748. https://doi.org/10.1080/09537325.2018.1549729.

Lim, J., Davis, A., Tang, A. R., Shannon, C. N., & Bonfield, C. M. (2019). Caregiver stress in children with craniosynostosis: A systematic literature review. *Child's Nervous System, 35*(2), 217–225.

Miozzo, M., Desyllas, P., Lee, H. F., & Miles, I. (2016). Innovation collaboration and appropriability by knowledge-intensive business services firms. *Research Policy, 45*(7), 1337–1351. https://doi.org/10.1016/j.respol.2016.03.018.

Mussi, C., Angeloni, M. T., & Faraco, R. A. (2014). Social networks and knowledge transfer in technological park companies in Brazil. *Journal of Technology Management and Innovation, 9*(2), 172–186. https://doi.org/10.4067/S0718-27242014000200013.

Nagano, M. S., Vick, T. E., & Madeira, L. M. M. (2017). Suporte da gestão do conhecimento em práticas de Ecoinovação. *RISTI - Revista Iberica de Sistemas e Tecnologias de Informacao, 22,* 37–56. https://doi.org/10.17013/risti.22.37-56.

Palmatier, R. W., Houston, M. B., & Hulland, J. (2018). Review articles: Purpose, process, and structure.

Park, M. M., Lencucha, R., Mattingly, C., Zafran, H., & Kirmayer, L. J. (2015). A qualitative study on the ethics of transforming care: Examining the development and implementation of Canada's first mental health strategy. *Implementation Science, 10*(1), 1–9. https://doi.org/10.1186/s13012-015-0297-y.

Qi, H., Liu, S., Qi, W., & Liu, Z. (2019). Geographical concentration of knowledge- and technology-intensive industries and city innovation in China. *Sustainability (Switzerland), 11*(18), 4840. https://doi.org/10.3390/su11184840.

Redaelli, E. J., Paiva, E. L., & Teixeira, R. (2015). The relationship between manufacturer and distributors: Knowledge transfer and performance. *BAR—Brazilian Administration Review, 12*(4), 421–441. https://doi.org/10.1590/1807-7692bar2015150049.

Rémillard, B. (2017). Goodness-of-fit tests for copulas of multivariate time series. *Econometrics, 5*(1), 1–23. https://doi.org/10.3390/econometrics5010013.

Schmitz, Q. T., Macedo, M., & Hatakeyama, K. (2015). Contributions of workflow for knowledge generation process. *Procedia Manufacturing, 3*(Ahfe). 904–911. https://doi.org/10.1016/j.promfg.2015.07.136.

Schomaker, M. S., & Zaheer, S. (2014). The role of language in knowledge transfer to geographically dispersed manufacturing operations. *Journal of International Management, 20*(1), 55–72. https://doi.org/10.1016/j.intman.2013.10.004.

Schreiber, D., Junior, D. C. V., Vargas, L. M., & Maçada, A. C. G. (2011). Knowledge transfer in product development: An analysis of Brazilian subsidiaries of multinational corporations. *BAR—Brazilian Administration*

Review, 8(3), 288–304. https://doi.org/10.1590/S1807-76922011000300005.

Sherman, D. K., Hartson, K. A., Binning, K. R., Purdie-Vaughns, V., Garcia, J., Taborsky-Barba, S., ... & Cohen, G. L. (2013). Deflecting the trajectory and changing the narrative: How self-affirmation affects academic performance and motivation under identity threat. *Journal of Personality and Social Psychology, 104*(4), 591.

Simpson, H. C., & de Loë, R. C. (2017). The agricultural community as a social network in a collaborative, multi-stakeholder problem-solving process. *Water (Switzerland), 9*(10), 750. https://doi.org/10.3390/w9100750.

Slikker, W., de Souza Lima, T. A., Archella, D., de Silva, J. B., Barton-Maclaren, T., Bo, L., ... & Zhao-Wong, A. (2018, July). Emerging technologies for food and drug safety. *Regulatory Toxicology and Pharmacology, 98,* 115–128. https://doi.org/10.1016/j.yrtph.2018.07.013.

Vick, T. E., & Nagano, M. S. (2018). Preconditions for successful knowledge creation in the context of academic innovation projects. *Journal of Information and Knowledge Management, 17*(1), 1–22. https://doi.org/10.1142/S0219649218500041.

Vinogradov, D., Shadrina, E., & Doroshenko, M. (2018). KIBS for public needs. *Economia e Politica Industriale* (Vol. 45). Springer International Publishing. https://doi.org/10.1007/s40812-018-0106-0.

Yergens, D. W., Tam-Tham, H., & Minty, E. P. (2016). Visualization of the IMIA yearbook of medical informatics publications over the last 25 years. *Yearbook of Medical Informatics*, (Suppl 1), S130.

Zaharia, M., Xin, R. S., Wendell, P., Das, T., Armbrust, M., Dave, A., ... & Ghodsi, A. (2016). Apache spark: A unified engine for big data processing. *Communications of the ACM, 59*(11), 56–65.

CHAPTER 10

Evaluating R&D Efficiency of Selected European Countries: A Dynamic Analysis for Period 2007–2017

Tihana Škrinjarić

10.1 Introduction

Although the endogenous growth model of Romer (1986) and Lucas (1988) is known in the literature for more than 30 years now, the interest in innovation and research and development (R&D) in academic research has been growing rapidly in the last couple of years. Literature nowadays recognizes that the economies are knowledge-based and those countries which invest in R&D are most successful in obtaining sustainable development, good GDP growth rates, and produce new value within the economic system itself. Furthermore, the knowledge economy asks for human capital with skills that are different from the traditional education approaches (Faria, Ferreira, Johnson, Mixon, & Wanke, 2020). Innovation represents an important role here as well, as

T. Škrinjarić (✉)
Department of Mathematics, University of Zagreb, Zagreb, Croatia
e-mail: tskrinjar@net.efzg.hr

J. J. M. Ferreira et al. (eds.), *Technological Innovation and International Competitiveness for Business Growth*, Palgrave Studies in Democracy, Innovation, and Entrepreneurship for Growth,
https://doi.org/10.1007/978-3-030-51995-7_10

it is based on the accumulation of knowledge and the process of innovation alongside aggressive R&D activities is often looked at as the main source of increasing the total factor productivity of countries (Coe & Moghadam, 1993; Griliches, 1979, 1988). Thus, literature explains that innovation-driven economies should reduce economic and social stagnation and risk (Joly, 2019; Pestre, 2019). It is not surprising that many world organizations, unions, institutions, and funds are recognizing the importance of innovation and R&D investments as basics for obtaining and remaining healthy economic growth. The European Union (EU) is among them, with some of the first formal documents brought in 1995 (Green Paper on Innovation) and Lisbon strategy in 2000 (historical details can be found in Weresa, 2018). OECD countries have to face two options in these terms: innovate or perish (Lechevalier & Laugier, 2019). Innovation and R&D are also linked to the environmental policy, a topic which importance has been recognized in the last couple of years (Popp, 2019); with policy relevance research (Stucki, Woerter, Arvanitis, Peneder, & Rammer, 2018). As seen in Hu, Liu, Li, and Li (2019), the innovation system concept is not an easy task, as it requires interactions between many intermediates, actors, firms, universities, policymakers, etc. Although, R&D is very important in the shaping of regional technical innovation capacities (Costantini, Crespi, Martini, & Pennacchio, 2015; Hu et al., 2019).

However, there is still not enough progress to meet the Europe 2020 target of R&D representing 3% of GDP (Eurostat, 2019a), although this goal was brought in 2000. Thus, an adequate analysis of sources of (in)efficiencies of EU member states is needed to see why 20 years later many problems still exist. Although, some progress is made on a regional level, as the European Commission (EC) brought a document Regional Policy Contributing to Smart Growth in Europe (EC, 2010), which focuses on local innovation processes, which should be specifically tailored with respect to local surroundings. CIFP (Competitiveness and Innovation Framework Program 2007–2013) had the goals to foster competitiveness of SMEs (small and medium enterprises), promoting innovation and especially eco-innovation, sustainable development, renewable energy resources, etc. (*Official Journal of the EU*, 2006). Cowan and Van de Paal (2000) define the innovation policy as set of actions which aim to rise quantity and efficiency of innovation (which includes creation, adaptation and adoption of new/improved products, services, and/or processes). Others add that human well-being should be the ultimate criterion that governs the direction of science (Gaudillière, 2019; Hiroi, 2019; Ruphy, 2019). UN (2019) emphasizes that the 2030 Agenda for Sustainable Development recognizes Science, Technology and Innovation (STI) as the main driving force for the environmentally sustainable and prosperous economies. This policy is trying to be measured via indicator systems such as the Global Innovation Index, International Innovation Index, the SarPIN project measurements (Statistical Reporting on Public Innovation, EU, 2019), etc. However, as Zabala-Iturriagagoitia, Voigt, Gutiérrez-Gracia, and Jiménez-Sáez (2007) state, traditional indicators offer partial views of the state of the innovation processes within countries. This sometimes results with different results and interpretations. This is one of the reasons on why the last couple of years have experienced a rise in number of papers which try to measure and quantify the extent of obtaining such goals regarding innovation and R&D investing. Many authors have tried to measure the efficiencies of different economies and regions in achieving and maintaining goals with respect to R&D and knowledge-based economy. As can be seen in the existing research, measuring and comparing the efficiencies with respect to innovation and R&D is not an easy task. That is why scientist and policymakers have to continuously work on these issues. Although the amount of literature on these topics is growing rapidly in the last couple of years (please see the next section), there still exist some gaps in the existing findings. Namely, research often concludes that efficient countries are those who have the most problems with important variables, which should be a warning that something in the analysis went wrong. That is why an objective comparison with reliable data and results should be a basis for future research and policy recommendations.

Thus, the main goal of this research is to objectively measure the (in)efficiency of 30 European countries with respect to R&D sector, in a dynamic context. The methodology used is Data Envelopment Analysis (DEA), as its main purpose is to measure relative efficiency of alternatives which are being contrasted one to another based on different criteria. As the majority of models within DEA are nonparametric ones, this methodology has several advantages over other approaches such as panel regression or stochastic frontier analysis (for details, see Coelli, 1995 or Guan & Chen, 2010). The novelties of this research include the following: this research includes relevant variables for measuring R&D and innovation, which are often neglected in the literature. Furthermore, a dynamic analysis is conducted which is, again, often ignored in the literature. This means that based on the results in this research, some conclusions on the (in)efficiency changes over time can be made. Next, a DEA model with a missing data approach is utilized which enables analysis with more countries and years included in the optimization process. Research often excludes relevant variables, years and/or countries from the analysis due to missing data. However, to retain as much data possible, this research uses the approach which deals with missing data. Finally, robustness checking of the results is performed in a detailed manner, which is also lacking in the previously existing literature. It is important to check for the robustness of the results; as previous literature findings often include contradictory results. In the end, detailed policy recommendations are given based on the results of the empirical part of the research. The gaps within this study include a relatively short time span included in the analysis due to data unavailability, using aggregate values of certain relevant variables instead of sector disaggregation and utilizing simple models within the DEA methodology (details are given in the conclusion section).

The rest of this research is structured as follows. The second section deals with literature overview of most relevant related papers. The third section describes the methodology used in the study, whilst the fourth section deals with empirical assessment of R&D efficiency of EU member states. The final, fifth section, gives recommendations and conclusions for future work.

10.2 Related Literature Overview

A very positive finding with respect to the topics of this research is that the literature within this area of research is growing. This means that the interest for these subjects is growing and the awareness as well. The focus of the literature overview was made on the research which dealt with EU and European countries, with rest of the related literature (in terms of methodology, main topic and question of the research and similar things) briefly being mentioned in this section. From a methodological point of view, the most common approaches of the empirical analysis include Data Envelopment Analysis (DEA), panel regression and Multiple Criteria Decision Model (MCDM) approaches. It is not surprising that the majority of the literature uses DEA due to it giving exact answers in comparisons of the alternatives which are contrasted one to another.

Other approaches with a detailed discussion can be found in Daraio (2019).

Some of the early studies include David, Hall, and Toole (2000), which is a review of empirical studies for a long period (1965–2000) with respect to the nature of R&D expenditures (public versus private). Thus, such research could be useful today to compare what countries have done in the long run, what are the effects today, etc. Bottazzi and Peri (2003) utilized econometric techniques to estimate knowledge spillovers between the EU regions (in the period 1977–1995). The authors found that the spillovers were very local: increase in R&D spending leads to increase in outputs of new ideas in neighbor regions within 300 km only by 2–3%. Regional level was in the focus of Zabala-Iturriagagoitia et al. (2007) as well. European region level data (for the years 2002 and 2003) was used in the mentioned study so that the authors could evaluate regional innovation system performance. Utilizing variables such as higher education (% of students), lifelong learning, public and business R&D expenditures, high-tech patent applications to the European Patent Office (EPO) and GDP per capita, authors found that the higher the technological level of a region, the greater is the need for system coordination. Authors also comment on methodological aspects within this area of research which are important part of the whole analysis as well. Sharma and Thomas (2008) utilized the DEA approach over 22 countries (both developed and developing ones) for the year 2002. Most efficient countries in the study were Japan, Republic of Korea, and China. However, a small number of inputs and outputs were used in the study, which was extended in the future research. The interest of R&D and patent efficiency exploration is found in Lee and Park (2005) as well, where authors use 2 inputs and 3 outputs over 27 world economies (period 1994–1998) with an emphasize on Asian countries. Here, authors found that the Chinese, South Korean, and Taiwanese industries have low R&D efficiencies in the observed period. This is an indication of conflicting results, when compared to Sharma and Thomas (2008) results. The reasoning could be due to using different variables in the model, observing different periods, etc. However, one must be careful when comparing such results. Here, some of the problems within this area of research are already visible. Which methodology should be used and what are the variables which will give most realistic results are some of the questions which a researcher needs to deal with in practice.

Other interesting studies include those which do not (solely) observe European countries, but give good discussions on the topic of interest: Guan and He (2005) focused on China; Lee, Park, and Choi (2009) on Korea; Chen, Hu, and Yang (2011) on different countries over the world; Szarowska and Žurkova (2017) made a 3-country specific focus (Czech Republic, Denmark and Slovakia); cross-country analysis was made in Guan and Zuo (2014). Furthermore, some analysis combines several approaches of modeling to get more insights into the matter: Cao, You, Shi, and Hu (2019) focused on China's 30 provinces, for the period 2016–2018 and combined the DEA approach with K-means clustering. Variables used in the study were such as number of researchers, number of R&D technical service institutions, total R&D funds, total value of technical achievements transformation, market share of leading products, etc. From the first part of the analysis (DEA) authors switched to the clustering of the provinces to see which provinces were similar concerning the pure technical efficiency and scale efficiency. Extensive research is also done in studies such as Guan and Zuo (2014), where which authors observed 35 countries (period: 2007–2011) via network-DEA approach, where technical and scale inefficiency was also in the focus of the analysis. Panel data approach can be found in the literature as well. However, it is used to focus on different types of questions compared to the DEA approach. Liu, Lu, and Cheng (2018) used 44 countries in the 1996–2013 period and panel regression and stochastic frontier analysis (SFA) to assess the effects of R&D spillovers on innovation efficiency of specific R&D outcomes. Other methodological approaches include PLSR (second step partial least squares regression) in conjunction relational network DEA, such as in Guan and Chen (2012) so that an upstream knowledge production process and a downstream knowledge commercialization process can be observed. Authors focused on 22 OCED countries, with main results indicating that the operation of internal independent subprocesses in modeling of national innovation systems should be taken into account. Some authors claim that before their research there were no studies which utilized the DEA approach in evaluating the efficiency of R&D performance (Karadayi & Ekinci, 2018, p. 229), which is not true, as seen already here in the literature review, but in other papers as well. de Rassenfosse, Jaffe, and Raiteri (2019) have examined patents arising from government financing in the USA and their characteristics. Based on an extensive descriptive statistics and regression analysis for the period 2000–2013 authors concluded that patents which are produced faster have greater value, decreasing returns to contract size. Leydesdorff and Porto-Gomez (2019) have used Shannon's information theory and entropy measuring in order to measure the synergy between technological, geographical, and organizational level in Spain. One million firms in 2010 have been included in the analysis. Main results show that firms in Spain are largely decentralized within the innovation system. Hu and Yongxu (2019) tried to answer the question if receiving a government R&D grant stimulates or crowds out firm's individual investments in China. A matching estimator and DiD (difference in differences) estimator were employed on a dataset for the period 2007–2011. Here, authors found that increase of government R&D grants led up to 4–9 million yuan increase of firm's own increase of R&D expenditures. Thus, cooperation and synthesis for surely exist.

The research which is closely related to this one is summarized in Table 10.1, which shows the basic characteristics of each paper. As can be seen, some of the most used variables in the analysis include a number of scientists, patents, and general expenditures with respect to R&D and innovation process. Although the common approach is to use the DEA methodology, several papers have some disadvantages such as observing just one year in the analysis or averaging an entire period for the analysis, the number of inputs and outputs with respect to a number of included countries is sometimes questionable (due to characteristics of DEA methodology). That is why often the results of different analyses are conflicting in finding that one country is inefficient with respect to R&D and in other times it is some of the best performing countries. Some of the gaps of previous literature here besides the mentioned problems include that in recent years there are no studies (to the knowledge of the author) with the newest data and a reasonable time period so that dynamic analysis can be conducted, alongside variables which are defined correctly.

10.3 Methodology

Data Envelopment Analysis (DEA) is part of the Operations Research, which consists of models and methods to evaluate the relative efficiency of decision-making units (DMUs). Based on mathematical programming, the model evaluates and calculates the efficiency value for each DMU, based on producing outputs by utilizing their inputs. The basic idea of being efficient is to produce as much output possible with little inputs

Table 10.1 Summary of related research results

Author(s)	*Countries/regions/time span*	*Variables*	*Main results*	*Methodology/comments*
Chen, Hu, and Yang (2011)	24 countries (of which 16 European); 1998–2005	Patents, scientific journal articles, royalty and licensing fee, total R&D manpower, R&D expenditure stocks. Note: no details given on variables such as "patents"—what exactly is measured by variable patents? Additional variables used in the panel regression: Intellectual property rights protection, per capita GDP, total education expenditure as % of GDP, number of personal computers per 100 people, overall and business R&D intensity, etc.	Best performers: USA, UK, Israel, Hungary, Ireland, Finland. Romania, Russia and Mexico are worst performing ones. Higher proportions of private R&D leads to greater DEA efficiency levels of a country	DEA in the first stage of the analysis, panel regression in the second stage. Note: some authors criticize using efficiency scores from DEA in regression. See Simar and Wilson (2007)

Author(s)	*Countries/regions/time span*	*Variables*	*Main results*	*Methodology/comments*
Aristovnik (2012)	EU members + Croatia and OECD members; 1999–2007	Expenditure per student, in% of GDP per capita (primary, secondary and tertiary education separated), school enrolment, pupil-teacher ratio, PISA 2006 average score, unemployment with tertiary education. Second part of the research: Total expenditure on R&D as a % of GDP, researchers in R&D (per million people), total European patent applications (per million people), scientific and technical journal articles (per million people), high-technology exports (% of manufactured exports)	Most inefficient: new member states of EU and Croatia and less developed OECD countries. Most efficient in the education system: Japan, Korea and Finland; in the R&D section: Switzerland and Netherlands	DEA, averaging the values for the observed period. No dynamics included

(continued)

Table 10.1 (continued)

Author(s)	*Countries/regions/time span*	*Variables*	*Main results*	*Methodology/comments*
Hudec and Procházková (2013)	19 EU countries; 2004–2010	Number of scientist and researchers employed full time, R&D expenditures of private and public sector, accumulated “knowledge stock”, international scientific papers (multiplied by the number of citations), number of patents, labour force out of the R&D, added value of industries, export of new products in high-tech industries	Luxembourg, Sweden, Denmark and Greece are best in production of knowledge Visegrad countries are in the high performing group of bringing innovations to the market	DEA

Author(s)	*Countries/regions/time span*	*Variables*	*Main results*	*Methodology/comments*
Aristovnik (2014)	EU-27 NUTS-2 regions (271 in total); 2005–2010	Total research expenditure in % of GDP, researchers as % of total employment, employment in high-tech sectors as % of total employment, human resources in science and technology in % of economically active population, patent applications to the EPO in number of applications per mil habitants, high-tech patent applications to the EPO	Most efficient regions in Netherlands, Belgium, Germany, Spain and France. Baltics, Eastern and Southern European regions worst performers	DEA, averaging the values for the observed period. No dynamics included

(continued)

Table 10.1 (continued)

Author(s)	*Countries/regions/time span*	*Variables*	*Main results*	*Methodology/comments*
Furková (2014)	EU member countries without Cyprus + Norway; 2012	Patent applications to the European Patent Office (per million of inhabitants), total intramural R&D expenditure (% of GDP), human resources in science and technology and employment in knowledge-intensive activities (% of active population), business enterprise R&D expenditure (% of GDP)	Best ranked countries are Sweden, Finland, Germany, Denmark; worst performers: Romania, Bulgaria, Croatia, Slovakia	MCDM, Topsis. Only year 2012 was observed
Ekinci and Ön (2015)	Review of literature on EU countries	Most used variables in previous studies include: Number of patents, R&D expenditure, institutional quality, number of full-time researches, number of scientific publications, number of MSc and PhD students hired, total educational expenditures, GDP, total R&D expenditures conducted business enterprises, % of R&D performed by the government, employment in technology and knowledge-intensive sectors, number of international scientific and technical articles published or accepted in journals listed on SCI, number of patents registered in domestic/foreign patent offices, high-technology exports		–

Author(s)	*Countries/regions/time span*	*Variables*	*Main results*	*Methodology/comments*
Tarnawska and Mavroeidis (2015)	25 EU member countries; 2009/2012	Annual expenditure on public and private educational institutions per student in PPPS, R&D personnel, by sectors of performance, intersectoral mobility of researchers, high-technology exports (% exports), scientific and technical publications per billion PPPS GDP, SME introducing marketing/organisational innovations (% of SMEs)	16 countries found to be efficient, worst performers: Bulgaria, Greece, Lithuania, Spain and Slovakia	DEA. Some variables were used from 2009, others from 2012
Halásková and Halásková (2015)	28 EU countries; 2004–2013	Total expenditure on R&D, business enterprise expenditure on R&D, expenditure on R&D in higher education sector, government expenditure on R&D, R&D expenditure on private non- profit, R&D total expenditure as % of GDP	Highest R&D intensity found for Finland, Sweden and Denmark, lowest: Romania, Cyprus, Bulgaria. Strong correlation found between total R&D expenditures and public expenditures and patent applications to the EPO	Descriptive statistics, coefficient of correlation

(continued)

Table 10.1 (continued)

Author(s)	*Countries/regions/time span*	*Variables*	*Main results*	*Methodology/comments*
Johansson, Lööp, and Savin (2015)	11 EU countries; 1991–2005	Number of granted USPTO patents per 1000 employees, R&D expenditures per 1000 employees, value added in industry as % of GDP, sum of exports and imports as % of GDP, stock market value as % of GDP, public expenditures on education per capita, institutional milieu promoting the development and application of new technology, Ginarte–Park index of intellectual property protection	Sweden, Finland, Germany and Denmark are top ranked in low and high technology industries	Panel regression
Kalapoutia, Petridisb, Malesiosc, and Deyd (2017)	192 EU regions; 1995–2006	Human Resources in science and technology as % of total population, total intramural R&D expenditure (Euro per inhabitant), knowledge transferred between regions because of geographical/technological proximity, patent applications at EPO	Best regions are in Austria (1), Belgium (1), Bulgaria (1), Germany (5), France (1), Hungary (2), Italy (3), Lativa (1), Poland (2), Portugal (1) and Romania (1). High innovative activity regions contribute more to own activity, but exploit knowledge spillovers from (geographical) neighbours	DEA and Structural Equation Modelling. Note: some authors criticize using efficiency scores from DEA in regression. See Simar and Wilson (2007)

Author(s)	*Countries/regions/time span*	*Variables*	*Main results*	*Methodology/comments*
Bednář and Halásková (2018)	178 Western European NUTS 2 regions; 2007–2012 (odd years only)	Patent applications to the EPO, intramural R&D expenditure as percentage of GDP	Divergence exists between the observed regions, beta convergence between regions is confirmed, but sigma convergence was rejected	Mixed spatial autoregressive model and DID model
Karadayi and Ekinci (2018)	28 EU countries, 2011–2013	Categorical data: frontier, secondary emerging, advanced emerging and developed country, total full time equivalent R&D personnel, postgraduates employed in science and technology (in 000), employment in high and medium-high technology manufacturing sectors, R&D expenditures (Euro per habitant) by government/business enterprises/education sector, total number of publications, patents granted by EPO and by US Patent and Trademark Office	Efficient countries were: Austria, Bulgaria, Croatia, Cyprus, Czech Republic, Germany, Hungary, Italy, Luxembourg, Malta, Netherlands, Poland, Romania, Slovenia, Sweden and UK. Worst performer: Lithuania	DEA. Since many input and output variables were included in the analysis, this could lead to misleading results, as the number of DMUs does not exceed 3(m + s) and 2 ms, and barely exceeds 2(m + s)

(continued)

Table 10.1 (continued)

Author(s)	*Countries/regions/time span*	*Variables*	*Main results*	*Methodology/comments*
Anderson and Stejskal (2019)	28 EU member states; 2018	New doctorate graduates per 1000 people, lifelong learning (population aged 25–64 involved in education), degree to which individuals pursue entrepreneurial activities, public sector R&D expenditures, venture capital investments and private sector R&D expenditure per GDP, non R&D expenditure, employment in knowledge intensive activities, sales of new-to-market and new-to-firm innovations	Half of the countries were found to be efficient in terms of DEA methodology. Unusual results such as Romania being efficient and UK being inefficient despite worst performances of inputs and outputs of Romania	DEA model. Only 2018 was observed. Since many input and output variables were included in the analysis, this could lead to misleading results, as the number of DMUs barely exceeds 2(m + s), 3(m + s) and does not exceed 2 ms

Note EPO denotes European Patent Office, DID difference in differences, m denotes number of inputs, s denotes number of outputs in the DEA model, MCDM denotes multiple criteria decision model, USPTO denotes United States Patent and Trademark Office, SME denotes small and medium enterprises, PPPS denotes Public–Private Partnerships put in the production process. Term relative refers to the comparisons between the DMUs themselves (not to a "super" unit). The terminology within this methodology is based on the production companies for which DEA was first developed. Thus, interested readers can refer to Cooper, Seiford, and Zhu (2011) for more details Two basic models often used in the literature are the CCR (Charnes-Cooper-Rhodes) model and the BCC (Banker-Charnes-Cooper) models. The basic description is as follows. Each DMU unit uses m inputs $(x_{1j},x_{2j},\ldots,x_{mj})$ and produces s outputs $(y_{1j},y_{2j},\ldots,y_{sj})$, where j denotes the unit, $j = 1, 2,\ldots, n$. In this study, the DMU unit is the EU country, whereas inputs and outputs are the selected variables. In the case of the greater the value of a variable is better, such a variable is considered as an output. The opposite is true for an input. Compactly, the data can be put in matrices $\boldsymbol{X}$ (inputs) and $\boldsymbol{Y}$ (outputs), as follows:

$$\boldsymbol{X} = \begin{pmatrix} x_{11} & x_{12} & \ldots & x_{1n} \\ x_{21} & x_{22} & \ldots & x_{2n} \\ \ldots & \ldots & \ldots & \ldots \\ x_{m1} & x_{m2} & \ldots & x_{mn} \end{pmatrix} \quad \text{and} \quad \boldsymbol{Y} = \begin{pmatrix} y_{11} & y_{12} & \ldots & y_{1n} \\ y_{21} & y_{22} & \ldots & y_{2n} \\ \ldots & \ldots & \ldots & \ldots \\ y_{s1} & y_{s2} & \ldots & y_{sn} \end{pmatrix} \tag{10.1}$$

$\boldsymbol{x}_{\mathrm{o}} = (x_{1\mathrm{o}}, x_{2\mathrm{o}}, \ldots, x_{m\mathrm{o}})^T$ and $\boldsymbol{y}_{\mathrm{o}} = (y_{1\mathrm{o}}, y_{2\mathrm{o}}, \ldots, y_{s\mathrm{o}})^T$ are the vectors of all inputs and all outputs of the j-th DMU, with the assumptions: $\boldsymbol{x}_{\mathrm{o}} \geq \mathbf{0}$, $\boldsymbol{x}_{\mathrm{o}} \neq \mathbf{0}$ and $\boldsymbol{y}_{\mathrm{o}} \geq \mathbf{0}$, $\boldsymbol{y}_{\mathrm{o}} \neq \mathbf{0}$. One of the basic problems is to define the returns to scale in production. This could be based on the true production process, previous experience, etc. However, when the researcher is dealing with non-production units, such as countries, this is not an easy task. The BCC model is characterized by the variable returns to scale (VRS), whilst CCR is based on constant returns to scale (CRS). Other relevant issues include determining whether the DMUs are input or output-oriented, i.e., are they aiming to minimize the inputs of the production with the given amount of outputs or vice versa. That is why several basic model specifications exist, based on the idea of the returns to scale and the orientation of the DMUs themselves.

If one assumes the model CCR-I (input), the first phase of the optimization can be written in what is called the envelope form:

$$\begin{aligned} &\min_{\lambda,\theta} \theta \\ &s.t. \theta x_o - X\lambda \geq \mathbf{0} \\ &Y\lambda \geq y_o \\ &\lambda \geq \mathbf{0}, \end{aligned} \tag{10.2}$$

where the goal function consists of value θ which is minimized such that the vector of inputs $\boldsymbol{x}_o$ is radially reduced toward value $\theta \boldsymbol{x}_o$, with constraints that the DMU stays within the production possibility set, and $\boldsymbol{\lambda} = (\lambda_1, \lambda_2, \ldots, \lambda_n)^T$ is the vector of nonnegative constants. The optimal value from (10.2), i.e. the efficiency score θ^* is in the interval [0,1], with the interpretation of the input reduction rate needed so that the DMU becomes more efficient. In the second phase of the optimization the sum of input surpluses and output slacks of the DMU is maximised. In that way, researcher can interpret the needed changes in input reduction and/or output increase so that the DMU can reach the efficient frontier:

$$\begin{aligned} &\max_{\lambda, s^-, s^+} w = es^- + es^+ \\ &s.t. \theta^* x_o - X\lambda = s^- \\ &Y\lambda - y_o = s^+ \\ &\lambda \geq \mathbf{0},\ s^- \geq \mathbf{0},\ s^+ \geq \mathbf{0}, \end{aligned} \tag{10.3}$$

where $\boldsymbol{s}^- = \left(s_1^-, s_2^-, \ldots, s_m^-\right)^T$ and $\boldsymbol{s}^+ = \left(s_1^+, s_2^+, \ldots, s_r^+\right)^T$ denote vectors of input surpluses and output slacks and $e = (1, 1, \ldots, 1)$ is the vector consisting of unit values. The optimal solution $\left(\lambda^*, \boldsymbol{s}^{-*}, \boldsymbol{s}^{+*}\right)$ is called the max-slack solution and if $\theta^* = 1$, $\boldsymbol{s}^{-*} = \mathbf{0}$ and $\boldsymbol{s}^{+*} = \mathbf{0}$ hold, the DMU is called CCR efficient. The CCR-O model can be observed in a similar fashion. For details please see Cooper, Seiford, and Tone (2006). By adding the assumption of variable returns to scale, additional constraint is added in models (10.2) and (10.3), $\sum_{j=1}^{n} \lambda_j = 1$, which makes the efficient frontier a convex piecewise linear function.

Sometimes a problem with data arises when the researcher cannot obtain all of the needed data (missing data problems). Thus, Kuosmanen

(2009) suggests giving penalties for missing data, depending on the information if the values for inputs or outputs are missing. Since all of the data for every DMU needs to be included so that the previously mentioned models can be optimized, missing output values will be set to most pessimistic value—zero, whilst the missing input values will be sufficiently large number so that they are greater than the maximal value of an input between the rest of DMUs for which input data is available. Kuosmanen (2009) showed that using such approximations for missing data results with a frontier which will be at least as good as a frontier with deleted observations from the original dataset.

Finally, since this research deals with data over time, a window analysis approach will be made, which means that dynamics are included in the analysis. This is important to obtain information on how do countries change their R&D (in)efficiencies over time.

10.4 Empirical Results

10.4.1 Data Description

To calculate efficiencies of selected European countries, yearly data on the following variables was collected from Eurostat (2019b) and OECD database (2019a): Intramural R&D expenditure in Euro per capita, all sectors; total R&D personnel and researchers by sectors of performance, as % of active population; patent applications to the EPO per million habitants; number of SRJ (Scientific Journal Rankings) publications per million habitants and high-tech exports % of total exports. A trade-off was made between the number of included years, variables and countries. Thus, the analysis included the range from 2007 until 2017 and the following countries: Austria, Belgium, Bulgaria, Croatia, Cyprus, Czech Republic, Denmark, Estonia, Finland, France, Germany, Greece, Hungary, Iceland, Ireland, Italy, Latvia, Lithuania, Luxembourg, Malta, Netherlands, Norway, Poland, Portugal, Romania, Slovakia, Slovenia, Spain, Sweden and the United Kingdom.

The variables included in the analysis are based on previous literature (see Sect. 10.2) and all of the variables are treated as output, with the reciprocal value of R&D expenditure as input values. The reasoning on why this research uses the mentioned reciprocal value as previous research which observes the value of R&D as inputs and not its reciprocal values obtains rather strange results (see Table 10.1): most efficient countries are those which are usually classified as modest innovators (e.g., European Innovation Scoreboard classification). Thus, the researcher needs to be very careful when defining input and output variables. Finally, in some years, missing data for some countries were treated as Kuosmanen (2009) suggested: missing output values were left to be equal to zero values, whilst missing input values were treated to be greater than the maximal value of all available input values. In total, 3% of all available data was missing.

10.4.2 *Main Results*

The BCC-I model was optimized via the window analysis, with a one-year window length. The efficient scores for every country in every year are shown in Table 10.2. Constant returns to scale (BCC model) were chosen as they are more rigorous (resulting in less number of efficient DMUs[1]). As can be seen from Table 10.2, the best performing countries over time include Denmark, Sweden, Luxembourg, Finland and Iceland. On the opposite side are countries such as Latvia, Poland, Croatia, Lithuania, Romania, and Bulgaria. Such ranking is in line with findings in Muizniece and Cepilovs (2017), where technology transfers are in the focus of the research (leaders here include Denmark, Sweden, Finland and Germany); Furková (2014) who obtained similar best ranked countries for 2012; Aristovnik (2014) who obtained similar results on a regional level and average values for the period 2005–2010; and Swedish Research Barometer (2017, p. 14).

Specific problems of the most inefficient countries include the transitional part from the planned to the market economy (Eastern European countries), which included slow changes and adjustment. Furthermore, the majority of those countries made greater changes in negotiations with the EU as a necessary condition for them to enter the EU. These changes in legislation, business practices, and other relevant fields were late compared to the Western and Northern Europe, which contributed to the differences which exist today. Romania and Bulgaria have problems with serious labor shortages in high-skill sectors and emigration of the highly educated population (Roman, 2010), with many firms closing research laboratories during the transition time (Bourdeau-Lepage & Kolarova,

[1] Although, the results of the CCR-I and O models are given in the Appendix.

Table 10.2 Efficiency scores, window analysis, BCC-I model

Country/year	*2007*	*2008*	*2009*	*2010*	*2011*	*2012*	*2013*	*2014*	*2015*	*2016*	*2017*
Austria	0.535	0.652	0.583	0.672	0.670	0.754	0.797	0.900	0.862	0.864	0.966
Belgium	0.344	0.697	0.344	0.340	0.402	0.486	0.412	0.605	0.490	0.624	0.606
Bulgaria	0.003	0.004	0.004	0.004	0.005	0.005	0.007	0.008	0.013	0.013	0.014
Croatia	0.025	0.026	0.027	0.022	0.025	0.026	0.029	0.026	0.029	0.045	0.040
Cyprus	0.044	0.922	0.048	0.061	0.057	0.050	0.074	0.039	0.050	0.047	0.063
Czech Republic	0.087	0.524	0.080	0.099	0.131	0.161	0.180	0.200	0.207	0.205	0.229
Denmark	0.806	0.594	1	0.895	1	0.861	1	1	1	1	1
Estonia	0.045	0.721	0.057	0.067	0.148	0.156	0.149	0.158	0.153	0.156	0.120
Finland	1	0.560	1	0.969	1	0.805	0.905	0.825	0.738	0.606	0.661
France	0.358	0.650	0.358	0.406	0.441	0.524	0.605	0.678	0.778	0.791	0.775
Germany	0.561	1	0.714	0.660	0.644	0.697	0.666	0.775	0.772	0.828	0.844
Greece	0.118	0.111	0.105	0.064	0.046	0.063	0.056	0.097	0.071	0.106	0.078
Hungary	0.054	0.050	0.045	0.066	0.079	0.077	0.094	0.093	0.101	0.108	0.109
Iceland	1	0.355	0.625	1	0.673	1	0.479	0.625	0.749	0.841	0.913
Ireland	0.481	0.464	0.346	0.394	0.451	0.490	0.516	0.586	0.702	0.956	1
Italy	0.117	0.800	0.124	0.107	0.126	0.111	0.129	0.123	0.134	0.132	0.170
Latvia	0.014	0.012	0.009	0.010	0.019	0.017	0.024	0.035	0.036	0.028	0.032
Lithuania	0.022	0.022	0.023	0.019	0.035	0.028	0.043	0.042	0.050	0.043	0.056
Luxembourg	1	0.464	1	1	1	1	1	1	1	0.890	0.603
Malta	0.082	1	0.052	0.086	0.105	0.147	0.161	0.180	0.168	0.117	0.138
Netherlands	0.506	1	0.466	0.492	0.542	0.601	0.588	0.691	0.737	0.849	0.788
Norway	0.716	0.331	0.979	0.555	0.860	0.595	0.845	0.809	0.841	0.784	0.928
Poland	0.009	0.010	0.011	0.014	0.017	0.022	0.026	0.036	0.041	0.045	0.051
Portugal	0.058	0.306	0.118	0.081	0.109	0.061	0.099	0.081	0.101	0.083	0.114
Romania	0.004	0.004	0.004	0.007	0.009	0.007	0.006	0.008	0.012	0.017	0.015
Slovakia	0.011	0.835	0.014	0.019	0.026	0.035	0.044	0.054	0.073	0.056	0.062
Slovenia	0.132	0.833	1	0.137	0.251	0.191	0.236	0.207	0.193	0.155	0.174
Spain	0.112	0.400	0.128	0.093	0.116	0.087	0.098	0.089	0.095	0.084	0.104
Sweden	1	0.673	1	1	1	1	1	1	1	1	1
United Kingdom	0.455	0.606	0.278	0.319	0.340	0.382	0.363	0.417	0.487	0.552	0.567

Source Author's calculation

2008). Latvia's enterprises have low productivity and low capacity to absorb new technologies (OECD, 2019b), with weak cluster formations that do not share expertise and knowledge (Arnold et al., 2014), low rates of entrepreneurship and risk-taking (Rodríguez-Pose, 2001). Poland experiences weak linkage between academia and the business sector, whit only 10% of innovative companies cooperating with universities

(Klincewicz, Szkuta, & Marczewska, 2017), as well as policy instability and restrictive tax rates, alongside slow digitalization (Klincewicz, Marczewska, & Szkuta, 2018). Furthermore, some problems have accumulated from the economic transition period, as science, technology and innovation were not in focus and were less important compared to reforms of the financial system, privatization, etc. (Grabowski, Pamukcu, Szczygielski, & Tandogan, 2013). Some of greater problems with Croatia include low levels of public funding of research projects, with a fragmented R&I (research and innovation) system which negatively affects its performance (EC, 2015; Račić, Švarc, & Testa, 2018), combined with emigration of highly skilled professionals, as well as low performance in applied science and mathematics (EC, 2017). Inefficient countries in the analysis are also those which have greater corruption perception indices, with lower PISA scores and lower average years of schooling, which has great effects not only on the R&D sector and innovativeness but also on the sustainable development and circular economy, as well as the eco-innovation system as well (Škrinjarić, 2020a, 2020b).

Best performing countries have the following main characteristics: Denmark has a healthy macroeconomic environment and great openness of the country, with the production being heavily knowledge-based and easy access to finance (Knudsen, Christensen, & Christensen, 2018). Sweden is characterized with great investing in general education and ICT (information and communications technology) which is complementary to the R&D sector, with good institutional framework, political stability, effective legislation, and high level of trust (Swedish Ministry of Enterprise, Energy and Communications, 2015). Furthermore, Swedish researchers are cooperating with foreign researchers (68% of total scientific publications are coauthored with foreign researchers, Swedish Research Barometer, 2017), which indicates great flexibility. Scandinavian countries, as well as Iceland implement innovation education which improves the creativity which facilitates innovation (Kerr et al., 2017). This is in line with Camagni (1991), where it is explained that knowledge is getting more complex in its nature, which means that networking and cooperation are greatly needed. Next, EC (2019) finds that one of the priorities in Iceland is public–private collaborative publications (per capita), as having more than 41 such publications per capita in 2018; and the priority sectors of the national economy include the following ones: industry, eco technologies, health technologies, logistics,

ICT, and space (Grotz, Walentiny, Boever, & Crean, 2017). Luxembourg is characterized with digital skills of the workforce, as well as great STEM (science, technology, engineering, and math) competences (EC, 2018); as well as the government spending on RDI has increased more than 11.4 times in the period from 2000 to 2015, which indicates the priorities of the government (Rumpf, Alexander, & del Rio, 2017) Generally speaking, best performing countries have better education levels, which are correlated with greater number of patents in an economy (see Arvemo & Gråsjö, 2014; Guerrero, Cunningham, & Urbano, 2015; Prokop, Stejskal, & Mikušová Meričková, 2017). Furthermore, the results are in line with Todaro and Smith's (2003) new growth theory, where the economic growth of an economy is mainly a result of the internal state of the system, where the knowledge has the biggest role. This knowledge includes not only basic education within the education system, but digital education as well: countries with lower digital skills are also worst performers in this study, whereas the opposite is true for best performers (see rankings of digital skills rankings in EC, 2018 for comparison).

Top five performing and worst five performing countries from Table 10.1 have been extracted and their efficiency scores have been plotted in Figs. 10.1 and 10.2 so that the dynamics can be observed over time. Figure 10.1 depicts the most efficient countries. It can be seen that all of them had a decline of efficiency score values in 2008 due to the crisis period; however, all of them had a relatively quick rebound in 2010. The decline of efficiency of Iceland in 2013 was due to smaller funds invested in R&D, which increased in 2015 onward which contributed to the increase of the efficiency score to the end of the observed period Finland experienced decline in the efficiency score in the last couple of years, for which the cause could be the decline of total factor productivity (EC, 2018).

On the other hand, the five worst performing countries' efficiencies have been plotted in Fig. 10.2. A promising result is that all of the countries experience an increase of the efficiency score over time, which means that some progress is made. Poland is experiencing the fastest increase of efficiency over the observed period. Reasoning could be increasing R&D collaboration between companies (Deloitte Poland, 2016) and increases of the FDI flow to Poland (PIFIA, 2011).

Finally, the projections of every country to the efficient frontier within the BCC-O model have been calculated for years 2007 and 2017 and are shown in Table 10.3. In that way, the needed changes, i.e., increases of

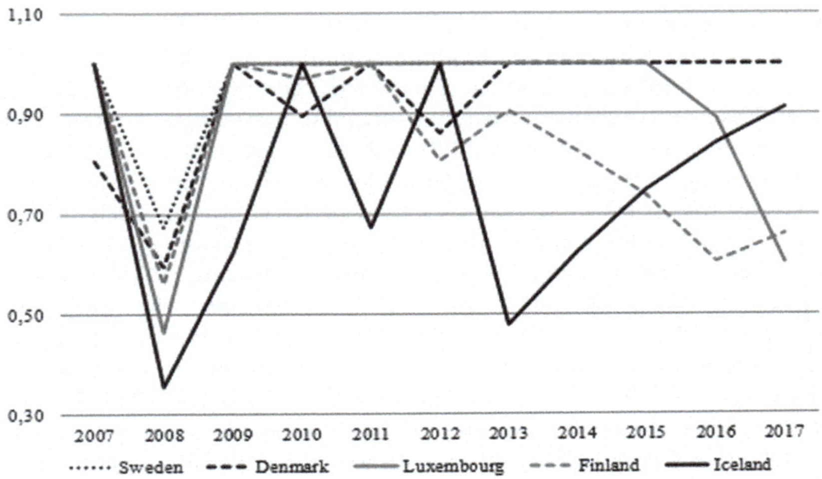

Fig. 10.1 Efficiency scores of 5 best performing countries (from Table 10.1) (*Source* Author's calculation)

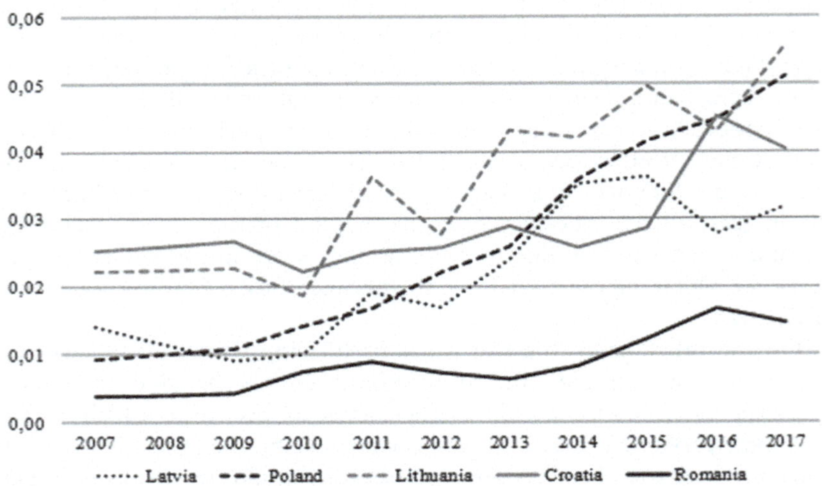

Fig. 10.2 Efficiency scores of 5 worst performing countries (from Table 10.1) (*Source* Author's calculation)

Table 10.3 Needed projections to the efficient frontier, BCC-O model, for 2007 and 2017

Country	*2007, in %*					*2017, in%*				
	1/R&D	*Exports*	*No publications*	*Patents*	*Employment*	*1/R&D*	*Exports*	*No publications*	*Patents*	*Employment*
Austria	−31.60	44.86	39.97	27.89	27.89	0.00	0.00	0.00	0.00	0.00
Belgium	−52.83	101.87	37.22	111.16	37.22	0.00	34.63	32.53	32.53	32.53
Bulgaria	−98.50	424.90	424.90	999.90	424.90	−91.80	294.63	294.63	999.90	294.63
Croatia	−93.28	156.27	156.27	999.90	219.66	−90.39	135.47	135.47	999.90	135.47
Cyprus	−78.74	81.37	81.37	437.01	103.74	−91.01	41.96	41.96	999.90	214.21
Czech R.	−39.04	68.15	68.15	857.26	68.15	−57.83	46.91	46.91	240.06	46.91
Denmark	−14.68	17.58	4.79	26.71	4.79	0.00	0.00	0.00	0.00	0.00
Estonia	−89.79	122.17	122.17	501.33	122.17	−80.01	66.34	66.34	661.06	67.91
Finland	0.00	0.00	0.00	0.00	0.00	−28.38	53.79	31.08	8.38	8.38
France	0.00	42.18	42.18	42.18	64.18	0.00	0.00	0.00	0.00	0.00
Germany	−41.32	4.64	80.96	4.64	38.49	−8.62	7.04	105.78	7.04	7.04
Greece	0.00	0.00	0.00	0.00	0.00	−70.62	258.76	93.58	710.30	93.58
Hungary	−27.00	54.34	54.34	475.89	54.34	−77.57	95.97	143.16	358.99	95.97
Iceland	0.00	0.00	0.00	0.00	0.00	0.00	0.00	0.00	0.00	0.00
Ireland	0.00	0.00	0.00	0.00	0.00	0.00	0.00	0.00	0.00	0.00
Italy	−73.69	185.69	112.37	193.06	112.37	−47.22	98.71	94.82	94.82	94.82
Latvia	−69.91	238.15	291.34	844.74	238.15	−89.58	154.59	154.59	616.87	154.59
Lithuania	−80.55	157.75	157.75	999.90	157.75	−77.78	132.45	132.45	999.90	132.45
Luxembourg	0.00	0.00	0.00	0.00	0.00	−4.40	35.71	35.71	106.99	35.71
Malta	0.00	0.00	0.00	0.00	0.00	−81.29	35.29	65.67	439.17	101.59
Netherlands	−36.42	3.28	3.28	4.36	101.55	0.00	0.00	0.00	0.00	0.00
Norway	−21.49	434.17	7.04	184.06	7.04	0.00	999.90	14.22	999.90	1.24
Poland	−96.17	443.27	288.57	999.90	288.57	79.90	154.03	154.03	378.33	154.03

(continued)

Table 10.3 (continued)

Country	*2007, in %*					*2017, in%*				
	I/R&D	*Exports*	*No publications*	*Patents*	*Employment*	*I/R&D*	*Exports*	*No publications*	*Patents*	*Employment*
Portugal	−84.76	153.96	153.96	999.90	153.96	−68.88	111.56	66.53	214.90	66.53
Romania	−97.53	553.26	553.26	999.90	553.26	−94.13	301.11	301.11	999.90	342.96
Slovakia	−96.14	244.78	244.78	999.90	244.78	−83.95	128.06	128.06	999.90	128.06
Slovenia	−80.45	189.13	47.64	423.16	71.36	−67.80	51.68	51.68	188.83	51.68
Spain	−75.61	305.25	106.27	502.31	106.27	−70.21	117.15	117.15	443.28	117.15
Sweden	0.00	0.00	0.00	0.00	0.00	0.00	0.00	0.00	0.00	0.00
UK	−46.51	6.71	6.71	153.07	77.02	0.00	0.00	0.00	0.00	0.00

Source Author's calculation

outputs and decreases of inputs can be seen for every country. Such analysis provides detailed insights into the strengths and weaknesses of every country with respect to the observed variables. Furthermore, a country can get a sense of its effectiveness of policies, legislation and its implementation in specific areas over time. For a comprehensive analysis, the projections should be made every year. As an example, Poland has shown an increase in efficiency over time (Fig. 10.2). Thus, results in Table 10.3 show that in 2007 the output increase of every variable was greater when compared to the corresponding values in 2017. This is a basic indicator that this country is going in the right direction with respect to the selected variables. Similar interpretations can be drawn for other countries as well. Thus, such calculations represent a valuable tool in tailoring and adjusting national policies on the topic of R&D and innovation.

10.4.3 Robustness Checking

In order to check for the robustness of the obtained results, the DEA efficiency scores from the previous subsection were contrasted to several ranking system values. The first comparison is made to the European Innovation Scoreboard (EIS, constructed by the European Commission) values in Fig. 10.3, for the year 2017. The correlation between both ranking systems is extremely high (over 90%). Since the EIS values are calculated based on over 27 different indicators, for which many variables are needed to be constructed, the obtained results and rankings in this research could provide more timely rankings, which are reliable, as due to the comparisons in Fig. 10.3.

Furthermore, the same DEA scores have been contrasted to the Global Innovation Index values (GII, constructed by Cornell University, INSEAD, and the World Intellectual Property Organization [WIPO, a specialized agency of the United Nations]) in Fig. 10.4. Again, the correlation between the scores/values is high (over 85%). The GII values are constructed based on 80 individual indicators. Thus, similar conclusions arise for using the ranking system and variables in this study as an approximation for the rankings within GII.

European Bank for Reconstruction and Development (EBRD) estimates the Knowledge Economy Index (KEI) for selected countries (46 in total) based on 38 indicators. Thus, for available countries, a comparison of DEA scores and the KEI scores was made and is shown in Fig. 10.5. Since data on KEI scores is available for years 2011 and 2018, the DEA

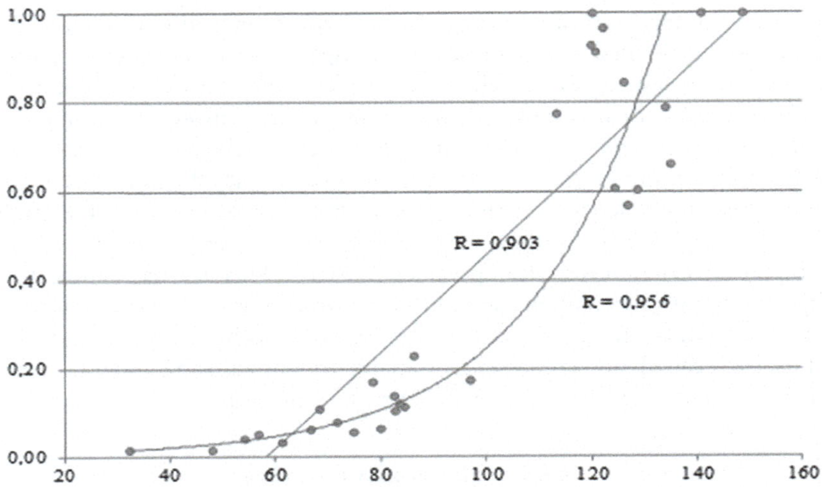

Fig. 10.3 Comparisons of 2017 DEA scores (y-axis) to the European Innovation Scoreboard values (x-axis) (*Source* Author's calculation, European Innovation Scoreboard [2019])

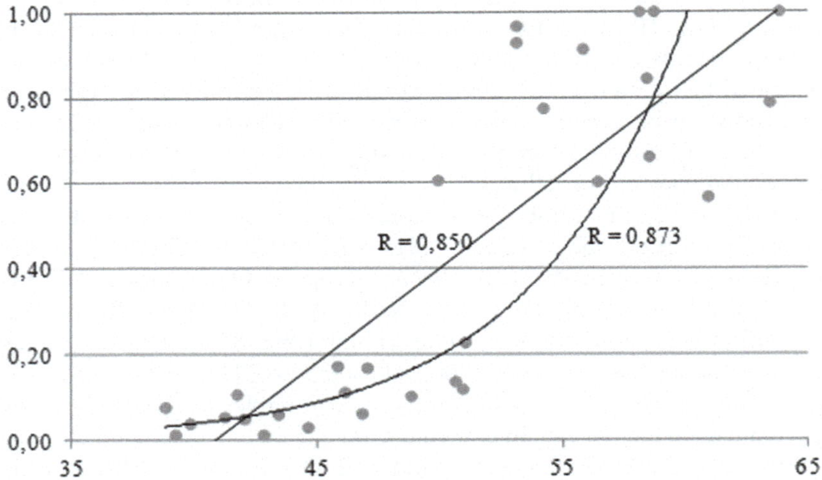

Fig. 10.4 Comparisons of 2017 DEA scores (y-axis) to the Global Innovation Index values (x-axis) (*Source* Author's calculation, Global Innovation Index [2019])

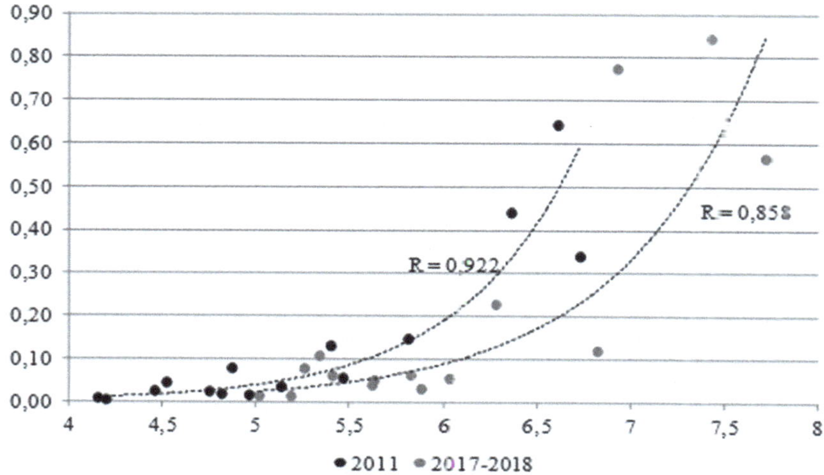

Fig. 10.5 Comparisons of DEA scores (y-axis) to the Knowledge Economy Index (x-axis) (*Source* Author's calculation, EBRD [2019]. *Note* Black dots denote 2011 data; grey dots denote 2017–2018 data)

scores from 2011 to 2017 were used for comparison purposes.[2] Again, the conclusions are similar, with great values of correlation coefficients among the ranking systems, even with using a smaller sample in this case.

Next, since both constant and variable returns to scale models have been optimized,[3] the rankings in each year for both approaches have been compared one to another. The correlation coefficients have been calculated and are shown in Tables 10.4 and 10.5. It can be seen that the values of the correlation coefficients are extremely high, which indicates that the rankings follow a similar fashion throughout the observed years. Smallest values are found for the year 2008 due to the financial crisis which affected some macroeconomic variables which were included in the calculation of variables used in this study.

[2] DEA 2017 scores were used as the latest data for this analysis was available for 2017, whilst the KEI data was not available for 2017, but 2018. Furthermore, the following countries are available within the KEI data: Bulgaria, Croatia, Cyprus, Czech Republic, Estonia, France, Germany, Greece, Hungary, Latvia, Lithuania, Poland, Romania, Slovakia and United Kingdom.

[3] Please see Tables 10.6, 10.7, and 10.8 in the Appendix for the full results.

Table 10.4 Correlation between efficiencies for CCR-I and BCC-I models

Year	*2007*	*2008*	*2009*	*2010*	*2011*	*2012*	*2013*	*2014*	*2015*	*2016*	*2017*
Correlation	0.806	0.537	0.985	0.880	0.894	0.901	0.892	0.900	0.979	0.993	0.977

Source Author's calculation

Table 10.5 Correlation between efficiencies for CCR-O and BCC-O models

Year	*2007*	*2008*	*2009*	*2010*	*2011*	*2012*	*2013*	*2014*	*2015*	*2016*	*2017*
Correlation	0.776	0.502	0.838	0.751	0.806	0.788	0.810	0.818	0.873	0.883	0.977

Source Author's calculation

Thus, it could be said that the results obtained in this study are fairly robust. Based on the fewer dataset, the rankings of the countries with respect to R&D are very similar to the rankings of different important world institutions. This means that the approach used in this study can be used in future research in order to obtain results quickly and with fewer data available so that dynamic changes over time can be monitored. In that way, more timely and efficient policy changes can be made over time if the results show a need for them.

10.5 Conclusion

R&D and innovation play an important role in the competitiveness of the European countries today, due to added value in the economy, obtaining sustainable growth, productivity growth, and efficient usage of all resources. That is why these areas have been in the focus of the European Commission for many years now. It is important to obtain an objective approach of measuring the achievement of given goals so that policymakers can make timely decisions on future directions of R&D and innovation policies and their implementations. This was the main focus of this research. Due to some of the shortfalls of previous research, the aim of this study was to provide a robust ranking system of the 30 European countries that can be used in future research as well. Namely, previous research often found that the countries with most problems within the whole economy (not only R&D sector) are just as efficient as the best performing ones (best innovators). Sometimes the results indicated that problematic countries are even better performers than some of the best ones according to different ranking systems. This should be alarming in the research process; as false or distorted results could be dangerous in policy implementation. The research and the results provided in this study are reliable, due to checking the robustness of the results via several approaches. So, the following discussion and conclusions arise

Firstly, the results in this research are in line with previous related work, which has been discussed in the previous section. The majority of related work focuses on some specific aspects of innovation or R&D, and the conclusions are similar to the comprehensive approach given here. Furthermore, the results are in line with rankings of different world organizations which focus on many indicators in their construction of the final index and rankings. This also indicates that by using fewer amounts of data, future researchers and policymakers could obtain specific results in a timelier manner.

Secondly, some of the recommendations for the worst performing countries and implications of this study for practice are as follows. Investments into (especially higher) education, especially concerning STEM competencies and ICT are crucial for greater productivity within the R&D sector and innovative behaviour (Elnasari & Fox, 2015; Vinding, 2006). Human capital represents is probably the most important factor within this area, as it determines the innovation capacity of firms (see Mariz-Pérez, Teijeiro-Álvarez, & García-Álvarez, 2012). R&D expenditures within the higher education system increases knowledge base of the economy (Pegkas, Staikouras, & Tsamadias, 2019). Previously stated means that the education systems should provide the workers and researches such skills which will be useful in a knowledge-based economy Some traditional approaches which cannot keep up with the fast pace need to fade out and new approaches which can enhance the productivity within the innovation and R&D system need to be implemented as soon as possible.

Since worst performing countries have low links between the universities and high-tech industry start-ups, a greater connectedness is required between the private sector and universities. Lew, Khan, and Cozzio (2018) suggest that highly skilled laborers such as new graduates can be employed in the whole innovation process, as they have fresh points of view. Furthermore, the connectedness of local knowledge bearers is important due to previous research finding positive effects of knowledge spillovers (Fariñas & Martín-Marcos, 2007; Trachuk & Linder, 2019).

This means that some policy measures need to be tailored specifically based on the characteristics of a local region. Such action will enable achieving the goals faster as the measures will be specifically be adjusted for a specific type of climate, industry, socio-demographic, and other relevant factors, which cannot be affected uniformly across all regions.

Connectedness with foreign researchers and all relevant agents within the area of R&D and innovation is shown to be important as well (see Anić, 2017 for literature overview), due to the more complex nature of knowledge and the necessity for such cooperation is growing (Camagni, 1991). Due to the increasing specialization within every area of science, cooperation is greatly needed in order to obtain benefits from the synergy. Besides the mentioned factors, the financing of the whole process is important as well (Buesa, Heijs, & Baumert, 2010, O'sullivan, 2005). Majority of businesses in Europe are SMEs (small and medium enterprises) which often do not have enough money, resources, skills and people to achieve certain goals. External financing is important to obtain enough money to prepare the needed infrastructure. Financial constraints do affect the level of R&D investing in European firms (Hall, Moncada-Paternò-Castello, Montresor, & Vezzani, 2015). Thus, improving the access to finance could help improving productivity and R&D skills. It is important to tailor specific measures, incentives, and taxes based on specific characteristics of firms and regions, as these measures depend on a variety of firm characteristics (see Moncada-Paternò-Castello, Vezzani, Hervás, & Montresor, 2014). Regarding the tax policies which focus on the R&D expenditures, empirical evidence shows that in the long run, these expenditures are responsive to fiscal incentives (see Da Rin, Nicodano, & Sembenelli, 2006). Some recent problems with worst performing countries also include the emigration of highly skilled workforce to other countries, which contributes to their problems (Atoyan et al., 2016; ICF, 2018). This also indicates fundamental problems within those countries. The quality of the overall institutional infrastructure has to be solved as soon as possible. Furthermore, Fleming, Greene, Li, Marx, and Yao (2019) advise that the research which is aiming toward fundamental understanding is a public good, which precedes commercialization. This means that it can be applied in different companies, industries for many years.

Finally, several shortfalls and limitations of this research include the following. A relatively short time span was observed due to data unavailability. This could be the reasoning on why the majority of previous research does not observe more than one or several years at once. The lack of data disables a better dynamic analysis, which is important for topics such as the one observed in this work. Next, a rather simple modeling approach was made with simple models within the DEA methodology. Although the parsimony approach of modeling is always advised, it cannot always capture all of the relevant real-world characteristics. Future research could look into other models that could perhaps provide other detailed results. Such models can include specifics which will model questions and topics which are relevant to a region or country. Moreover, some of the variables included in the research were on an aggregate level. Future work is going to include the analysis of the efficiencies on disaggregated data, such as the R&D investments from the private, government, and the high education sectors separately. In such case, specific sources of inefficiencies will be detected. This can enable focusing only on those sources which are relevant with respect to the inefficiency. This could save time and money, which are very valuable within this area of research and policymaking. Questions regarding these individual sectors are also important for the policymakers and specific tailoring of the needed measures to facilitate obtaining needed goals.

Appendix

See Fig. 10.6, Tables 10.6, 10.7, and 10.8.

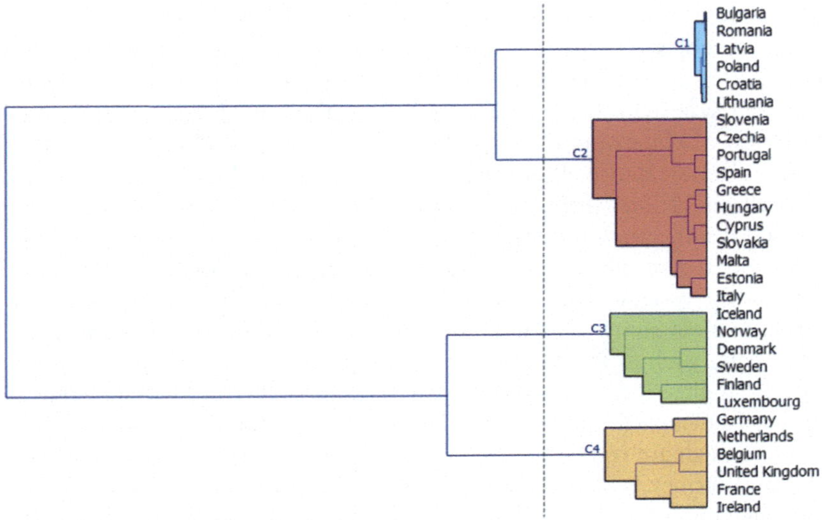

Fig. 10.6 Clustering of efficiency scores from Table 10.1, Ward distance (*Source* Author's calculation)

Table 10.6 Efficiency scores, window analysis, CCR-I model

Country/Year	*2007*	*2008*	*2009*	*2010*	*2011*	*2012*	*2013*	*2014*	*2015*	*2016*	*2017*
Austria	0.644	0.768	0.700	0.672	0.708	0.754	1	0.900	0.911	0.866	1
Belgium	0.464	0.729	0.502	0.422	0.532	0.486	0.545	0.605	0.599	0.624	0.651
Bulgaria	0.014	1	0.019	0.015	0.021	0.018	0.024	0.033	0.040	0.034	0.034
Croatia	0.062	0.842	0.069	0.043	0.056	0.045	0.055	0.057	0.059	0.062	0.063
Cyprus	0.071	1	0.082	0.073	0.077	0.066	0.080	0.074	0.067	0.076	0.080
Czech Republic	0.135	0.671	0.144	0.131	0.179	0.203	0.204	0.226	0.223	0.206	0.242
Denmark	0.840	0.916	1	0.905	1	1	1	1	1	1	1
Estonia	0.099	0.884	0.115	0.103	0.209	0.203	0.176	0.173	0.167	0.157	0.144
Finland	1	1	1	1	1	0.842	1	0.846	0.745	0.705	0.705
France	0.478	0.657	0.522	0.483	0.524	0.580	0.613	1	1	0.817	1
Germany	0.586	1	1	0.660	0.674	0.697	0.689	0.775	0.772	0.835	0.864
Greece	1	1	0.105	0.064	0.090	0.063	0.088	0.097	0.104	0.106	0.117
Hungary	0.076	0.943	0.084	0.081	0.093	0.097	0.107	0.108	0.110	0.109	0.127
Iceland	1	1	0.626	1	1	1	1	1	1	1	1
Ireland	1	1	0.475	0.409	0.452	0.503	0.526	1	1	1	1
Italy	0.240	0.836	0.254	0.181	0.239	0.198	0.233	0.254	0.242	0.249	0.243
Latvia	0.044	0.921	0.031	0.027	0.049	0.041	0.046	0.058	0.051	0.036	0.044
Lithuania	0.055	0.877	0.055	0.037	0.066	0.056	0.074	0.091	0.089	0.074	0.082
Luxembourg	1	1	1	1	1	1	1	1	1	0.900	0.755
Malta	1	1	0.061	1	1	1	1	1	0.236	0.120	0.148
Netherlands	0.513	1	0.498	1	0.546	1	0.593	1	1	1	1
Norway	0.755	0.697	1	0.616	0.863	0.662	0.854	0.894	0.874	0.852	0.965
Poland	0.036	0.831	0.043	0.037	0.053	0.051	0.060	0.072	0.076	0.070	0.079
Portugal	0.144	0.424	0.205	0.130	0.174	0.115	0.143	0.152	0.143	0.150	0.155
Romania	0.024	0.643	0.021	0.016	0.023	0.018	0.019	0.020	0.026	0.027	0.030
Slovakia	0.036	1	0.044	0.042	0.062	0.065	0.075	0.088	0.114	0.077	0.085
Slovenia	0.191	1	1	0.192	0.312	0.250	0.301	0.306	0.275	0.256	0.240
Spain	0.229	0.486	0.246	0.163	0.217	0.157	0.185	0.195	0.189	0.186	0.187
Sweden	1	1	1	1	1	1	1	1	1	1	1
United Kingdom	0.460	1	0.367	0.332	0.369	0.402	0.386	0.457	0.510	0.565	1

Source Author's calculation

Table 10.7 Efficiency scores, window analysis, CCR-O model

Country/year	*2007*	*2008*	*2009*	*2010*	*2011*	*2012*	*2013*	*2014*	*2015*	*2016*	*2017*
Austria	0.782	0.966	0.811	0.989	0.892	1	1	1	0.951	1	1
Belgium	0.729	0.854	0.628	0.722	0.724	1	0.718	1	0.735	1	0.755
Bulgaria	0.191	0.206	0.221	0.204	0.222	0.180	0.253	0.193	0.237	0.252	0.253
Croatia	0.390	0.366	0.342	0.426	0.443	0.439	0.438	0.397	0.412	0.436	0.425
Cyprus	0.551	0.526	0.501	0.740	0.684	0.628	0.804	0.519	0.640	0.605	0.704
Czech republic	0.595	0.871	0.531	0.639	0.677	0.652	0.746	0.706	0.737	0.642	0.681
Denmark	0.954	0.978	1	0.980	1	1	1	1	1	1	1
Estonia	0.450	0.904	0.495	0.554	0.649	0.627	0.684	0.748	0.711	0.666	0.601
Finland	1	1	1	1	1	0.932	1	0.975	0.963	0.862	0.923
France	0.703	0.803	0.662	0.733	0.803	0.828	0.962	1	1	1	1
Germany	0.956	1	1	0.997	0.951	1	0.927	1	0.954	1	0.934
Greece	1	1	0.998	0.988	0.482	1	0.573	1	0.559	1	0.517
Hungary	0.648	0.953	0.530	0.682	0.738	0.607	0.686	0.568	0.631	0.554	0.510
Iceland	1	1	0.996	1	1	1	1	1	1	1	1
Ireland	1	1	0.597	0.927	0.998	0.941	0.951	1	1	1	1
Italy	0.471	0.847	0.487	0.477	0.489	0.451	0.528	0.439	0.480	0.454	0.513
Latvia	0.296	0.294	0.292	0.293	0.360	0.268	0.424	0.424	0.462	0.355	0.393
Lithuania	0.388	0.399	0.410	0.418	0.516	0.383	0.540	0.423	0.422	0.390	0.430
Luxembourg	1	1	1	1	1	1	1	1	1	1	0.737
Malta	1	1	0.840	1	1	1	1	1	0.988	0.645	0.739
Netherlands	0.968	1	0.849	1	0.990	1	0.977	1	1	1	1
Norway	0.934	0.943	1	0.873	0.941	0.876	0.899	0.874	0.915	0.876	0.988
Poland	0.257	0.253	0.249	0.290	0.285	0.296	0.348	0.360	0.382	0.351	0.394
Portugal	0.394	0.672	0.571	0.586	0.597	0.474	0.631	0.506	0.608	0.545	0.600
Romania	0.153	0.672	0.196	0.318	0.327	0.254	0.249	0.275	0.299	0.289	0.249
Slovakia	0.290	1	0.323	0.346	0.380	0.373	0.446	0.463	0.450	0.426	0.438
Slovenia	0.677	1	1	0.669	0.738	0.708	0.713	0.651	0.667	0.632	0.659
Spain	0.485	0.643	0.517	0.511	0.506	0.463	0.494	0.443	0.460	0.441	0.461
Sweden	1	1	1	1	1	1	1	1	1	1	1
United Kingdom	0.937	1	0.629	0.924	0.908	0.897	0.864	0.821	0.863	0.834	1

Source Author's calculation

Table 10.8 Efficiency scores, window analysis, BCC-O model

Country/year	*2007*	*2008*	*2009*	*2010*	*2011*	*2012*	*2013*	*2014*	*2015*	*2016*	*2017*
Austria	0.535	0.652	0.583	0.672	0.670	0.754	0.797	0.900	0.862	0.864	0.966
Belgium	0.344	0.697	0.344	0.340	0.402	0.486	0.412	0.605	0.490	0.624	0.606
Bulgaria	0.003	0.004	0.004	0.004	0.005	0.005	0.007	0.008	0.013	0.013	0.014
Croatia	0.025	0.026	0.027	0.022	0.025	0.026	0.029	0.026	0.029	0.045	0.040
Cyprus	0.044	0.046	0.048	0.061	0.057	0.050	0.074	0.039	0.050	0.047	0.063
Czech Republic	0.087	0.524	0.080	0.099	0.131	0.161	0.180	0.200	0.207	0.205	0.229
Denmark	0.806	0.594	1	0.895	1	0.861	1	1	1	1	1
Estonia	0.045	0.050	0.057	0.067	0.148	0.156	0.149	0.158	0.153	0.156	0.120
Finland	1	0.560	1	0.969	1	0.805	0.905	0.825	0.738	0.606	0.661
France	0.358	0.650	0.358	0.406	0.441	0.524	0.605	0.678	0.778	0.791	0.775
Germany	0.561	1	0.714	0.660	0.644	0.697	0.666	0.775	0.772	0.828	0.844
Greece	0.118	0.111	0.105	0.064	0.046	0.063	0.056	0.097	[illegible]	0.106	0.078
Hungary	0.054	0.050	0.045	0.066	0.079	0.077	0.094	0.093	0.101	0.108	0.109
Iceland	1	0.355	0.625	1	0.673	1	0.479	0.625	0.749	[illegible]	0.913
Ireland	0.481	0.464	0.346	0.394	0.451	0.490	0.516	0.586	0.702	0.955	1
Italy	0.117	0.800	0.124	0.107	0.126	0.111	0.129	0.123	0.134	0.132	0.170
Latvia	0.014	0.012	0.009	0.010	0.019	0.017	0.024	0.035	0.036	0.028	0.032
Lithuania	0.022	0.022	0.023	0.019	0.036	0.028	0.043	0.042	0.050	0.043	0.056
Luxembourg	1	0.464	1	1	1	1	1	1	1	0.890	0.603
Malta	0.082	1	0.052	0.086	0.105	0.147	0.161	0.180	0.168	[illegible]	0.138
Netherlands	0.506	1	0.466	0.492	0.542	0.601	0.588	0.691	0.737	0.849	0.788
Norway	0.716	0.331	0.979	0.555	0.860	0.595	0.845	0.809	0.841	0.734	0.928
Poland	0.009	0.010	0.011	0.014	0.017	0.022	0.026	0.036	0.041	0.045	0.051
Portugal	0.058	0.306	0.118	0.081	0.109	0.061	0.099	0.081	0.101	0.083	0.114
Romania	0.004	0.004	0.004	0.007	0.009	0.007	0.006	0.008	0.012	0.017	0.015
Slovakia	0.011	0.012	0.014	0.019	0.026	0.035	0.044	0.054	0.073	0.056	0.062
Slovenia	0.132	0.833	1	0.137	0.251	0.191	0.236	0.207	0.193	0.165	0.174
Spain	0.112	0.400	0.128	0.093	0.116	0.087	0.098	0.089	0.095	0.084	0.104
Sweden	1	0.673	1	1	1	1	1	1	1	1	1
United Kingdom	0.455	0.606	0.278	0.319	0.340	0.382	0.363	0.417	0.487	0.552	0.567

Source Author's calculation

References

Anderson, H. J., & Stejskal, J. (2019). Diffusion efficiency of innovation among EU Member States: A data envelopment analysis. *Economies, 7*(34), 1–19.

Anić, I.-D. (2017). Facilitating effective science-industry collaborative research: A literature review. *Economic Trends and Economic Policy, 26*(1), 7–40.

Aristovnik, A. (2012). The relative efficiency of education and R&D expenditures in the new EU member states. *Journal of Business Economics and Management, 13*(5), 832–848.

Aristovnik, A. (2014). Efficiency of the R&D sector in the EU-27 at the regional level: An application of DEA. *Lex Localis—Journal of Local Self-Government, 12*(3), 519–531.

Arnold, E., Knee, P., Angelis, J., Giarraca, F., Griniece, E., Javorka, Z., & Reid, A. (2014). *Latvia innovation system review and research assessment exercise: Final report.* Technopolis Group. http://izm.gov.lv/images/zinatne/ZISI/Latvia-systems-review_2014.pdf.

Arvemo, T., & Gråsjö, U. (2014). University colleges' effect on economic growth in Swedish middlesized municipalities. In C. Karlsson (Ed.), *Knowledge, innovation and space* (pp. 287–304). Cheltenham: Edward Elgar.

Atoyan, R., Christiansen, L., Dizioli, A., Ebeke, C., Ilahi, N., Ilyina, A., … Zakharova, D. (2016). *Emigration and its economic impact on Eastern Europe* (IMF Staff Discussion Note, SDN/16/07).

Bednář, P., & Halásková, M. (2018). Innovation performance and R&D expenditures in Western European regions: Divergence or convergence? *Journal of International Studies, 11*(1), 210–224.

Bottazzi, L., & Peri, G. (2003). Innovation and spillovers in regions: Evidence from European patent data. *European Economic Review, 47*(4), 687–710.

Bourdeau-Lepage, L., & Kolarova, D. (2008). Knowledge society and transition economies: The Bulgarian challenge. *The Journal of the Romanian Regional Science Association, 2*(2), 53–79.

Buesa, M., Heijs, J., & Baumert, T. (2010). The determinants of regional innovation in Europe: A combined factorial and regression knowledge production function approach. *Research Policy, 39*(6), 722–735.

Camagni, R. (1991). Technological change, uncertainty and innovation networks: Towards dynamic theory of economic space. In R. Camagni (Ed.), *Innovation networks: Spatial perspectives* (pp. 121–144). London: Belhaven-Pinter.

Cao, Y., You, J., Shi, Y., & Hu, W. (2019). Evaluating R&D and transformation functional platforms' operational performance using a data envelopment analysis model: A comparative study. *Sustainability, 11*(5023), 1–14.

Chen, C.-P., Hu, J.-L., & Yang, C.-H. (2011). An international comparison of R&D efficiency of multiple innovative outputs: The role of the national innovation system. *Innovation, 13*(3), 341–360.

Coe, D. T., & Moghadam, R. (1993). *Capital and trade as engines of growth in France: An application of Johansen's cointegration methodology* (IMF Staff Paper No. 40), pp. 542–666.

Coelli, T. J. (1995). Recent developments in frontier modelling and efficiency measurement. *Australian Journal of Agricultural and Resource Economics, 39*(3), 219–245.

Cooper, W. W., Seiford, L. M., & Tone, K. (2006). *Introduction to data envelopment analysis and its uses: With DEA-solver software and references*. New York: Springer.

Cooper, W. W., Seiford, L. M., & Zhu, J. (2011). *Handbook on data envelopment analysis*. New York: Springer.

Costantini, V., Crespi, F., Martini, C., & Pennacchio, L. (2015). Demand-pull and technology-push public support for eco-innovation: The case of the biofuels sector. *Research Policy, 44*(3), 577–595.

Cowan, R., & Van de Paal, G. (2000). *Innovation policy in a knowledge based economy*. The Commission of the European Communities no. EUR 17023, Luxembourg.

Da Rin, M., Nicodano, G., & Sembenelli, A. (2006). Public policy and the creation of active venture capital markets. *Journal of Public Economics, 90*(8–9), 1699–1723.

Daraio, C. (2019). Econometric approaches to the measurement of research productivity. In W. Glänzel, H. F. Moed, U. Schmoch, & M. Thelwall (Eds.), *Springer handbook of science and technology indicators*. Springer Handbooks. Cham: Springer.

David, P. A., Hall, B. H., & Toole, A. A. (2000). Is public R&D a complement or substitute for private R&D. *Research Policy, 29*(4–5), 497–529.

de Rassenfosse, G., Jaffe A., & Raiteri, E. (2019). The procurement of innovation by the U.S. government. *PLoS One, 14*(8), e0218927.

Deloitte Poland. (2016). *Poland corporate R&D report 2016*. https://www2.deloitte.com/content/dam/Deloitte/pl/Documents/Reports/pl_RD-2016-Poland-EN%20(1).pdf.

EBRD. (2019). *European Bank for reconstruction and development*. https://www.ebrd.com/news/publications/brochures/ebrd-knowledge-economy-index.html.

EC. (2010). *Commission of the European Communities: Regional policy contributing to smart growth in Europe*, COM(2010)553, Brussels.

EC. (2015). *Country report Croatia 2015: Including an in-depth review on the prevention and correction of macroeconomic imbalances* (European Semester), SWD (2015) 30 final. Brussels: European Commission. http://ec.europa.eu/europe2020/pdf/csr2015/cr2015_croatia_en.pdf.

EC. (2017). *Country report Croatia 2017: Including an in-depth review on the prevention and correction of macroeconomic imbalances* (European Semester),

COM SWD (2017) 76 final. Brussels: European Commission. https://ec.europa.eu/info/sites/info/files/2017-european-semester-country-report-croatia-en.pdf.

EC. (2018). *Science, research and innovation performance of the EU 2018: Strengthening the foundations for Europe's future*. https://ec.europa.eu/info/sites/info/files/srip-report-full_2018_en.pdf.

EC. (2019). *European research area progress report 2018 country profile Iceland*. https://ec.europa.eu/info/sites/info/files/research_and_innovation/era/era-2018_country_profile_is.pdf.

Ekinci, Y., & Ön, R. M. (2015). A review on the comparison of EU countries based on research and development efficiencies. *World Academy of Science, Engineering and Technology International Journal of Industrial and Manufacturing Engineering, 9*(7), 2437–2440.

Elnasari, A., & Fox, K. J. (2015). R&D, innovation and productivity: The role of public support. *KDI Journal of Economic Policy, 37*(1), 73–96.

EU. (2019). European Union. In *Measuring public innovation in the EU: the STARPIN methodology*. Luxembourg: Publications Office of the European Union.

European Innovation Scoreboard. (2019). https://ec.europa.eu/growth/industry/innovation/facts-figures/scoreboards_en.

Eurostat. (2019a). *Europe 2020 indicators—R&D and innovation*. https://ec.europa.eu/eurostat/statistics-explained/index.php/Europe_2020_indicators_-_R%26D_and_innovation#R.26D_intensity_in_the_EU_is_growing_too_slowly_to_meet_the_Europe_2020_target.

Eurostat. (2019b). *Database*. https://ec.europa.eu/eurostat/data/database.

Fariñas, J. C., & Martín-Marcos, A. (2007). Exporting and economic performance: Firm-level evidence of Spanish manufacturing. *The World Economy, 30*(4), 618–646. https://doi.org/10.1111/j.1467-9701.2007.01007.x.

Faria, J. R., Ferreira, J. J., Johnson, K. H., Mixon, F. G., Jr., & Wanke, P. F. (2020, Forthcoming). Agglomeration economies and university program creation in the knowledge economy. *Socio-Economic Planning Sciences*. https://www.sciencedirect.com/science/article/abs/pii/S0038012119304288.

Fleming, L., Greene, H., Li, G., Marx, M., & Yao, D. (2019). Government-funded research increasingly fuels innovation. *Science, 364*(6446), 1139–1141.

Furková, A. (2014). Multiple selections of alternatives under constraints: Case study of European countries in area of research and development. *Trendy v podnikání = Business trends: vědecký časopis Fakulty ekonomické ZČU v Plzni, 5*(1), 73–88.

Gaudillière, J. P. (2019). From crisis to reformulation: Innovation in the global drug industry and the alternative modernization of Indian Ayurveda. In

S. Lechevalier (Ed.), *Innovation beyond technology* (pp. 121–139). Berlin: Springer.

Global Innovation Index. (2019). https://www.globalinnovationindex.org/analysis-indicator.

Grabowski, W., Pamukcu, T., Szczygielski, K., & Tandogan, S. (2013). *Does government support for private innovation matter? Firm-level evidence from Turkey and Poland*. CASE Network Studies and Analyses 0458, CASE-Center for Social and Economic Research.

Griliches, Z. (1979). Issues in assessing the contribution of R&D to productivity growth. *Bell Journal of Economics, 10*(1), 92–116.

Griliches, Z. (1988). Productivity puzzles and R&D: Another nonexplanation. *Journal of Economic Perspectives, 2*(4), 9–21.

Grotz, M., Walentiny, M., Boever, E., & Crean, G. (2017). *Research and innovation smart specialization strategy (RIS3)*. The Government of the grand Duchy of Luxembourg. https://meco.gouvernement.lu/dam-assets/publications/rapport-etude-analyse/minist-economie/ris3/luxembourg-research-and-innovation-smart-specialisation-strategy-2017.pdf.

Guan, J. C., & Chen, K. H. (2010). Modeling macro-R&D production frontier performance: An application to Chinese province-level R&D. *Scientometrics, 82*(1), 165–173.

Guan, J. C., & Chen, K. H. (2012). Modeling the relative efficiency of national innovation systems. *Research Policy, 41*(2), 102–115.

Guan, J. C., & He, Y. (2005). Comparison and evaluation of domestic and international outputs in information science & technology research of China. *Scientometrics, 65*(2), 215–244.

Guan, J. C., & Zuo, K. (2014). A cross-country comparison of innovation efficiency. *Scientometrics, 100*(2), 541–575.

Guerrero, M., Cunningham, J. A., & Urbano, D. (2015). Economic impact of entrepreneurial universities' activities: An exploratory study of the United Kingdom. *Research Policy, 44*(3), 748–764.

Halásková, R., & Halásková, M. (2015). Current issues of research and development policy in EU countries. In *Proceedings of 13th International Scientific Conference "Economic Policy in the European Union Member Countries"* (pp. 161–174). Karolinka, Czech Republic. ISBN 978-80-248-3796-3.

Hall, B. H., Moncada-Paternò-Castello, P., Montresor, S., & Vezzani, A. (2015). Financing constraints, R&D investments and innovative performances: New empirical evidence at the firm level for Europe. *Economics of Innovation and New Technology, 25*(3), 183–196.

Hiroi, Y. (2019). Science as care: Science and innovation in post-growth society. In S. Lechevalier (Ed.), *Innovation beyond technology* (pp. 301–324). Berlin: Springer.

Hu, A. G. Z., & Yongxu, D. (2019). Does government R&D stimulate or crowd out firm R&D spending? Evidence from Chinese manufacturing industries. *Economics of Transition, 27*(2), 497–518.

Hu, S., Liu, S., Li, D., & Li, Y. (2019). How does regional innovation capacity affect the green growth performance? Empirical evidence from China. *Sustainability, 11*(5084), 1–21.

Hudec, O., & Prochádzková, M. (2013). The relative efficiency of knowledge innovation processes in EU countries. *Studies in Regional Science, 43*(1), 145–162.

ICF. (2018). *Study on the movement of skilled labour*. Luxembourg: Publications Office of the European Union.

Johansson, B., Lööf, H., & Savin, M. (2015). European R&D efficiency. *Economics of Innovation and New Technology, 24*(1–2), 140–158.

Joly, P. B. (2019). Reimagining innovation. In S. Lechevalier (Ed.), *Innovation beyond technology* (pp. 25–45). Berlin: Springer.

Kalapoutia, K., Petridisb, K., Malesiosc, C., & Deyd, P. K. (2017). Measuring efficiency of innovation using combined data envelopment analysis and structural equation modeling: Empirical study in EU regions. *Annals of Operations Research*. https://doi.org/10.1007/s10479-017-2728-4.

Karadayi, M. A., & Ekinci, Y. (2018). Evaluating R&D performance of EU countries using categorical DEA. *Technology Analysis & Strategic Management, 31*(2), 227–238.

Kerr, B. A., Birdnow, M., Hallaert, J., Alexander, K., Malmsten, R., Stull, O., ... Claiborn, G. J. (2017). Creativity and innovation in Iceland: Individual, environmental, and cultural variables. *Gifted and Talented International, 32*(1), 27–42.

Klincewicz, K., Marczewska, M., & Szkuta, K. (2018). *RIO country report 2017: Poland, EUR 29150 EN*. Luxembourg: Publications Office of the European Union. ISBN 978-92-79-81197-5, JRC111282.

Klincewicz, K., Szkuta, K., & Marczewska, M. (2017). *RIO country report 2016: Poland; EUR 28481 EN*. Luxembourg: Publications Office of the European Union.

Knudsen, M. P., Christensen, J. L., & Christensen, P. (2018). *RIO country report 2017: Denmark; EUR 29187 EN*. Luxembourg: Publications Office of the European Union. ISBN 978-92-79-81276-7.

Kuosmanen, T. (2009). Data envelopment analysis with missing data. *Journal of the Operational Research Society, 60*(12), 1767–1774.

Lechevalier, S., & Laugier, S. (2019). Innovation beyond technology—Introduction. In S. Lechevalier (Ed.), *Innovation Beyond Technology, Creative Economy*. Cham: Springer.

Leydesdorff, L., & Porto-Gomez, I. (2019). Measuring the expected synergy in Spanish regional and national systems of innovation. *The Journal of Technology*

Transfer, 44, 189–209. https://link.springer.com/article/10.1007/s10479-017-2728-4#citeas.
Lee, H., Park, Y., & Choi, H. (2009). Comparative evaluation of performance of national R&D programs with heterogeneous objectives: A DEA approach. *European Journal of Operational Research, 196*(3), 847–855.
Lee, H.-Y., & Park, Y.-T. (2005). An international comparison of R&D efficiency: DEA approach. *Asian Journal of Technology Innovation, 13*(2), 207–222.
Lew, Y. K., Khan, Z., & Cozzio, S. (2018). Gravitating toward the quadruple helix: International connections for the enhancement of a regional innovation system in Northeast Italy. *R&D Management, 48*(1), 44–59.
Liu, J., Lu, K., & Cheng, S. (2018). International R&D spillovers and innovation efficiency. *Sustainability, 10*(3974), 1–23.
Lucas, R. E. (1988). On the mechanics of economic development. *Journal of Monetary Economics, 22*(1), 3–42.
Mariz-Pérez, R. M., Teijeiro-Álvarez, M. M., & García-Álvarez, M. T. (2012). The importance of human capital in innovation: A system of indicators, soft computing in management and business economics. *Studies in Fuzziness and Soft Computing, 278*, 31–44.
Moncada-Paternò-Castello, P., Vezzani, A., Hervás, F., & Montresor, S (2014). *Financing R&D and innovation for corporate growth: What new evidence should policymakers know?* (European Commission Policy Brief).
Muizniece, L., & Cepilovs, A. (2017). Supporting university technology transfer—Struggles and barriers in Latvia. *Economic Thought and Practice Dubrovnik, 26*(1), 321–342.
O'sullivan, M. (2005). Finance and innovation. In J. Fagerberg, D Mowery, & R. Nelson (Eds.), *The Oxford handbook of innovation*. Oxford: Oxford University Press.
OECD. (2019a). *Database*. https://data.oecd.org/.
OECD. (2019b). *OECD economic surveys—Latvia*. https://www.oecd.org/economy/surveys/Latvia-2019-OECD-economic-survey-overview.pdf.
Official Journal of the European Union. (2006). *Decision No. 1639/2006/EC of the European Parliament and of the Council of 24 October 2006 establishing a competitiveness and innovation framework programme (2007 to 2013)* (OJ L 310/15, 9.11.2006). http://eur-lex.europa.eu/legal-content/EN/TXT/PDF/?uri=CELEX:32006D1639&from=EN.
Pegkas, P., Staikouras, C., & Tsamadias, C. (2019). Does research and development expenditure impact innovation? Evidence from the European Union countries. *Journal of Policy Modeling, 41*(5), 1005–1025.
Pestre, D. (2019). Environment and social innovation: Why technology never was the solution. In S. Lechevalier (Ed.), *Innovation beyond technology* (pp. 175–194). Berlin: Springer.

PIFIA. (2011). *Polish information and foreign investment agency*. R&D Sector in Poland.

Popp, D. (2019). *Environmental policy and innovation: A decade of research* (NBER Working Paper Series, No. 25631). National Bureau of Economic Research.

Prokop, V., Stejskal, J., & Mikušová Meričková, B. (2017). *Determinants of the number of patents in the Czech Republic*. Scientific papers of the University of Pardubice. Series D, Faculty of Economics and Administration. 41/2017.

Račić, D., Švarc, J., & Testa, G. (2018). *RIO country report 2017: Croatia, EUR 29155 EN*. Luxembourg: Publications Office of the European Union. ISBN 978-92-79-81200-2, JRC111260.

Rodríguez-Pose, A. (2001). Is R&D investment in lagging areas of Europe worthwhile? Theory and empirical evidence. *Papers in Regional Science, 80*(3), 275–295.

Roman, M. (2010). Regional efficiency of the knowledge economy in the new EU countries: The Romanian and Bulgarian case. *Romanian Journal of Regional Science, 4*(1), 33–53.

Romer, P. M. (1986). Increasing returns and long-run growth. *The Journal of Political Economy, 94*(5), 1002–1037.

Rumpf, G., Alexander, S., & del Rio, J.-C. (2017). *RIO country report 2016: Luxembourg; EUR 28506 EN*.

Ruphy, S. (2019). Public participation in the setting of research and innovation agenda: Virtues and challenges from a philosophical perspective. In S. Lechevalier (Ed.), *Innovation beyond technology* (pp. 243–261). Berlin: Springer.

Sharma, S., & Thomas, V. J. (2008). Inter-country R&D efficiency analysis: An application of data envelopment analysis. *Scientometrics, 76*(3), 483–501.

Simar, L., & Wilson, P. W. (2007). Estimation and inference in two-stage semi-parametric models of production processes. *Journal of Econometrics, 136*(1), 31–64.

Škrinjarić, T. (2020a). Re-examining sustainable development in Europe: A data envelopment approach. *International Journal of Environment and Sustainable Development, 19*(1), 72–108.

Škrinjarić, T. (2020b). R&D in Europe: Sector decomposition of sources of (in)efficiency. *Sustainability, 12*(1432), 1–20.

Stucki, T., Woerter, M., Arvanitis, S., Peneder, M., & Rammer, C. (2018). How different policy instruments affect green product innovation: A differentiated perspective. *Energy Policy, 114*, 245–261.

Swedish Ministry of Enterprise, Energy and Communications. (2015). *The Swedish innovation strategy*. https://www.government.se/contentassets/cbc9485d5a344672963225858118273b/the-swedish-innovation-strategy.

Swedish Research Barometer. (2017). *The Swedish research system in international comparison*. https://www.vr.se/download/18.5639980c162791bbfe69788d/1555334890011/Swedish-Research-Barometer_VR_2017.pdf.

Szarowska, I., & Žurkova, D. (2017). Public expenditure on research and development and its relationship with economic growth in the Czechia, Denmark and Slovakia. *Scientific Papers of the University of Pardubice—Series D, 24*(39), 211–222.

Todaro, M. P., & Smith, S. C. (2003). *Economic development* (8th ed.). Harlow, England: Pearson Education.

Trachuk, A., & Linder, N. (2019). Knowledge spillover effects: Impact of export learning effects on companies' innovative activities. In M. Wickham (Ed.), *Current issues in knowledge management* (pp. 1–16). London, UK: IntechOpen.

UN. (2019). *A framework for science, technology and innovation policy reviews harnessing innovation for sustainable development*. United Nations: Geneva.

Vinding, A. L. (2006). Absorptive capacity and innovative performance: A human capital approach. *Economics of Innovation and New Technology, 15*(4–5), Empirical Studies of Innovation in the Knowledge Driven Economy.

Weresa, M. A. (2018). Innovation Union initiative—An overview. In M. A. Weresa (Ed.), *Strengthening the knowledge base for innovation in the European Union*. Warsaw, Poland: Polish Scientific Publishers PWN.

Zabala-Iturriagagoitia, J. M., Voigt, P., Gutiérrez-Gracia, A., & Jiménez-Sáez, F. (2007). Regional innovation systems: How to assess performance. *Regional Studies, 41*(5), 661–672.

PART IV

Empirical Case Studies

CHAPTER 11

Middle-Technology Trap: The Case of Automotive Industry in Turkey

İbrahim Semih Akçomak and Serkan Bürken

11.1 Introduction

A group of engineers produced three functioning prototypes of the first domestic car in Turkey in 1961 through reverse engineering. The project *Devrim* ("Revolution") was a short-lived but commendable effort. Turkish automotive industry has developed extensively since. Turkey is now a production base for the global automotive industry hosting manufacturing operations of global brands such Ford, Toyota, and Renault. A large supplier network and research centers that started operating recently complement the manufacturing operations. Turkey manufactures approximately 1.7 million vehicles annually and ranks 15th

İ. S. Akçomak (✉)
Middle East Technical University, Ankara, Turkey
e-mail: akcomak@metu.edu.tr

S. Bürken
OSTIM Technical University, Ankara, Turkey
e-mail: serkan.burken@ostimteknik.edu.tr

J. J. M. Ferreira et al. (eds.), *Technological Innovation and International Competitiveness for Business Growth*, Palgrave Studies in Democracy, Innovation, and Entrepreneurship for Growth,
https://doi.org/10.1007/978-3-030-51995-7_11

in terms of car and 9th in terms of commercial vehicle production in the world (OICA, 2018). This chapter aims to investigate whether this manufacturing success created an impetus for technological learning and to what extent the sector has gained R&D and innovation capabilities.

Globalization creates various opportunities for developing countries many of which are constrained by weak Innovation Systems (IS) and strong Global Value Chains (GVCs). Technological learning occurs in a local "natural" interactive process where knowledge diffuses and actors learn. In most developing countries, IS produces innovations that are predominantly incremental because of capability and interaction problems (e.g., Alcorta & Peres, 1998; Pietrobelli & Rabellotti, 2011; Viotti, 2002). GVCs may provide an "artificial" global environment where domestic firms can learn through foreign interaction (e.g., Callegari, Massaroli Melo, & Carvalho, 2018; De Marchi, Giuliani, & Rabellotti, 2018; Gereffi, Humphrey, & Sturgeon, 2005; Gereffi & Kaplinsky, 2001; Morrison, Pietrobelli, & Rabellotti, 2008). During technological upgrading, however, developing countries may stuck in a middle-technology trap between a weak IS and strong GVCs.

Gaining capabilities that would help to build a strong IS, while integrating into the GVCs, is key to technological upgrading, which only a number of countries, such as South Korea, has achieved (Amendolagine, Presbitero, Rabellotti, & Sanfilippo, 2019; Lee, Szapiro, & Mao, 2018; Gehl Sampath & Vallejo, 2018). With particular to the automotive industry, many countries suffer from being trapped in a vicious circle where capability building and learning is not sufficient to tap into higher segments of the GVCs, which further limits learning and upgrading (Alcorta & Peres, 1998; Pietrobelli & Rabellotti, 2011). Literature on automotive industry argues that the capability gap between the country and the GVC, localization strategies and learning opportunities from foreigners (Gereffi et al., 2005) affect indigenous capability building in a weak IS (e.g., Albornoz & Yuguel, 2004; Brimble & Doner, 2007; Lim, Han, & Ito, 2013; Lorentzen, 2005; Motohashi & Yuan, 2010; Nam 2011; Özatağan, 2011; Pavlinek & Zenka, 2011). However, lead firms drive GVCs where tacit knowledge and strategic codified knowledge is very much centralized and local firms are generally allowed to learn and upgrade in particular directions, which seldom helps building a strong IS (e.g., Barnes & Morris, 2004; Pavlinek, Domanski, & Guzik, 2009; Pietrobelli & Rabellotti, 2011; Quadros, 2004). This chapter aims to investigate capability building process of the Turkish automotive industry under a state where weak IS interacts with strong GVC.

While the limiting forces of IS and GVC are discussed in the literature, treating the co-existence of weak IS and strong GVC forming middle-technology trap for developing countries is the first contribution of this chapter. We specifically refer to this situation as a "trap" since it is very difficult yet not impossible to escape from because of the vicious circle that the co-existing weak IS and strong GVC create. This chapter analyses Turkey as a case to illustrate this framework, further investigates why Turkey has fallen into a middle-technology trap and generates lessons for other developing countries on how technological progress could be achieved in the co-existence of weak IS and strong GVCs. Why and how questions necessitate a qualitative research design which aims to understand the actual mechanisms. The literature on the automotive industry mostly use econometric (e.g., Albornoz & Yuguel, 2004; Hu, Xiao, & Zhou, 2014, Motohashi & Yuan, 2010; Simona & Axele, 2012) and descriptive analysis (e.g., Catalan, 2010; Pavlinek, 2012). Qualitative designs (and/or mixed method designs) are rare (Contreras, Carrillo, & Alonso, 2012; Hassler, 2009; Nam, 2011; Zhao, Anand, & Mitchell, 2005). Thus, blending two qualitative research designs together with actual data this chapter also addresses a gap in the literature in the methodological sense.

Initial impetus after the 1980s led by the Joint Venture (JV) and Foreign Affiliate (FA) structure and extensive production support (and to some extent R&D and innovation) served to enhance learning in manufacturing and create a wide local supply chain in Turkey compatible with the export-led growth strategy. Strategic policy choices favoring short-term gains over long-term capability building created a homegrown state-industry agreement on gaining manufacturing capabilities, which created a vicious circle within the weak IS. On the other hand, increased integration to automotive GVCs with strong entry–exit barriers and predetermined profit margins (e.g., Sturgeon, Van Biesebroeck, & Gereffi, 2008) meant delegation. The interplay of these national and global forces created a middle-technology trap for the Turkish automotive industry.

To identify and understand how this occurred, we followed a mixed research design with both quantitative and qualitative analyses. Data is collected on the automotive sector-specific technology development projects from 1995 to 2011 using the Turkish Technology Development Foundation (TTGV) database. This unique longitudinal data enables the comparison of certain characteristics of the R&D projects over time. The quantitative part was complemented by two qualitative designs based on 13 detailed face-to-face interviews with beneficiary firms on the specifics of R&D and innovation process and 14 interviews with experts: R&D managers, CEOs of automotive firms, and industry professionals. The expert interviews are instrumental in presenting a micro to macro framework of the Turkish automotive industry. This novel research design presents information at the project, firm and macro levels providing internal and external validity and robustness to our findings.

Section 11.2 of this chapter briefly discusses learning in the IS and the GVCs. Section 11.3 describes the methodology with details of TTGV data and firm and expert interviews, followed by an overview of the Turkish automotive industry. Section 11.5 presents the primary results, emphasizing the three mechanisms that collectively created the middle-technology trap followed by a synthesis of the results. Policy implications contextualizing the Turkish automotive industry globally conclude the study.

11.2 Middle-Technology Trap on the Borders of IS and GVC

Development requires industrial upgrading and technological learning (Altenburg, Schmitz, & Stamm, 2008; Bell, 2006; Giuliani, Pietrobelli, & Rabellotti, 2005; Kim, 1999; Lee & Kim, 2001; Lema, Quadros, & Schmitz, 2015). Current technology, economy, and geography create opportunities for the developing world as well as local and global barriers for learning (Archibugi & Pietrobelli, 2003).

Technological learning occurs in IS where actors and interaction between actors are significant. IS provides a "natural" interactive process of learning where firms and formal and informal institutions blend (e.g., Lundvall, 1992). The system's inherent locality is conducive to technological learning but may also create lock-in situations (Bathelt, Malmberg, & Maskell, 2004; Narula, 2002). Contrariwise, GVCs provide an "artificial" organized global environment where local firms can learn from their foreign counterparts. However, GVCs may also hinder technological learning depending on how much knowledge the lead firms are willing to transfer. Lee et al. (2018), for instance, conclude that building a strong local IS is key to upgrading while integrating into the GVCs, which only some developing countries such as South Korea have accomplished. Gehl

Sampath and Vallejo (2018) and Amendolagine et al. (2019) further highlight the role of capabilities and a strong IS in benefiting from GVCs. Thus, developing countries may face a middle-technology trap on the borders of local natural systems such as the IS and global artificial organizations such as the GVCs.

11.2.1 Learning in IS

Innovation occurs in a socially embedded learning system where actors interact (Edquist, 1997; Freeman, 1995; Lundvall, 1992). Part of the extensive literature on IS pertains to developing countries (e.g., Arocena & Sutz, 1999; Edquist, 2001; Lundvall, Joseph, Chaminade, & Vang, 2009).

Pietrobelli and Rabellotti (2011) argue that innovation in developing countries is predominantly incremental and occurs in weak IS where external knowledge is important. To reach technological maturity, firms have to absorb new knowledge by creating significant new-to-the-firm knowledge that entails incremental steps (Bell, 1984; Ernst, Mytelka, & Ganiatsos, 1998). Countries that govern the learning-by-doing and learning-by-using phases can increase active learning where transition to an innovative environment is possible (Chiarini, Rapini, & Silva, 2017; Viotti, 2002).

Technological learning in developing countries occurs in weak IS where either the actors or their interactions are missing, which creates barriers for successful firms. Comparing India and Brazil, Guennif and Ramani (2012) argue that how actors in an IS perceive windows of opportunity determines divergence that reduces to forming new capabilities. In another comparative study of Brazil, China, and India, McMahon and Thorsteinsdóttir (2013) observe that the capabilities of local actors are pivotal for learning. Various studies show that actors in developing countries lack capability, and their interactions are low (Alcorta & Peres, 1998; Crespi & Zuniga, 2012; Dantas & Bell, 2011).

An important difference in IS between the developed and developing worlds is the quantity and quality of knowledge in the system. Limited technological knowledge of actors in the system and non-existent or weak interactions, interrupts the knowledge diffusion process. Introducing external knowledge in the system helps alleviate the knowledge diffusion process to enhance learning and technological upgrading (Carlsson, 2006; Fromhold-Eisebith, 2007; Iammarino, Padilla-Pérez, & von Tunzelmann,

2008). Thus, GVC is viewed as a form of learning through interaction with foreign firms (Lundvall et al., 2009; Pietrobelli & Rabellotti, 2011) compared with others such as learning from exporting (e.g., Wagner, 2007) and learning from spillovers as a result of Foreign Direct Investment (FDI) (e.g., Navaretti & Venables, 2004). Local firms can learn from foreign firms participating in GVCs and upgrade their technologies, thereby enhancing the variety and quality of knowledge in IS. When the government actively enables interactions and/or when local firms demand such soft policies, even upgrading of IS is a possibility.

Literature on automotive industry has emphasized the importance of capability building in weak IS where learning is difficult. Research on Argentina (Albornoz & Yuguel, 2004), South Africa (Lorentzen, 2005), Thailand (Brimble & Doner, 2007), South Korea (Oh & Rhee, 2010), Central and Eastern Europe (Pavlinek & Zenka, 2011), India (D'Costa, 2004; Lim et al., 2013), China (Motohashi & Yuan, 2010; Nam 2011; Zhao et al., 2005), and Turkey (Özatağan, 2011) illustrate that indigenous capability building is affected by capability gap, localization strategies under active and passive governments and various forms of learning opportunities from foreigner firms that the next subsection discusses.

Brimble and Doner (2007) highlight the role of weak university–industry linkages to explain why learning and technological upgrading in weak IS is difficult. Similarly, Albornoz and Yuguel (2004) report weak knowledge flows within the automotive network while Pamukçu and Sönmez (2012) and Sönmez (2013) suggest poor backward and forward linkages. Given the capability gap, successful learning is possible if local firms collaborate with foreign firms in an early stage of technology and product development, focus on niche products and actively demand climbing the value chain (D'Costa, 2004; Karabag, Tuncay-Celikel, & Berggren, 2011; Lim et al., 2013; Oh & Rhee, 2010; Okada, 2004; Pavlinek, 2012; Ray & Ray, 2011).

Finally, weak IS demands a more active government policy. While the government in developed countries focuses on fixing systemic failures, developing countries have to actively create the system. Barnes and Kaplinsky (2000) for South Africa, Park (2003) for South Korea, Catalan (2010) for South Korea and Spain, Depner and Bathelt (2005), Chu (2011) and Hu et al. (2014) for China show that active government policy (i.e., localization strategies, active JV policy, late liberalization, policy experimentation, creating forced competition, active deregulation) is an important determinant of successful learning and approaching higher value-added segments of the GVC.

11.2.2 Learning in GVC

Essentially, the concept of GVCs is related to how global production is organized. Technological advancement and a favorable political climate enabled large firms to divide the production process and distribute the pieces geographically based on cost and quality standards. Multinational Corporations (MNC) view this vertically integrated and fragmented production as a value chain where stages of production is performed in a network of firms globally (Gereffi et al., 2005; Gereffi & Kaplinsky, 2001; Pietrobelli & Rabellotti, 2007). This governance of global production provides various technological learning opportunities for developing countries (Morrison et al., 2008).

GVC may transfer technical and managerial knowledge to local firms. When such knowledge is combined with local capabilities, developing countries can climb the value ladder (Amendolagine et al., 2019; Pietrobelli & Rabellotti, 2007). Such development entails a significant amount of technological learning and capability building. When GVC meets a fairly developed IS, firms can obtain new higher value-added skills such as design and R&D and can even learn to tap into new value chains (Humphrey & Schmitz, 2002; Pietrobelli & Rabellotti, 2011).

Gereffi et al. (2005) list various forms of learning mechanisms in GVCs. Developing countries can access global markets via GVCs to leverage the learning effects from exporting. For instance, Kumar and Subrahmanya (2010) show that the subcontracting relations of Indian firms with MNCs can help firms to upgrade technology. Meeting standards, regulations, and technical specifications of the lead firms is an important learning mechanism that forces firms to adopt certain skills just to tap into the value chains. Okada (2004), Pavlinek et al. (2009), Motohashi and Yuan (2010), and Oh and Rhee (2010) identify this channel of learning in the automotive industry for various countries. Another form of learning is via technical and managerial knowledge transfer. This can be a by-product of interactions or can be deliberately organized by the lead firm. Training and turnover of key employees can also help local firms to learn from the lead firms in the GVC. For instance, Contreras et al. (2012) show that the spin-off process of locally established lead firms in Mexico can result in the emergence of knowledge-intensive firms within the automotive supply chain. By transferring complex manufacturing, managerial, and knowledge-related tasks, GVCs can boost the development process, assuming that firms learn from and/or imitate their counterparts and that knowledge spreads to local firms through spillovers (e.g., Dutrenit & Vera-Cruz, 2005). The idea of development enhancing GVC is based on the assumption that local firms and supplier industry learn from the subsidiaries, FAs, and JVs to the extent of creating backward and forward linkages (Pavlinek, 2018).

Automotive industry is an example of GVCs with complex and dynamic interactions. Sturgeon et al. (2008) define the industry as global in codified knowledge (i.e., production) but local in tacit knowledge (i.e., design and R&D). Though technical (and even R&D) centers of lead firms are located in developing countries such as China, core design, R&D, and engineering remain centralized. After completing conceptual design and modularization, suppliers that meet technical specifications are integrated into the value chain. Pietrobelli and Rabellotti (2011) refer to GVCs in the automotive sector as "modular chains" where capable suppliers produce technical modular parts under highly complex codified transactions. Usually, lead firms readily provide specs and force the suppliers to commit to stringent technical specifications and standards (Barnes & Morris, 2004; Hassler, 2009; Nam, 2012; Pavlinek, 2012; Pavlinek et al., 2009; Simona & Axele, 2012). To fulfill the standards, suppliers need to learn and acquire certain technological and managerial skills. Automotive GVCs are considered as captive and quasi-hierarchical value chains in which lead firms drive the value chain and decide whom to support and what to produce (Gereffi et al., 2005; Nam, 2011; Pavlinek & Zenka, 2011). Such conceptualizations define a well-structured value chain driven by lead firms where tacit knowledge is centralized and codified knowledge is decentralized only if certain standards and specifications are met.

The process of learning and technological upgrading that enables climbing the value ladder in a well-structured GVC seldom includes active involvement of the lead firms. As in Argentina (Albornoz & Yuguel, 2004), Brazil (Quadros, 2004), Central and Eastern Europe (Pavlinek et al., 2009; Pavlinek & Zenka, 2011), South Africa (Barnes & Morris, 2004; Lorentzen, 2005), Thailand (Brimble & Doner, 2007), Turkey (Özatağan, 2011) and even in the JV case of China (Nam, 2011, 2012), suppliers and local firms upgrade to an extent but mostly in a particular direction to become a "technology colony" (Barnes & Morris,

2004). Learning and technological upgrading at such a stage is possible depending on the firms' capability and the state of IS in the developing countries (Pietrobelli & Rabellotti, 2011), active government policy such as in China (Chu, 2011; Liu & Dicken, 2006) and South Korea (Catalan, 2010; Park, 2003) and ownership of the technology (Lorentzen, 2005).

11.2.3 Middle-Technology Trap

We conceptualize middle-technology trap in a narrative where IS meets GVC (e.g., Pietrobelli & Rabellotti, 2011). To our knowledge, the term was initially used by Robert Wade to refer to situations where firms in middle-income countries are stuck in low value-added segments of the global production chain (Wade, 2010). A variation of the concept "middle innovation trap" has recently been used to highlight the role of innovation capability to explain the source of middle-income trap (Lee, 2017).

Weak IS with capability and interaction problems limits technological learning in developing countries. Local firms engage in GVCs to create new learning opportunities but face strong reluctance from the foreign lead. Thus, firms in developing countries are internally (i.e., the weak IS pulls down such firms to average), as well as externally (i.e., pushed away by the GVCs) constrained. Literature on the automotive industry reports that GVCs delegate roles to developing countries and allow learning to an extent that further supports the position of the lead firms in GVCs (Barnes & Morris, 2004; Brimble & Doner 2007; Contreras et al., 2012; Nam, 2011, 2012; Okada, 2004; Pavlinek & Zenka, 2011; Petison & Johri, 2008). We argue that developing countries can be trapped in producing middle-technology products from which it is difficult yet not impossible to escape because a weak IS coupled with strong GVCs create a vicious circle.

Thus, a strong middle-technology trap fosters on the borders of IS and GVC where both restrict technological learning opportunities. The concept is related to transition from a passive by-product "doing-based" learning to a more active "non-doing-based" learning where firms deliberately invest in technological upgrading (Bell, 1984). A similar transition occurs from active learning to building innovation capabilities (Viotti, 2002), but most developing countries are trapped between the two.

11.3 Methodology

We employ a mixed-methods research approach that includes both quantitative and qualitative analyses. The quantitative part is based on TTGV data that provides information at the project level. Detailed information on technology development at the firm level is gathered by conducting face-to-face semi-structured interviews. Expert interviews assess the position of Turkish automotive industry globally. Variety within the selected firms and experts is ensured for internal validity and robustness (e.g., Yin, 2003). We follow an explanatory sequential design where the qualitative part is employed to further interpret and contextualize the findings of the quantitative part (Creswell & Plano Clark, 2011). Figure 11.1 depicts the research design.

There are two primary advantages to using mixed-methods research designs. First, mixed-methods research designs provide complementarity. In our setting, TTGV data provides compelling evidence that proved instrumental in reaching interim findings but also provided space for further analysis. The two case study designs provide information on the aspects that TTGV data could not corroborate, thereby proving complementary in nature. The second advantage of using mixed-methods research design is triangulation. The three research designs provide information at the project, firm, and expert levels. The main findings and three mechanisms identified are mostly validated at all three levels that contributed to the novelty of this research.

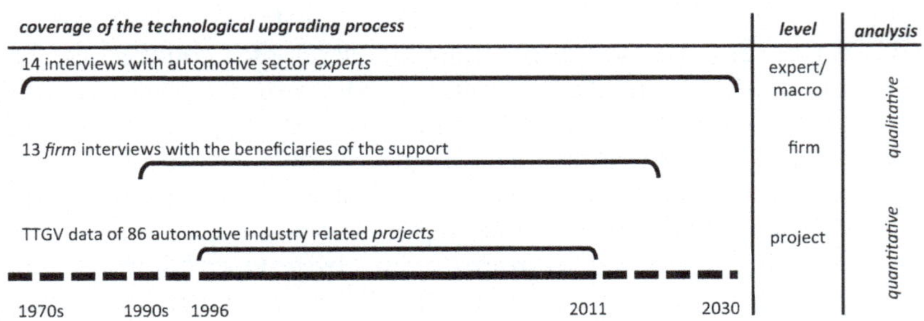

Fig. 11.1 Research methodology

11.3.1 TTGV Data

Technology Development Foundation (the Turkish acronym being TTGV) was founded as a non-profit organization in 1991 to support technological development by providing seed capital and R&D funds to Turkish industrial firms.

TTGV's funding is the antecedent of all R&D support mechanisms in Turkey. The data set covers the entire R&D support period of Turkey, starting from the early 1990s, thereby enabling comparisons over time. Data on automotive projects is sourced from the Technology Development Support Program of TTGV that provides R&D loans of up to one million US dollars for industrial firms. The repayment commences one year after the project is officially completed and continues for three years. By 2011, there were approximately 2400 project applications and 938 of these were supported. The total amount of contracted support under this scheme was approximately 320 million US dollars. With the development of firm and entrepreneurship support programs in TUBITAK by 2010, TTGV support gradually turned inconsequential and eventually stopped by 2012. Previous research has showed that TTGV support was successful in creating awareness for R&D and innovation (Özçelik & Taymaz, 2008).

The project reports detail the R&D activities provided by the performer firm that seeks approval from the field committee members who evaluate the projects. Within approximately 500 projects that may be related to automotive, 102 projects were identified by carefully examining the fact sheets and the evaluation reports. However, due to missing information, only 86 projects were analyzed. The first project was initiated in 1996. There were, in total, 86 projects on automotive till 2011. Our data set comprises information on firm characteristics (size, capital structure, location, etc.) and project characteristics (budget, involvement in design, technology field, target markets, targeted automotive component, innovation level, etc.). Table 11.1 summarizes these projects' information.

Despite the program being primarily aimed at increasing the capability of the SMEs, big firms, OEMs, and JVs also benefitted from the R&D support. Table 11.1 shows that approximately 60% of automotive projects are initiated by SMEs. Most firms are suppliers, but OEMs and JVs constitute one-fourth of the project applicants. Beneficiaries are mostly domestic, have quality certificates such as the ISO9001 and ISO16949 and are involved in R&D activities before applying to TTGV. The firms

Table 11.1 Summary of TTGV automotive projects, 1996–2011

SMEs	52	(0.60)
Has R&D department?	57	(0.66)
Applications by domestic firms	73	(0.85)
Applications from Doğu Marmara region	50	(0.58)
Firms having quality certificates (ISO9001; ISO16949 etc.)**	67	(0.81)
Firms that are involved in R&D activities before application	61	(0.71)
Core business of applicants		
OEMs and JVs	19	(0.22)
Auto-suppliers	53	(0.62)
Engineering and consulting firms	8	(0.09)
Core business other than automotive	6	(0.07)
Projects by auto-component classification		
Body & body equipment	30	(0.35)
Power transmission	13	(0.15)
Electronic component	1	(0.01)
Safety component	1	(0.01)
Engine	6	(0.07)
Whole vehicle	16	(0.19)
Others	19	(0.22)

Note The numbers in parentheses are the percentages (over 86 projects). ** indicates that the percentages are calculated over 83 projects because of data availability

are generally located in the Doğu Marmara Region (Bursa, Istanbul, Gebze and Izmit), which is the heart of the Turkish automotive industry.

We additionally matched each R&D project to an automobile component to verify whether over time there is an inclination toward contemporary technologies such as safety technologies, electronics component, software, engine, etc., rather than traditional technologies such as body and body equipment. Table 11.1 shows that over the years, most project applications involved traditional technologies. Approximately, one-third of all project applications were on body and body equipment. Only 8 projects (i.e., approximately one-tenth of all applications) in the whole period were on electronics, safety component, and engines. This subtly indicates toward the technological sophistication level of the Turkish automotive industry.

11.3.2 Firm and Expert Interviews

Two separate designs are used to cross-validate the findings of the TTGV data. In both designs, we presented the interviewee brief information regarding the research project but did not specifically mention the interim results obtained from the TTGV data.

The qualitative part focuses on three aspects. First, firms are asked to evaluate their last five R&D projects to understand the evolution of R&D content. The interviews are tailored to investigate whether the R&D activities of firms are based on more design-oriented contemporary automotive technologies. Second, we focus on the content of innovation and decision-making in commercialization. Finally, the impact of foreign presence on decision-making in domestic firms is examined. The presence of design-oriented R&D activities in contemporary technologies in which the decision-making power on commercialization activities is retained by domestic firms is perceived as a sign of increased technological sophistication.

Firm interviews aim to collect detailed information regarding the R&D context (content of R&D, novelty, OEM presence in decision-making, etc.), R&D output (customers, decision-making in commercialization, etc.) and firm strategy on R&D and innovation. 15 firms that benefitted from the TTGV support mechanism were selected on the basis of size, location, capital structure (domestic, JV, FA), and core competencies (suppliers, design, and engineering firms, etc.). 13 of these firms responded our interview request (5 SMEs, 6 big firms, 1 JV, and 1 FA). The face-to-face semi-structured interviews with the R&D managers (or top-level managers) of these firms lasted for one and a half hours on average. The firms vary in terms of size, location, capital structure, core competency, and type of end-product. Table 11.6 in the appendix summarizes information regarding the selected firms.

To complement the project and firm level information, we conducted interviews with experts to gather information on the development of the Turkish automotive industry, its position in the GVC and the future of the industry with reference to R&D and innovation activities. 20 names were initially drafted of which 14 responded. Table 11.7 in the appendix presents the general characteristics of the selected 14 experts. Interviews averaged 45 minutes. Interviewees have either previously worked in automotive firms or automotive NGOs or still actively work in automotive firms and organizations. The backgrounds of the experts vary in terms of job status (e.g., managerial position), past and current work experience (from production, engineering, and design activities to top-level management), and background (policy-makers, consultants, R&D managers, etc.).

11.4 Turkish Automotive Industry at a Glance

In the 1960s closed economy, infrastructural limitations, political, and bureaucratic problems as well as shortage of physical, human, and intellectual capital prevented industry formation. Before the 1960s, only minor attempts were made such as Ford assembling trucks by 1930s, the Otomarsan assembling buses, and Turk Tractor assembling tractors by 1950s in very small quantities. Traces of the first organized governmental intervention can be located in the five-year development plans (DP). The import substitution, credits to manufacturing industry, ban on bus imports (1963–1967 DP), creating national automotive industry and especially domestic supply industry (1968–1972 DP), increasing scale and capacity usage ratios (1973–1977 DP) and various other policies were emphasized in DPs, most of which were rarely implemented. Unlike other developing countries such as Argentina, China, South Africa, and South Korea, the government did not even administer a local-content ratio. Most strategies, targets, and policies remained on paper except the import substitution.

The government supported the industry by subsidizing business groups to foster (automotive specific) capital accumulation. Backed by the import substitution policies, this process led to the first organized attempts at production by the late 1960s and the emergence of JVs such as Tofaş-Fiat and Oyak-Renault in the early 1970s. By investing and accumulating financial, physical, and human capital, the import substitution period from 1960s to 1980s attempted to build capabilities. By mid-1980s, Turkey started implementing export-oriented policies aimed at establishing a fully functioning market economy. The industry reached a commendable level of capital accumulation in the 1990s, which together with increased investment in assembly production meant expertise in manufacturing. The customs union with the European Union in 1996 tested ability to survive in global competition. The industry passed this test by obtaining licenses from foreigners to produce cars that can sell immensely in the domestic market and even exported at a later stage (e.g., Fiat-Tempra produced by Tofaş-Fiat). In the last 40 years, Turkish share in global vehicle production rose from a mere 0.1% to approximately 1.8%.

Table 11.2 depicts the current state of the Turkish automotive industry. Three phases of production can be observed from the table: 1960s assembly of trucks, busses, midi-busses and tractors; 1970s creation of JVs Oyak-Renault and Tofas-Fiat that produced passenger cars; and the establishment of fully or partially foreign-owned production facilities of Ford, Honda, Hyundai, and Toyota in the second-half of the 1990s. In 2018, a total of 1.58 million vehicles were produced in Turkey while the maximum production was achieved in 2017 with 1.75 million units. The utilization rate in 2018 in passenger car producers is 81% that is higher than non-passenger vehicle producers (73%). 64% of total production are passenger cars and 27% are pick-ups. The automotive industry exports reach 21.9 billion US dollars in 2018, which is approximately 13% of Turkey's total exports. The firms in Table 11.2 altogether employ approximately 52,000 employees, of which 12% are engineers. The ratio of engineers in the total workforce reached a maximum of 14% in 2014 and declines since then.

The average foreign ownership in non-passenger automotive production industry is 33%. There are 9 producers, 4 of which are fully domestically owned (Hattat Traktor, Karsan, Otokar, and TEMSA). Considering only foreign companies, average foreign ownership in non-passenger automotive industry is 73%. There are six passenger car producers with average foreign ownership of 66%. The passenger car industry is concentrated in the Marmara Region (Bursa, Kocaeli and Sakarya), whereas the non-passenger automotive industry is more distributed since production occurs in various cities such as Aksaray, Ankara, Adana, Eskisehir, and Kocaeli.

11.5 Results

The analyses start by considering 6 indicators that reflect the quality of the R&D projects: (a) R&D content (whether the R&D involves modeling and design activities), (b) auto-component the project addresses (traditional vs. contemporary), (c) the users of the R&D results (OEMs & JVs, domestic firms), (d) market orientation of the projects (domestic vs. abroad), (e) type of intended innovative activity (process, product, or both), and (f) intended level of innovation (new to the firm, country, world). To observe development over time, TTGV data is divided into

Table 11.2 The current state of automotive industry in Turkey

Firms	*Production place and starting year of production*	*License*	*Ratio of foreign capital (%)*	*Type(s) of vehicles produced*	*Total production capacity (2018)*	*Total production (2018)*
Anadolu Isuzu Otomotiv Sanayi	Kocaeli—1966	ISUZU	29.74	Truck, Pick-up, Bus, Mini-Bus	19,012	4461
Ford Otosan	Eskişehir—1983 Gölcük/Kocaeli—2001 Yeniköy/Kocaeli—2014	Ford	41.04	Passenger Car, Truck, Pick-up, Mini-bus	455,000	373,702
Hattat Traktör	Tekirdağ—2002	Valtra, Hattat	0.00	Tractor	25,000	3572
Honda Türkiye	Kocaeli—1997	Honda Motor Europe Ltd.	100.00	Passenger Car	50,000	38,319
Hyundai Assan	Kocaeli—1997	Hyundai Motor Company	70.00	Passenger Car	245,000	203,000
Karsan	Bursa—1966	Hyundai Motor Company, Breda Menarini Bus	0.00	Pick-up, Bus, Mini-bus, Midi-bus	52,225	6724
M.A.N. Türkiye	Ankara—1966	MAN Truck and Bus AG	99.90	Bus	2400	2558
Mercedes Benz Turk	Istanbul—1968 Aksaray—1985	Mercedes Benz	84.99	Truck, Bus	22,000	20,856
Otokar	Sakarya—1963	Land Rover, Fruehauf	0.00	Pick-up, Bus, Truck, Midi-bus	10,300	2369
OYAK Renault	Bursa—1971	Renault	51.00	Passenger Car	375,000	336,778
TEMSA Global	Adana—1987	TEMSA	0.00	Truck, Bus, Midi-bus	10,500	2549
TOFAŞ	Bursa—1971	Fiat	37.80	Passenger Car	450,000	301,750
Toyota	Sakarya—1994	Toyota	100.00	Passenger Car	280,000	257,084

Firms	*Production place and starting year of production*	*License*	*Ratio of foreign capital (%)*	*Type(s) of vehicles produced*	*Total production capacity (2018)*	*Total production (2018)*
Türk Traktör	Ankara—1954 Sakarya—2014	New Holland	37.50	Tractor	50,000	34,114

Source Automotive Manufacturers' Association (OSD) in Turkey. Statistics in 2018 and 2019 http://www.osd.org.tr/sites/1/upload/files/2018_YILLIK-3299.pdf

2 sub-periods. The first period (1996–2003) characterizes the strengthening of the manufacturing capabilities with the first examples of R&D activities. In this period, TTGV supports were instrumental in not only funding the industrial automotive R&D but also in improving the image of the participants since obtaining funding from TTGV signaled capability. The latter (2004–2011) characterizes a period where the number of automotive R&D performers increase and funding opportunities expand.

Table 11.3 summarizes the results. Since more projects are available in the second period, we present absolute numbers as well as column percentage shares. Intended level of innovation that reflects novelty does not display a clear pattern. In the entire 16-year period, only 5 projects can be classified as new-to-the-world. 3 of these belong to foreign OEMs and JVs. Initially, the R&D projects predominantly aimed at product innovation while in the second period, process as well as product innovations were in focus. Process innovations are considered as a trigger of productivity increase. In this manner, Turkish automotive R&D projects are more inclined toward augmenting productivity at the expense of increasing product variety. This result is inline with earlier findings reporting that process upgrading is integral to integrating with GVCs while product upgrading is mostly limited (Okada, 2004; Pavlinek & Zenka, 2011; Simona & Axele, 2012).

Considering the content of R&D projects, we assessed the presence of design-oriented and market-signaled R&D activities independent of foreign partners. Design and design confirmation processes are considered as significant determinants of technological capability (Barnes & Morris, 2004; Nam, 2012; Ray & Ray, 2011). The project may either involve domestic efforts of modeling, design and design verification or such activities can be in the form of readily available specs, knowhow and technology that are provided by the foreigners. Table 11.3 indicates design components in almost all projects. However, performers are increasingly inclined to obtain know-how from abroad in the second period compared to the first. This pattern became more apparent after the global crisis; more than 40% of the R&D projects used ready specs and know-how sourced from OEMs and JVs. Moreover, approximately 60% of automotive R&D projects are intended for foreign OEMs and JVs. This signifies foreign dependency that may affect strategic R&D and commercialization decisions of domestic firms.

Table 11.3 R&D, innovation and technology in automotive projects, 1996–2011

	1996–2003	*Column %*	*2004–2011*	*Column %*	*Row total*
R&D content					
modelling, design and design verification (domestic)	12	0.75	45	0.64	57
know-how, specs and technology transfer from abroad	3	0.19	23	0.33	26
no design activity	1	0.06	2	0.03	3
Type of intended innovation					
process	1	0.06	12	0.17	13
product	15	0.94	42	0.60	57
process and product	0	0.00	16	0.23	16
Intended level of innovation					
new to the firm	5	0.31	32	0.46	37
new to the country	11	0.69	33	0.47	44
at the world frontier	0	0.00	5	0.07	5
Projects by auto-component classification					
traditional	11	0.69	48	0.69	59
contemporary	4	0.25	22	0.31	26
both	1	0.06	0	0.00	1
Intended use of the R&D output					
OEMs and JVs	10	0.63	40	0.57	50
other (end users, subcontractors, firms, etc.)	6	0.38	30	0.43	36
Market orientation of projects					
domestic	4	0.25	13	0.19	17
abroad	5	0.31	8	0.1[illegible]	13
domestic and abroad	6	0.38	48	0.69	54

Note columns 1, 3, and 5 present the project numbers in two different time periods and the row total. Columns 2 and 4 present the column percentages such that the column sum of each indicator panel sum to 1.00

Matching each R&D project to an automotive component can show how contemporary the R&D projects are. 70 sub-groups of automotive components belong to 2 main groups: (i) contemporary—electric and electronic component, safety component, engine, and emerging engine technologies such as recyclability and telematics and (ii) traditional—body, body equipment, and power transmission technologies. As

Table 11.3 shows, almost 70% of the automotive R&D projects are in traditional components and there is no difference between the two periods.

Two important findings emerge from the TTGV data. First there is no significant difference in the projects between the two time periods regarding R&D content and output, auto-component technology and innovation type and level. Project portfolio around 2010 resembles the project portfolio around 2000. Second, Turkish automotive firms depend on global OEMs and lead firms in GVC on strategic R&D and innovation decisions. Automotive R&D in Turkey is usually sustained with the provision of specs from foreigners that may restrict domestic R&D efforts to traditional technologies and components with less value-added.

Why Turkish automotive R&D efforts are stuck in low value-added components and the role of foreign presence in explaining this can be comprehensively understood by exploring the role of Turkey in automotive GVCs. Current global automotive industry has a well-organized structure with high entry/exit barriers and pre-determined profit margins that are consolidated by lead firms in GVCs, allowing little space for latecomers such as Turkey. *INT1* describes the current state referring to the value chain and the role of JVs in Turkey: "*A branded car is manufactured at a cost of 75 percent of its sale price. JV has rights to sell it to a dealer or export it with 3-5 percent margin. Main branch of the JV is determining what part of the production is sold abroad and what part will remain inside. JV has rights to sell the part that is left for the domestic market with a margin of extra 12 percent. For a car sold in domestic market, the profit margin for JV is reaching nearly to 17 percent. The last 8 percent is acquired by the dealer. The growth of domestic market refers more value-added for JVs.*"

In such a well-organized scheme, foreign firms establish branches in developing countries mainly for reasons of exploitation of the domestic market and manufacturing (e.g., Barnes & Morris, 2004; Brimble & Doner, 2007; Contreras et al., 2012; Liu & Dicken, 2006; Nam, 2011; Okada, 2004). Interviewees agree that Turkey gained competence in manufacturing over the years (see also Table 11.5 in Sect. 11.6). For instance, *INT3* argued that "*With about 50 years of experience, we learned how to produce efficiently in good quality, how to implement production methods and produce a ready-made product.*" In a similar manner *INT7* argues that "*Reaching a certain level of intellectual capital has been an accumulated process during the past 50 years. Turkey has reached this level by manufacturing. Now, manufacturing has reached a certain level of maturity. On tier 2 (supplier industry), quality, planning and lean manufacturing is well-developed. Before 2000, no one was expecting this kind of development.*" *INT8* emphasizes further that Turkey gained capabilities primarily on manufacturing but not on technology development. "*Turkey is highly capable of automobile mass manufacturing. But this is the least profitable part. Government frequently refers to the association between the automotive industry and export performance. However, we are manufacturing cars without absorbing R&D and developing technology.*"

Our initial analysis leads us to argue that Turkey has become an excellent manufacturing center but Turkish automotive R&D as well as production efforts are stuck in low value-added components, which is very difficult to recover from. We identify three mechanisms to further explain how this has occurred. (1) The delegated manufacturing role within the GVC has been accepted by the governments for job creation and export revenue, which shapes the content of R&D activities and binds them to incremental innovations that further strengthens the position of lead firms; (2) lack of indigenous electronics and/or ICT sector that complements the automotive sector; (3) foreign presence enhances technological upgrading at a decreasing rate and saturates well below the frontier.

11.5.1 Automotive Manufacturing as a Delegated Role

Being part of GVCs may create an industry with stable employment and export prospects but can hinder further development of the industry as in the case of Turkey. Especially for developing countries, manufacturing or process upgrading is a delegation problem rather than a choice *INT7* illustrates this emphatically, stating "*Common transport is still on four wheels. Boundary conditions are certain and in this well-organized industry, corners are held by big players. The needs are determined and the prices are fixed. Turkey has accepted the rules that the western counterparts has established and has no power to change them. Developed countries are continuously changing and developing these rules in order to protect their leadership.*"

Neither the government nor the firms and NGOs could design strategies and policy tools transforming manufacturing capabilities to innovation capabilities. Especially in the 1990s, the governments left the playing field void which strengthened the position of lead firms in the GVCs and tied Turkish firms to the lower segments of value chain. The governments could have retaliated, but this delegated position in the GVC was accepted because the automotive industry created jobs and export revenue that had political connotations especially in the 1990s where both elections and economic crises were frequent. We argue that this delegated role shapes the content of R&D and innovation that Turkish firms conduct.

Approximately half of the firms in the TTGV sample indicated that their products involve solely traditional technologies and little R&D effort has been invested in producing knowledge at the world frontier. Knowing why firms perform R&D, how R&D process is initiated, and how much decision-making power firms have on commercialization is vital to assess the potential for further development. Firms perform R&D either for cost reduction (i.e., improving production processes) or to achieve higher quality or produce new (and niche) products. As a quality check, we specifically seek concept design and design confirmation processes.

The R&D and innovation processes in Turkish automotive firms are not nurtured by basic and experimental R&D accompanying design and design confirmation processes. Most ideas emerge from foreign partners/firms or outsourcers. Incremental R&D and innovation for survival are common elements. To illustrate further, *INT3* argued that the source of innovation is not basic or experimental R&D that is an important handicap for the industry's further growth. "*Turkish firms are performing R&D for survival. Turkish firms are investing on projects involving lower risks…one of the weakest side of the innovation system is that experimental R&D is not supported…Turkey also seems weak in basic research. In contrast, newly developed countries such as Taiwan are highly specialized in generic and advanced contemporary technologies such as nanotechnology and in basic sciences.*" If not basic and experimental R&D, what is the source of R&D in the Turkish automotive industry?

The first step toward answering this is locating the source of ideas i.e., whether R&D activities are initiated by market signals or by (direct commissioning of) foreign firms, JVs, and FAs. Using market signals is an important phase of nurturing concept design capabilities unless the domestic firm is assigned for this process by the foreign lead. As *INT1* puts it, "*design and design confirmation are the most eminent processes of automotive manufacturing today. If you have presence in design, you take royalty and as a result, higher positions in the GVC.*" *INT8* emphasizes this, stating "*Designing concepts requires collecting data from the field—signals from markets, passengers, car users, dealers, manufacturers,* etc., *so that you are able to design brand new models accompanying the needs of the stakeholders. Data help you design new concepts. However, developing countries such as Turkey are skipping this phase since the designs have been readily served by JVs. Without market analysis, it is impossible to develop concepts.*" *INT5* similarly argues that design and innovation capabilities are of instrumental in the automotive industry, "*Given the ease of reaching capital, investment, technology and resources today, design and innovation are of vital importance to provide competency in the global industry.*"

Though data collection for concept design and design confirmation processes are vital for gaining design and innovation capabilities, *INT8* argues that most Turkish firms are far from reaching such understanding. "*We lack in design and design confirmation. We cannot develop concepts maybe because the industry is highly dependent on JVs. We are not even developing engine or power transmission.*" *INT3* also emphasizes the significance of designing concepts rather than designing whole vehicles (or components). Interviewers usually associate concept designs with a sophisticated phase of technological development that is nurtured by market signals. Firm interviews further corroborate this finding. Table 11.4 shows that firms seldom adopt signals from the market but rather depend on foreign partners and outsourcers.

Tables 11.2 and 11.3 (TTGV data), Table 11.4 (firm interviews), and quotes from expert interviews show that design and design confirmation processes are usually skipped because firms use ready specs made available by foreigners. Most firms rely on signals (and mostly delegation) from the outsourcers to determine the technological area and content of R&D activities. Only one firm in the interviews (*BIG1*) states that they completely rely on market signals to conduct R&D. Some firms use mixed R&D strategies where the original idea either comes from the JV, OEM, FA, or the market. Thus, Turkish firms (domestic, FA, or JV) are missing a vital step in routine formation for developing technology. This finding parallels the findings of Ölmezoğulları (2011), citing a lock-in situation in Turkey on co-designing activities. Özatağan (2011) also argues that using ready specs and neglecting the concept design phase makes the performing firm more dependent on the lead firms in GVC. The only exceptions to this rule are large firms (*BIG1*, *BIG4* and *BIG5*, see Table 11.4) that conduct R&D in niche technologies apart from their core areas.

In conclusion, the delegated role of being a manufacturing center shapes the main characteristics of R&D and innovation. Turkish firms

Table 11.4 Summary results of the firm interviews: R&D content, R&D output and innovation

Firm	*Core specialization*	*Core technology*	*How R&D projects are initiated?*	*Product/process innovation*	*Ready specs from foreigners*	*Commercialization decision*	*Projects in niche or sophisticated products*	*Innovation level*	*Diversified core competency?*	*Technological sophistication*
SME1	Design and engineering firm of a domestic OEM	Contemporary	Affiliated OEM and market signals	Product	Yes	Dependent on OEM	Yes	National	Yes	Yes
SME2	Supplier	Traditional	Outsourcer	Both	Yes	Dependent on OEM	No	Firm	No	No
SME3	Supplier	Traditional	Outsourcer	Both	Yes	Dependent on OEM	Yes	Firm	Failed	No
SME4	Supplier	Traditional	Outsourcer	Both	Yes	Dependent on OEM	Yes	Firm	No	Yes (due to its phase of being a co-designer)
SME5	Supplier	Traditional	Outsourcer	Product	Yes	Dependent on OEM	No	Firm	No	No
Procurer BIG1	Engineering firm/assembly line procurer for global OEMs	Contemporary	Outsourcer and market signals	Both	Yes (niche projects—No)	Dependent on OEM	Yes	National	Yes	Yes
BIG2	Supplier	Traditional	Outsourcer	Both	Yes	Dependent on OEM	Yes	Firm	No	No
BIG3	Supplier	Traditional	Outsourcer	Both	Yes	Dependent on OEM	No	National	Failed	No
BIG4	End product manufacturer	Contemporary	Market signals	Product	Yes (niche projects—No)	Independent	Yes	National/international	Yes	Yes

Firm	*Core specialization*	*Core technology*	*How R&D projects are initiated?*	*Product/process innovation*	*Ready specs from foreigners*	*Commercialization decision*	*Projects in niche or sophisticated products*	*Innovation level*	*Diversified core competency?*	*Technological sophistication*
BIG5	Supplier/end product manufacturer	Traditional/contemporary	Outsourcer and market signals	Both	Yes (niche projects—No)	Dependent (for niche projects—independent)	Yes	National	Yes	Yes
BIG6	Supplier	Traditional/contemporary	Outsourcer and market signals	Both	Yes	Semi-Dependent	Yes	National	Yes	Yes
FA1	Supplier of an affiliated MNE	Traditional/contemporary	Affiliated MNE	Both	Yes	Dependent on headquarter	NA	National	No	No
JV1	Supplier of an affiliated MNE	Traditional/contemporary	Affiliated MNE and firm's own initiative	Both	Yes	Dependent on headquarter	NA	National	Yes	Yes

conduct R&D and innovation for survival, hardly participate in basic and experimental R&D and mostly skip concept design and design confirmation processes. These findings support literature on automotive industry in India (Okada, 2004), South Africa (Barnes & Morris, 2004), Thailand (Brimble & Doner, 2007; Hassler, 2009), Central and Eastern Europe (Pavlinek, 2012; Pavlinek et al., 2009), and on automotive JVs in China (Nam, 2012).

11.5.2 Lack of Complementarities

The reason for the Turkish automotive industry's inability to ascend the value ladder can be the accompanying developments in the electronics industry. *INT11* cites the lack of physical infrastructure, qualified workforce, and intellectual capital as the main reasons behind Turkey's failure to establish a strong electronics industry. "*By 1980s, there was a critical threshold; unfortunately, privatization had slowed down the national efforts towards electronics. We speeded up in automotive but Turkish electronics declined. I strongly think that the failure in the adoption of electronics technologies in automotive has decreased the value-added being created in national automotive industry, particularly the suppliers'. This has also impeded the system design processes. The result is products with lower value-added.*" The initial attempts at establishing R&D labs and conducting R&D in state-owned (electronics) companies were interrupted by privatization attempts (e.g., the Teletaş case—see Yücel, 2016).

Similarly, *INT8* emphasizes the role of electronics in engine design and in designing and integrating smart systems in automobiles. "*Electronics industry is a prerequisite for producing 'smart automotive systems.' Without a good electronics and software industry, it is impossible to design and produce engine control unit.*" *INT1* approaches the issue with a wider perspective, arguing that there are hardly any domestic producers of components predominantly involving electronics and software. "*We have no manufacturers in automatic transmissions, engines, vehicle control units, software integrating with mechanic parts, brake systems. Furthermore, Turkey has no manufacturer producing boards and cards that are being used in automotive software. Unless you are uniting mechanics with software, it is hard to have more value-added.*" *INT9* emphasizes the (future) role of telematics as well as electronics. "*Among international projects, the most important ones are from the technological fields of telematics and telecommunication...ICT-driven technologies are driving innovation in automobile industry.*"

Almost all interviewers cite the importance of electronics and ICT especially with the developments in electric and autonomous vehicles. Moreover, most technologies related with customer-based tendencies on safety and comfort (such as heating, air-conditioning, entertainment, parking-assistance, ABS, and ESP, etc.,) are predominantly related to electronics. Since customer satisfaction for the adoption of electrical vehicles and the attainment of rage extension targets seemingly increase the probability of substitution of internal combustion engine technologies with electrical engines, electronics could become axial to automobiles.

Turkey seems to have ignored the strong effect of electronics (and ICT) on the national automotive industry. Privatization policies that emerged after the 1980s weakened the national electronics industry, particularly in hardware and component development. Thus, failure to establish a competitive electronics industry is a missed opportunity for Turkey, which thereby significantly hinders the automotive industry's technology development attempts.

11.5.3 Foreign Dependence on Strategic Decisions

When the sources and content of R&D activities and decision-making in commercialization are considered, our findings reveal that Turkish firms are highly dependent on foreign OEMs and JVs. The JV/FA structure in the automotive industry hinders Turkish manufacturers and suppliers from participating in decision-making processes. Firms are unable to participate in design confirmation, regulation and homologation processes.

The supplier industry in Turkey managed to survive in export-oriented market policy regime by merging with foreign firms and/or performing R&D and innovation led by foreign firms and JVs. This helped Turkish firms to survive amidst fierce global competition at the expense of independence on strategic decision-making. JVs took advantage of this structure by gaining R&D capabilities (up to the extent that lead firms allow). However, the foreign-dependent structure in the industry affects the R&D efforts of the local suppliers. *INT3* summarizes the current situation as "*Between 1995 and 2005, in addition to the main industry, the supplier industry integrated with the foreign markets through mergers and acquisitions. This impedes Turkey's presence on decision-making processes of the global automotive industry. R&D efforts have seriously been lowered because both JVs and the supplier industry are based on foreign partners… This situation has inevitably made Turkey dependent upon foreigners.*" As discussed in Sect. 11.5.1, Turkey accepted the delegated role of manufacturing rather than easily for short-term economic gains. This process inevitably increased foreign dependence of Turkish firms. As *INT5* argues, "*If you are highly dependent on the JV structure, it is not allowed to make your own R&D. Your innovations remain at the firm-level or at best national level.*"

Involving R&D projects of the lead firms and head-quarters could enhance local in-house R&D capabilities. *INT6* presents an example for this. "*In TOFAŞ (JV of FIAT), Doblo was the very first car that was fully designed and manufactured in a JV in Turkey. TUBITAK supports were effective in manufacturing the prototype. R&D department in TOFAŞ started up with 10-15 persons and then dramatically increased to 350-400 persons.*" The R&D performers, rather than "*dancing with foreign affiliates,*" as *INT3* illustrates, should be involved in comprehensive learning and interactions at an early phase in order to benefit from such commissioned R&D. Fiat Doblo and Ford Transit Connect cases reveal that when manufacturing cooperates with decision-making in design and design confirmation processes and when domestic firms are integrated in the process at a much earlier phase, sophisticated capabilities can be nurtured. Özatağan (2011) shows that for several suppliers in Bursa (central hub of the automotive industry in Turkey), a co-designer phase has created opportunities in the upper segments of GVC. Similarly, Ray and Ray (2011) argue that collaboration in design activities with suppliers in the early phase was important for the success of Nano in India. Lim et al. (2013) further illustrate the role of early phase collaboration for TATA.

Big firms try operating a dual structure; one related to their core areas that generates most revenue (survival) and another where they invest in niche technologies to penetrate into new markets (growth). In the former, the firms, though big, are primarily dependent on OEMs and outsourcers regarding technology production. In the latter, firms are more independent in decision-making. For example, *BIG1,* a design and engineering-oriented firm, has developed R&D projects in niche areas such as electrical vehicle components but in their core business (building custom-made automation lines for Turkish JVs and global OEMs), they are highly dependent on foreign partners. Similarly, *BIG4* is rather independent in the decision-making process of R&D and innovation activities because it operates in niche areas that are not driven by global OEMs.

When we consider the commercialization decisions on the performed R&D, the structure does not change. Table 11.4 shows that almost all firms are either dependent on the OEM or the head-quarter (in the cases of *FA1* and *JV1*) for commercialization decisions. *INT9* bluntly states, "*Innovative projects are not being developed within the sector. For international projects, innovative ideas are coming from foreign firms and research centers. Main car manufacturers are operating as test-beds of these projects.*"

Summarizing, most Turkish automotive firms rely on ideas and specs readily available from lead firms in the GVC that outsource non-core R&D activities. Local firms are not independent in commercialization decisions even though such R&D activities produce incremental innovations. Firms that rely on market signals and invest in concept design and design confirmation processes are more likely to produce niche product innovations in which they have full authority on commercialization. This, however, is an exception.

11.6 Synthesis of Results

Table 11.5 summarizes the findings of the analyses. The first column lists statements based on findings. The robustness of each statement is analyzed by investigating whether the statements are supported at different levels (project, firm, and expert) of analysis. In this manner, firm and expert interviews show within-level and Table 11.5 shows between-level robustness.

The between-level results indicate extensive learning in the industry being used for establishing excellent manufacturing capabilities. However, for catching-up (or leap-frogging) an IS should be formed based on manufacturing capabilities where the industry can indigenously design, commercialize, and sell (radical or niche) new products/processes. Our results show that Turkish automotive industry is predominantly involved in R&D activities on traditional components; conduct applied R&D; invest in incremental (process) innovations; rely on ideas generated by foreign actors and possesses less power in strategic decision-making. Through gains in manufacturing capabilities after 2000, this structure prevailed in R&D and innovation activities. With this portfolio, expecting

Table 11.5 Consolidation of results at the project, firm and macro levels

Automotive industry characteristics	*Project level data*	*Firm interviews*	*Expert interviews*
Manufacturing excellence	Hard to observe from the data	Strong support	Strong support
Inclination from process toward product innovation (cost reduction versus product variety)	Increased number of recent projects with process innovation focus	Mostly process innovation but cases of niche product innovations	Mostly process innovation
Inclination toward contemporary technologies	Mostly traditional technologies. Almost no change through time	Mostly traditional. Some cases of contemporary technologies in niche products	Mostly traditional. Existence of exceptions (niche products)
Existence of basic and experimental R&D	Weak support. Some exceptions	Weak support. Number of exceptional cases niche products with new technologies	No support
Existence of domestic local concept design and design confirmation processes	Weak support. No significant differences through time	No support. Some exceptions	No support
Independence (from foreigners) in strategic decisions on R&D and innovation	Hard to observe from the data	No support. Some exceptions	No support. Except cases of transport vehicle companies with niche products
Signs of increased technological sophistication	The project characteristics did not change between two time periods	Weak support in the case of firms with niche products	Almost no support. There are cases which are by and large exceptions

radical innovations or niche innovative products from the automotive industry is hard.

The delegated role of being a manufacturing center has resulted in learning and increased capability. However, as our results reveal, the Turkish automotive industry did not succeed in making the next leap toward indigenous capability building in design, R&D, and innovation that implies retaliation against delegation. Governments and the industry made strategic mistakes in the process that became the seedbed for middle-technology trap. Strategic policy choices that favored short-term gains coupled with the acceptance of such choices by the firms fed a homegrown state-industry agreement process. This whole process detailed above led the industry to a position from which it is difficult or impossible to recover. It is rather difficult to recover from such a trap given the dual national and international forces that work in the same direction. Weak IS could not nurture and strong automotive GVC inherently prevents such forward leaps.

Complementarities among industries are crucial for the sustainability of the automotive industry. Privatization attempts in the 1990s especially in the state-led electronics sector was an important strategic mistake, considering the increased convergence of electronics, ICT, and automotive. Lacking complementarities coupled with the decision to maintain temporary competitive positions for export revenue and employment, the foreign presence that was crucial for learning gradually became a handicap. Thus, foreign presence initially enhanced technological upgrading. However, this effect decelerated through time and saturated significantly below the frontier. Current dependence structure impedes attempts to form indigenous technological capabilities.

11.7 Conclusion

This research shows that on the borders of weak IS and strong GVCs, the Turkish automotive industry has fallen into a middle-technology trap. Our novel research design involves both quantitative and qualitative methods to improve the validity of the findings. The main finding is that the manufacturing capabilities gained over the years have not been translated into innovation capabilities and national and global forces work in the same direction, making indigenous technological and innovation capabilities difficult to form. Considering between-sector complementarities, success in producing niche products and penetrating into niche markets, involvement in joint production at an earlier stage and active government policies, a divide between the Latin American and East Asian experience is traced in building indigenous technological capabilities in the automotive industry. Our results show that Turkey rather resembles to the Latin American case. This result is compatible with the findings of Timmer, Miroudot, and de Vries (2019), claiming that Turkey plays a "fabrication only" role in functional specialization on trade similar to the case of Brazil and Mexico.

11.7.1 Implications for Theory

There is a recent attempt to bring IS and GVC literatures together, despite their contradictions, to study and understand economic development (Jurowetzki, Lema, & Lundvall, 2018; Pietrobelli & Rabellotti, 2011). Theoretically, this research fits into such an agenda. The impact of three identified mechanisms, delegation, complementarities, and foreign dependence can best be understood in a setting where IS and GVCs meet. Our nuanced view is that especially in the case of "innovation for economic development" in less developed countries weak IS and strong GVCs co-exist to form vicious circles of middle-technology trap.

To understand the role of interactive learning on technological upgrading this co-existence should be further investigated. For instance, in the case of Turkey weak national IS coupled with state-automotive industry agreement favoring short-term economic gains at the expense of forming long-term indigenous technological capabilities left the playing field void, creating scope for increased GVC operations in Turkey. Thus, it might be the case that GVCs favor weak IS. As evident from other cases such as Thailand (Petison & Johri, 2008), China (Nam, 2011, 2012), Mexico (Contreras et al., 2012), South Africa (Barnes & Morris, 2004), Central and Eastern Europe (Pavlinek & Zenka, 2011), GVCs seldom care about the local industry unless building local capabilities strengthen the position of lead firms. Weak IS lacking complementarities, passive governments, and strong GVCs that increased foreign presence all together may weaken the bargaining power of nations. Recent findings suggest that position rather than participation in GVCs determines success in productivity gains and local sourcing (Amendolagine et al., 2019; Montalbano, Nenci, & Pietrobelli, 2018). However, climbing up the GVC requires strong local capabilities which GVCs hardly help to build. Thus, we argue that, to benefit from GVCs in terms of interactive learning for innovation, a certain level of "initial" or "starting-level" local capability is required. How such capabilities can be obtained by limiting the role GVCs or under strong GVCs is fertile soil for research. As co-existence of IS and GVCs in an economy creates context specificities, translating success stories or best practices becomes even more difficult.

11.7.2 Implications for Policy

Our research reveals four important lessons for developing countries. First, complementarity among sectors is crucial for long-run sustainability that entails technology production. We show that lack of a strong electronics industry hindered technology development in the automotive industry. Park (2003) argues that capability building in electronics and automotive industries was a combined effort in South Korea and was aggressively supported by the government. Similar complementarities can be found in China (automotive-electronics-IT). Thus, to further enhance interactive learning governments can consider developing complementarities among sectors. Second, firms that can diversify especially in niche products and markets become more independent in terms of R&D, innovation, and commercialization. Our results are comparable to earlier findings on India regarding the importance of niche products and markets for indigenous capability building (D'Costa, 2004; Lim et al., 2013). Third, firm interviews reveal that joint product development in which domestic firms involve in initial stages is not only important for capability building but also for bargaining power over strategic decisions. Motohashi and Yuan (2010) and Ray and Ray (2011) report similar findings for China and India, respectively. Thus, while production capabilities develop, governments can induce (or even force) local-foreign partnerships on R&D and innovation in niche products.

Finally, the findings hint at the difficulty of escaping the middle-technology trap without active government involvement. Several cases are available where governments actively created, governed, and restructured the automotive industry. Catalan (2010) argues that early liberalization attempts in Argentina as opposed to South Korea and Spain were decisive in forming an indigenous automotive industry. A similar story can be found in South Africa (Barnes & Kaplinsky, 2000; Barnes & Morris, 2004). Part of the success in creating indigenous technological capabilities in South Korea and China is due to the state's active regulation and structuring of the industry (Chu, 2011; Depner & Bathelt, 2005; Hu et al., 2014; Liu & Dicken, 2006; Nam, 2012; Park, 2003).

11.7.3 Limitations and Future Research

This work has several limitations which invite further research. The first limitation is that we have used data from R&D support program of TTGV. In the period we analysed TTGV was the dominant public support agency in Turkey. However especially after 2010, it lost ground to TUBITAK R&D and innovation support programs. A similar analysis on the TUBİTAK data may produce different results. In a similar manner selection of a different sector such as machinery or energy may also produce interesting findings. It has been already emphasized that the interaction of government policy, national IS, and GVC produce context-specific results. Our main result of middle-technology trap could be a special case to Turkey. It is essential to look at various industries in other countries to generalize the findings of this research. Thus, the context-specificity argument necessitates researching more cases from different countries. Lastly, this chapter investigates only one aspect of an IS–GVC interaction, where we specifically look at the weak IS–strong GVC interface. It would be interesting to look at the cases where strong IS interacts with strong GVC, and further investigate the possibility of other options such as strong IS–weak GVC.

Acknowledgements The authors would like to thank Erkan Erdil, Jeong-Dong Lee, Tarmo Lemola, Franco Malerba, Teoman Pamukçu, Eddy Szirmai, and the participants of the 15th Globelics Conference in Athens and 9th European Meeting on Applied Evolutionary Economics (EMAEE) for comments and suggestions.

Appendix

See Tables 11.6 and 11.7.

Table 11.6 Characteristics of selected firms

Firm	*Description of the firm*	*Category*	*City*	*Position of the interviewee*
SME 1	A domestic design and engineering firm affiliated with the domestically owned midi-bus and military vehicle manufacturer	SME	Kocaeli	R&D Manager
SME2	A domestically owned clutch procurer for automobiles and buses	SME	İzmir	R&D Manager
SME3	A domestically owned brake components manufacturer for the global brands under foreign license	SME	İzmir	R&D Manager
SME4	A domestically owned front/rear axle procurer for global OEMs	SME	Bursa	R&D Manager
SME5	A domestically owned procurer manufacturing plastic assembly parts for automobiles	SME	Bursa	Vice Manager
BIG1	A reputable company specialized in automation and installing robotics on mass production lines in JVs	Big Enterprise	Kocaeli	Vice Manager
BIG2	A reputable domestically owned spring supplier for heavy vehicle OEMs	Big Enterprise	Manisa	R&D Manager
BIG3	A domestically owned supplier for global heavy vehicle manufacturers that operates in a niche market	Big Enterprise	İzmir	R&D Manager

(continued)

Table 11.6 (continued)

Firm	*Description of the firm*	*Category*	*City*	*Position of the interviewee*
BIG4	A renowned accumulator and battery producer that is operating worldwide (former shareholder was foreign)	Big Enterprise	Manisa	R&D Manager
BIG5	A domestically owned tractor, customised automobile, wagon parts, and heavy parts manufacturer	Big Enterprise	Eskişehir	R&D Manager
BIG6	A globally owned domestic cord fabric manufacturer for international tire brands	Big Enterprise	Kocaeli	R&D Manager
FA1	A foreign-affiliate of a renowned bus manufacturer	Foreign Affiliate	Ankara	R&D Manager
JV1	A joint venture, which is a sub-branch of a globally renowned automobile manufacturer	Joint Venture	Bursa	R&D Manager

Table 11.7 Expert characteristics

Interviewee	*Title*	*Firm/Institution*	*Rationale behind selection*
INT1	General Manager	University test/homologation center	Highly qualified expert
INT2	General Secretary	An umbrella organization	Experienced and well-known in the automotive industry
INT3	General Manager	An R&D design/engineering firm affiliated with an OEM	Experienced specialist in the automotive industry
INT4	R&D Director	A JV in Turkey	Specialized experience in automotive R&D
INT5	Technology Consultant	Former R&D director of a bus manufacturer	Experience in automotive industry, entrepreneur, and consultant
INT6	Professor	Former R&D director and an academic member in a university	One of the first R&D managers in Turkish automotive industry
INT7	R&D Director	R&D director in a Turkish manufacturer	Experienced specialist in the automotive industry
INT8	Technology consultant and specialist	Former senior expert in R&D funding, Automotive Specialist, Technology Policy Maker	Respected in the automotive industry; former policy-maker of the very first R&D grant program

(continued)

Table 11.7 (continued)

Interviewee	*Title*	*Firm/Institution*	*Rationale behind selection*
INT9	General Manager	Former manager in an EU program, General Manager in a consulting firm	Specialized in networking and clustering
INT10	General Secretary	Technology specialist, business developer, General Secretary in a former R&D-funding institution	Possession of wide array of knowledge and vision about several sectors and technologies
INT11	Former Board President	The founder of one of the first R&D departments in electronics in Turkey	Expert in a complementary sector to automotive
INT12	General Manager	Manager in an automotive procurer	Experienced in auto supplier industry
INT13	Vice Manager	Financial manager in an engineering firm	Experienced professional in the automotive industry
INT14	Former General Coordinator	An umbrella organization of Turkish Automotive Suppliers	Experienced professional in the supplier industry

References

Albornoz, F., & Yuguel, G. (2004). Competitiveness and production networks: The case of Argentine automotive sector. *Industrial and Corporate Change, 13*(4), 619–641.

Alcorta, L., & Peres, W. (1998). Innovation systems and technological specialization in Latin America and the Caribbean. *Research Policy, 26*(7–8), 857–881.

Altenburg, T., Schmitz, H., & Stamm, A (2008). Breakthrough: China's and India's transition from production to innovation. *World Development, 36*(2), 325–334.

Amendolagine, V., Presbitero, A. F., Rabellotti, R., & Sanfilippo, M. (2019). Local sourcing in developing countries: The role of foreign direct investments and global value chains. *World Development, 113*, 73–88.

Arocena, R., & Sutz, J. (1999). Looking at national innovation systems from the South. *Industry and Innovation, 7*(1), 55–75.

Archibugi, D., & Pietrobelli, C. (2003). The globalisation of technology and its implications for developing countries: Windows of opportunity or further burden? *Technological Forecasting and Social Change, 70*(9), 861–883.

Barnes, J., & Kaplinsky, R. (2000). Globalization and the death of the local firm? The automobile components sector in South Africa. *Regional Studies, 34*(9), 797–812.

Barnes, J., & Morris, M. (2004). The German connection: Shifting hegemony in the political economy of the South African automotive industry. *Industrial and Corporate Change, 13*(5), 789–814.

Bathelt, H., Malmberg, A., & Maskell, P. (2004). Clusters and knowledge: Local buzz, global pipelines and the process of knowledge creation. *Progress in Human Geography, 28*(1), 31–56.

Bell, M. (1984). Learning and the accumulation of industrial technological capacity in developing countries. In M. Fransman & K. K. King (Eds.), *Technological capability in the third world* (pp. 187–209). London: Palgrave Macmillan.

Bell, M. (2006). Time and technological learning in industrialising countries: How long does it take? How fast is it moving (if at all)? *International Journal of Technology Management, 36*(1–3), 25–39.

Brimble, P., & Doner, R. F. (2007). University–industry linkages and economic development: The case of Thailand. *World Development, 35*(6), 1021–1036.

Callegari, J., Massaroli Melo, T., & Carvalho, C. E. (2018) The peculiar insertion of Brazil into global value chains. *Review of Development Economics, 22*(3), 1321–1342.

Carlsson, B. (2006). Internationalization of innovation systems: A survey of the literature. *Research Policy, 35*(1), 56–67.

Catalan, J. (2010). Strategic policy revisited: The origins of mass production in the motor industry of Argentina Korea and Spain, 1945–87. *Business History, 52*(2), 207–230.

Chiarini, T., Rapini, M. C., & Silva, L. A. (2017). Access to knowledge and catch-up: Exploring some intellectual property rights data from Brazil and South Korea. *Science and Public Policy, 44*(1), 95–110.

Chu, W. W. (2011). How the Chinese government promoted a global automotive industry. *Industrial and Corporate Change, 20*(5), 1235–1276.

Contreras, O., Carrillo, J., & Alonso, J. (2012). Local entrepreneurship within global value chains: A case study in the Mexican automotive Industry. *World Development, 40*(5), 1013–1023.

Crespi, G., & Zuniga, P. (2012). Innovation and productivity: Evidence from six Latin American countries. *World Development, 40*(2), 273–290.

Creswell, J. W., & Plano Clark, V. L. (2011). *Designing and conducting mixed methods research*. London: Sage.

Dantas, E., & Bell, M. (2011). The co-evolution of firm-centered knowledge networks and capabilities in late industrializing countries: The case of Petrobras in the offshore oil innovation system in Brazil. *World Development, 39*(9), 1570–1591.

D'Costa, A. (2004). Flexible practices for mass production goals: Economic governance in the Indian automobile industry. *Industrial and Corporate Change, 13*(2), 335–367.

De Marchi, V., Giuliani, E., & Rabellotti, R. (2018). Do global value chains offer developing countries learning and innovation opportunities? *European Journal of Development Research, 30*(3), 389–407.

Depner, H., & Bathelt, H. (2005). Exporting the German model: The establishment of a new automobile industry cluster in Shanghai. *Economic Geography, 81*(1), 53–81.

Dutrenit, G., & Vera-Cruz, A. (2005). Spillovers from MNCs through worker mobility and technological and managerial capabilities of SMEs in Mexico. *Innovation: Management, Policy and Practice, 7*(2–3), 274–297.

Edquist, C. (Ed.). (1997). *Systems of innovation: Technologies, institutions and organisations*. London: Pinter.

Edquist, C. (2001). *Systems of innovation for development* (Background Paper for UNIDO World Industrial Development Report 2002/3). UNIDO.

Ernst, D., Mytelka, L., & Ganiatsos, T. (1998). Technological capabilities in the context of export-led growth—A conceptual framework. In D. Ernst, L. Mytelka, & T. Ganiatsos (Eds.), *Technological capabilities and export success in Asia* (pp. 5–45). New York: Routledge.

Freeman, C. (1995). The 'National System of Innovation' in historical perspective. *Cambridge Journal of Economics, 19*(1), 5–24.

Fromhold-Eisebith, M. (2007). Bridging scales in innovation policies: How to link regional, national and international innovation systems. *European Planning Studies, 15*(2), 217–233.

Gehl Sampath, P., & Vallejo, B. (2018). Trade, global value chains and upgrading: What, when and how? *European Journal of Development Research, 30*(3), 481–504.

Gereffi, G., Humphrey, J., & Sturgeon, T. J. (2005). The governance of global value chains. *Review of International Political Economy, 12*(1), 78–104.

Gereffi, G., & Kaplinsky, R. (2001). The value of value chains: Spreading the gains from globalization. *IDS Bulletin, 32*(3), 1–12.

Giuliani, E., Pietrobelli, C., & Rabellotti, R. (2005). Upgrading in global value chains: Lessons from Latin American clusters. *World Development 33*(4), 549–573.

Guennif, S., & Ramani, S. V. (2012). Explaining divergence in catching-up in pharma between India and Brazil using the NSI framework. *Research Policy, 41,* 430–441.

Hassler, M. (2009). Variations of value creation: Automobile manufacturing in Thailand. *Environment and Planning A, 41*(9), 2232–2247.

Hu, W.-M., Xiao, J., & Zhou, X. (2014). Collusion or competition? Interfirm relationships in the Chinese Auto Industry. *Journal of Industrial Economics, 62*(1), 1–40.

Humphrey, J., & Schmitz, H. (2002). How does insertion in global value chains affect upgrading in industrial clusters? *Regional Studies, 36*(9), 1017–1027.

Iammarino, S., Padilla-Pérez, R., & von Tunzelmann, N. (2008). Technological capabilities and global-local interactions: The electronics industry in two Mexican regions. *World Development, 36*(10), 1980–2003.

Jurowetzki, R., Lema, R., & Lundvall, B.-A. (2018). Combining innovation systems and global value chains for development: Towards a research agenda. *European Journal of Development Research, 30*(3), 364–388

Karabag, F., Tuncay-Celikel, A., & Berggren, C. (2011). The limits of R&D internationalization and the importance of local initiatives: Turkey as a critical case. *World Development, 39*(8), 1347–1357.

Kim, L. (1999). Building technological capability for industrialization: Analytical frameworks and Korea's experience. *Industrial and Corporate Change, 8*(1), 111–136.

Kumar, R. S., & Subrahmanya, M. H. B. (2010). Influence of subcontracting on innovation and economic performance of SMEs in Indian automobile industry. *Technovation, 30*(11–12), 558–569.

Lee, J.-D. (2017, October 11–13). *Middle innovation trap: Transition failure from implementation capability to concept design capability as a source of the middle income trap* [Conference presentation]. Paper presented at the GLOBELICS 2017 Conference, Athens, Greece.

Lee, K., & Kim, C. S. (2001). Technological regimes, catching-up and leapfrogging: Findings from the Korean industries. *Research Policy, 30*(3), 459–483.

Lee, K., Szapiro, M., & Mao, Z. (2018). From global value chains (GVC) to innovation systems for local value chains and knowledge creation. *European Journal of Development Research, 30*(3), 424–441.

Lema, R., Quadros, R., & Schmitz, H. (2015). Reorganising global value chains and building innovation capabilities in Brazil and India. *Research Policy, 44*(7), 1376–1386.

Lim, C., Han, S., & Ito, H. (2013). Capability building through innovation for unserved lower end mega markets. *Technovation, 33*(12), 391–404.

Liu, W., & Dicken, P. (2006). Transnational corporations and "obligated embeddedness": Foreign direct investment in China's automobile industry. *Environment and Planning A, 38*(7), 1229–1247.

Lorentzen, J. (2005). The absorptive capacities of South African automotive component suppliers. *World Development, 33*(7), 1153–1182.

Lundvall, B.-A. (Ed.). (1992). *National systems of innovation: Towards a theory on innovation and interactive learning*. London: Pinter.

Lundvall, B.-A., Joseph, K. J., Chaminade, C., & Vang, J. (Eds.). (2009). *Handbook of innovation systems and developing countries: Building domestic capabilities in a global setting*. Cheltenham: Edward-Elgar.

McMahon, D., & Thorsteinsdóttir, H. (2013). Pursuing endogenous high-tech innovation in developing countries: A look at regenerative medicine innovation in Brazil, China and India. *Research Policy, 42*(4), 965–974.

Montalbano, P., Nenci, S., & Pietrobelli, C. (2018). Opening and linking up: Firms, GVCs, and productivity in Latin America. *Small Business Economics, 50*(4), 917–935.

Morrison, A., Pietrobelli, C., & Rabellotti, R. (2008). Global value chains and technological capabilities: A framework to study learning and innovation in developing countries. *Oxford Development Studies, 36*(1), 39–58.

Motohashi, K., & Yuan, Y. (2010). Productivity impact of technology spillover from multinationals to local firms: Comparing China's automobile and electronics industries. *Research Policy, 39*(6), 790–798.

Nam, K.-M. (2011). Learning through the international joint venture: Lessons from the experience of China's automotive sector. *Industrial and Corporate Change, 20*(3), 855–907.

Nam, K.-M. (2012). Out of passivity: Potential role of OFDI in IFDI-based learning trajectory. *Industrial and Corporate Change, 22*(3), 711–743.

Narula, R. (2002). Innovation systems and 'inertia' in R&D location: Norwegian firms and the role of systemic lock-in. *Research Policy, 31*(5), 795–816.

Navaretti, G. B., & Venables, A. (2004). *Multinational firms in the world economy*. Princeton: Princeton University Press.

Oh, J., & Rhee, S.-K. (2010). Influences of supplier capabilities and collaboration in new car development on competitive advantage of carmakers. *Management Decision, 48*(5), 756–774.

OICA. (2018). *Production statistics 2017* [Data set]. International Organization of Motor Vehicle Manufacturers. http://www.oica.net/category/production-statistics/2017-statistics/. Accessed 8 Feb 2019 at 10:23.

Okada, A. (2004). Skills development and interfirm learning linkages under globalization: Lessons from the Indian automobile industry. *World Development, 32*(7), 1265–1288.

Ölmezoğulları, T. (2011). *Türk otomotiv sanayi'nde firma ölçeğinde teknolojik yetenek düzeyinin araştırılması ve sektörün eleceğine yönelik politika önerileri* [Conference presentation]. Paper presented at EconAnadolu 2011: Anadolu International Conference in Economics, Eskişehir, Turkey.

Özatağan, G. (2011). Dynamics of value chain governance: Increasing supplier competence and changing power relations in the periphery of automotive production—Evidence from Bursa, Turkey. *European Planning Studies, 19*(1), 77–95.

Özçelik, E., & Taymaz, E. (2008). R&D support program in developing countries: The Turkish experience. *Research Policy, 37*(2), 258–275.

Pamukçu, M. T., & Sönmez, A. (2012). Technology transfer in the global automotive value chain—The case of Turkish automotive industry. In D. Audretsch, L. Lehmann, A. Link, & A. Starnecker (Eds.), *Technology transfer in a global economy* (pp. 303–334). New York: Springer.

Park, B.-G. (2003). Politics of scale and the globalization of the South Korean automobile industry. *Economic Geography, 79*(2), 173–194.

Pavlinek, P. (2012). The internationalization of corporate R&D and the automotive industry R&D of east-central Europe. *Economic Geography, 88*(3), 279–310.

Pavlinek, P. (2018). Global production networks, foreign direct investment, and supplier linkages in the integrated peripheries of the automotive industry. *Economic Geography, 94*(2), 141–165.

Pavlinek, P., Domanski, B., & Guzik, R. (2009). Industrial upgrading through foreign direct investment in Central European automotive manufacturing. *European Urban and Regional Studies, 16*(1), 43–63.

Pavlinek, P., & Zenka, J. (2011). Upgrading in the automotive industry: Firm-level evidence from Central Europe. *Journal of Economic Geography, 11*(3), 559–586.

Petison, P., & Johri, L. M. (2008). Localization drivers in an emerging market: Case studies from Thailand. *Management Decision, 46*(9), 1399–1412.

Pietrobelli, C., & Rabellotti, R. (2007). *Upgrading to compete. Global value chains, clusters and SMEs in Latin America*. Cambridge, MA: Harvard University Press.

Pietrobelli, C., & Rabellotti, R. (2011). Global value chains meet innovation systems: Are there learning opportunities for developing countries? *World Development, 39*(7), 1261–1269.

Quadros, R. (2004). Global quality standards and technological upgrading in the Brazilian auto-components industry. In H. Schmitz (Ed.), *Local enterprises in the global economy: Issues of governance and upgrading* (pp. 265–296). Cheltenham: Edward-Elgar.

Ray, S., & Ray, P. K. (2011). Product innovation for the people's car in an emerging economy. *Technovation, 31*(5–6), 216–227.

Simona, G.-L., & Axele, G. (2012). Knowledge transfer from TNCs and upgrading of domestic firms: The polish automotive sector. *World Development, 40*(4), 796–807.

Sönmez, A. (2013). *Multinational companies, knowledge and technology transfer: Turkey's automotive industry in focus*. Cham: Springer.

Sturgeon, T., Van Biesebroeck, J., & Gereffi, G. (2008). Value chains, networks and clusters: Reframing the global automotive industry. *Journal of Economic Geography, 8*(3), 297–321.

Timmer, M. P., Miroudot, S., & de Vries, G. J. (2019). Functional specialisation in trade. *Journal of Economic Geography, 19*(1), 1–30.

Viotti, E. (2002). National learning systems: A new approach on technological change in late industrializing countries. *Technological Forecasting and Social Change, 69*(7), 653–680.

Wade, R. (2010). After the crises: Industrial policy and the developmental state in low-income countries. *Global Policy, 1*(2), 150–161.

Wagner, J. (2007). Exports and productivity: A survey of evidence from firm level data. *World Economy, 30*(1), 60–82.

Yin, R. K. (2003). *Case study research, design and methods* (3rd ed.). Thousand Oaks, CA: Sage.

Yücel, F. (2016). *Telekomünikasyonun Öyküsü*. TTGV.

Zhao, Z., Anand, J., & Mitchell, W. (2005). A dual networks perspective on inter-organizational transfer of R&D capabilities: International joint ventures in the Chinese automotive industry. *Journal of Management Studies, 42*(1), 127–160.

CHAPTER 12

Kaiser Permanente Internet of Things (IoT) Roadmap

Tugrul U. Daim, Mohammed Marthed, and Marina Dabić

12.1 Introduction

The healthcare industry is one of the fastest increasing and biggest sectors in the world. According to the United States (US) Department of Health and Human Services, US healthcare spending grew 3.9% in 2017, the total national health expenditure $3.5 trillion or $10,739 per person (CMSgov, 2019). By consuming more than 17.9% of gross national product (GDP) in 2017, health care can form a huge portion of a country's economy (CMSgov, 2019). According to the Bureau of Labor

T. U. Daim · M. Marthed
Portland State University, Portland, OR, USA
e-mail: ji2td@pdx.edu

M. Dabić (✉)
University of Zagreb, Zagreb, Croatia
e-mail: mdabic@net.efzg.hr; marina.dabic@ntu.ac.uk

Nottingham Trent University, Nottingham, UK

J. J. M. Ferreira et al. (eds.), *Technological Innovation and International Competitiveness for Business Growth*, Palgrave Studies in Democracy, Innovation, and Entrepreneurship for Growth,
https://doi.org/10.1007/978-3-030-51995-7_12

Statistics the growth in healthcare employment is expected to continue its steady growth and to reach almost 26% by 2022.

The perception of the quality of healthcare service users is a direct indicator of the quality and efficiency of health care, which consequently determines customer satisfaction and consumption of the service. Healthcare professionals focused on the quality and success in health services through patient satisfaction (Meesala & Paul, 2018; Moretta Tartaglione, Cavacece, Cassia, & Russo, 2018; Vogus & McClelland, 2016), patient safely (Aiken et al., 2012), employee engagement (Tóth, Jónás, & Dénes, 2019), and continuous improvement of delivered service like the patient-centered care concept (Rathert, Vogus, & McClelland, 2016), costs, etc. (Weiss et al., 2015).

Cost justification of PHM systems—The cost justification can esteem maintaining or increasing quality (Weiss et al., 2015). Health information technologies, which hold software and infrastructure used in the clinical practice of medicine have been promoted as vital components to reduce healthcare costs and also to improve healthcare quality, increase admission, safety, and quality health outcomes (Davidson, Baird, & Prince, 2018).

Improvements with Internet of Things (IoT) health monitoring devices continuously create more health-related data. IOT promises healthcare professionals and patients to be connected in real time(Cognizant, 2016). This type of connection will save lives, time and money. This technology will enable many health information technologies to their ideal performance (N. Behkami & Daim, 2016; Hogaboam & Daim, 2018; Spatar, Kok, Basoglu, & Daim, 2019).

In this chapter we focused on IoT for one of the biggest healthcare organizations in United States Kaiser Permanente.

Kaiser Permanente is an American integrated managed care group established in 1945 by industrialist Henry J. Kaiser and physicist Sidney Garfield, based in Oakland, California, United States. Kaiser Permanente consists of three separate but interdependent groups of organizations: the Kaiser Foundation Health Plan, Inc. (KFHP) and its regional operating subsidiaries; the Kaiser Foundation Hospitals; and the Permanente Medical Regional Groups. Kaiser Permanente has been operating in eight countries (Hawaii, Washington, Oregon, California, Colorado, Maryland, Virginia, Georgia) and the District of Columbia since 2017 and is the biggest managed care organization in the United States. With the development of the IoT in today's connectivity globe, all entities are linked by some means of communication. The IoT for medical equipment will generate information that can go a long way in enhancing not only the effectiveness of machinery, but also the safety of patients. Industry and various services are increasingly recognizing the IoT primarily in healthcare (Yeole & Kalbande, 2016).

As pointed out by Spatar et al. (2019), Jungwirth and Haluza (2019), Hogaboam and Daim (2018), and Behkami and Daim (2016), health information technologies have not reached their ideal performance. Studies focusing on adoption of such technologies (Basoglu, Daim, & Topacan, 2012; Başoglu, Işkın, Aydınog, & Öztürk, 2012; Daim, Al-Mulla, Sengupta, Shah, & Demchig, 2015) as well as those exploring the future prospects (N. A. Behkami & Daim, 2012) agree that there are still barriers to be brought down and technologies to be commercialized to enable these technologies to their maximum performance. Technology roadmapping is presented as an ideal framework to address this gap (Hansen, Daim, Ernst, & Herstatt, 2016; Romanski & Daim, 2019; Sourav, Daim, & Herstatt, 2018).

In this chapter, the authors focused on IoTs in Kaiser Permanente and how they can develop their services and options using IoT. Trying to answer one of the biggest questions facing all the healthcare market "How can we compete with other healthcare organization and catch the fast growth opportunity?" The answer is using roadmap to put a good future for the next 20 years and start working on this roadmap.

The purpose of this chapter to develop a roadmap for Kaiser Permanente to drive them to the next level and be sure this big health organization and insurance provider is on the right track.

12.2 Technology Roadmapping

One of the most important parts in business planning is the inclusion of technology into strategy of business. According to Bitondo and Frohman (1981) and Matthews (1992) technology strategies should integrate with business plan in any technology-based business. With regard to business strategy, all activities in any organization should be adjusted to provide the company with a secure and strong market position (Porter, 2008). A roadmap is a far-reaching plan or a clarification to control advance toward a specific objective. Roadmap act as choice guides to enhance the coordination among activities and resources in complex environment (Albright & Kappel, 2003; Alcantara & Martens, 2019) Roadmap consists of two major workshops S and T workshop. And those two roadmaps are used in different fields of business such as industries, government, and academia. An S&T roadmap consists of nodes and links. These roadmaps nodes and links may have both quantitative and qualitative attributes. A generic S&T roadmap consists of dimensions of time and space. The spatial dimension describes at a given point in time the relationship between S&T disciplines. The time dimension takes the evolution of S&T capabilities into consideration. S&T roadmap nodes and links are actually vectors that require a complete description of both magnitude and direction. Because roadmaps are used to perform both prospective and retrospective studies, the vectors can take forward as well as backward directions in time. Different types of roadmaps are implemented in large technology-centric firms. A comprehensive report was released as a digest on industry roadmaps (Force, 1997). Some roadmaps are roadmaps for science and study, cross-industry roadmaps, roadmaps for product technology, roadmaps for industry, product roadmaps, roadmaps for technology, and roadmaps for project/issue, some of which were outlined briefly below. Motorola and Corning created the early origins of this strategy in the US automotive industry. In the late 1970s and 80s, they created systematic methods (Probert & Radnor, 2003). Philips (Groenveld, 1997), Lucent Technologies (Albright & Kappel, 2003), and the Semiconductor Industry Association (SIA) (Kostoff & Schaller, 2001) have further adopted the Motorola approach. Product planning; it is the most prevalent form of roadmap technology and addresses the introduction of technology into produced products and deals with more than one product being generated. Service/capacity planning: This sort of roadmap is most appropriate for service-based sectors. Strategic planning: This sort of roadmap is best suited for strategic overall evaluation. It helps to analyze the possibilities and threats at the stage of company. This roadmap focuses on market, product, technology, development of future company, etc. By comparing the future vision with the present state, the gaps are recognized. Long-range planning: This long-range scheduling approach is pursued. In order to recognize disruptive technologies and markets, this sort of roadmapping is carried out at domestic or industry level. Knowledge asset planning: This form aligns knowledge management projects with company goals. Program planning: this planning methodology focuses on execution of strategies. Process planning: This form of planning is used to assist information management and focuses on a specific process region (e.g., fresh product development). It promotes product planning and focuses on the information flow that promotes the creation of fresh products. Integration planning: This form focuses on technology inclusion and how it is possible to combine distinct technologies with goods and services. Technology Roadmapping (TRM) is a strategic instrument used by a company to integrate science and technology with the company and products of the company. According to (Winebrake & Creswick, 2003), TRM is a technique of strategic planning that details the goals, obstacles, and strategies for achieving the mission of the firm. TRM is also used as a scheduling instrument for achieving a set of required goals (Jeffrey, Sedgwick, & Robinson, 2013). Motorola first integrated the roadmapping strategy to align technology with innovation (Willyard & McClees, 1987) After applying this methodology at Motorola, other businesses, governments, and organizations embraced its apps. The roadmapping method, which is the implementation and the final outcome of the application, which is the roadmap, is two main elements of the roadmapping strategy. The final resulting roadmap is a summary of the maps depicted in the form of technology and science plans. Roadmapping is the method of developing this map. As stated by Barker and Smith (1995) and EIRMA (1997), roadmapping has been implemented in multiple sectors. EIRMA (1997) described the most prevalent strategy. Overtime, the TRM has evolved and is displayed by Fenwick, Daim, and Gerdsri (2009), where a value-driven roadmap for Internet safety systems has been established using suitable assessment instruments. As process steps on the y-axis and instruments and applicability on the x-axis, the value-driven technology roadmap comprises of evaluation, market analysis, service availability, and needed innovations. The roadmap is a multi-layer plan depiction that links the product to market drivers (Wells, Phaal, Farrukh, & Probert, 2004). Although technology roadmaps have been helpful in creating connections between technology and business, the company has been struggling to use roadmaps. The reason for this is the existence of many particular types of roadmaps tailored to the requirements of the particular companies. Practical assistance is scarce for the process, and the businesses are reinventing the procedures. Groenveld (1997) summarizes the main measures for the roadmapping method of technology. However, these sources do not function as a guidance instrument on how to proceed with the roadmapping strategy. Thus, to fill this gap, the T-Plan approach is implemented. There may be two groups within a product-based business. Researchers, technicians, and individuals connected with market growth and exploitation, i.e., marketing and sales personnel, are connected with science and technology. There is always an imbalance in corporate history between "push" technology and "pull" market, resulting in company mistakes. A balanced integration of all these variables can lead to a more solid growth plan. TRM, which aims at integrated business planning, is used to tackle this challenge.

12.3 Methodology

Technology roadmapping is a well proven methodology to develop integrated planes for service, product and technology development to address emerging market trends and a future vision in technology-driven industries (Daim, Amer, & Brenden, 2012; Daim et al., 2018; Khanam & Daim, 2017; Schimpf & Abele, 2019).

As demonstrated in the literature, technology roadmapping is dependent on both published data and expert interviews or workshops (Amer, Daim, & Jetter, 2016; Rivero & Daim, 2017). The units of analyses have been standard in the literature for this kind of analyses: Market Drivers, Product Features, Technologies and Resources (Daim, Gomez, Martin, & Sheikh, 2013; Lamb, Daim, & Leavengood, 2012; Martin & Daim, 2012).

In this chapter, we used S roadmap to identify all the market drivers and what Kaiser Permanente needs in order to be on the top of the healthcare market supporting with all product features needed to reach out the goal. All the nodes of drivers and product features links together and then perform a quality function deployment QFD table to rank all those product features from the most important features for drivers to the lowest one. The market drivers are mentioned on the *x*-axis on the QFD graph and the product characteristics are listed on the *y*-axis. The organization's specialists assign weights to market drivers on a scale of 1–10. The QFD graph also shows a correlation between market drivers and product characteristics with 4 representing a strong co-relationship, 2 a medium co-relationship, 1 a low correlation, and 0 indicating no relationship. In S plan also science-Technology-Application and market transformation was used to decide what time was suitable for the transformation in the S timeline plan.

After finishing the S plan, we need to start on T-plan to decide the technologies that are needed to cover all features we have and what resources and materials or new business are needed to partnership with to cover all those technologies. With another QFD to rank the technology chosen to cover all product features and then link all nodes together in the timeline.

Finally, we need to analyze all the gaps in all the 4 main groups to identify what we need and what we have before starting deal with other companies or partnership with different organization. After that we should have a complete roadmap for any organization not just Kaiser Permanente.

12.4 Technology Roadmap Development

12.4.1 Market Driver

In this chapter, we found 7 main market drivers for Kaiser Permanente and their plan to use IoT to satisfy all these drivers.

First business driver is the efficiency, this driver is very important for any industry to reduce all the waiting time and trying to give the patients a real time consult, eliminate redundancy and trying to decrease the cost of consult by reducing the cost of tests and cost of transportation to hospitals and vice versa. Also, efficiency focuses on reducing all errors and making sure the results are right and the investigation is as close to the optimum as possible by improving the data collection and using the technology and software to collect all data available without long waiting time.

Second one is the capability, Kaiser Permanente is one of the biggest insurance providers and healthcare organization needs to increase the scope of medicine and reach the patient base very quickly to provide suitable care and insurance at the same time by diversifying healthcare offering and delivery option such as home treatment, hospital care, and small centers deals. Creating new systems to catch the market by generating health and personal data to make management is easier now. Health management needs to shift from cure care to make all the procedure and tests to prevent the customers and decrease the cost of treatment and make more profit from other offers.

Interoperability is very important especially in healthcare organization. One of the biggest market driver for Kaiser Permanente is to give the patients multiple doctors servicing and best care in healthcare industry by spending a fair amount of time on the patients with best facilities and make sure the facilities are always ready and have the capability to exchange all the data with labs, pharmacy, doctors, and every single elements in the interoperability circle in real-time services.

Fourth market driver is improving the communication services by developing two main strategies to enhance the communication; first one is patient involvement and trying to involve the patient in the whole process to make them aware and second one is enhancing the doctor–patient communication using the healthcare utility with patient and doctor interface. These strategies need high technologies to make sure there is continuous development in communication.

Defragmentation is another important driver especially in the investigation phase to satisfy customers. According to the United Nations, the US' Chronic disease patients end up in the hospital more than they do in other OECD countries. While chronic disease sufferers are more likely to receive preventive medicine, Kaiser Permanente believes in treatment by primary care physicians rather than having their problems addressed by emergency physicians. This driver needs artificial intelligent (AI) to expect the preventive actions.

Business environment in general respond very quickly to standardization of organizations (Materla, Cudney, & Antony, 2019). Kaiser Permanente must be standardized in terms of procedure of data collection and analyze all the data to anticipate the problems to find common patterns. The goal of standards is to have complete functional healthcare platform.

Last market driver is making Kaiser Permanente innovative and creative. Healthcare industry is one of the biggest industries in terms of innovation and development especially in facility—home integrations and the ability to improve basic support and complicated procedure to reach the goal of more time dedicated to patient care. All the market drivers and the codes for them are shown in Table 12.1.

12.4.2 Technologies and Product Feature

The product characteristics listed in this section are used to determine how the market and company drivers can be satisfied. This section also focuses on product characteristics that will ensure the highest possible mix of drivers and product characteristics while taking into consideration

Table 12.1 Market driver

Code	*Market and business driver*
D1	Efficiency
D2	Capability
D3	Interoperability
D4	Communication
D5	Defragmentation
D6	Standardization
D7	Innovation

time and economic considerations. The authors came up with 11 main features that needed to be satisfied.

First feature is adaptability, new technology should adapt with all systems in the region. Technologies like regional alert system and regional emergency support should be as adaptable as possible.

Second feature of product is the mobility of the new product, Kaiser Permanente needs the product to be flexible and has ability of mobility to use new technology in hospital, home, and any Kaiser's clinic such as patient's wearable to connect with any device and enhance communication with doctors and pharmacist and emergency team. Kaiser could use cloud-based doctor as mobile appointment and trying to create mobile scanning devices. All those technologies should be connected with other treatment circle elements.

Third product feature is Automation one, using new technologies is one of the most important goal for Kaiser Permanente such as AI to collect all the data automatically and connect AI system with wearable devices. Using drones for delivering the prescriptions to patients or the questions from patients to doctors in a very quick and easy way.

Kaiser Permanente accepts any new product as long as it's secure enough to pass the procedure and security tests. Kaiser could use blockchain-encrypted data to increase the level of security and with automation and AI they could use patient's fingerprint to collect all the data needed in a secure way.

Fifth, one is home healthcare capability. With wearable and mobile devices, Kaisers wants to decrease the response time for home-based patients and with AI the response should be automated while this response is so critical in this kind of industry.

Diagnostic feature is also very important. With AI, the system can predict right diagnosis and prescription especially with all the data collected from patient fingerprint. After fair amount of time all prediction should be more trusted.

Feature number seven is trying to do all treatment, data collection, and communication in real time. Using telemedicine technology supported by AI, wearable devices and cloud-based doctors. This feature drives Kaiser Permanente to do Automatic recommendation for diagnosis and emergency support decisions.

Another feature is how to customize the treatment and technology to specific patient. How to create health dashboard for each patient and make a clock countdown for his or her life using all the technologies that support these actions such as AI. Table 12.3 shows all technology needed and the gaps on each one now.

Last two features are affordability and comfort, respectively, trying to make offers for insurance coverage and create a low-cost wearable to be affordable for everyone and through the time make sure that all these technologies and devices are very comfortable for patients. Table 12.2 shows all the product features with the technology supported by codes of required technologies Table 12.3.

12.4.3 Quality Function Deployment (QFD)

The authors give scores for market driver depending on what extent those market drivers are important for Kaiser Permanente. Communication, fragmentation, and innovation got high or 4, then efficiency and capability got medium, and the lowest two are interoperability and standardizations. Quality function deployment has been performed between market driver and product features and adaptability has the biggest score then automation and mobile with the same score. Security is also very important and home health care, respectively. All these features make diagnosis safer and easier in a real-time response to give the patients suitable customized recommendation. Last two features comparing with market drivers are affordability and comfort at number 10 and 11, respectively in ranking table (Table 12.4).

Another QFD has been developed to know the most important technology to cover the product features by giving adaptability, mobile tech, automation, security, real time and affordability a high ranking

Table 12.2 Product features with technologies needed

Code	*Product features*	*Tech support with code*
PF1	Adaptability	1a Regional Alert System 1b Regional Emergency Support
PF2	Mobility	2a Wearables 2b Cloud-Based Doctors 2c Mobile scanning devices
PF3	Automation	3a Wearable Devices 3b Drone Delivery 3c AI
PF4	Security	4a Blockchain Encrypted Data 4b Biometric "Fingerprints"
PF5	Home Health Care	5a Wearables 5b Mobile Devices 5c Automated Response System
PF6	Diagnostic	6a Tricorder Biometric Analysis Device 6b AI Diagnostic
PF7	Realtime	7a Wearables 7b Cloud-Based Doctors 7c Telemedicine
PF8	Recommendation	8a Cloud-Based Doctors 8b AI Prescriptions 8c Wearable Device Procedures 8d Cloud-based Emergency Support
PF9	Customization	9a Health Dashboard 9b Delivery Options 9c AI Support 9d Life Countdown Clock
PF10	Affordability	10a Low-Cost Medical Grade Wearables (Family) 10b IoT's Insurance Coverage
PF11	Comfort	11a Automated Reminder System 11b Family Health Dashboard 11c Progress Reports/Actions required

according to customers' surveys. Homecare diagnostic and customization are medium, and comfort got very low compared to other features.

After calculating everything, we found out that the mobile devices and wearable devices have the biggest score then cloud services and telemedicine technology, respectively. Technology number five at the ranking list is blockchain to make all data secured enough to make an automated alert response and emergency support systems secured and

Table 12.3 Technologies and gap analysis

Code	*Technology*	*Gap*
T1	Mobile	Medical data not directly linked to healthcare providers
T2	Wearables	Not Medically Validated (Inaccurate) Uncomfortable
T3	Cloud services	Lack of Support Software Unsecured data
T4	Telemedicine	Lack of internet coverage Lack of Training
T5	Health dashboard	Clinical Data Architecture (CDA)
T6	Blockchain	Sparse high-speed internet infrastructure Lack of trials
T7	Automated alert system	REQD Individual & mass alert capabilities
T8	Automated emergency	Need IoT's capable smart 911 system
T9	Bio clock	Proof that health can be predicted with sensor & device data
T10	Drone delivery	Lacks FAA regulations, FDA approval
T11	Data driven cost structure	Lacks Clinical Data Architecture & Medical Validations
T12	Artificial intelligent	Undeveloped for consumers use Lack of platform
T13	Biometric fingerprint	Database, CDA

real. For decreasing the time and focusing on efficiency, drone delivery got number seven. Artificial intelligent and the biometric fingerprint have a least score, respectively. Table 12.5 shows all the scores and ranking for all technologies.

12.4.4 Resources

In this section, the authors decided all the resources needed and some examples for these resources such as starting with sensor development to build a good and effective wearable device. There are a lot of companies that develop healthcare sensors such as HUMON. Sensors could help all system in terms of collecting data and communicate with lab to increase the real-time capability.

Government is another very useful and important resource. Kaiser could use military testing department before using new systems in commercial specially sensors and drone delivery.

Table 12.4 Market drivers vs product features QFD

		Drivers							*Score*	*Ranking*
		Efficiency (Medium 1)	*Capability (Medium 2)*	*Interoperability (Low 1)*	*Communication (High 4)*	*Fragmentation (High 4)*	*Standardisation (Low 1)*	*Innovation (High 4)*		
Product feature	Real Time	(4 × 2) 8	(2 × 2) 4	(4 × 1) 4	(4 × 4) 16	(1 × 4) 4	(1 × 1) 1	(4 × 4) 16	53	7
	Mobile	(4 × 2) 8	(4 × 2) 8	(4 × 1) 4	(4 × 4) 16	(1 × 4) 4	(2 × 1) 2	(4 × 4) 16	58	2
	Home Health Care	(2 × 2) 4	(4 × 2) 8	(4 × 1) 4	(4 × 4) 16	(1 × 4) 4	(2 × 2) 4	(4 × 4) 16	56	5
	Comfort	(1 × 2) 2	(1×2) 2	(1 × 1) 1	(1 × 4) 4	(1 × 4) 4	(2 × 2) 4	(2 × 4) 8	25	11
	Security	(4 × 2) 8	(4 × 2) 8	(4 × 1) 4	(4 × 4) 16	(1 × 4) 4	(1 × 1) 1	(4 × 4) 16	57	4
	Affordability	(4 × 2) 8	(2 × 2) 4	(2 × 1) 2	(2 × 4) 8	(1 × 4) 4	(1 × 1) 1	(4 × 4) 16	43	10
	Customization	(1×2) 2	(4 × 2) 8	(2 × 1) 2	(4 × 4) 16	(1 × 4) 4	(1 × 1) 1	(4 × 4) 16	49	9
	Automatization	(4 × 2) 8	(4 × 2) 8	(4 × 1) 4	(4 × 4) 16	(1 × 4) 4	(2 × 1) 2	(4 × 4) 16	58	2
	Adaptability	(4 × 2) 8	(4 × 2) 8	(2 × 1) 2	(4 × 4) 16	(4 × 4) 16	(2 × 2) 4	(2 × 4) 8	62	1
	Diagnostic	(4 × 2) 8	(4 × 2) 8	(4 × 1) 4	(2 × 4) 8	(2 × 4) 8	(1 × 2) 2	(4 × 4) 16	4	6
	Recommendation	(2 × 2) 4	(4 × 2) 8	(4 × 1) 4	(2 × 4) 8	(2 × 4) 8	(1 × 2) 2	(4 × 4) 16	50	8

Table 12.5 Product features vs technologies QFD

		Product features											*Score*	*Ranking*
		Adaptability (High 4)	*Mobile Tech (High 4)*	*Automated (High 4)*	*Security (High 4)*	*Home Care (Medium 2)*	*Diagnostic Services (Medium 2)*	*Real Time (High 4)*	*Intervention Services (Medium 2)*	*Customization (Medium 2)*	*Affordability (High 4)*	*Comfort (Low 1)*		
Technologies	Automated Alert & Response System	(4 × 4) 16	(4 × 4) 16	(4 × 4) 16	(4 × 4) 16	(4 × 2) 8	(4 × 2) 8	(4 × 4) 16	(4 × 2) 8	(1 × 2) 2	(1 × 4) 4	(4 × 1) 4	114	6
	Automated Emergency Support Systems	(4 × 4) 16	(4 × 4) 16	(4 × 4) 16	(4 × 4) 16	(4 × 2) 8	(4 × 2) 8	(4 × 4) 16	(4 × 2) 8	(1 × 2) 2	(1 × 4) 4	(4 × 1) 4	114	6
	Wearables Devices	(4 × 4) 16	(4 × 4) 16	(4 × 4) 16	(4 × 4) 16	(4 × 2) 8	(4 × 2) 8	(4 × 4) 16	(4 × 2) 8	(4 × 2) 8	(4 × 4) 16	(4 × 1) 4	132	1
	Cloud Services	(4 × 4) 16	(4 × 4) 16	(4 × 4) 16	(4 × 4) 16	(4 × 2) 8	(4 × 2) 8	(4 × 4) 16	(4 × 2) 8	(4 × 2) 8	(4 × 4) 16	(2 × 1) 2	130	2
	Mobile Devices	(4 × 4) 16	(4 × 4) 16	(4 × 4) 16	(4 × 4) 16	(4 × 2) 8	(4 × 2) 8	(4 × 4) 16	(4 × 2) 8	(4 × 2) 8	(4 × 4) 16	(4 × 1) 4	132	1
	Drone Delivery Options	(1 × 4) 4	(4 × 4) 16	(4 × 4) 16	(4 × 4) 16	(4 × 2) 8	(1 × 2) 2	(4 × 4) 16	(2 × 2) 4	(1 × 2) 2	(2 × 4) 8	(4 × 1) 4	96	7
	AI	(4 × 4) 16	(1 × 4) 4	(4 × 4) 16	(4 × 4) 16	(4 × 2) 8	(1 × 2) 2	(2 × 4) 8	(2 × 2) 4	(4 × 2) 8	(1 × 4) 4	(1 × 1) 1	87	9
	Blockchain	(4 × 4) 16	(2 × 4) 8	(4 × 4) 16	(4 × 4) 16	(2 × 2) 4	(2 × 2) 4	(4 × 4) 16	(4 × 2) 8	(4 × 2) 8	(4 × 4) 16	(4 × 1) 4	116	5
	Biometric Fingerprints	(2 × 4) 8	(1 × 4) 4	(4 × 4) 16	(4 × 4) 16	(1 × 2) 2	(1 × 2) 2	(1 × 4) 4	(4 × 2) 8	(4 × 2) 8	(2 × 4) 8	(2 × 1) 2	78	10
	Telemedicine Prescriptions	(4 × 4) 16	(4 × 4) 16	(4 × 4) 16	(4 × 4) 16	(4 × 2) 8	(2 × 2) 4	(4 × 4) 16	(4 × 2) 8	(4 × 2) 8	(2 × 4) 8	(4 × 1) 4	120	3

	Product features											*Score*	*Ranking*
	Adaptability (High 4)	*Mobile Tech (High 4)*	*Automated (High 4)*	*Security (High 4)*	*Home Care (Medium 2)*	*Diagnostic Services (Medium 2)*	*Real Time (High 4)*	*Intervention Services (Medium 2)*	*Customization (Medium 2)*	*Affordability (High 4)*	*Comfort (Low 1)*		
Dashboard Progress Reports	(4 × 4) 16	(4 × 4) 16	(4 × 4) 16	(4 × 4) 16	(2 × 2) 4	(4 × 2) 8	(4 × 4) 16	(1 × 2) 2	(2 × 2) 4	(4 × 4) 16	(4 × 1) 4	118	4
Bioclock Forecasting	(4 × 4) 16	(1 × 4) 4	(4 × 4) 16	(4 × 4) 16	(2 × 2) 4	(1 × 2) 2	(4 × 4) 16	(1 × 2) 2	(4 × 2) 8	(2 × 4) 8	(4 × 1) 4	96	7
Data Driven Cost Structure	(4 × 4) 16	(1 × 4) 4	(4 × 4) 16	(4 × 4) 16	(1 × 2) 2	(1 × 2) 2	(1 × 4) 4	(2 × 2) 4	(4 × 2) 8	(4 × 4) 16	(1 × 1) 1	89	8

FDA is the department responsible for space regulation. Drone delivery needs approval and adapt with FDA regulation. Another very important government partnership is with police and 911 systems to enhance the emergency alert system and automatic alert system with real-time response for patients by reducing all errors and waiting time. Another resource is new software. Kaiser roadmap should goes to computerize all systems to be automated and trusted, In order to create complete and trusted system, Kaiser should develop a new and strong software to run all applications and detect locations such as customized GIS. Using blockchain to enhance communication and secure the data also needs good and developed software.

Fourth resource is cloud services. As we explained, one of the biggest challenges in healthcare systems is how to make the data more secure and trusted. Cloud services not only make this function possible, but make the doctor–patient communication easier now. Using this technology make the home health care the best way to treat the emerging situation. IBM, AWS, and Intel are biggest companies in this kind of services. So, Kaiser should use one of these companies to develop their own cloud services.

In order to searching new technology and innovation driver, Kaiser must partner with research's centers or university to develop R&D department and be on top of new technologies. Boston dynamics is the most famous researching institute that Kaiser should open links with them to make sure that they have a good research resource.

Test all systems in sport league could be bifacial for healthcare institute in terms of media part and technical adjustment (Table 12.6).

Table 12.6 The resources

Code	*Resources*	*Examples*
R1	Sensor Development	Humon, Brainscope, Dash, Catapult,
R2	Government	Military, FDA, Smart 911, FAA
R3	Software	GIS, Apps, Blockchain
R4	Cloud Services	AWS, Intel, IBM
R5	Research	Boston Dynamics, University, DARPA
R6	Integrated Healthcare Enterprises	CDISC, OMG, NCPDP/SCRIPT, DICom, ASTM-CCD
R7	Testing	All Professional Sporting Leagues

Last resources that the authors came up with are Integrated Healthcare Enterprises such as:

CDISC Clinical Data Interchange Standardization consortium
OMG Object Management Group
NCPD National Council for Prescription Drug Programs (script)
DiCom Digital Imaging and Communications in Medicine
ASTM—CCR Continuity of Care Record.

12.5 Conclusion

Roadmaps are an important instrument for identifying important assets within and outside the organization. TRM aligns business with technology policies. They helped us to answer the following question:

"How can we compete with other healthcare organization and catch the fast growth opportunity?"

The answer is to follow the plan on Fig. 12.1.

Technology Roadmap Model was implemented in this research, which focuses on defining market drivers, creating a link between market drivers, and the product characteristics that could assist accomplish market drivers. This research also indicates the techniques that could close the product characteristics gap and highlights the resources needed to connect the product characteristics to the new techniques. QFD method was used to map characteristics of technology with product characteristics and product characteristics with market drivers. The final technology roadmap is set up after analyzing each part of the roadmap, as shown in Fig. 12.1.

Final roadmap is divided into 5 main time periods:

1. Present–5 years:

Main market drivers in this period are communication, Innovation and capability with starting efficiency and defragmentation after 2 years. In order to cover these market drivers. product should have mobility and be home-based used and reducing the waiting time as much as possible by transforming those features from science to technology and using the mobile, wearables, cloud services and home dashboard for home-based communication with telemedicine and data-driven. In this period Kaiser Permanente should start using all resources that they have and discuss.

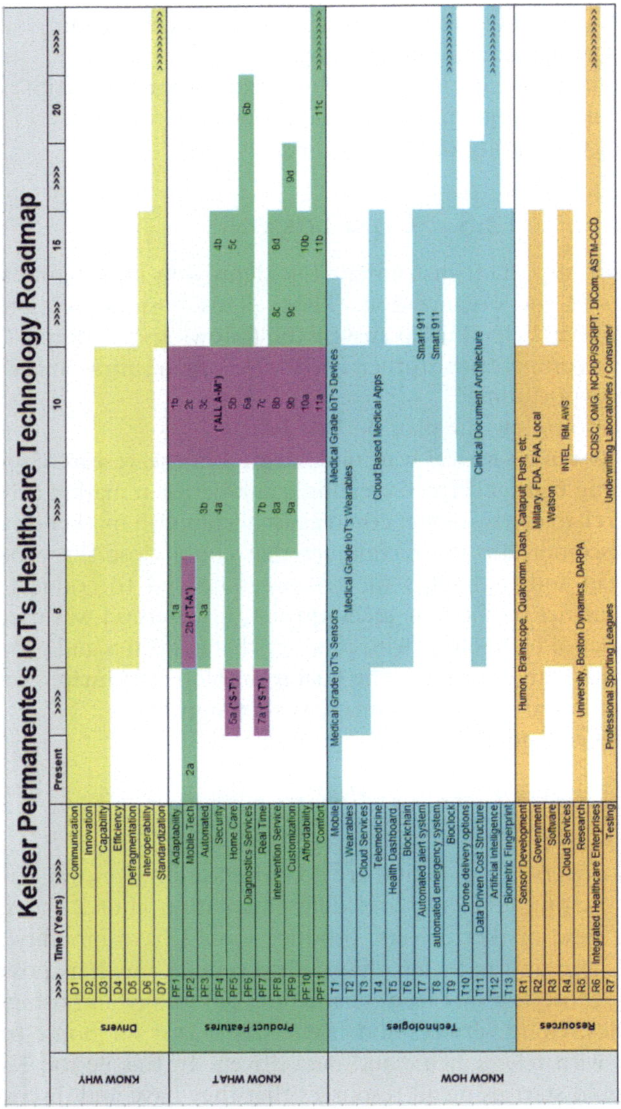

Fig. 12.1 Human resources

2. 5–10 years:

In this period, Kaiser's drivers add interoperability to all market drivers that they have. All technology should start transforming from technology to application phase. By using all technology except bio clock, Kaiser starts new level of management.

3. 10–15 years:

At this time, Kaiser should focus on standardization and interoperability drivers using the security and customized every product to specific patient and trying to enhance their services to be comfortable with all alert systems from government or FDA approvals products.

4. 15–20 years:

After 15 years, Kaiser Permanente should continue focusing on the standards and develop these standards to be acceptable for patients by using self-diagnosis systems, customized treatment, and delivery to be on comfort zone with bio clock technology and collect data with data-driven using AI technology.

5. After 20 years:

Using all integrated healthcare enterprises, Kaiser should continue developing the AI systems and bio clock technology to create more comfortable standards for doctors, patients, nurses, and technicians.

This chapter has important implications for practitioners since it provides a template for future technology roadmaps in the healthcare industry involving IOTs. The template can easily be adapted to other sectors such as sports, entertainment, smart homes or smart cities where IOTs are the major enabling technologies.

References

Aiken, L. H., Sermeus, W., Heede, K., Sloane, D. M., Busse, R., McKee, M., … Tishelman, C. (2012). Patient safety, satisfaction, and quality of hospital care: Cross sectional surveys of nurses and patients in 12 countries in Europe and the United States. *Bmj, 344,* 1717.

Albright, R. E., & Kappel, T. A. (2003). Roadmapping in the corporation. *Research-Technology Management, 46*(2), 31–40.

Alcantara, D. P., & Martens, M. L. (2019). Technology Roadmapping (TRM): A systematic review of the literature focusing on models. *Technological Forecasting and Social Change, 138,* 127–138.

Amer, M., Daim, T. U., & Jetter, A. (2016). Technology roadmap through fuzzy cognitive map-based scenarios: The case of wind energy sector of a developing country. *Technology Analysis & Strategic Management, 28*(2), 131–155.

Barker, D., & Smith, D. J. (1995). Technology foresight using roadmaps. *Long Range Planning, 28*(2), 21–28.

Başoglu, A. N., Işkın, İ., Aydınog, B., & Öztürk, M. (2012). New product development for the healthcare industry: A case study of diet software. *Health Policy and Technology, 1*(2), 93–104.

Basoglu, N., Daim, T. U., & Topacan, U. (2012). Determining patient preferences for remote monitoring. *Journal of Medical Systems, 36*(3), 1389–1401.

Behkami, N., & Daim, T. U. (2016). Exploring technology adoption in the case of the patient-centered medical home. *Health Policy and Technology, 5*(2), 166–188.

Behkami, N. A., & Daim, T. U. (2012). Research forecasting for health information technology (HIT), using technology intelligence. *Technological Forecasting and Social Change, 79*(3), 498–508.

Bitondo, D., & Frohman, A. (1981). Planning tools for effective research management in the '80s: Linking technological and business planning. *Research Management, 24*(6), 19–23.

CMSgov. (2019). *No Title*. Retrieved from https://www.cms.gov/Research-Statistics-Data-and-Systems/Statistics-Trends-and-Reports/NationalHealthExpendData/NationalHealthAccountsHistorical.html.

Cognizant. (2016). *How the Internet of Things is transforming medical devices.*

Daim, T. U., Al-Mulla, N., Sengupta, S. B., Shah, K., & Demchig, B. (2015). Technology assessment: Case of the wearable computing for fitness. *International Journal of Medical Engineering and Informatics, 7*(4), 321–364.

Daim, T. U., Amer, M., & Brenden, R. (2012). Technology roadmapping for wind energy: Case of the Pacific Northwest. *Journal of Cleaner Production, 20*(1), 27–37.

Daim, T. U., Gomez, F. A., Martin, H., & Sheikh, N. (2013). Technology roadmap development process (TRDP) in the medical electronic device industry. *International Journal of Business Innovation and Research, 7*(2), 228–263.

Daim, T. U., Yoon, B. S., Lindenberg, J., Grizzi, R., Estep, J., & Oliver, T. (2018). Strategic roadmapping of robotics technologies for the power industry: A multicriteria technology assessment. *Technological Forecasting and Social Change, 131*, 49–66.

Davidson, E., Baird, A., & Prince, K. (2018). Opening the envelope of health care information systems research. *Information and Organization, 28*(3), 140–151.

E.I.R.M.A. (1997). *Technology roadmapping—Delivering a business vision*. Paris, France: EIRMA.

Fenwick, D., Daim, T., & Gerdsri, N. (2009). Value-driventechnology road map (VTRM). *PICMET: Portland International Center for Management of Engineering and Technology, Proceedings* (pp. 2517–2529). https://doi.org/10.1109/PICMET.2009.5261808.

Force, N. G. M. R. T. (1997). Next-generation manufacturing: A framework for action. In *Digest of US industry roadmaps* (Vol. III). Bethlehem, PA, USA: NGM Project Office.

Groenveld, P. (1997). Roadmapping integrates business and technology. *Research-Technology Management, 40*(5), 48–55.

Hansen, C., Daim, T., Ernst, H., & Herstatt, C. (2016). The future of rail automation: A scenario-based technology roadmap for the rail automation market. *Technological Forecasting and Social Change, 110*, 195–212

Hogaboam, L., & Daim, T. (2018). Technology adoption potential of medical devices: The case of wearable sensor products for pervasive care in neurosurgery and orthopedics. *Health Policy and Technology, 7*(4), 409–419.

Jeffrey, H., Sedgwick, J., & Robinson, C. (2013). Technology roadmaps: An evaluation of their success in the renewable energy sector. *Technological Forecasting and Social Change, 80*(5), 1015–1027. https://doi.org/10.1016/j.techfore.2012.09.016.

Jungwirth, D., & Haluza, D. (2019). Information and communication technology and the future of healthcare: Results of a multi-scenario Delphi survey. *Health Informatics Journal, 25*(1), 161–173.

Khanam, M., & Daim, T. U. (2017). A regional technology roadmap to enable the adoption of CO_2 heat pump water heater: A case from the Pacific Northwest, USA. *Energy Strategy Reviews, 18*, 157–174.

Kostoff, R. N., & Schaller, R. R. (2001). Science and technology roadmaps. *IEEE Transactions on Engineering Management, 48*(2), 132–143.

Lamb, A. M., Daim, T. U., & Leavengood, S. (2012). Wood pellet technology roadmap. *IEEE Transactions on Sustainable Energy, 3*(2), 218–230.

Martin, H., & Daim, T. U. (2012). Technology roadmap development process (TRDP) for the service sector: A conceptual framework. *Technology in Society, 34*(1), 94–105.

Materla, T., Cudney, E. A., & Antony, J. (2019). The application of Kano model in the healthcare industry: A systematic literature review. *Total Quality Management & Business Excellence, 30*(5–6), 660–681.

Matthews, W. H. (1992). Conceptual framework for integrating technology into business strategy. *International Journal of Vehicle Design, 13*(5–6), 524–532.

Meesala, A., & Paul, J. (2018). Service quality, consumer satisfaction and loyalty in hospitals: Thinking for the future. *Journal of Retailing and Consumer Services, 40,* 261–269.

Moretta Tartaglione, A., Cavacece, Y., Cassia, F., & Russo, G. (2018). The excellence of patient-centered healthcare: Investigating the links between empowerment, co-creation and satisfaction. *The TQM Journal, 30*(2), 153–167.

Porter, M. E. (2008). *Competitive strategy: Techniques for analyzing industries and competitors*. USA: Free Press.

Probert, D., & Radnor, M. (2003). Frontier experiences from industry-academia consortia. *Research-Technology Management, 46*(2), 27–30.

Rathert, C., Vogus, T. J., & McClelland, L. E. (2016). Re-humanizing health care. In *The Oxford handbook of health care management* (p. 141). Oxford: Oxford University Press.

Rivero, A. R. G., & Daim, T. (2017). Technology roadmap: Cattle farming sustainability in Germany. *Journal of Cleaner Production, 142,* 4310–4326.

Romanski, B., & Daim, T. (2019). A technology roadmap to uncontested market space using autonomous vehicles in the transportation industry. *IEEE Engineering Management Review, 47*(1), 67–76.

Schimpf, S., & Abele, T. (2019). How German companies apply roadmapping: Evidence from an empirical study. *Journal of Engineering and Technology Management, 52,* 74–88.

Sourav, K., Daim, T., & Herstatt, C. (2018). Technology roadmap for the single-aisle program of a major aircraft industry company. *IEEE Engineering Management Review, 46*(2), 103–120.

Spatar, D., Kok, O., Basoglu, N., & Daim, T. (2019). Adoption factors of electronic health record systems. *Technology in Society, 58,* 101144.

Tóth, Z. E., Jónás, T., & Dénes, R. V. (2019). Applying flexible fuzzy numbers for evaluating service features in healthcare–patients and employees in the focus. *Total Quality Management & Business Excellence, 30*(supl), 240–254.

Vogus, T. J., & McClelland, L. E. (2016). When the customer is the patient: Lessons from healthcare research on patient satisfaction and service quality ratings. *Human Resource Management Review, 26*(1), 37–49.

Weiss, B. A., Vogl, G., Helu, M., Qiao, G., Pellegrino, J., Justiniano, M., & Raghunathan, A. (2015). Measurement science for prognostics and health management for smart manufacturing systems: key findings from a roadmapping workshop. In *Proceedings of the Annual Conference of the Prognostics and Health Management Society. Prognostics and Health Management Society Conference* (Vol. 6). NIH public Access.

Wells, R. D., Phaal, R., Farrukh, C., & Probert, D. (2004). Technology roadmapping for a service organization. *Research Technology Management, 47*(2), 46–51.

Willyard, C. H., & McClees, C. W. (1987). Motorola's technology roadmap process. *Research Management, 30*(5), 13–19.

Winebrake, J. J., & Creswick, B. P. (2003). The future of hydrogen fueling systems for transportation: An application of perspective-based scenario analysis using the analytic hierarchy process. *Technological Forecasting and Social Change, 70*(4), 359–384.

Yeole, A. S., & Kalbande, D. R. (2016). Use of internet of things (IoT) in healthcare: A survey. In *Proceedings of the ACM Symposium on Women in Research 2016* (pp. 71–76). ACM.

CHAPTER 13

BNDES' Impact on the Steel Industry's Efficiency: A Two-Stage Malmquist Model Usage

Ricardo Kalil Moraes and Peter F. Wanke

13.1 Introduction

This chapter examines the possible impacts on the efficiency of the firms resulting from financing offered by public banks of economic development (development banks). This issue is part of a wider scope of public–private relations in which the State operates through institutional regulations or in a more active way either by public spending or by providing public financing. In developing economies, in particular by means of development banks, this type of activity by the State in promoting industrialization and productive infrastructure has the objective of productive modernization and economic development (Aghion,

R. K. Moraes (✉) · P. F. Wanke
Rio de Janeiro Federal University, Rio de Janeiro, Brazil
e-mail: ricardo.kalil@coppead.ufrj.br

P. F. Wanke
e-mail: peter@coppead.ufrj.br

J. J. M. Ferreira et al. (eds.), *Technological Innovation and International Competitiveness for Business Growth*, Palgrave Studies in Democracy, Innovation, and Entrepreneurship for Growth,
https://doi.org/10.1007/978-3-030-51995-7_13

1999; Lazzarini, Musacchio, Bandeira-de-Mello, & Marcon, 2015). Until recently, a significant part of the long-term credit was provided by these banks, especially the Brazilian National Development Bank (BNDES) being one of the largest banks in terms of number and volume of transactions (Torres & Zeidan, 2016).

However, the most recent quantitative studies have concentrated on assessing the effects of public spending on private investment (Melo & Rodrigues, 1998; Shanmugan, 2017; Sonaglio, Braga, & Campos, 2010; Tadeu & Silva 2013). Alternatively, as for development banks, there is a gap of quantitative studies with the largest part of the research being in public banks in general (Andrianova, Demetriades, & Shortland, 2008; Carvalho, 2014; La Porta, López-De-Silanes, & Shleifer, 2002; Yeyati, Micco, & Panizza, 2007), or following theoretical and qualitative scopes (Bond 2013; Bruck 1998; Gutierrez, Rudolph, Homa, & Beneit, 2011; Hochstetler & Montero, 2013; Torres & Zeidan, 2016).

One of the few quantitative studies on development banks focuses the impact on the level of investments (Lazzarini et al., 2015). However, there is still a gap in the research in relation to the impact from the role of the development banks on the efficiency of the firms receiving financing.

Extensive research has been carried out over the past few years on sector efficiency based on parametric and nonparametric approaches. The main sectors to be studied have been banking (Azad, Musinamy, Masum, Saona, & Wanke, 2016; Bahrini, 2015; Barros & Wanke, 2014; Fukuyama & Matousek, 2017; Lee & Kim, 2013; Rezvanian, Rao, & Mehdian, 2008), insurance (Barros, Dumbo, & Wanke, 2014; Wanke & Barros, 2016), infrastructure (Estache, De La Fé, & Trujillo, 2004; Marchetti & Wanke, 2017; Sarkis, 2000), and industry (He, Zhang, Lei, Fu, & Xu, 2013; Li & Lin, 2015; Ma, Evans, Fuller, & Stewart, 2002).

The objective of this chapter is to complement the line of research on public banks by addressing the impact on the efficiency of the firms based on nonparametric modeling of Data Envelopment Analysis (DEA). In particular, the Malmquist model of DEA and later nonlinear regression to test the effects of contextual variables on the Malmquist efficiency indexes for companies in the steel sector. The study of this sector of economic activity can be justified due to its relevance in both economic growth and for increasing industrialization due to the spillover effects (Huh, 2011). Due to the remarkable increase of China and India production on last decades, steel sector has put an environmental challenge for the next years, mainly due to energy consumption and gas emission (Debnath &

Sebastian, 2014; Feng, Huang, Wang, & Song, 2018; Yu, Li, Qiao, & Shi, 2015). Furthermore, the steel industry in Brazil is one of the main recipients of funding from BNDES in the period considered, 3% of all lendings, with a peak in 2007 (11%). Thus, by using Malmquist-DEA methodology, our research search for the impact from BNDES lendings on Brazilian steel firms, in terms of efficiency through modernization (catching-up effect) and innovation (frontier shift effect).

In addition to this introduction, the chapter is organized as follows: Sect. 13.2 presents the role of BNDES and of the steel industry, Sect. 13.3 presents the literature review covering studies on public development banks as well as the recent literature applying efficiency modeling with an emphasis on the Malmquist models, Sect. 13.4 presents the data and methodology applied, and Sect. 13.5 analyzes and discusses the results highlighting the significance of the contextual variables. Finally, the conclusions suggest implications of public policies, the study's limitations, and possibilities for future research.

13.2 Context

13.2.1 Brazilian National Development Bank (BNDES)

BNDES is one of the largest development banks in the world and has taken on a significant role in offering long-term credit in Brazil in recent years (Torres & Zeidan, 2016). According to Colby (2012), the bank's three main activities can be listed as: (a) complement the offer of credit, (b) economic restructuring, and (c) countercyclical policies. While the first and the third would have a horizontal nature, the second would take on a vertical nature aiming at the productive structure by means of reorientation or creation of new competitive advantages.

The magnitude of its participation in the Brazilian economy has increased since the global financial crisis of 2008 in three aspects: (a) financing of productive investment, (b) granting of guarantees, and (c) sectoral consolidations through mergers and acquisitions of companies. The bank has also taken on a key role in making major infrastructure projects feasible in the sectors of oil & gas, energy, and logistics. Consequently, this set of capital intensive projects began to have a growing weight in the bank's portfolio of assets. This growth in the bank's role corresponded to a growth in financial resources by the National Treasury and from specific funds such as the Worker's Welfare Fund (FAT, acronym in Portuguese).

In particular, the bank provides two main financial instruments to support investment in R$D in order to promote innovation: entrepreneurship financing (FINEM) and technological solutions. FINEM settled specific interest rates by theme. Its cheaper rate focuses on[1]: social investment; environment; inclusive connectivity; innovation (advanced manufacturing); human resource qualification; public safety; sewage and energy (solar).

The bank is currently in a paradigm shift due to the coming together of three factors: (a) retraction of the Brazilian economy, (b) the impeachment process, and (c) upward trend of public deficit. This situation reflects in a reduction of productive activity and consequently the demand for financing for productive investment along with a new round of divestiture of assets and concession of public services in infrastructure that require different instruments of institutional action on the part of BNDES.

Parallel to this, a debate begins about the size of the Brazilian State and consequently about the standard of BNDES's recent actions. Some of the main issues that arise in this debate refer to the selection of projects—strategy of the "national champions", return of resources to the National Treasury, and readjusting the long-term interest rate (LTIR).

13.2.2 The Steel Sector

Throughout the twentieth century, the standard of industrial mass production was built around capital-intensive industries and of scale focused on the production of consumer durables and capital goods. The steel industry arose among the intermediate industries supplying inputs because of its relation with the construction industry through the production of long products (cables, rebars) and with the metal-mechanical complex through flat products (plates, coils). Economic development was interpreted as the increasing incorporation of these industries into the productive matrix, hence the relevance of the steel sector for building more complex and dynamic productive matrices (Huh, 2011).

[1] 0.9% a.a.

Waves of forced development and industrialization were observed by different groups of developing countries with the application of industrial policies focused on setting up steel complexes integrated with their respective economies. In chronological order we can list Japan, subsequently South Korea, and in recent decades mainly China and India (Debnath & Sebastian, 2014; Huh, 2011; Lee & Ki, 2017; Wu, 2000). Specifically regarding the South Korean and Chinese companies, there are specific sites that have been interpreted as relevant for their productive and economic performance. While the former presents economic integration with the metal-mechanical chain geared to exports, especially the automobile industry, household appliances, and shipbuilding (Huh, 2011), the latter is linked to the growth of domestic demand, bringing together both the metal-mechanics industry and civil construction while increasing the offer of infrastructure services (Sun, Dong, & Zhao, 2017; Wu, 2000).

In Brazil, the incorporation of the steel industry was directly linked to its industrial policy of putting in place a set of state companies. Beginning in the 1990s, simultaneous processes took place of economic opening, deregulation of markets, and privatization resulting in the formation of three large private economic groups: Companhia Siderúrgica Nacional (CSN), Usiminas, and Gerdau (Montero, 1998). Later on the multinational company Arcelor Mittal entered the market through acquisition and consolidation of the former state productive capacity (Companhia Siderúrgica de Tubarão—CST) and private companies (Mendes Junior). The Brazilian steel sector also presents characteristics that are relevant to its performance such as productive integration with the main raw material, iron ore, as well as with the logistics infrastructure for the distribution of steel products to the domestic market and of iron ore abroad.

13.2.3 Innovations in the Steel Sector

In the last two decades, R&D spending and innovations have been driven by environmental issues, focusing on energy consumption and gas emission (Feng et al., 2018; He et al., 2013; Liu & Gao, 2016; Ozawa, Sheimbaum, Martin, Worrell, & Price, 2002; Pardo & Moya, 2013; Yu et al., 2015). Following these two drivers, mainly process innovation has taken place, such as the usage of direct reduction of iron (DRI), basic oxygen furnace (BOF), and electric arc furnace (EAF), allowing improvements in energy efficiency rate (Ozawa, op.cit). In addition, changes in input and fuel mix, by larger use of scrap, natural gas and electricity, paved the way to gas emission reduction (Ozawa et al., 2002; Pardo & Moya, 2013).

In particular, due to its huge increase of steel production in the last decade, China has shown to be concerned about these environmental issues. In this sense, Chinese public policies have gradually supported investments on energy-saving technology and scrap usage (Feng et al., 2018; Yu et al., 2015).

In Brazil, in spite of BNDES offering particular financial instrument to support research and development (R&D) spending, the steel sector investments have been strongly focused on capacity expansion and modernization. Between 2002 and 2016, from the total amount of projects that got financial support from BNDES less than 1% corresponded to innovation. Capacity expansion and modernization concentrated 58.27 and 24.25%, respectively.[2] This implies that steel sector investment has been driven more to a catching up process, if we assume that capacity expansion and modernization would made use of the more up to date technology available, than to a innovative or frontier shift process.

13.3 Literature Review

13.3.1 Development Banks

The debate about the interaction of the State with the market implies in arguments that oppose complementarity—correction of market failures and competition for economic resources (Hicks, 1937). Quantitative researches on the effect of public spending on the private sector conducted mainly in developing economies reach different results depending on the sample of countries and temporal space considered. There is a set of studies indicative of crowding-out of public spending on private spending (Melo & Rodrigues, 1998; Sonaglio et al., 2010) and another indicating crowding-in specifically in relation to the infrastructure sector (Shanmugan, 2017; Tadeu & Silva, 2013).

As for development banks, an evolution can be observed both in their way of operating as well as in the line of research. After an initial period of

[2] Data of each project, its description and amount of money borrowed are available at www.bndes.gov.br.

an active public policy geared to industrialization characterized by long-term financing, the next phase was one of financing the privatization of infrastructure along with a countercyclical role in response to the international financial crisis, adopting new forms of intervention such as minority shareholding and providing guarantees (Hochstetler & Montero, 2013; Torres & Zeidan, 2016). Recent research, however, on the role of development banks considers a series of risks and costs as an effect that distorts investment decisions, as well as crowding-out on the private banking sector, resulting in a negative impact on economic growth, hoping to stimulate a rent-seeking behavior on the part of the market (Lazzarini et al., 2015). As for the quantitative research (Lazzarini et al., 2015) on the other hand, neither was significance found of BNDES on the private investment, nor a rent-seeking behavior by the economic agents in relation to electoral financing.

In the last years, national development banks worldwide have been promoting industrial policy focused on environmental issues, such as energy efficiency and gas emissions reduction. Larger banks such as german KFW, China Development Bank, Asian Development Bank and the European Union has been offering aid to projects of clean energy and inputs substitution which increased power generation from solar, eolic and natural gas sources in Europe and Asia, and improved scrap usage, mainly in Europe and China (Delina, 2011; Geddes, Schmidt, & Steffen, 2018; Naqvi, Henoq, & Chang, 2018).

In spite of the risks and costs related to the development banks, their presence in many countries indicates a function of providing long-term credit that would be relevant for projects of social value to the extent that they would mitigate the effect of market failures and externalities (Yeyati et al., 2007) and address problems related to the insufficiency of effective demand due to radical uncertainty (Ferraz, Além, & Madeira, 2013). According to the post-Keynesian approach, the presence of radical uncertainty would be relevant for forming the investment decisions of the private agent, which corresponds to a negative impact on the level of effective demand. In this sense, by providing long-term funding, the development banks could play a fundamental role for enabling and sustaining the level of investments, especially in activities more subject to the negative impact of uncertainty, corresponding to high capital expenditures, long periods of maturation of the investment, and significant social impacts such as externalities resulting from innovations.

Of the roles assigned to these banks of correcting market failures, sustaining the level of investments, and promoting development, this last one is viewed as being the most efficient use of economic resources. So, the following research questions can be proposed:

- BNDES credit promotes the efficiency of the recipient steel firm?
- This efficiency gain comes equally form modernization (catching-up) and innovation (frontier shift)?

13.3.2 The Steel Sector

Recent research on the steel sector indicates intensive use of energy and capital (Debnath & Sebastian, 2014; Nielsen, 2017) as well as a correlation with the dynamics of growth of the gross domestic product (GDP) and industrial competitiveness by creating integrated productive chains (Huh, 2011). This dynamic would have a positive impact on the steel sector by stimulating the investment and feasibility of larger production scales. In this sense, scale economies would have an important role in the performance and efficiency of the steel sector (Debnath & Sebastian, 2014; Huh, 2011; Kim, Lee, Kim, & Lee, 2006; Nielsen, 2017; Wu, 2000). This growth dynamic, however, would induce an asymmetric mechanism to increase capacity, resulting in inefficient allocation of resources in the long term (Sun et al., 2017).

Furthermore, the investment would have a positive impact on efficiency, to the extent that it represents production modernization, by incorporating newer equipment and plants (Kim et al., 2006). This modernization effect specifically would be inserted into contexts of windows of opportunity, which would explain the catching up, for example, of the Japanese and South Korean companies (Lee & Ki, 2017).

On innovation and modernization themes, special focus on environmental issues such as energy efficiency and gas emission has taken place, mainly the use of time series models to estimate the impact of new technologies on energy consumption and gas emission (Ozawa et al., 2002) and DEA models to evaluate energy efficiency (Feng et al., 2018; He et al., 2013).

13.3.3 Efficiency Analysis

Since the establishment of the DEA methodology (Charnes, Cooper, & Rhodes, 1978), there has been a significant growth in research concerning the efficiency of firms in various sectors of economic activity. A significant part of the articles focuses on the sectors of infrastructure and financial services, which are subject to regulation by the State and therefore potentially indicative of direction for public policies. Furthermore, as for the industrial sectors, there is a tendency for research to be done with a focus on environmental issues or energy efficiency (He et al., 2013; Li & Lin, 2015). Specifically regarding the steel sector, the research has focused on financial indicators, energy consumption, and emission of pollutants (Debnath & Sebastian, 2014; Kim et al., 2006; Nielsen, 2017). Table 13.1 presents the literature review on efficiency analysis.

Traditionally the research has concentrated on the estimation of the efficiency frontiers and in identifying the positioning of the firms in relation to the frontier (Barros et al., 2014; Estache et al., 2004; He et al., 2013; Li & Lin, 2015; Ma et al., 2002; Sarkis, 2000). In general, the Malmquist Productivity Index (MPI) is used for evaluating the interfirm performance, highlighting the dynamic effects of displacing the efficiency frontier.

More recently, especially in the banking sector, the DEA methodology of estimating efficiency has been used in two stages associated with econometric methods such as generalized linear models, panel data, and bootstrap truncated regression. Thus, relations can be identified between the efficiency indexes and explanatory contextual variables (Azad et al., 2016; Bahrini, 2015; Lee & Kim, 2013; Marchetti & Wanke, 2017). This greater complexity of the research allows implications for formulating public policies and for decision-making processes.

In particular, Bahrini (2015) and Lee and Kim (2013), respectively, applied two-stage MPI models in order to identify the explanatory contextual variables on the performance of Islamic and Koreans banks. While the performance of the Islamic system is related to the banking variables (capitalization, size, profitability, credit risk), the performance of the Korean banking sector would be more related to the type of the bank's ownership—international or public.

Due to the growing application of two-stage models for estimating efficiency, especially in the banking sector that include accounting variables, the choice of the methodology of this research uses this type of procedure

Table 13.1 Literature review—analysis of efficiency and public policy to the steel industry

See sample MS for how to insert callouts in MS

Author/year	*Research proposal*	*DMU/period*	*Method*	*Country*	*Inputs/independent variables*	*Products/dependent variables*	*Context variables/findings*
Feng et al. (2018)	Evaluation of the energy efficiency (EE) in iron an steel sector	27/2001–14	DEA metafrontier, TGI, SEI and PEI	China	Labour, capital sock, energy consumption	Gross output and CO_2 emission	–
Geddes et al. (2018)	Clean energy policy by national development banks		Qualitative case study—52 interviews and design of a risk matrix	Australia, UK and German	Bank instruments and activities	Barriers to investment (political, technical, commercial, novelty and proficiency	Mainly activities addressed the most part of barriers
Nielsen (2017)	Efficiency of the steel sector	21	DEA CRS and VRS	Market and planned economies	Energy and raw materials (coal, iron, and scrap)	Production of crude steel and pig iron	
Liu and Gao (2016)	The effect of carbon price on low carbon technology difusion in steel industry	60	Survey MDBC	China	Payback	Investment in low carbon technologies	–

See sample MS for how to insert callouts in MS

Author/year	*Research proposal*	*DMU/period*	*Method*	*Country*	*Inputs/independent variables*	*Products/dependent variables*	*Context variables/findings*
Li and Lin (2015)	Method for measuring growth of green productivity	504	MLPI	China	Capital stock, use, energy	Gross industrial product, CO_2 emissions	–
Yu et al. (2015)	Relationship among carbon emission, investment, technology expenditure in steel industry and GDP	1990–2010	VAR	China	Control and command policy, market-based policy	Carbon emissions, investment, technology expenditure, GDP	–
Debnath and Sebastian (2014)	Efficiency in the steel sector	22	BCC Model	India	Employment, fixed assets, current assets, and energy	Income, profits before and after taxes, sales	–
He et al. (2013)	Energy efficiency and productivity variation in the steel sector	400	MPI and MPLI	China	Net fixed assets, employment, energy	Added value, gaseous waste, liquid waste, solid waste	–
Pardo and Moya (2013)	Technology innovation impact on energy and CO_2 emission efficiency		Simulation and forecasting model	European Union	Innovative technologies and best practices; scrap, energy, CO_2 prices; steel demand	Energy consumption and CO_2 emission	Net scrap imports

(continued)

Table 13.1 (continued)

See sample MS for how to insert callouts in MS

Author/year	*Research proposal*	*DMU/period*	*Method*	*Country*	*Inputs/independent variables*	*Products/dependent variables*	*Context variables/findings*
Huh (2011)	Steel consumption and economic growth	1975–2008	VEC and VAR	South Korea	–	–	Steel consumption and economic activity of steel consumers (long, flat and pipes) Reinforcemnt growth mechanism
Ghosh (2006)	Steel consumption and economic growth consumption	1951–2004	Vector autoregressive (VAR)	India	–	–	No long run relationshionship. Economic growth foster steel
Kim et al. (2006)	Sources of productive efficiency in steel industry	22	SFA	Several countries	Employment, productive capacity, raw material	Production of crude steel	Ownership (private or public), plant age, scale
Ma et al. (2002)	Operational efficiency of the steel sector	711	MPI	China	Employment, fixed capital, energy, age, working capital	Production	–

See sample MS for how to insert callouts in MS

Author/year	*Research proposal*	*DMU/period*	*Method*	*Country*	*Inputs/independent variables*	*Products/dependent variables*	*Context variables/findings*
Ozawa et al. (2002)	Efficiency in energy use and CO_2 emission in iron and steel	1970–1996	Time series estimation	Mexico	Production volume; (+) product and process mix (−); efficiency(−); fuel mix(−)	Electricity consumption CO_2 emission	DRI technology through changed fuel consumption to natural gas and electricity, and scrap usage. These foster energy efficiency, product and fuel mix

DEA = data envelopment analysis; CRS = constant return of scale; VRS − variable return of scale; TGI = technology gap; SEI = scale inefficiency; PEI = pure technology inefficiency; MDBC = multibounded discrete choice; MPI = Malmquist productivity index; MPLI = Malmquist-Luenberger productivity index; VAR = vector autoregressive; VEC = vector errors correction; SFA = stochastic frontier analysis in order to fill the gap of quantitative studies regarding the impact of the financing from development banks in the performance of the steel firms.

13.4 Methodology

This research applies a two-stage model to estimate the role of efficiency. The growth ratio method of Malmquist productivity oriented to the product will be used to obtain the productivity indexes (Malmquist Index), as well as the portions corresponding to the frontier approximation effect (Technical Change) and frontier displacement (Frontier Shift). Next a nonlinear robust regression approach is applied to test the impact of the contextual variables on the Malmquist index. All estimates were performed in R using the following packages: *nonparaeff* (Malmquist index); mgcv, gamlss, MCMCpack, MCMCglmm, and DEoptim (robust regression).

13.4.1 Malmquist Index

The Malmquist Productivity Index can be broken down into two components related to interfirm efficiency gain (catching up effect) and displacement of the efficiency curve (technological change) between period t and $t + 1$ (Fare, Grosskopf, Norris, & Zhang, 1994) according to Eq. (13.1):

$$PRODch = EFFch \times TECHch \tag{13.1}$$

with,

$$PRODch = \left(\frac{D_0^t(x^{t+1}, y^{t+1})}{D_0^t(x^t, y^t)} \frac{D_0^{t+1}(x^{t+1}, y^{t+1})}{D_0^{t+1}(x^t, y^t)} \right)^{1/2} \tag{13.2}$$

$$EFFch = D_0^{t+1}\left(x^{t+1}, y^{t+1}\right) / D_0^t\left(x^t, y^t\right) \tag{13.3}$$

$$TECHch = \left(\frac{D_0^t\left(x^{t+1}, y^{t+1}\right)}{D_0^{t+1}\left(x^{t+1}, y^{t+1}\right)} \frac{D_0^t\left(x^t, y^t\right)}{D_0^{t+1}\left(x^t, y^t\right)} \right)^{1/2} \tag{13.4}$$

where:

D0—maximizing function of relative distance (Fare et al., 1994).

These indexes are allocated to the following function to which the robust regression is applied:

$$\begin{aligned} Y_{jz} = & \beta_0 + \beta_i \sum X_i + \beta_2 BNDES + Brasil + China \\ & + Coreia + \beta_i \sum Z_i + \varepsilon_j \end{aligned} \tag{13.5}$$

being,

j—DMU

z—*PRODch*, *EFFch*, *TECHch*

Xi—accounting-financial contextual variables specific for the firms (price of labor, cost of capital, EBITDA/asset ratio, CAPEX/assets ratio, leverage)

Zi—socioeconomic contextual variables (GDP growth, GDP by purchasing power parity—GDP PPP, inflation, Human Development Index (HDI), Gini Index, Foreign Direct Investment—FDI, energy use, life expectancy, infant mortality, global innovation, and logistics performance)

BNDES—dummy variable (financing granted by the bank in year *t*)

Brazil—dummy variable for Brazilian company

China—dummy variable for Chinese company

Korea—dummy variable for South Korean company.

While the dummy BNDES represents the hypothesis to be tested by the model, the dummies for Brazil, China, and Korea were applied due to the specifications mentioned in the section Context. In turn, the socioeconomic contextual variables would be related to greater economic development and competitiveness as mentioned in the section Context regarding the relevance of the level of business activities.

13.4.2 Nonlinear Stochastic Robust Regression Approach

In this approach, the following regression methods were combined for applying the bootstrapping and nonlinear stochastic programming technique: ordinary least squares (OLS), generalized linear model (GLM), generalized additive model (GAM), generalized additive model for location, scale, and shape (GAMLSS), Markov chain Monte Carlo and generalized linear mixed model (MCMC-GLMM) and Markov chain Monte Carlo and Gaussian linear model (MCMC-Gaussian Linear). All these methods are properly described in Faraway (2006). This combination is justified because most of the regression approaches generate biased results in the two-stage DEA. This can be mitigated by using the bootstrapping technique (Simar & Wilson, 2007, 2011) and by the combination of forecasts to return to a smaller variance of errors (James, Witten, Hastie, & Tibshirani, 2013; Ledolter, 2013).

The problem of nonlinear stochastic optimization for combining the regressions after applying the bootstrapping is presented in model (6) where w_1, w_2, w_3, w_4, w_5, and w_6 represent weights between 0 and 1 are assigned to the vectors of the regression residuals. This model optimizes the values of w so that the variance (*Var*) of the combined residuals (***Ri***) is minimal. Bootstrapping was applied to all regressions and were recombined 100 times, allowing a distribution of the profile w to be collected for the best estimates of efficiency scores and of the weight division model. The residual variances were collected assuming the linear model for each of these regressions, linking the efficiency/division of weights estimates with the contextual variables.

$$
\begin{aligned}
&\min Var(w_1\boldsymbol{R}1 + w_2\boldsymbol{R}2 + w_3\boldsymbol{R}3 + w_4\boldsymbol{R}4 + w_5\boldsymbol{R}5 + w_5\boldsymbol{R}6)\\
&S.T.\\
&\sum_{i=1}^{6} w_i = 1\\
&0 \le w_1 \le 1\\
&0 \le w_2 \le 1\\
&0 \le w_3 \le 1\\
&0 \le w_4 \le 1\\
&0 \le w_6 \le 1
\end{aligned}
\qquad (13.6)
$$

Model (13.6) was solved by means of the differential evolution (DE) technique (Mullen, Ardia, Gil, Windover, & Cline, 2011; Thangaraj, Pant, Bouvry, & Abraham, 2010). Additional references can be found at Ardia, Boudt, Carl, Mullen, and Peterson (2011).

13.5 Data Analysis and Discussion of the Results

13.5.1 Data

In recent years, projects in the steel sector have been some of the main recipients of funding from BNDES.[3] Because of this, the companies in this sector were selected as the object of analysis in this study. Considering the small number of Brazilian firms, we opted for a sample that included some of the largest international competitors. The sample selected of 34 companies was obtained based on a pre-selected sample made by Bloomberg.[4,5] Furthermore, due to the availability of data for the variables considered, the analysis was restricted to the period 2010–2015.

The raw data set was worked on to make it possible to be used with the MPI model, specifically regarding the restriction to nonzero values for inputs and products. The application of the model to the natural logarithms of the variables also required treatment for negative and zero values. The procedure adopted was the transformation of the data to a 0–1 scale, adding 2 to each observation for posterior logarithmic transformation.

13.5.2 Results

As for fitting the distributions into the MPIs, Fig. 13.1 describes the adjustments of the OLS, GLM, GAM, GAMLSS, MCMC-GLMM, and MCMC-Gaussian Linear regressions for their non-conditional inverse accumulated distributions. However, it is not possible to affirm in principle if a specific distribution is preferred in detriment to another. This suggests that a combination of results from these regressions would be a more appropriate approach. In fact, the results for the Kullback-Leibler (KL) divergence test presented in Table 13.2 for conditional distributions of MPIs indicates that the differences between both the adjustments

[3] The file of contracts is available at www.bndes.gov.br.

[4] Anyang, Arcelor, Azovstal, Baosteel. Beijing, China, CSN, Eregli, Gerdau, Guangri, Hesteel, Hunan, Hyundai, JFE, Kobe, Liuzhou, Maanshan, Magnito, Mechel, Nippon, Novolipetsk, Nucor, Pangang, Posco. SAAB, Severstal, Shandong, Steel Dynamics, Ternium, TSK, US Steel, Usiminas, Voestalpine, and Xinyu.

[5] Data collected from Bloomberg and complemented with information provided in the Annual Reports and Financial Forms available on the websites of the firms.

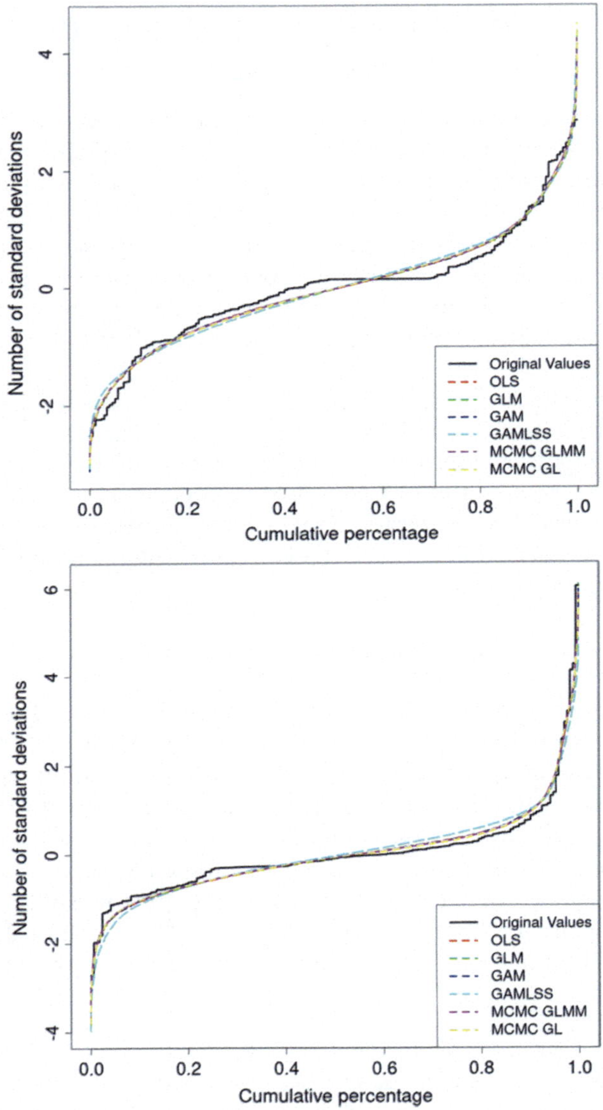

Fig. 13.1 KL divergence for Technical Change (high), Frontier Shift (mean), and Malmquist Index (low)

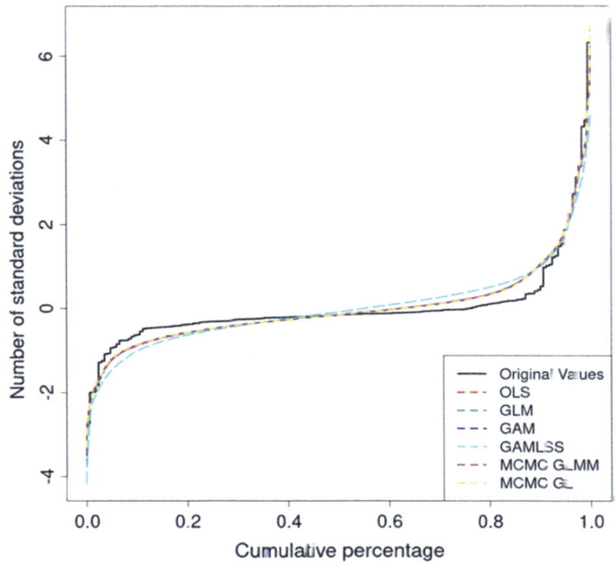

Fig. 13.1 (continued)

Table 13.2 Results of the KL divergence

	OLS	*GLM*	*GAM*	*GAMLSS*	*MCMC GLMM*	*MCMC GL*
Technical Change	0.1791	0.1675	0.1773	0.1863	0.1780	0.1696
Frontier Shift	0.0472	0.0469	0.0471	0.1110	0.0449	0.0430
Malmquist Index	0.1325	0.1325	0.1301	0.2694	0.1321	0.1241

is minimal for most distributions assumed, sometimes favoring a distribution, which means a specific type of regression, in detriment to another.

The results for the nonlinear stochastic optimization on the residuals of 100 bootstrap regressions according to the OLS, GLM, GAM, GAMLSS, MCMC-GLMM, and MCMC-Gaussian Linear methods are presented in Fig. 13.2 for the MPIs of the different steel companies around the

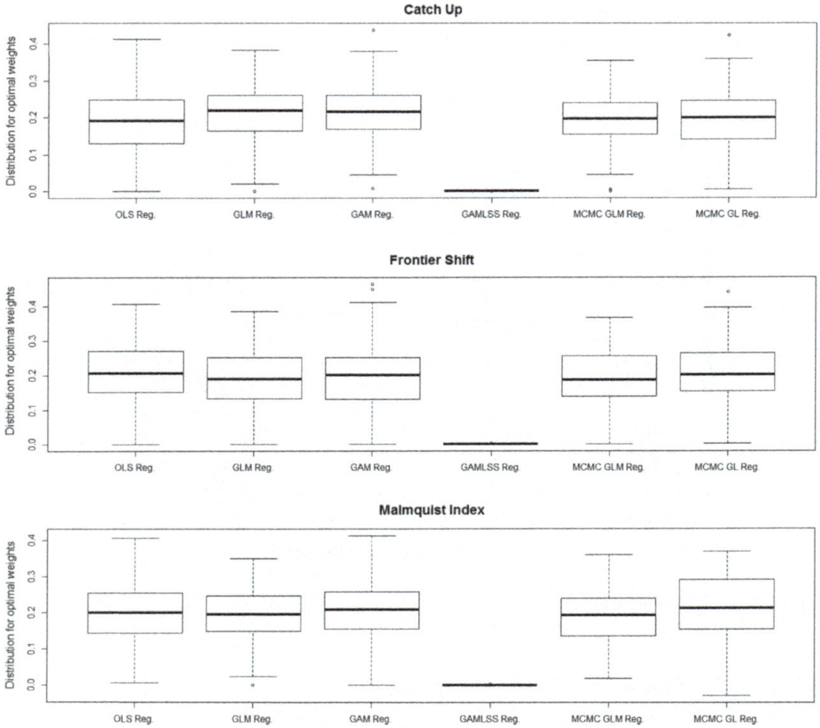

Fig. 13.2 Optimal distribution of weights

world. The results suggest, with the exception of the GAMLSS regression, almost the same dispersion among the weights assigned to the other 5 regressions. Also interesting to note are the best performances of the OLS and GAM models for the displacement of the frontier and the change of productivity. These results suggest the importance of a combination of different methods not only in terms for removing bias, but also in terms of capturing the benefits of mixing different distribution formats for the prediction of efficiency.

The results from the bootstrap combined regression for the contextual variable coefficients used to predict the MPIs are presented in Fig. 13.3. Readers should note that if the distribution of the bootstrap coefficients

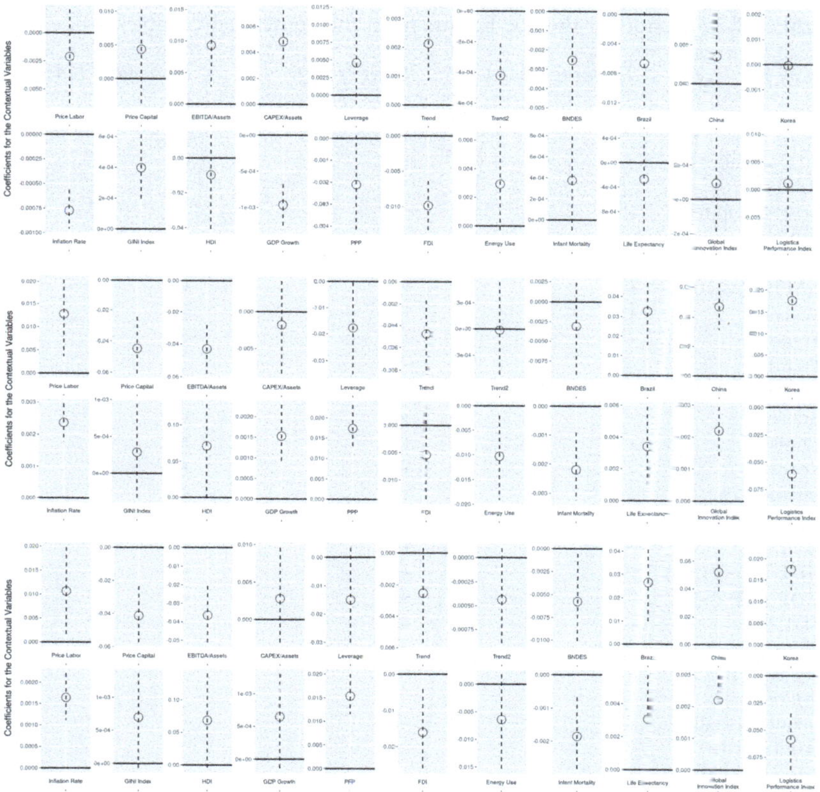

Fig. 13.3 Results of the coefficients for Technical Change (high), Frontier Shift (mean), and Malmquist Index (low)

crosses the solid line that marks zero in each graph in Fig. 13.3, the variable should be interpreted as not significant. This is the case for some contextual variables analyzed in the context of the three models, implying that productivity in the steel producers is driven by the economy of various factors such as the change in total productivity and the effects of Technical Change and Frontier Shift. The results regarding the significance and the direction of the impact on the indexes are summarized in Table 13.3.

Table 13.3 Results of the coefficients from the contextual variables

Variable	*Technical Change*		*Frontier Shift*		*Malmquist Index*	
	Sign	*Significant*	*Sign*	*Significant*	*Sign*	*Significant*
Price of labor (LN)	–		+	*	+	*
Cost of capital (LN)	+		–	*	–	*
EBITDA/assets	+	*	–	*	–	*
CAPEX/assets	+	*	–		+	
Leverage	+		–	*	–	
Trend	+	*	–	*	–	
Trend^2	–	*	–		–	
BNDES	–	*	–		–	*
Brazil	–		+	*	+	*
China	+		+	*	+	*
Korea	–		+	*	+	*
Inflation (%)	–	*	+	*	+	*
Gini Index	+	*	+		+	
HDI	–		+		+	
GDP growth (%)	–	*	+	*	+	
GDP PPP ($)	–		+	*	+	*
FDI ($)	–	*	–		–	*
Energy use (kg eq. oil *per capita*)	+		–	*	–	
Infant mortality (1000 births)	+		–	*	–	*
Life expectancy (years)	–		+	*	+	*
Global innovation index	+		+	*	+	*
Logistics performance index	+		–	*	–	*

A greater relevance of the Frontier Shift effect can be observed in the definition of the Malmquist index to the extent that the respective coefficients have the same signs for most of the contextual variables. In addition, compared to most of the contextual variables, the significance for the Malmquist index comes from the significance for its respective *Frontier Shift*. The two effects are strengthened in response to the contextual variables BNDES, China, Gini, FDI, and the global innovation index.

As for the Technical Change effect, only nine contextual variables were considered significant. The positive impact was because of EBITDA/assets (cash generation) and CAPEX/assets (investment) ratios, the short-term trend, and the Gini index. According to the literature review, the results corroborate the expectation as to the positive impact insofar as in the short term a greater volume of investment would enable productive modernization and larger scales of production on the one hand, while the growth of the Gini index, representing an improvement in the distribution of income, reinforces the inductor power represented by the GDP through the incorporation of steel consumption *per capita*. Additionally, in the short term, the greater cash generation can represent greater operational efficiency, providing resources that contribute to the schedule of investments.

As for the variables of negative impact, the long-term trend would corroborate to the inefficient allocation of resources (Sun et al., 2017). The inflationary effect can be interpreted as symmetrical to the Gini index effect, and in fact this effect has been considered negative for the distribution of income. In principle, the negative effect of the growth in GDP and the foreign direct investment (FDI) would be contrary to the expectations regarding the inducer role of the GDP and investment. However, it should be considered that the first, if on the one hand would have an inducer effect, on the other hand it represents an increase in the level of activity that would affect the economy as a whole, opening up space for stronger competition with the allocation of resources and the consequent pressure of costs represented by the inflationary impact. The interpretation of the second would follow this same line of competition for allocation of resources in other productive activities. Additionally, unlike the CAPEX/assets ratio, this index does not fully translate into investment in the expansion and modernization of capacity. In general, portions of this investment have been used to acquire existing assets and portfolio investments (shares on the stock exchange).

As for the research's questions, however, the results inasmuch as BNDES financing has a negative impact on the Technical Change effect.

But as for the Frontier Shift, its fourteen variables showed to be significant. The positive impact would come from the price of labor, the dummies of the countries, the inflation rate, GDP growth, GDP by purchasing power parity (GDP PPP), life expectancy, and global innovation index. This corroborates the expectations with regard to the specificities of the countries and the development indicators with effects on modernization and incorporation of technology. Specifically, the positive impact of the price of labor in a capital-intensive industry can represent an incentive to the commitment of more qualified workers (Wanke, Azad, Barros, & Hassan, 2016). Furthermore, the growth and level of economic activity would provide new scales of production, allowing for the displacement of the efficiency frontier.

The negative impact from the variables of the price of capital, cash generation, indebtedness, trend, energy use, infant mortality, and logistics performance index corroborates some of the expectations discussed in the literature review. Considering the capital-intensive nature of the steel sector, the negative sign of the cost of capital corroborates with the theoretical hypothesis of a negative impact of this cost on the firm's efficiency, as well as the negative impact from the leverage on the indicators of technological frontier may indicate that the financial cost of the indebtedness on the part of the companies in the sample would be related to a worse performance in the generation of financial results, thus impacting the products profit and dividends. In the case of an energy-intensive sector in which various studies emphasize the relevance of energy efficiency, the negative impact of the intensity of using energy would be consistent with the representation of an environment of high energy consumption, thus competing with the steel sector. The negative impact of infant mortality is consistent with greater social development. In turn, the negative impact from the logistics performance index seems to be representing the correlation between the use of logistics and the level of activity. The higher the latter, while keeping constant with the infrastructure available, would cause a worsening in the index. In this sense, highlighting the positive impact from the level of activity on the Frontier Shift represented by the coefficients of the inflation rate, GDP growth, and GDP PPP, the negative impact from the logistics performance index would be consistent.

As for the contextual variable BNDES, this would not be significant for displacing the frontier. This result would be consistent with the expectation from this public policy instrument, which would be toward reducing the technological gap that exists and not for the displacement of the frontier. As can be seen in the context section, a few R&D projects in steel sector has been financially supported by this bank.

The impact from BNDES specifically can also be understood in light of the behavior of the dummy Brazil. It should be pointed out that during the period analyzed, there were not BNDES disbursements in the steel sector neither for all the Brazilian companies (CSN) nor in all the years. The relevance of the dummy Brazil for defining the frontier efficiency would be an indication that, as a whole, Brazilian companies have contributed more to the displacement of the efficiency frontier than for the Technical Change effect. Therefore, for Brazil, the Frontier Shift effect would be more significant, indicating that the financing from BNDES would not be relatively significant for this productive sector.

13.6 Conclusions

The wide use of two-stage DEA models for estimating efficiency frontiers and identifying contextual variables that explain the performance of firms, in particular as regards the various studies on the banking sector, seems to be promising for assessing the impact of development banks on the productive performance of industries. The implications of public policies may indicate a reorientation of the loan transactions from these banks, implying, for example, in the systematization of institutional instruments that focus on the resources according to pre-defined objectives.

No positive impact was identified in this study from the BNDES loans on the efficiency of the firms in the recent period, specifically regarding reducing the efficiency gap through a possible Technical Change effect. However, this study has limitations because it represents a specific sector sample, the steel sector. Complementary studies with a focus on other industrial sectors receiving financing from BNDES may contribute to evaluating the hypothesis proposed.

Furthermore, it should also be noted that the actions of BNDES and other development banks could have an impact on other social objectives (Yeyati et al., 2007) that are beyond the scope of this chapter. To broaden this scope, future research should consider the projects financed by BNDES and their respective social impacts.

References

Aghion, B. A. (1999). Development banking. *Journal of Development Economics, 58*(1), 83–100.

Andrianova, S., Demetriades, P., & Shortland, A. (2008). Government ownership of banks, institutions, and financial development. *Journal of Development Economics, 85*(1), 218–252.

Ardia, D., Boudt, K., Carl, P., Mullen, K., & Peterson, B. (2011). Differential evolution with DEoptim: An application to non-convex portfolio optimization. *The R Journal, 3,* 27–34.

Azad, A. K., Musinamy, S., Masum, A. K. M., Saona, P., & Wanke, P. (2016). Bank efficiency in Malaysia: A use of Malmquist meta-frontier analysis. *Eurasian Business Review, 7*(2), 287–311.

Bahrini, R. (2015). Productivity of MENA Islamic banks: A bootstrapped Malmquist index approach. *International Journal of Islamic and Middle Eastern Finance and Management, 8*(4), 508–528.

Barros, C., Dumbo, S., & Wanke, P. (2014). Efficiency determinants and capacity issues in Angolan insurance companies. *South African Journal of Economics, 82*(3), 455–467.

Barros, C., & Wanke, P. (2014). Banking efficiency in Brazil. *Journal of International Financial Markets, Institutions & Money, 28,* 54–65.

Bond, P. (2013). The BRICS bank and shifts in multilateral finance: A view from South Africa. In *SouthGovNet Conference Panel: Institutions of South-South Cooperation*. Shanghai. [s.n.]. Shanghai: Fudan University Institute of International Relations.

Bruck, N. (1998). The role of development banks in the twenty-first century. *Journal of Emerging Markets, 3,* 39–68.

Carvalho, D. (2014). The real effects of government-owned banks: Evidence from an emerging market. *Journal of Finance, 69*(2), 577–609.

Charnes, A., Cooper, W., & Rhodes, E. (1978). Measuring the efficiency of decision making units. *European Journal of Operational Research, 2*(6), 429–444.

Colby, S. (2012). Explaining the BNDES: What it is, what it does and how it works. *CEBRI Artigos, 8*(3), 3–31.

Debnath, R. M., & Sebastian, V. J. (2014). Efficiency in the Indian iron and steel industry: An application of data envelopment analysis. *Journal of Advances in Management Research, 11*(1), 4–19.

Delina, L. L. (2011). Clean energy financing at Asian Development Bank. *Energy for Sustainable Development, 15,* 195–199.

Estache, A., De La Fé, B., & Trujillo, L. (2004). Sources of efficiency gains in port reform: A DEA decomposition of Malmquist TFP index for Mexico. *Utilities Policy, 12,* 221–230.

Faraway, J. (2006). *Extending the linear model with R: Generalized linear, mixed effects and nonparametric regression models*. Boca Raton, FL: Taylor and Francis.

Fare, R., Grosskopf, S., Norris, N., & Zhang, Z. (1994). Productivity growth, technical progress and efficiency changes in industrial countries. *American Economic Review, 84,* 66–83.

Feng, C., Huang, J., Wang, M., & Song, Y. (2018). Energy efficiency in China's iron and steel industry: Evidence and policy implications. *Journal of Cleaner Production, 177,* 837–845.

Ferraz, J. C., Além, A. C., & Madeira, R. F. (2013). A contribuição dos bancos de desenvolvimento para o financiamento de longo prazo. *Revista Do BNDES, 40,* 5–42.

Fukuyama, H., & Matousek, R. (2017). Modelling bank performance: A network DEA approach. *European Journal of Operational Research, 259,* 721–732.

Geddes, A., Schmidt, T. S., & Steffen, B. (2018). The multiple roles of state investment banks in low-carbon energy finance: An analysis of Australia, the UK and Germany. *Energy Policy, 115,* 158–170.

Ghosh, S. (2006). Steel consumption and economic growth: Evidence from India. *Resources Policy, 31,* 7–11.

Gutierrez, E. Rudolph, H. P., Homa, T., & Beneit, E. T. (2011). *Development banks: Role and mechanisms to increase their efficiency* (World Bank Policy Research Working Paper Series, 5729). World Bank. http://documents.worldbank.org/curated/en/912941468045550498/Development-banks-role-and-mechanisms-to-increase-their-efficiency. Accessed 29 Apr 2020.

He, F., Zhang, K., Lei, J., Fu, W., & Xu, X. (2013). Energy efficiency and productivity change of China's iron and steel industry: Accounting for undesirable outputs. *Energy Policy, 54,* 204–213.

Hicks, J. (1937). Mr. Keynes and the "Classics": A suggested interpretation. *Econometrica, 5*(2), 147–149.

Hochstetler, K., & Montero, A. P. (2013). The renewed developmental state: The National Development Bank and the Brazil model. *Journal of Development Studies, 49*(11), 1484–1499.

Huh, K. (2011). Steel consumption and economic growth in Korea: Long-term and short-term evidence. *Resources Policy, 36,* 107–113.

James, G., Witten, D., Hastie, T., & Tibshirani, R. (2013). *An introduction to statistical learning: With application in R*. New York. NY: Springer.

Kim, J. W., Lee, J. Y., Kim, J. Y., & Lee, H. K. (2006). Sources of productive efficiency: International comparison of iron and steel firms. *Resources Policy, 31,* 239–246.

La Porta, R., López-De-Silanes, F., & Shleifer, A. (2002). Government ownership of banks. *Journal of Finance, 57*(2), 265–301.

Lazzarini, S. G., Musacchio, A., Bandeira-de-Mello, R., & Marcon, R. (2015). What do state-owned development banks do? Evidence from BNDES, 2002–09. *World Development, 66*, 237–253.

Ledolter, J. (2013). *Data mining and business analytics with R*. Hoboken, NJ: Wiley & Sons.

Lee, J. K., & Kim, D. (2013). Bank performance and its determinance in Korea. *Japan and the World Economy, 27*, 83–94.

Lee, K., & Ki, J. (2017). Rise of latecomers and catch-up cycles in the world steel industry. *Research Policy, 46*, 365–375.

Li, K., & Lin, B. (2015). Measuring green productivity growth of Chinese industrial sectors during 1998–2015. *China Economic Review, 36*, 279–295.

Lin, X., & Gao, X. (2016). A survey analysis of low carbon technology diffusion in China's iron & steel industry. *Journal of Cleaner Production, 129*, 88–101.

Ma, J., Evans, D. G., Fuller, R. J., & Stewart, D. F. (2002). Technical efficiency and productivity change of China's iron and steel industry. *International Journal of Production Economics, 76*, 293–312.

Marchetti, D., & Wanke, P. (2017). Brazil's rail freight transport: Efficiency analysis using two-stage DEA and cluster-driven public policies. *Socio-Economic Planning Sciences, 59*, 26–42.

Melo, G. M., & Rodrigues, W., Jr. (1998). *Determinantes do investimento privado no Brasil: 1970–1995* (Texto para Discussão Ipea n. 605). Brasília, DF: Instituto de Pesquisa Econômica Aplicada.

Montero, A. P. (1998). State interests and the new industrial policy in Brazil: The privatization of steel, 1990–1994. *Journal of Interamerican Studies and World Affairs, 40*(3), 27–62.

Mullen, K., Ardia, D., Gil, D., Windover, D., & Cline, J. (2011). DEoptim: An R package for global optimization by differential evolution. *Journal of Statistical Software, 40*(6), 1–26.

Naqvi, N., Henoq, A., & Chang, H. (2018). Kicking away the financial ladder? German development banking under economic globalization. *Review of International Political Economy, 25*(5), 672–698.

Nielsen, H. (2017). Productive efficiency in the iron and steel sector under state planning: The case of China and former Czechoslovakia in a comparative perspective. *Applied Energy, 85*, 1732–1743.

Ozawa, L., Sheimbaum, C., Martin, N., Worrell, E., & Price, L. (2002). Energy use and CO_2 emissions in Mexico's iron and steel industry. *Energy, 27*, 225–239.

Pardo, N., & Moya, J. A. (2013). Prospectie scenarios on energy efficiency and CO_2 emissions in the European Iron & Steel industry. *Energy, 54*, 113–128.

Rezvanian, R., Rao, N., & Mehdian, S. (2008). Efficiency change, technological progress and productivity growth of private, public and foreign banks in India:

Evidence from the pos-liberalization era. *Applied Financial Economics, 18*, 701–713.

Sarkis, J. (2000). An analysis of the operational efficiency of major airports in the United States. *Journal of Operations Management, 18*, 335–351.

Shanmugan, M. (2017). Does public investment crowd-out private investment in India? *Journal of Financial Economic Policy, 9*(1), 1–23.

Simar, L., & Wilson, P. (2007). Estimation and inference in two-stage, semi-parametric models of production processes. *Journal of Econometrics, 136*, 31–64.

Simar, L., & Wilson, P. (2011). Two-stage DEA: *caveat emptor*. *Journal of Productivity Analysis, 36*(2), 205–218.

Sonaglio, C. M., Braga, M. J., & Campos, A. C. (2010). Investimento público e privado no brasil: evidências dos efeitos *crowding-in* e *crowding-out* no período 1995–2006. *Revista de Economia, 11*(2), 383–404.

Sun, W., Dong, K., & Zhao, T. (2017). Market demand dynamic induced mechanism in China's steel industry. *Resources Policy, 51*, 13–21.

Tadeu, H., & Silva, J. (2013). The determinants of the long term private investment in Brazil: An empirical analysis using cross-section and a Monte Carlo simulation. *Journal of Economics, Finance and Administrative Science, 18*, 11–17.

Thangaraj, R., Pant, M., Bouvry, P., & Abraham, A. (2010, December 16–18). Solving multi objective stochastic programming problems using differential evolution. In *Swarm, Evolutionary, and Memetic Computing: First International Conference on Swarm, Evolutionary, and Memetic Computing, SEMCCO 2010* (pp. 54–61), Chennai, India. Proceedings. Berlin, Heidelberg: Springer Berlin Heidelberg.

Torres, E., & Zeidan, R. (2016). The life-cycle of national development banks: The experience of Brazil's BNDES. *The Quarterly Review of Economics and Finance, 62*, 97–104.

Wanke, P., Azad, M. A. K., Barros, C. P., & Hassan, M. K. (2016). Predicting efficiency in Islamic banks: An integrated multi-criteria decision making (MCDM) approach. *Journal of International Financial Markets, Institutions & Money, 45*, 126–141.

Wanke, P., & Barros, C. P. (2016). Efficiency drivers in Brazilian insurance: A two-stage DEA meta frontier-data mining approach. *Economic Modelling, 53*, 8–22.

Wu, Y. (2000). The Chinese steel industry: Recent developments and prospects. *Resources Policy, 26*, 171–178.

Yeyati, E., Micco, A., & Panizza, U. (2007). A reappraisal of state-owned banks. *Economía, 7*(2), 209–247.

Yu, B., Li, Z., Qiao, Y., & Shi, L. (2015). Low-carbon transition of iron and steel industry in China: Carbon intensity, economic growth and policy intervention. *Journal of Environmental Sciences, 28*, 137–147.

CHAPTER 14

Fostering Business Growth and Innovation Through Internationalization: The Interesting Illustration of the Indian IT Industry

Santoshi Sengupta, Parth Patel, and Sawlat Zaman

14.1 Introduction

India is rising as a country of vast business and industrial power (Oskarsson & Lahiri-Dutt, 2019; Thakur & Hale, 2013) as it is actively pursuing the progressive policies of technological innovation, economic liberalization, deregulation and privatization of the service sector (Alam, 2007; Sehgal & Gupta, 2019). These policies have given a boost to

S. Sengupta
School of Management, Graphic Era Hill University, Bhimtal, India

P. Patel (✉) · S. Zaman
Newcastle University Business School, Newcastle University, Newcastle upon Tyne, UK
e-mail: parth.patel@ncl.ac.uk

S. Zaman
e-mail: sawlat.zaman@ncl.ac.uk

J. J. M. Ferreira et al. (eds.), *Technological Innovation and International Competitiveness for Business Growth*, Palgrave Studies in Democracy, Innovation, and Entrepreneurship for Growth,
https://doi.org/10.1007/978-3-030-51995-7_14

various Indian industries, especially the knowledge-intensive information technology (IT) industry (MacKenzie, 2006), which has witnessed unprecedented growth. Such escalation of the Indian IT industry has brought velocity in the innovativeness of the country; boosted its technological transformations; accelerated its economic growth; and lifted India as an attractive alternative for foreign investors (Sheshabalaya, 2004). According to India Brand Equity Foundation (IBEF, 2018), a trust established by the Department of Commerce, Ministry of Commerce and Industry, and Government of India; this country is the most preferred sourcing destination across the world, accounting for approximately 55% market share of the US$185–190 billion global services sourcing business. Indian IT & IT-enabled services companies have set up more than 1000 global delivery centers in about 80 countries across the world (IBEF, 2018). With such unparalleled growth, India has become the center of digital capabilities of the world with around 70% of global digital talent in the form of human resources present in the country.

The phenomenal growth of the Indian software industry in terms of sales, employment, and exports has been unprecedented as compared to the performance of other industrial sectors in India (Athreye, 2005). The hidden saga behind this success revolves around the abilities of the pioneer firms in the industry that transformed the programming skills of their labor force into firm-specific capabilities that gave them a competitive advantage to become credible competitors of international firms in the outsourced-software market. The ability of Indian firms to assemble their teams of talented engineers, and deliver strong, high-quality technical service to customers anywhere in the world has given them a strong point. Also, the way firms have leveraged their capabilities to derive maximum economic value through the adaptation and perfection of a new business model called the global delivery model (GDM).

In the Indian IT industry, there are a lot of successful examples of global delivery centers that facilitate in extending the technological services and digital capabilities to global markets. Companies combine their innovation and competitive actions to create new opportunities for business growth as both technological innovation and competitiveness are imperative for business growth in the global market through internationalization. Internationalization of ventures received accelerated research focus in the era of the 1980s wherein scholars centered on finding the differences between modern international business frameworks and traditional international business frameworks (Oviatt & McDougall, 1994;

Saiyed, Fernhaber, Basant, & Dhandapani, 2020). However, understanding internationalization in the context of emerging economies has received only underdeveloped research attention (Kiss, Danis, & Cavusgil, 2012). Thus, we attempt to study the IT industry which is a competent example of internationalization that has fostered business growth in the context of the emerging economy of India. The Indian IT industry has grown due to the combined role of technology, innovation, and global competitiveness (Papazoglou & Spanos, 2018) which have eventually driven many firms to success (Chen, Yin, & Mei, 2018). So how do these firms that operate globally through a distributed network use their business model to gain international competitive advantages? While literature is abundant with the growth of IT industry in India and the rise of the GDM, this chapter attempts to bring a consolidated and comprehensive overview about the evolution of the IT industry in the globe, followed by global dominance of Indian IT industry, the business model of Indian IT industry, and their competitive advantage.

14.2 The Evolution of IT and Its Global Industry

IT refers to any system, product, or process whose underlying technology base is composed of computer-based hardware and software. IT is the use of computers to store, protect, retrieve, process, transmit, and manipulate data, or information, often in the context of a business or other enterprise. It is considered a subset of information and communications technology. Owing to its strong reliance on the use of computer systems for managing information, it is also called management information systems (MIS).

IT has had an interesting evolution story that began in the early 30s of the past century. Punched card units and record machines started getting increasing attention as they began to be widely used for limited data processing. This was followed by the University of Pennsylvania in the US, building and unveiling the first electronic digital computer in 1946. The computer, as stated in Forester's research (1986) weighed around 30 tons, contained 18,000 vacuum tubes, and cost approximately 500 thousand dollars. It gave way to the computer industry that gradually expanded during the 1950s and the 1960s. The major turnaround came when Intel Inc. invented the computer chip (microprocessor) in 1971, which boosted the mass-scale production of personal computers. This was followed by the emergence of cellular radios and satellites and the rise of professional computers and integrated software in the 80s (Forester,

1986). By the early 1990s, the computer market witnessed substantial growth as computing power and memory beyond basic user needs also increased, thus making personal computers a household commodity (Fig. 14.1).

With the expansion of computing and the internet, software applications also started getting prominence as they began to be extensively used by business organizations for enterprise resource planning, database, and internet communications (Eischen, 2000). This was further escalated by the transformation of the internet into a global phenomenon that occurred with the creation of "HTTP" and internet "browser" (or the World Wide Web) in the 1990s. This simply changed the course of things as a vast network of computing power could then (in the 2000s) be accessed locally, via ethernet and globally, via the internet (Eischen, 2000). An array of technologies was developed following the union of internet and wireless communications which changed the basic way IT was developed, shared, and used between consumers across the globe. These consumers could be individual users and business firms using technologies such as web 3.0, social networking, p2p networks, online

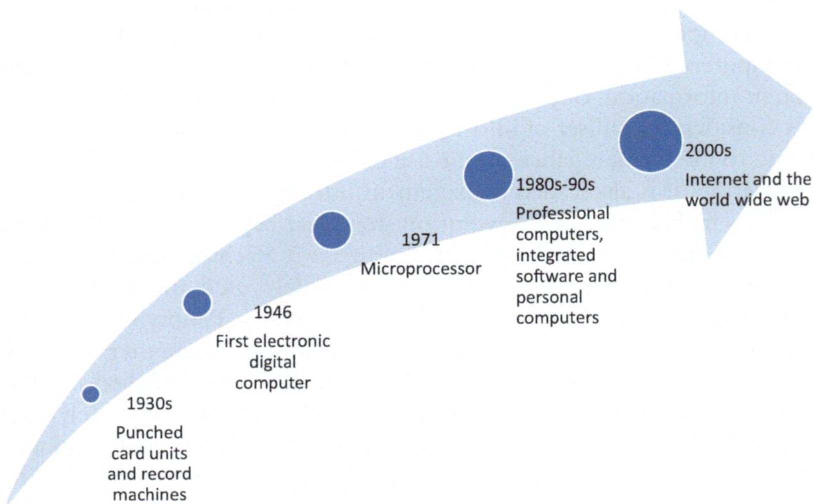

Fig. 14.1 Evolution of information technology (Developed by the authors for this chapter)

markets, cloud computing, mobile and touch computing, tablets, and apps.

As IT grew, businesses around computers also grew. Many companies entered into the business of designing, manufacturing, installing, and servicing computers which eventually emerged as one of the fastest-growing industries across the world. Many of these companies are Multinational corporations (MNCs) (Roche, 1992) that include excellent examples of companies from emerging economies that are seeking to expand into value-added products and services world-wide (Moghaddam, Sethi, Weber, & Wu, 2014). For instance, a country such as India, an emerging economy, has experienced significant growth in its software and services industry. India's IT & ITeS industry grew to US$181 billion in 2018–19. In India, production of software was virtually non-existent during the early 1980s, but by the early 2000s, the Indian IT industry was employing more than 450,000 employees (Arora & Gambardella, 2005).

14.3 The IT Industry of India

The Indian IT industry is one of the most swiftly growing IT industries in the world. Started in the 1970s under the encouragement of the Indian government, the industry initially comprised of firms that were asked to develop software in exchange for computer hardware imports (Athreye, 2005). In the beginning, the Indian IT industry focussed on a few clusters, with Bangalore being the main hub for its location—branded as the Silicon Valley of India (Arora & Bagde, 2006). With time, as technology progressed, the Indian software industry witnessed noteworthy growth around the country and progressed much faster than other industrial sectors in India (Athreye, 2005; Larsen, Manning, & Pedersen, 2019). The IT industry which was worth $US5.7 billion during the 1990s and 2000s, rose to a worth of $US150 million in the past decade showing the velocity at which it has grown. In recent times, this domestic share of the Indian IT industry has grown substantially from $US15 billion approximately to $US17.4 billion [excluding hardware sales] making it one of the largest sectors of the country (Kathpalia & Raman, 2014; Ray & Sharma, 2019).

While India's domestic IT market is on a quick rise, it is India's IT exports in the form of software and services exports that have become its chief growth indicator (Chakraborty & Dutta, 2003; Jain, Celo, & Kumar, 2019). India's IT & ITeS industry has grown to US$181 billion in 2018–19. Exports from the IT industry rose to US$137 billion in FY19 while domestic revenues (including hardware) jumped up to US$44 billion (SESEI, 2019). Revenue from the digital segment is expected to comprise 38% of the forecasted US$350 billion industry revenue by 2025 (IBEF, 2020). Overall, India's IT and business services market is likely to grow by over 8% to reach US$13.1 billion by the year-end and expand further to US$14.3 billion by 2020, according to research firm IDC (*Economic Times*, 2019). The Indian IT industry has become a significant contributor to growth within the Indian economy—one that has changed the image of the country from being a rural, agricultural and heavy industries-based economy to one that is knowledge and technology orientated (Chatterjee & Heuer, 2006) (Fig. 14.2).

14.4 Overview of the Indian IT Service Sector

The IT/ITeS Sector comprises of IT services, Business Process Management, Software products and engineering services, and Hardware. IT services dominate the market as it has a market size of US$86 billion and, over 81% of revenue comes from the export market (IBEF, 2019). Indian IT/ITeS's core competencies and major strengths have attracted noteworthy investments from major countries all over the world. Both the computer hardware and software sector in India accumulated cumulative Foreign Direct Investment (FDI) inflows worth US$37.23 billion between April 2000 and March 2019 (IBEF, 2019). Leading Indian IT firms such as Tata Consultancy Services, Infosys, Wipro, and Tech Mahindra, are diversifying their offerings and projecting leading ideas in artificial intelligence and blockchain to clients using innovation hubs, research, and development centers to create distinctive offerings.

The growth of this industry was not by accident, in fact, it was the outcome of a carefully planned Indian government initiative to set up software technology parks [STP], where 100% export-oriented firms were given tax-free exemptions and admission to office-space, equipment related to computers and internet connections (Athreye, 2005; Hobbs, Link, & Scott, 2017; Vaidyanathan, 2008). The outcome was that Indian firms started exporting their IT and IT-enabled services to more than 50 countries around the world, with two-thirds being clients from the US market, including half of fortune 500 firms (Chaudhuri, Hirudayaraj, & Ardichvili, 2018). Such swift developments have augmented India's status as a trustworthy provider of IT and IT-enabled services which has

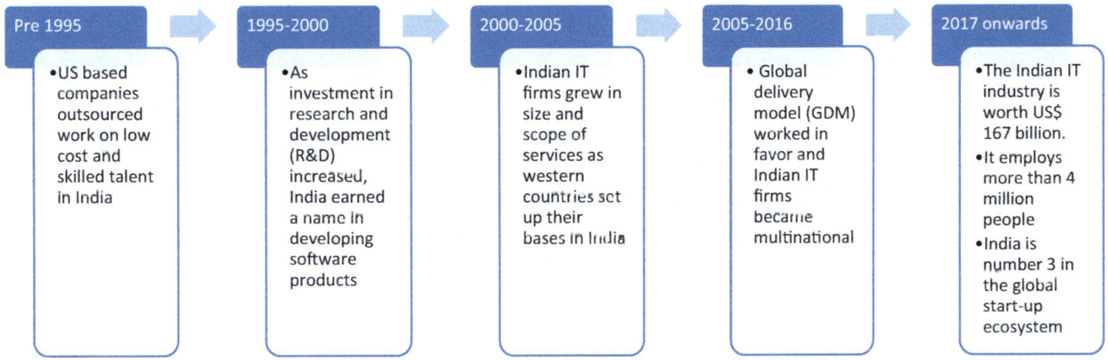

Fig. 14.2 Evolution of the Indian IT industry (Developed by the authors for this chapter)

led India to become a preferred destination for outsourcing operations to overseas firms and organizations. As a result, India now delivers its IT products and services at a global level competitively in such quantity that is much more than any other domestic industry of India (Taeube, 2004). It is projected that by 2020, the export of IT services from India will reach $US200 billion as it has been forecasted by India's National Association of Software and Services Companies (NASSCOM) (Gupta, Pande, & Wang, 2014).

According to the reports from IBEF (2019, 2020), there have been some significant developments in the Indian IT and ITeS sector in the past few years. Few of them are as follows:

- NASSCOM has launched an online platform that is aimed at enhancing the skills of over 2 million technology professionals and skilling another 2 million potential employees and students.
- Revenue growth in the banking, financial services, and insurance (BFSI) verticals stood at 6.80% year-over-year between July–September 2018.
- As of March 2018, over 1140 GICs were operating out of India.
- Private Equity investments in the sector stood at US$2400 million in Q4 2018.
- Venture Capital (VC) investments in the IT & ITeS sector stood at US$53.0 million during Q4 2018.

While government-related economic factors have boosted the growth of the IT industry, it was opportunities in outsourcing that gave the major push. Foreign-based organizations got the option of reducing their costs, increasing productivity, and using Indian firm's large pool of resources that spurted the growth of the outsourcing industry (Chiamsiri, Bulusu, & Agarwal, 2005; Kathpalia & Raman, 2014). Owing to the labor-market conditions in India, there is a huge cost arbitrage for Indian IT firms that have allowed them to offer their services at reduced prices (Kumar, 2011). Besides, the simplicity with which Indian IT firms have managed to scale their operations has also positively affected their overall growth and success (Kumar, 2011). Consequently, Indian firms have managed to create competitive organizations that not only operate within their home country but also in countries where their clients are located (Cappelli, Singh, Singh, & Useem, 2010) (Fig. 14.3).

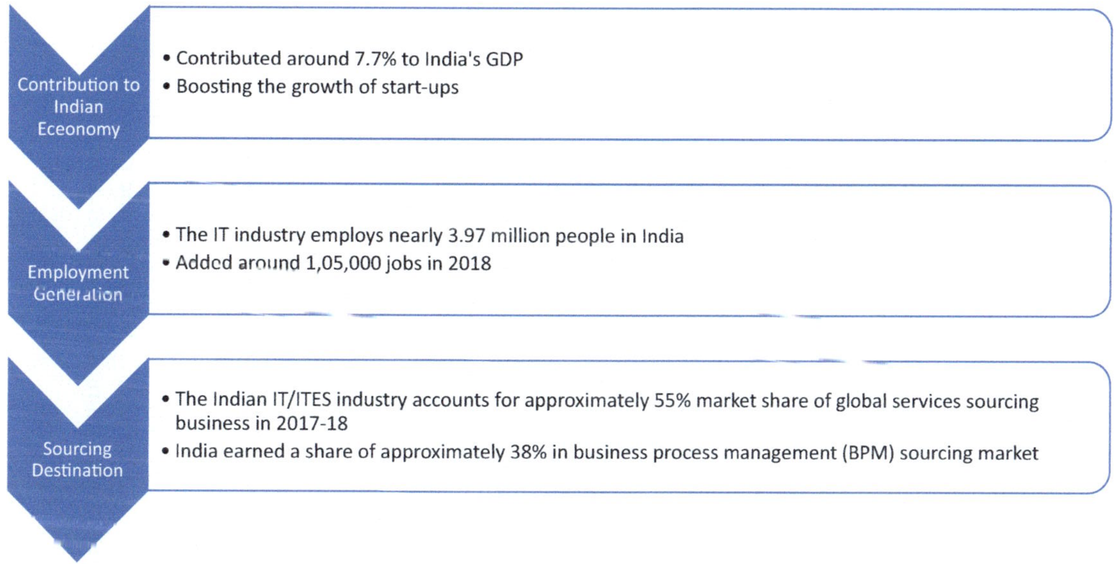

Fig. 14.3 Significant developments in the Indian IT industry (Developed by the authors for this chapter)

14.5 Global Dominance of the Indian IT Industry

The Indian IT industry has had some exceptional advantages due to which this industry has acquired global dominance. The four major reasons for getting the global leverage are: the increasing demand for IT/ITTES services; the global presence of Indian IT firms; competitive advantage, and policy support.

- **Increasing demand for IT/ITeS**: There has been strong growth in demand for IT/ITeS exports from new verticals such as banking, financial services, and insurance; telecommunication, retail, e-commerce, etc. Also, as urban infrastructure is on the rise, it has fostered several IT centers in the country. The expansion in the economy has propelled growth in local demand of IT/ITeS, thereby giving it a push in the international market too.
- **Global presence of Indian IT firms**: Indian IT firms are present all around the world as they have delivery centers spread across almost every continent. IT/ITeS industry is well-diversified across verticals, thus catering to different types of industries in different markets. As the strategic alliance between domestic and international players is on the rise, Indian firms can deliver solutions across the globe.
- **Competitive advantage**: India has a low-cost advantage by being 5–6 times inexpensive than the US as far as the labor cost is considered (IBEF, 2020). As a preferred destination for IT/ITeS in the world, India continues to be a clear leader in the global sourcing industry with almost 55% market share (IBEF, 2018).
- **Policy support**: Interestingly, in the past few years a few policies support have also worked in India's favor. Tax exemption of three years in a block of seven years to tech start-ups under "Start-up India" was well received by start-up firms and it also boosted their growth. To add to this, a liberal system for raising global capital, ease of getting seed capital, and ease of doing business has spurted the growth of many Indian IT firms. As a whole, there has been a cumulative FDI inflow of US$30.82 billion for the period of April 2000 to March 2018 in the computer software and hardware industry.

14.6 Theoretical Frameworks Explaining the Success of the IT/ITeS Sector

Decades of in-depth research in the IT/ITeS industry has resulted in a few theoretical frameworks/models that club the factors under broad classification to form a generalized structure that can explain the dynamics emerging from the interaction of the factors that result in a competitive advantage for countries that deal in the IT/ITeS industry (Bhattacharjee & Chakrabarti, 2015). Four of the important ones are listed below:

(a) **Porter's diamond model (1990)**: Porter's model stressed upon the need for increasing productivity to retain the competitive edge in the industry through continuously upgrading technology which is a result of favorable factor conditions that form the diamond. The diamond includes high domestic demand; firm strategy, structure, and rivalry; and the existence of related and supporting industries, along with "chance" factors and government policies that often play an important role in strengthening the diamond.

(b) **The Heeks–Nicholson model (2002)**: Heeks and Nicholson (2002) scrutinized the factors that contributed to the success of three top software exporting nations, viz India, Ireland, and Israel. Heeks and Nicholson (2002) proposed a software export success model based on a comparative analysis of these three countries. The model has five factors, demand (both, domestic and foreign); national vision and strategy; international linkages and trust; software industry characteristics; and domestic input factors/infrastructure.

(c) **The oval model (2003)**: Carmel (2003) propounded the oval model, which was an enhancement of Heeks and Nicholson (2002). The model identified eight factors that contributed to software export success: government vision and policies; human capital; wages; quality of life; linkages; technological infrastructure; capital; and industry characteristics.

(d) **The offshore attractiveness framework (2008)**: The offshore attractiveness framework was propounded by Joshi and Mudigonda (2008) to evaluate a country's attractiveness for offshore work. The framework is based on three key factors: primary motivating factors (accelerator); inhibitors (brakes); and facilitating conditions (steering). Primary motivating factors are fundamental drivers for offshore work; inhibiting factors are deterrents; and the facilitating conditions support initial entry, smooth transition, and efficient trouble-free delivery (Fig. 14.4).

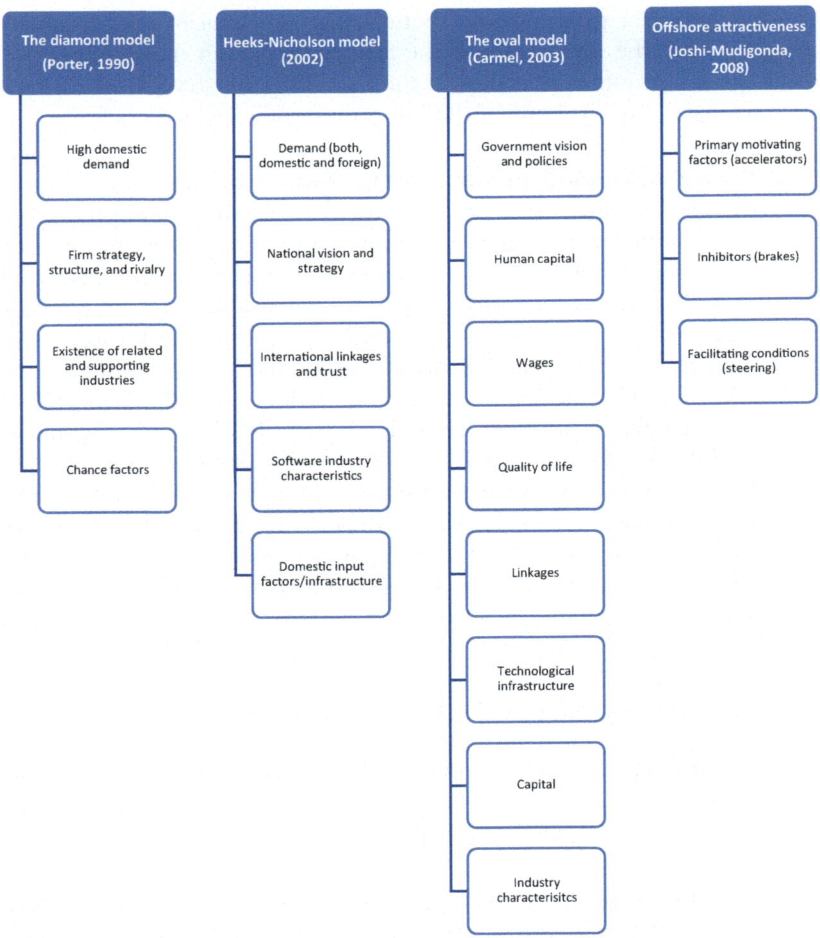

Fig. 14.4 Models/frameworks for the success of IT/ITES sector (Adapted from Bhattacharjee & Chakrabarti, 2015)

14.7 The Business Model of Indian IT Firms

Since the start of this millennium, several organizations worldwide are in the process of continuously advancing their technology-enabled services. As the business needs are on the rise, firms may sometimes need a business partner or a consulting firm in IT which is willingly available with its specialized set of skills required to accomplish those technical needs. A great solution for this is a global delivery approach, which provides the flexibility of owning the resources onshore or offshore. This approach is referred to as the GDM and is most common among the Indian IT firms.

The GDM has surfaced as an important path in the IT industry and has also fostered the birth and growth of global outsourcing. Global outsourcing in the current times is generally accepted by many organizations as it serves an important purpose of reducing investment—which, in turn, generates more revenue for the company. Also, operational teams work together to develop their performance and provide quality work to the client. GDM has been successful in achieving most of the organizational goals, and offers the benefits of mitigated risk and enhanced productivity.

The GDM can be defined as "the process of executing IT projects using resources located at multiple sites across the globe" (Prime Consulting, 2019), which may involve collecting, and analyzing customer requirements at the client site and then executing the project using technical teams located at a remote site, which may be either onshore or offshore. Work tasks may be divided among various operational teams and the same may be controlled by distributed project management.

Indian IT firms typically follow the GDM which is essentially a technology project using a team that is distributed globally. These IT firms have globally distributed resources and a globally distributed team. Gartner, a global research and advisory firm providing information, advice, and tools for leaders in IT, defines GDM as a "focus on the technical skills, process rigor, tools, methodologies, overall structure and strategies for seamlessly delivering IT-enabled services from global locations" (Gartner, 2020).

Many of the IT services and consulting firms across the globe refer to this model of global delivery to suggest one or more of the following value propositions they offer to their clients:

i. A global presence enables companies to address changing customer requirements faster.
ii. A global presence that gives the organization access to resources of varying costs allowing it to deliver services to its customers at a favorable cost, which is normally a mix of more expensive "on-site" resources combined with less expensive "offshore" resources.
iii. A GDM that implies an IT firm can work round the clock for its clients, managing work from one location to another thereby providing more work capacity as compared to working only from one single location/time-zone.
iv. A GDM that decreases the gaps between cultural diversity.

14.8 Various Categories of the Global Delivery Model

14.8.1 On-Site Delivery Model

The on-site delivery model is one in which IT consultants are deployed at the client site. These consultants work from the initial phases of the consultation until the final delivery of the project. They generally interact physically, face-to-face with their clients to have a clear understanding of the client's requirements and policies. Since the consultants are placed on-site, there is no room for the communication gap, thus facilitating better project control and management (Fig. 14.5).

14.8.2 Offsite/Nearshore Delivery Model

The offsite or nearshore delivery model is one in which the consultant resides in the same area (city or country) as that of the client and works rather remotely. Since there is a possibility to have more than one onshore work site, few consultants may work at the client side while others may work little away but within the same territory. This model is a combination of on-site and offsite but onshore business model.

14.8.3 Offshore Delivery Model

The offsite delivery model is one which all major tasks related to a project from the start until its completion is accomplished at various (or one) offshore sites utilizing a whole outsourcing team. In such models, project

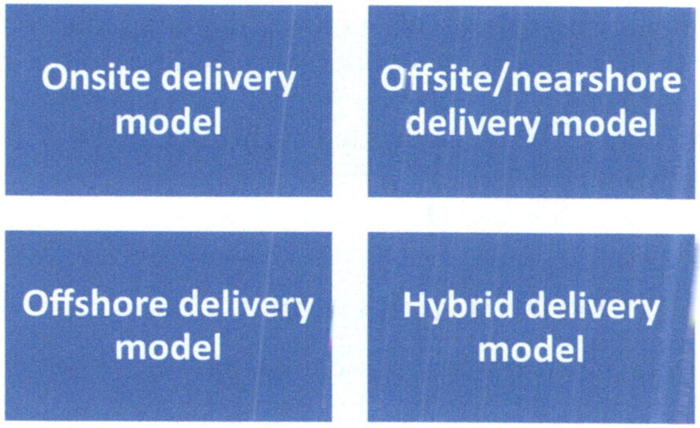

Fig. 14.5 Various categories of the global delivery model (Developed by the authors for this chapter)

managers or delivery managers may be assigned at both onsite (client) and offshore site to have greater project control and management.

14.8.4 Hybrid Delivery Model

The hybrid delivery model is a combination of all three—onsite, offsite and onshore. This model provides cost-effectiveness of the offshore model while utilizing the physical presence and benefits of face-to-face contact which is critical in the prevention of gaps of understanding and important for projects' success. The final solution of the project is usually the integrated onsite-nearshore model because it reaps the best of both the worlds, the effectiveness of the on-site model, and the cost efficiency of offshore development.

Of all these GDMs, Indian IT firms rely on the third one—i.e., hybrid or more popularly known as the "onsite-offshore" model. This, as discussed above, allows members of a project team to divide work among different locations and effectively utilize their strengths. To elaborate further, while the "onsite" team works with the client, which is often situated at the host location to define project requirements and to coordinate on regular intervals, the "offshore" team, which is situated at the home location, i.e., India, works on the main essence of the project (Agrawal, Khatri, & Srinivasan, 2012). This model forms the basic crux of delivery of IT services for Indian firms since it allows them to adopt a continuous mode of working, where they work nonstop day and night to utilize their large pool of human resources to work on projects round the clock (Kathpalia & Raman, 2014). This delivery model is crucial for understanding because it theoretically provides many insights that are specific to the IT industry and that may help explain the control/coordination and human resource (HR) decisions made by Indian IT firms.

14.9 Benefits of the Global Delivery Model

IT firms generally institute development centers and development teams in multiple locations all around the world because of the following benefits:

- Reduction of investment cost
- Round the clock resource availability
- Accessibility of expertise and knowledge
- Intuitive distribution and integration of human capital and task workload
- Swift response to changing client requirements
- Toggle between on-site and offshore resources
- Flexible work arrangements for faster project completion
- Minimizing risk
- Back-up facilities in global locations
- Improved transparency and visibility
- Communication Smoothness
- A diverse cultural work environment.

14.10 Domains and Verticals in the Indian IT Industry

Besides the GDM, there are two additional constructs that are critical to understanding in the delivery process of the IT services by Indian firms. They are domains and verticals. "Domains" are a certain type of service (e.g., cloud computing, java, oracle, etc.) delivered and set of skills associated with it (Choure, 2004). "Verticals," on the other hand, are the various markets or industries (e.g., financial, banking, infrastructure, etc.) to which the services are delivered. For example, Indian IT firms utilize their IT software and service-specific skills and competencies to deliver their IT solutions across a large span of domains, such as Java, Oracle, or Cloud computing. Likewise, some of the vertical markets in which Indian IT services firms may have specialization include industry sectors such as finance, hospitality, or health care. Over the past many years Indian IT software and services firms have gained expertise in various skill-based domains and industry verticals to increase their efficiency and effectiveness in the delivery of software and services.

To explain with an example, Indian IT firms develop customized software using their expert domain knowledge for various organizations falling in different verticals (Arora & Athreye, 2002). The software then needs to be maintained and this is when Indian IT firms offer support services [examples include BPO, IT consulting, and infrastructure management]. This entire process adds another dimension to the delivery of IT services (Kathpalia & Raman, 2014).

14.11 Internationalization and the Global Competitive Advantage of Indian IT Firms

Internationalization speed is the amount of overseas expansion by a firm in a given period (Vermeulen & Barkema, 2002). Referring to Indian IT firms that have gone international, it is stated that firms need time to absorb new knowledge learned from a typical characteristic environment of a host country, without which firms are unlikely to learn from internationalization (Jain et al., 2019). Generally, a multinational enterprise gets an advantage from internationalization because it can create a repository of knowledge-based routines by accumulating unique context-driven knowledge transferred by various subsidiaries to headquarters. The accumulated knowledge is, then, relayed to a new subsidiary attenuating its survival hazards in a host country (Foss & Pedersen, 2002; Gao & Pan, 2010). In this context of internationalization, Indian IT firms have gained several global advantages such as cost arbitrage, favorable resource endowments, lower infrastructural costs boosting entrepreneurship, the presence of Indian diaspora, and MNCs imparting positive externalities.

14.11.1 Cost Arbitrage

An industry can be said to have an upper hand or in other words, cost arbitrage, on solid ground, that is, skilled yet cost-effective labor which is in abundance. Interestingly, Indian software professionals have enjoyed (absolute) wage advantages in comparison with their US and European counterparts. Indian software professionals in 1997 were about one-third to one-fifth of estimated wage cost in comparison with the employees of the same skill set present in the US and Europe (Chandrasekhar, 2005; OECD, 2000). This differential still exists despite the wage inflation and a decline of rates by 5% in the last half decade (NASSCOM, 2013). What complements this is the large buffer of a workforce which is well-equipped with the latest technological advancements and fluent in English, which helps the multinational companies have a free supply of workforce without any lingual barrier (Athreye, 2005; Heeks, 2006). The evolution of the IT-ITeS industry was possible only because of the bulk orders of outsourced software production to India. Outsourcing was advantageous because of the easily available quality workforce at a cost-effective price (Arora & Athreye, 2002). As a result, the Indian economy moved from agriculture to services. It was a forced-choice for the entrepreneurs to move toward service sectors like IT/IteS because of the dearth of basic physical infrastructure in India (Arora & Athreye, 2002; Athreye, 2005). Indian software industry reached its first US$100 billion mark because of the Wage arbitrage. IT-ITeS industry touched its next landmark US$100 billion mark because of the blend of the high valued services and an increase in non-linear play which facilitated a shift from enterprise services to enterprise solutions (Bhattacharjee & Chakrabarti, 2015). To boost the competitiveness of the industry numerous measures were taken such as the inclusion of agile delivery models, automation and standardization of business processes, the inclusion of delivery in lower-tier cities, excellence in innovation processes, excellence in delivery, and expertise in various domains. Starting from a cost arbitrage country, India without any doubt, gradually but firmly, has reached a height where it gives tough competition to the other software industries around the world. This position is attained because India offers value-based and high-end services as an IT consulting provider at an effective cost.

14.11.2 Favorable Resource Endowments

The Indian IT-IteS industry, by using the readily available resource such as quality workforce, can gain a competitive edge rather than struggle for the not-so-sufficient and less flourished resources such as physical infrastructure or financial capital (Arora & Athreye, 2002; Coward, 2002; Kapur, 2002; Kapur & Ramamurti, 2001). It is quite observable that the relevant skill sets, fluent ability to speak English, high technological knowledge, and the quality of education which Indians go through are tailor-made to suit the requirement of this industry (Joshi & Mudigonda, 2008). For instance, India has around 347 higher education institutions and approximately 16,885 colleges with a total enrollment of over 9.9 million students (D'Cruz & Noronha, 2010). This means that each year, India produces 495,000 technical graduates, about 2.3 million other graduates and over 300,000 postgraduates (D'Cruz & Noronha, 2010) Along with the technical skills, the Indian workforce is preferred for their soft skills as well. Due to the socio-cultural setup, Indians readily give respect and space to others and do not hesitate in being submissive. A sincere and disciplined approach to work, designing, and project management skills just add more to a demanding workforce. Having outsourced the work to a competent and diligent workforce in India, most of the western countries have gained doubly by getting the work effectively done without any trade union entanglements. Government of India's focus and planned initiatives to boost the infrastructure for the IT industry and public–private partnership model have encouraged the private partnership to invest in building robust infrastructure.

14.11.3 *Lower Infrastructural Costs Boosting Entrepreneurship*

In comparison to the factories and manufacturing units, the overall cost of software infrastructural set is relatively very low. For setting a software infrastructure the basic system requirements (i.e., laptops/personal computers), space for office set up, and internet connectivity (Coward, 2002) are very less. Therefore, a large number of entrepreneurs, mostly engineers and technicians were the products of the major "brain–drain" in the 1960s and 70s who after acquiring sufficient funds and practical knowledge came to India and started their companies in India (Balasubramanyam & Balasubramanyam, 1997). Software giants such as Infosys, Wipro, Mahindra Satyam, Polaris, etc. are the newcomer entrepreneurs or first-generation entrepreneurs in the IT/IteS industry.

14.11.4 *Presence of the Indian Diaspora*

A huge number of the Indian diaspora in the US's Silicon Valley represent Indians. Not only has the diaspora represented the Indians in the US but has also accelerated reverse migration i.e., skilled people returning to India with their enhanced skills and investments (Kapur & McHale, 2005). The representational number helps in building the "reputational and credibility intermediaries" which ultimately increases the chances of professional advantages (Coward, 2002; Kapur, 2002; Kapur & Ramamurti, 2001; Patibandla, Kapur, & Petersen, 2000). Almost 1/4th of the Silicon Valley population is an investor in India and almost half of them have professional contacts in India (Saxenian, Motoyama, & Quan, 2002).

14.11.5 MNCs Imparting Positive Externalities

In the 1980s, the Indian IT industry, which was in a very formative stage, had a great influence of MNCs. These MNCs came to India and left their mark in the way business models in India worked. Software leaders in India such as Infosys, TCS, Wipro, etc. followed the business models of Texas Instruments (TI). TI, which came to India around the 80s, had advanced and robust communication facilities and extraordinary offshore R&D activities. The positive externalities of MNCs affected the overall Indian market by enhancing the skillset and knowledge of the workforce in general, especially in the field of knowledge and sub-contracting, which caused "demonstration effects" (Giarratana, Torrisi, & Pagano, 2003).

14.12 Indian IT Firms, Internationalization, and Their Human Assets

An important feature of the IT/ITeS industry is the accelerated growth in the number of MNCs that have almost become identical to the country's economic growth and is the reason behind the emergence of India as a global leader in IT (Gupta & Shapiro, 2014). These MNCs were created when local Indian firms operating in India's domestic IT services sector began setting up their subsidiaries in foreign host countries. For example, IT giants such as Infosys, Tata Consultancy Services [TCS], and Wipro, all of which are headquartered in India, established their extensive operations overseas. Ever since then, these firms have moved beyond their national borders and have looked for resources and technology to serve customers in high-end segments (Singal & Jain, 2012).

The emergence of these Indian IT MNCs has produced many studies, especially about the methods by which they adopt equity-based entry mode strategies. This includes strategic alliances, joint ventures, and acquisitions which have been particularly important in the context of the IT industry (Singal & Jain, 2012). The entry mode strategies adopted by Indian IT MNCs are important to understand how they internationalize both, in theory, and practice. It is also quite different from the control and coordination systems and the HR practices used by Indian IT firms once they have established their operations overseas.

With the rise in technological advancement as firms develop a deeper international focus, effective management of human assets also become quite challenging and it demands inevitable adaptation. As firms have gone overseas in their operations, management of human resources in the foreign countries has posed a hydra-headed dilemma to the management, dealing with complex issues such as developing human resource management practices in the host countries where different cultures, economic systems, and different legal systems exist. All-encompassing demographic changes along with millions of women pouring in the global IT workforce imply that Indian IT firms face an ever-increasing pressure to generate innovative ideas aimed at integrating and retaining the diverse global workforce.

Interestingly, while there are a large number of Indian IT firms that are growing both domestically and internationally, the industry is still largely dominated by just a few indigenous firms, due to its pyramidal structure (Bhatnagar, 2007; Budhwar, Luthar, & Bhatnagar, 2006). In fact, among the total number of firms exporting IT services from India, three of its largest firms have more than $US1 billion in annual sales, while the other has an average of less than $US10 million (Bhatnagar, 2007). An example of this is TCS, which has risen to annual revenues of $US1.17 billion; over 80% of which comes from outside India (Das, 2007). A vast number of firms operating in the Indian IT industry are in fact medium–to–smaller size organizations. There are many Indian MNCs in the IT services sector that has adopted a unique strategy in the delivery of their IT-centric solutions, which is quite popularly known as "body-shopping" (Malik & Blumenfeld, 2015). This term refers to a practice whereby IT firms recruit workers [on casual contracts] and send them to work on client premises for a particular project, while the firm itself may not be directly involved (Xiang, 2001). This practice of body-shopping has created huge employment opportunities for Indian IT professionals; thus, Indian IT services firms have become the largest providers of temporary migrant workers from India (Thite & Russell, 2010; Xiang, 2001).

14.13 Conclusion

The Indian IT/ITeS industry has witnessed unparalleled growth in the past four decades. A growing international position with Indian firms competing internationally in the global market is a result of high-speed technological advancements and the ever-growing demand for quality software and software services. The large-scale outsourced business model pools in complementary dynamic organizational capabilities such as the capability to scale up volumes in response to demand growth; capability to manage HR in the context of internationalization; capability to manage high-quality software processes; and capability to manage offshore business model. To add to it, the supporting role of the government and reforms initiated by it has also been quite instrumental to boost its formation stage and bring it to a mature and robust stage where it is now. By utilizing the various GDMs, the IT industry of India has indeed fostered unprecedented growth through internationalization. While most of the aspects of the Indian IT industry give a promising picture, internationalization comes with its host of challenges too. Rapid internationalization provides firms with quick access to global markets; however, it constrains their capacity to absorb expansion (Jain et al., 2019). Business growth is smooth but the kind of work being performed by the engineers is mundane with only limited potential for sustained professional growth. To add to this, external barriers in the form of home-market and the host-market environments along with industry characteristics can challenge the aspect of internationalization (Kahiya, 2018; Leonidou, 1995, 2004; Tesfom & Lutz, 2006). Notwithstanding the challenges to internationalization, the Indian IT industry has reaped numerous benefits out of it and has showcased an unparalleled business growth by leveraging on its flexibility, responsiveness, and speed.

References

Agrawal, N. M., Khatri, N., & Srinivasan, R. (2012). Managing growth: Human resource management challenges facing the Indian software industry. *Journal of World Business, 47*(2), 159–166.

Alam, I. (2007). New service development process: Emerging versus developed markets. *Journal of Global Marketing, 20*, 43–55.

Arora, A., & Athreye, S. (2002). The software industry and India's economic development. *Information Economics and Policy, 14*(2), 253–273.

Arora, A., & Bagde, S. (2006). *The Indian software industry: The human capital story*. Conference Paper, Danish Research Unit for Industrial Dynamics, Copenhagen, Denmark.

Arora, A., & Gambardella, A. (2005). The globalization of the software industry: Perspectives and opportunities for developed and developing countries. *Innovation Policy and the Economy, 5,* 1–32.

Athreye, S. S. (2005). The Indian software industry and its evolving service capability. *Industrial and Corporate Change, 14*(3), 393–418.

Balasubramanyam, A., & Balasubramanyam, V. N. (1997). Singer, services and software. *World Development, 25*(11), 1857–1861.

Bhatnagar, J. (2007). Talent management strategy of employee engagement in Indian ITES employees: Key to Retention. *Employee Relations, 29*(6), 640–663.

Bhattacharjee, S., & Chakrabarti, D. (2015). Investigating India's competitive edge in the IT-ITeS sector. *IIMB Management Review, 27*(1), 19–34.

Budhwar, P., Luthar, H. K., & Bhatnagar, J. (2006). The dynamics of HRM systems in Indian BPO firms. *Journal of Labor Research, 27*(3), 339–360.

Cappelli, P., Singh, H., Singh, J., & Useem, M. (2010). The India way: Lessons for the US. *Academy of Management Perspectives, 24*(2), 6–24.

Carmel, E. (2003). The new software exporting nations: success factors. *The Electronic Journal of Information Systems in Developing Countries, 13*(1), 1–12.

Chakraborty, C., & Dutta, D. (2003). Indian software industry: Growth patterns, constraints and government initiatives. In J. Raghbendra (Ed.), *Indian economic reforms* (pp. 317–333). New York: Palgrave Macmillan.

Chandrasekhar, C. P. (2005). The diffusion of information technology and implications for development: A perspective based on the Indian experience. In A. Saith & M. Vijayabaskar (Eds.), *ICTs and Indian economic development: Economy, work, regulation*. New Delhi: Sage India.

Chatterjee, S. R., & Heuer, M. (2006). Understanding Indian management. In S. R. Chatterjee & M. Heuer (Eds.), *Management in India: Trends and transition* (p. 11). Thousand Oaks: Sage.

Chaudhuri, S., Hirudayaraj, M., & Ardichvili, A. (2018). Borrow or grow: An overview of talent development/management practices in Indian IT organizations. *Advances in Developing Human Resources, 20*(4), 460–478.

Chen, J., Yin, X., & Mei, L. (2018). Holistic innovation: An emerging innovation paradigm. *International Journal of Innovation Studies, 2*(1), 1–13.

Chiamsiri, S., Bulusu, S. D., & Agarwal, M. (2005). Information technology offshore outsourcing in India: A human resources management perspective. *Research and Practice in Human Resource Management, 13*(2), 105–114.

Choure, T. (2004). *Information technology industry in India*. Delhi: Kalpaz Publications.

Coward, C. (2002). *Obstacles to developing an offshore IT-enabled services industry in Asia: The view from the US*. Center for Internet Studies, University of Washington, USA.

Das, N. (2007). The emergence of Indian multinationals in the new global order. *International Journal of Indian Culture and Business Management, 1*(1–2), 136–150.

D'Cruz, P., & Noronha, E. (2010). Employee dilemmas in the Indian ITES-BPO sector. In J. C. Messenger & N. Ghosheh (Eds.), *Offshoring and working conditions in remote work* (pp. 60–100). The International Labour Organization. London: Palgrave Macmillan.

Economic Times. (2019). *India IT & business services market to reach $14.3 billion by 2020: IDC*. Retrieved December 20, 2019, from https://economictimes.indiatimes.com/tech/ites/india-it-business-services-market-to-reach-14-3-bn-by-2020-idc/articleshow/69221249.cms?from=mdr.

Eischen, K. (2000, January 11). *Information technology: History, practice and implications for development* (Working Paper Series No. 2000-4). Centre for Global International & Regional Studies. Santa Cruz, USA: University of California.

Forester, T. (1986). *The evolution of information technology* (3rd ed.). Cambridge, MA: MIT Press.

Foss, N. J., & Pedersen, T. (2002). Transferring knowledge in MNCs: The role of sources of subsidiary knowledge and organizational context. *Journal of International Management, 8*(1), 49–67.

Gao, G. Y., & Pan, Y. (2010). The pace of MNEs' sequential entries: Cumulative entry experience and the dynamic process. *Journal of International Business Studies, 41*(9), 1572–1580.

Gartner. (2020). *Information technology: Gartner glossary*. Retrieved September 16, 2019, from https://www.gartner.com/en/information-technology/glossary/global-delivery-model-gdm.

Giarratana, M. S., Torrisi, S., & Pagano, A. (2003). *Links between multinational firms and domestic firms: A comparison of the software industry in India, Ireland and Israel* (LEM Working Paper No. 2003–22). Laboratory of Economics and Management, Sant'Anna School of Advanced Studies. Madrid, Spain: Universidad Carlos III. https://papers.ssrn.com/sol3/papers.cfm?abstract_id=571363.

Gupta, A., Pande, G., & Wang, J. (2014). *The silk road rediscovered*. San Francisco, CA: Jossey-Bass.

Gupta, S., & Shapiro, D. (2014). Building and transforming an emerging market global enterprise: Lessons from the Infosys journey. *Business Horizons, 57*(2), 169–179.

Heeks, R. (2006). Using competitive advantage theory to analyze IT sectors in developing countries: A software industry case analysis. *Information Technologies & International Development, 3*(3), 5.

Heeks, R., & Nicholson, B. (2002). *Software export success factors and strategies in developing and transitional economies* (Paper No. 12). Institute for Development Policy and Management, University of Manchester, UK. https://papers.ssrn.com/sol3/papers.cfm?abstract_id=3477760.

Hobbs, K. G., Link, A. N., & Scott, J. T. (2017). Science and technology parks: An annotated and analytical literature review. *The Journal of Technology Transfer, 42*(4), 957–976.

IBEF. (2018). *IT & ITes*. IBEF Report. Retrieved September 25, 2018, from https://www.ibef.org/download/IT-ITeS-Report-July-2018.pdf.

IBEF. (2019). *IT & ITes*. IBEF Report Retrieved July 28, 2019, from https://www.ibef.org/download/it-ites-feb-2019.pdf.

IBEF. (2020). *Indian IT & ITES report*. Retrieved January 5, 2020, from https://www.ibef.org/industry/information-technology-india.aspx

Jain, N. K., Celo, S., & Kumar, V. (2019). Internationalization speed, resources and performance: Evidence from Indian software industry. *Journal of Business Research, 95*, 26–37.

Joshi, K., & Mudigonda, S. (2008). An analysis of India's future attractiveness as an offshore destination for IT and IT-enabled services. *Journal of Information Technology, 23*(4), 215–227.

Kahiya, E. T. (2018). Five decades of research on export barriers: Review and future directions. *International Business Review, 27*(6), 1172–1188.

Kapur, D. (2002). The causes and consequences of India's IT boom. *India Review, 1*(2), 91–110.

Kapur, D., & McHale, J. (2005). Mobile human capital and high-tech industry development in India, Ireland, and Israel. In S. Kapur (Ed.), *From underdogs to tigers: The rise and growth of the software industry in Brazil, China, India, Ireland, and Israel* (p. 236). Oxford, UK: Oxford University Press.

Kapur, D., & Ramamurti, R. (2001). India's emerging competitive advantage in services. *Academy of Management Perspectives, 15*(2), 20–32.

Kathpalia, L., & Raman, R. (2014). The road ahead for the Indian IT and ITES: Industry considering its service offerings, domestic market and technology trends. *Journal of Theoretical and Applied Information Technology, 60*(2), 263–273.

Kiss, A. N., Danis, W. M., & Cavusgil, S. T. (2012). International entrepreneurship research in emerging economies: A critical review and research agenda. *Journal of Business Venturing, 27*(2), 266–290.

Kumar, N. A. (2011). Impact of global recession on Indian IT industry and effectiveness of e-business in the era of recession. *Global Journal of Business Management and Information Technology, 1*(1), 9–25.

Larsen, M. M., Manning, S., & Pedersen, T. (2019). The ambivalent effect of complexity on firm performance: A study of the global service provider industry. *Long Range Planning, 52*(2), 221–235.

Leonidou, L. C. (1995). Empirical research on export barriers: Review, assessment and synthesis. *Journal of International Marketing, 3*(1), 29–43.

Leonidou, L. C. (2004). An analysis of the barriers hindering small business export development. *Journal of Small Business Management, 42*(3), 279–302.

MacKenzie, D. W. (2006). Outsourcing America: What's behind our national crisis and how can we reclaim American jobs. *Journal of Applied Management and Entrepreneurship, 11*(1), 89.

Malik, A., & Blumenfeld, S. (2015). Skills, strategy and people management in the Indian IT industry. In A. Malik & C. Rowley (Eds.), *Business models and people management in the Indian IT industry: From people to profits* (pp. 55–77). New York, NY: Routledge.

Moghaddam, K., Sethi, D., Weber, T., & Wu, J. (2014). The smirk of emerging market firms: A modification of the Dunning's typology of internationalization motivations. *Journal of International Management, 20*(3), 359–374.

NASSCOM. (2013). *The IT-BPM sector in India*. New Delhi: Strategic Review.

OECD. (2000). *OECD information technology outlook: ICTs, E-commerce and the information economy*. Paris: OECD Publications.

Oskarsson, P., & Lahiri-Dutt, K. (2019). India's resource (inter) nationalism: Overseas mining investments shaped by domestic conditions. *The Extractive Industries and Society, 6*(3), 747–755.

Oviatt, B. M., & McDougall, P. P. (1994). Toward a theory of international new ventures. *Journal of International Business Studies, 25*(1), 45–64.

Papazoglou, M. E., & Spanos, Y. E. (2018). Bridging distant technological domains: A longitudinal study of the determinants of breadth of innovation diffusion. *Research Policy, 47*(9), 1713–1728.

Patibandla, M., Kapur, D., & Petersen, B. (2000). Import substitution with free trade: Case of India's software industry. *Economic and Political Weekly, 35*(15), 1263–1270.

Porter, M. E. (1990). *The competitive advantage of nations: With a new introduction*. New York: The Free Press.

Prime Consulting. (2019). *Global delivery*. Retrieved September 15, 2019, from http://www.primeconsulting-inc.com/global-delivery/.

Ray, K., & Sharma, M. (2019). Qualitative study of challenges and strategies of Indian IT organizations toward global branding. *Benchmarking: An International Journal, 27*(2), 708–731.

Roche, E. M. (1992). *Managing information technology in multinational corporations*. New York: Macmillan Publishing.

Saiyed, A. A., Fernhaber, S. A., Basant, R., & Dhandapani, K. (2020). The internationalization of new ventures in an emerging economy: The shifting role of industry concentration. *Asia Pacific Journal Management*. https://doi.org/10.1007/s10490-020-09712-2.

Saxenian, A., Motoyama, Y., & Quan, X. (2002). *Local and global networks of immigrant professionals in Silicon Valley*. San Francisco, CA: Public Policy Institute of California.

Sehgal, S., & Gupta, G. (2019). Converging resources and co-producing for innovation: Evidence from healthcare services. *European Journal of Innovation Management, 23*(3), 429–453.

SESEI. (2019). *Indian ICT sector profile report*. Seconded European Standardisation Expert in India. Published Jan 1, 2019. Retrieved July 5, 2019, from http://www.sesei.eu/wp-content/uploads/2019/02/ICT_Sector-Profile-Report.pdf.

Sheshabalaya, A. (2004). *Rising elephant: The growing clash with India over white-collar jobs*. USA: Common Courage Press.

Singal, A., & Jain, A. K. (2012). Outward FDI trends from India: Emerging MNCs and strategic issues. *International Journal of Emerging Markets, 7*(4), 443–456.

Taeube, F. A. (2004). *Proximities and innovation: Evidence from the Indian IT industry in Bangalore* (Working Paper No. 04–10). Aalborg, Copenhagen: Danish Research Unit for Industrial Dynamics.

Tesfom, G., & Lutz, C. (2006). A classification of export marketing problems of small and medium sized manufacturing firms in developing countries. *International Journal of Emerging Markets, 1*(3), 262–281.

Thakur, R., & Hale, D. (2013). Service innovation: A comparative study of US and Indian service firms. *Journal of Business Research, 66*(8), 1103–1123.

Thite, M., & Russell, B. (2010). The next available agent: Work organisation in Indian call centers. *New Technology, Work and Employment, 25*(1), 2–18.

Vaidyanathan, G. (2008). Technology parks in a developing country: The case of India. *Journal of Technology Transfer, 33*(3), 285–299.

Vermeulen, F., & Barkema, H. (2002). Pace, rhythm, and scope: Process dependence in building a profitable multinational corporation. *Strategic Management Journal, 23*(7), 637–653.

Xiang, B. (2001). Structuration of Indian information technology professionals' migration to Australia: An ethnographic study. *International Migration, 39*(5), 73–90.

CHAPTER 15

Decoding Management Practices of Women Entrepreneurs with or Without Technological Skills in Emerging Economies: Evidence from India

Ranjana Singh-Nagpal and Tania Sebastian

15.1 Introduction

The knowledge of Information and Communications Technology (ICT) contributes to the overall efficiency of entrepreneurs to perform numerous tasks. This means that although they need not be an expert in one particular skill to do a task, a wide variety of skills enables that the business does not fail (Lazear, 2004). It is here that ICT and related changes have been the prime mover behind entrepreneurial ventures beginning from the 1960s to the last quarter of the twentieth century,

R. Singh-Nagpal (✉)
School of Social Sciences—Centre for Studies in Social Management, Central University of Gujarat, Gandhinagar, India

T. Sebastian
VITSOL, Vellore Institute of Technology, Chennai, India

J. J. M. Ferreira et al. (eds.), *Technological Innovation and International Competitiveness for Business Growth*, Palgrave Studies in Democracy, Innovation, and Entrepreneurship for Growth,
https://doi.org/10.1007/978-3-030-51995-7_15

albeit in different sectors and different ways (Bosma, De Wit, & Carree, 2003). ICT creates numerous possibilities for small businesses thereby creating a trend for favouring independent producers over large corporations (Bernardt & Muller, 2000). It also helps in reducing barriers to access of information and costs related to the classical mode of running of businesses (Prljić, Vučeković, & Vujačić, 2015). Additionally, it also increases the share of products that is positioned at an early stage of the product life cycle (Bosma et al., 2003). We insert the scenario of emerging economies in the narrative of ICT and entrepreneurs by stating that the untapped prowess of the emerging economies has always been lucrative for investment to the developed economies. Large market potential and the low cost of labour in developing economies continue to attract investments (Avgerou, 2008). These have been thwarted by the gaps in use and form of technology that further affects the developed-developing countries relationships. There is also the added aspect of differences in cultural, social, political, economic, technological and legal positions. Solutions exist for bridging these gaps sustainability from the point of view of developing economies by technologically driven solutions thereby further resulting in economic growth.

The negative side of this exists in research that states the role of ICT in improving the competitiveness and productivity of enterprises as a disillusionment. This research is said to be riddled with the maladies of small sample size and noisy data (Brynjolfsson, Hitt, & Bresnahan, 2002). Numerous studies have debunked the negative co-relation between ICT and progress, and have shown the positive effects of ICT on the investment costs and its contribution to the nation's economy (Alshubiri, Jamil, & Elheddad, 2019; APEC, 2018; Toader, Firtescu, Roman, & Anton, 2018).

This chapter argues that an understanding of the adaptation of ICT by developing economies is important so that the rewards of innovation are realized to its full potential through adaptation, diffusion or leapfrogging of technology. We provide this understanding from the perspective of the state of Gujarat and in the context of women entrepreneurs.

In the context of women, it is unfortunate that much of the writing on the topic of women entrepreneurs is lacking in the given context and is even stereotypical in nature (Veiga & Yanouzas, 1976) and hence this study contributes to the status of ICT skills and its impact on managerial skills of women entrepreneurs across industries in the small business sector. This then brings out the positive effects to planning, decision making, communication, motivation to employees and controlling, all of which forms the core of this research.

This study puts Gujarat at the epicentre of research as a result of its uniqueness embedded in its culture and abundant spirit of entrepreneurship, among other suitable conditions that include geographical location and focus on promotion of women entrepreneurs as a result of government policies (Singh & Sebastian, 2018). This study is mindful of the fact that challenges that women entrepreneurs face are manifold, in terms of lack of family support, lack of education, etc. making the entrepreneurial ecosystem hostile for women. However, change is eminent and the aid of technology will provide an initial advantage in relation to exposure to business practices and a tacit knowledge of business (Junare & Singh, 2016a, 2016b).

15.2 Theory Building

15.2.1 Women Entrepreneurs as Small Business Owner-Manager and ICT Entrepreneurial Ecosystem

The field of small business is a challenging field to capture and comprehend, with its ever-changing facets and divergence (Papulová & Mokroš, 2007). Being undermined for its potential in the past, subsequent literature has underlined the economic gravity of small businesses (Newton, 2001; Papulová & Mokroš, 2007). Small businesses are significant economic agents that will shape future economics across the globe (Kot, 2018; Energy, 2010) and this chapter explores a sub-field of small business, i.e. the application of ICT in small businesses.

It focuses upon ICT application in small businesses and ICT-enabled operations not only inside the business (across sub-systems of business) but in transactions and business operations of supply chain or Porter's '*Value chain*'[1] (Auramo et al., 2005; Feller, Shunk, & Callarman, 2006; Kumar & Rajeev, 2016; Niu, 2010; Tseng, Wu, & Nguyen, 2011). Building upon the framework of Isenberg's (2011) widely recognized 'Entrepreneurship Ecosystem', further cited and developed by Bramann

[1] Value chain encompasses the complete set of activities and services that is essential to take a product or service from its conception to consumption and beyond in its final market. It necessarily includes producers, input suppliers, operation, processors, retailers and buyers who are assisted by a range of technical, business and financial service providers.

(2017), there is a seventh condition of '*ICT infrastructure*' added to the six existing conditions, '***conducive sociocultural norms around entrepreneurship, availability of entrepreneurial support systems, availability of qualified human capital, presence of appropriate financing sources, relevant entrepreneurship policy, and venture-friendly markets for new products***'.

Analogous to the ICT entrepreneurial ecosystem, Singh (2017), proposes '*Chief Facilitator Process*' as a possible solution to create an empowering environment to women entrepreneurs encompassing four important *facilitators*' whose efficient participation can be instrumental in the prospect of women entrepreneurs and women entrepreneurship as a process. This process includes '*Self, Family and Society, Government Bodies and NGOs, and Other Women Entrepreneurs as Role Models*'. Among these, '*Self*' should be '*Keen to learn ICT skills*' (Singh, 2017), along-with Government Bodies and NGOs active provision of ICT subsidies/infrastructure to facilitate women entrepreneurs.

Discourse on women entrepreneurship with the quest of forming a conducive and sustainable entrepreneurial ecosystem with policymakers attempting to track down and address appropriate ICT conditions and barriers to access and use of ICT has increased in the past decade (Madanda, Kabonesa, & Bantebya-Kyomuhendo, 2007). Limitations have been identified that include weaker managerial and business skills in women entrepreneurs and the role of traditional cultural norms that result in hurdles in managing a business in low-growth and low-income sectors of economy (Deborah, Wilhelmina, Oyelana, & Ibrahim, 2015; Martínez & Nguyen, 2014; Singh, 2017). Subjugating these limitations is likely by investment in ICT and learning-related skills that has the potential to improve the working of women entrepreneurs anticipated managerial and business responsive solutions (Junare & Singh, 2016a; Locust, 2018; Spanos, Prastacos, & Poulymenakou, 2002).

In Indian context, ICT Entrepreneurial ecosystem has geared up in the last quarter of the twentieth century with the establishment of dedicated institutes like National Science and Technology Entrepreneurship Development Board (NSTEDB) and GoI (NSTEDB, 2013), with nearly 120 Technology Business Incubators (TBIs) across India. There are no studies pertaining to assessment of impact and effectiveness of all the incubation mechanisms put together (NSTEDB, n.d.). NSTEDB has, nevertheless, identified the pertinent role a support system for innovation can play, with four crucial key areas, i.e. government support, sponsored R&D institutions, societal acceptance and regulatory aid that are at the epicentre of developing entrepreneurship and innovation (NSTEDB, n.d.). India just follows China and US in having the maximum number of start-up incubators and accelerators ('Incubators/Accelerators (I/As) Driving the Growth of Indian Start-up Ecosystem–2017'©@), and has seen 40% growth only in the year 2016 (Swissnex India, 2017) and therefore we can see potential to work more aggressively towards facilitating women entrepreneurs with an enriched entrepreneurial and technological ecosystem.

15.2.2 Managerial Functions and ICT

Having received flak from those in favour of competency-based management education (CBME), the American Assembly of Collegiate Schools of Business (AACSB), the functional view of managerial job even today forms the framework for basic management job in most text-books (Clement, 1992). The functional approach was first proposed by Henry Fayol in 1916 and stated that managerial jobs can be divided into five common functions—planning, organizing, command, coordination and control. Fayol's form of function then evolved to planning, organizing, staffing, directing, coordinating, reporting and budgeting (POSDCORB) and five-step view of planning, organizing, staffing, leading and controlling (POSLC) and further to 'PRINCESS' factors (Planning, Representing, Investigating, Negotiating, Coordinating, Evaluating, Supervising, Staffing) and finally to the now accepted four-step approach of planning, organizing, leading and controlling (Carroll & Gillen, 1987; Caskey, 1972; Clement, 1992).

Owing to the easy comprehension of the concept and terminologies that functional approach of management portrays, as against the Mintzberg's 'Role of Managers' (Clement, 1992) this study uses four-step approach by Golson (1977) to critique.

15.2.2.1 Planning and Decision-Making Vis-à-Vis Technological Skills

Technological changes have resulted in unsteadiness in market conditions on one hand and rise in demand on the other (Golson, 1977; Spanos et al., 2002; Subashini, Rita, & Vivek, 2012). This compels organizations, irrespective of its size, to capture and blend the internal and external information appropriately to the right person at right time (Subashini et al., 2012), to execute evaluated planning and decision making. Referring to enterprise computing, end-user computing, strategic computing and ubiquitous computing, i.e. the four stages of ICT in the digital era (Cascio & Montealegre, 2016), organizations linked internet and enterprise application systems, *viz.* enterprise resource planning, customer relationship management, supply chain management (Auramo et al., 2005; Cascio & Montealegre, 2016; Niu, 2010; Shavazi, Abzari, & Mohammadzadeh, 2009; Tseng et al., 2011), material requirement planning and the like. Also, computer associated technological change has a wide-ranging effect on control and coordination of information systems as inputs for planning and decision-making (Golson, 1977). Thus, testing $H1_0$ and $H2_0$ for women entrepreneurs of MSMEs in Gujarat.

$H1_0$ Managerial skills of planning is independent of technological skills in women entrepreneurs.

$H2_0$ Managerial skills of decision-making is independent of technological skills in women entrepreneurs.

15.2.2.2 Communication Vis-à-Vis Technological Skills

In the current digital era, different stages of advancement of ICT facilitated businesses to improve communications and create augmented B2B and B2C communications in strategic computing stage (mid 90s to later part of 2010s) that resulted in an amplified international outreach resulting in heterogenous computers and communication interfaces (Cascio & Montealegre, 2016). Higher growth is expected from the latter half of the decade of 2010, with a computing stage that integrates physical and electronic space, and delimits the international boundaries and trade barriers (Cascio & Montealegre, 2016). These advancements in technologies and enhanced utility of ICT can be employed for mundane activities of business (Golson, 1977) thereby increasing time availability for better communications and relationship building with stake holders.

The fast pace of technology and hence ICT, does it have equal upshot on managers' realization of self-actualization is debatable (Golson, 1977). When self-actualized, people have better understanding of people, are in a state of building relationships and focus more on duty as a result of enhanced inner consciousness. Therefore, from the discussions above, we formulate the following hypothesis

$H3_0$ Managerial communication skill is independent of the technological skills in women entrepreneurs.

15.2.2.3 *Motivating Employees Vis-à-Vis Technological Skill*

Human resource management gets easier with improved technologies (Cascio & Montealegre, 2016). But improved technologies bring with it challenges and bottlenecks in the management of employees. Integration of new technologies in businesses should be done after certain preconditions are met, for instance, prior awareness among employees, modified management system consistent with the demand of technological progress, etc. It should be a rational decision to instal new technology and not mere fad. It is important that employees are able to relate individual goals with organizational goals in the backdrop of technological upgradation (Ghosh, 1980). It is equally important that employees' access to decision making in the organization is a constant feature. It is also marked that ICT creates a sensation of urgency in organizations keeping employees demoralized in stressed environment (Leduc, Guilbert, & Vallery, 2015). This leads us to test the next hypothesis

$H4_0$ Managerial skills to motivate employees is independent of technological skills in women entrepreneurs.

15.2.2.4 *Controlling Vis-à-Vis Technological Skills*

Today the global commerce atmosphere has blurred terrestrial, political and cultural borders. This makes it easier for accessibility of ICT by remote locales (Alderete, 2015; Carayannis, Popescu, Sipp, & Stewart, 2006) resulting in better control over organizational operations. Complex administrative application businesses undoubtedly support ICT installation for improved managerial control, operational control and administration (Islam, 2016; Kushwaha, 2011). Increased usage of ICT and changes owing to its disruptive nature leading to managerial functions will demand frequent changes. Management will have elevated responsibilities for profitable organizational outcomes leaving management strained and stressed, affecting their morale, productivity and output (Golson, 1977). This reflection derives to frame the next hypothesis

$H5_0$ Managerial skill to control is independent of technological skills in women entrepreneurs.

15.3 Empirical Section

15.3.1 Selection Criteria for Inclusion in the Study and Research Instrument

The sample size of 401 women entrepreneurs has been collected from 6 districts of Gujarat, i.e. *Gandhinagar (North Gujarat), Vadodara (East Gujarat), Ahmedabad (Central Gujarat), Kachch (West Gujarat), Rajkot (Saurashtra Peninsular) and Surat (South Gujarat)*. These women have their establishments in Micro, Small and Medium Enterprises (MSMEs) and are selected to be part of the data by snowball sampling technique. Structured interview schedule is administered by the researchers to register the responses of the women entrepreneurs. This is done in two stages. The first stage is the pre-test and pilot test stage which becomes instrumental in designing the interview schedule for the final stage of data collection (Singh, 2019). Second stage involved the final data collection and collation. Data hence collected is primarily nominal in nature which led to the entire bi-variate analysis based on *chi square* test to assess the independence or otherwise, and *Phi* and *Cramer's* value analysis to analyze the strength of relationship so established between the dependent and independent variable.

15.3.2 Important Terms

For the purpose of the study following definitions has been considered applicable

Women entrepreneur 'A women entrepreneur in MSME sector can be defined as that economic entity who is vigorously involved in non-agricultural industrial activity, owns and manages the functions of the business enterprise, new or already established by investing most of the days' time or otherwise towards business activities, invests her own (or borrowed) capital resources, even if in lower proportion (in case of micro enterprises of informal 15 sector), identifies opportunity and bear risk to organize and mobilize the factors of production and the resources of the enterprise, individually as a self-employed or in collaboration or as a member of a family business and produces goods/services to the customers with a primary motive of profit maximization' (Singh, 2017).

ICT in business ICT include any communication device or application such as radio, television, cellular phones, computers, satellite systems as well as network hardware and software and associated services (UN, n.d.).

Management The concept as used by Golson (1977) motivates us to use managerial function chiefly in the form planning, decision-making, coordination (managerial communication and motivation to employees) and controlling.

15.4 Data Corroboration and Statistical Treatment

15.4.1 General Profile of Women Entrepreneurs of Gujarat

The demographic analysis of women entrepreneurs of Gujarat shows that 47.9% of women entrepreneurs are with establishments set-up only after 2011. Age composition exhibits 34.9 and 33.9% of women entrepreneurs between the age group of 36–45 years and 26–35 years, respectively indicating that majority of women entrepreneurs are young. Women entrepreneurs have decent educational qualification, with 43.4% holding a Bachelor's degree, i.e. an education of 10 + 2 + 3 years or 10 + 2 + 4 years and 25.2% holding a Master's degree, i.e. an education of 10 + 2 + 3 + 2 years or 10 + 2 + 4 +2 years depending on the discipline of study. 80.5% of women entrepreneurs are married. Majority (48.9%) among married women entrepreneurs' husbands' run business as their primary occupation. They either work with their husband as co-entrepreneur or have a different business set-up. Analysis also shows that father of 52.1% women entrepreneurs have business as their primary occupation while 78.8% of women entrepreneurs have/had stay-at-home mother.

15.4.2 Business Profile of Women Entrepreneurs of Gujarat

In Gujarat, the major share of business of women entrepreneurs is in micro sector (81.5%) rather than in small (15.2%) and medium sector (3.2%). Majority of them own one business (83.8%) rather than two (10.5%) or three (4%) or more (1.7%). In Gujarat pull motivations (Van der Zwan et al., 2016) dominates push-factor as 57.8% of women entrepreneurs commenced their establishments as they were desirous of a venture of their own to shape and deliver their ideas. Funds to start the venture surfaced from their personal savings (68.6%), followed by funds borrowed from family members/relatives (28%). Women entrepreneurs preferred the service sector (55.9%) over the manufacturing sector

(33.9%) or both (7.2%). Among women entrepreneurs in the service industry, the widely practiced activity is retail store/home-based retail (51.6%). In the manufacturing sector, the widely practiced business among women entrepreneurs is home-based manufacturing of handicraft items/ handmade jewellry/ Medical Product for Sale (44.1%), followed by business of manufacturing textiles/customized clothing (33.9%). Among this set of women entrepreneurs, 69.3% recognizes themselves to be using technology (ICT) for business operations against rest 30.7%, who do not. The fact central to the study is, among these women entrepreneurs 54.1% have acknowledged owning technological skills against rest 45.9%, who do not. The gap in between using technology (ICT) in business operations and owning the technological skills is evident in this revelation. This forms the very foundation of this study to examine linkages of managerial skills/practices with knowledge of technological skills among women entrepreneurs in existing context.

15.4.3 Managerial Functions Vis-à-Vis Technological Skills

Managerial functions of technological skills have been analyzed based on the self-identified perception of women entrepreneurs that was then recorded in the interview schedule of the researchers.

In the following section, each of the hypotheses will be tested. Identify of the dependence/independence of variables will be tested. The strength of the established relationship by analyzing *Phi* (φ) or *Cramers V* depending upon the table size will also be analyzed.

The questions asked to the participating women entrepreneurs prompted them to share, in form of their input to the interviewer, their credence on selves' managerial capabilities. To be specific, the capabilities of planning (V_1), decision-making (V_2), communication (V_3), motivation to employees (V_4) and controlling (V_5). Similarly, they were also asked about their perception of selves' technological skill (V_0) that they possess. V_1, V_2, V_3, V_4, V_5 are dependent variables and V_0 is the independent variable for the study. The data collected will be treated for dependency/independency in this paper.

$H1_0$ Managerial skill of planning is independent of technological skills in women entrepreneurs.

Chi square test with V_1 as dependent and V_0 as independent variable with a 5% level of significance, i.e. $\alpha = .05$, shows that the *Pearson chi square* value is 12.457 and *p-value* is .000. Evidently *p-value* is less than the α value. It means this test is statistically significant and we would accept the alternate hypothesis, ie, in this case 'managerial skill of planning is dependent of technological skills in women entrepreneurs'. If we further proceed to evaluate the size of effect of V_0 on V_1, we will look at the value of *phi* (φ) *value* (and not *Cramer's V* owing to the size of the table which is bigger than 2 × 2) which is simply a *Pearson* correlation computed for dichotomous variables (SPSS Tutorials, n.d.). The *phi* (φ) *value* is significant with strength of .176 (see Fig. 15.1) meaning there is a strong association (Akoglu, 2018) between V_1 and V_0.

H2$_0$ Managerial skills of decision-making is independent of technological skills in women entrepreneurs.

Dependence/independence of V_2 on V_0 is analyzed and *chi square* value unleashes the dependence of V_2 on V_0 with a *Pearson chi square* value equal to 28.940 and *p-value* (.000) < α value (.05). Therefore, we accept the alternate hypothesis concluding managerial skill of decision-making getting affected by technological skills possessed among women entrepreneurs. *Phi* (φ) value is also significant with a strength of .269 (see Fig. 15.1) which means the relationship between the variables in question is very strong (Akoglu, 2018).

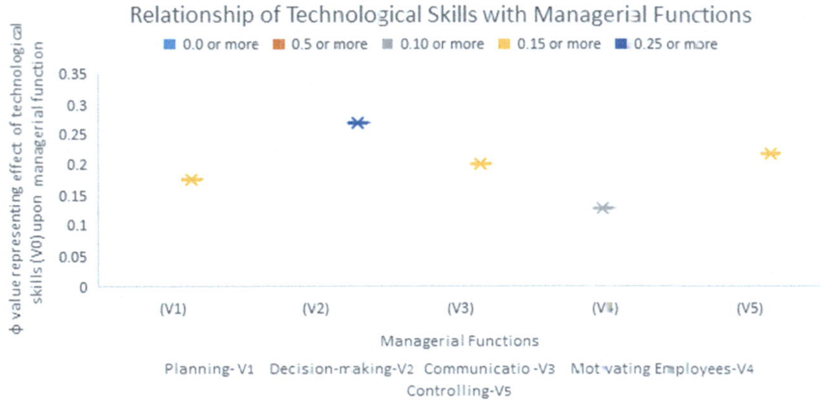

Fig. 15.1 Strength of relationship between technological skills and managerial functions represented in terms of phi-value

$H3_0$ Managerial communication skill is independent of the technological skills in women entrepreneurs.

In this section, women are asked about the managerial communication skills they possess and their perception of the technological skills that they carry (as separate questions). Data collected is treated for bi-variate analysis testing the dependence/independence with *chi square* test. It reveals that V_3 is dependent on V_0 as the *p-value* (.000) is less than the α value (.05). *Pearson chi square* value is 16.412. *Phi (φ) value* is significant suggesting the strength of the effect of V_0 on V_3 is strong as it is .202 (see Fig. 15.1).

$H4_0$ Managerial skills to motivate employees is independent of technological skills in women entrepreneurs.

When there is a *chi square* analysis to check the relationship between V_4 and V_0, it surfaces that *Pearson chi square* value is 6.614 with a *p-value* (.010) $< \alpha$ value (.05) denoting its statistical significance. Therefore, we choose the alternate hypothesis, i.e. Managerial Skills to motivate employees is dependent on technological skills of women entrepreneurs. Furthering the quest to reveal the strength of the relationship, the significance of *phi (φ) value* at .128 (see Fig. 15.1) depicts moderate association (Akoglu, 2018) between V_0 and V_4.

$H5_0$ Managerial skills to control is independent of technological skills in women entrepreneurs.

In this category of analysis, the *p-value* (.000) is less than the α value (.05) and the alternate hypothesis is accepted to unveil the dependence of V_5 on V_0. Alternatively, we can say that managerial skill to control is independent of technological skills in women entrepreneurs. So, what is the strength of this relationship? *Phi (φ) value* answers this question with its significance at .219 (see Fig. 15.1) indicating a strong relationship (Akoglu, 2018) between V_5 and V_0.

15.5 Finding & Discussion

This study aims to examine association of managerial functions among women entrepreneurs against selves' self-identified technological skills. To achieve this, participating women entrepreneurs were asked direct questions like 'Do you have knowledge of technological skills?' or

'Do you have required planning skills?' This might have made women entrepreneurs conscious and reserved in revealing to the interviewer their actual state of mind, at least among few of the respondents. We consider this to be a possible limitation of this study.

Gujarat is the land of incubators and accelerators managed by the premier educational institutions, has NGOs like SEWA and is the land to technology led white revolution (NSTEDB, n.d.), however, in analyzing V_0 there is no noticeable gap between those who do not self-identify having less knowledge of technological skills (54.1%), against those who identify themselves having less knowledge of technological skills (45.9%) To add to the status of ICT embeddedness in the SME sector of Gujarat this group displays promising figure of 69.3% of women entrepreneurs making use of ICT technology in their day to day businesses (see Sect. 15.4.2).

As represented in Fig. 15.1, Managerial planning (V_1) displays a significant, strong and accepted association with technological skills (V_0) as an independent variable. Analysis of Table 15.1 portrays a positive relation between V_1 and V_0 signifying the likelihood of dependability of planning skills if technological skills are sound. This confirms the propositions of referred literature (Golson, 1977; Subashini et al., 2012).

Managerial decision-making (V_2) pitted against technological skills (V_0) present a positive relationship. There is a positive relationship between V_2 and V_0 as presented in Table 15.2, but the intensity is more than V_1 (see Fig. 15.1) and is therefore a desirable outcome. This suggests that if women entrepreneurs have better technological skills, the probability of improvement in decision-making skills than planning skills is high. There is a dearth of studies that compare planning with decision-making; it rather considers decision-making a part of planning. There is a possibility of study to explore the comparative analysis of association of managerial planning function/praxis with technological skills versus association of decision-making skill with technological skills and its impact overall. This carves the path for subsequent research.

An exploration of the communication skills (V_3) and technological skills (V_0), like the relationship between V_1 and V_0 show strong and accepted association (see Fig. 15.1). Table 15.3 underlines a positive link between communication skills not independent on technological skills. This is a widely accepted phenomenon and also stands proven in current context.

Table 15.1 Managerial planning vis-a-vis technological skills

*Technological problems—lack of technological skills * managerial problems—lack of proper planning cross-tabulation*

			Managerial problems—lack of proper planning		*Total*
			Yes	*No*	
Technological problems—lack of technological skills	Yes	Count	82	102	184
		Expected count	65.2	118.8	184
		% within technological problems—lack of technological skills	44.60%	55.40%	100%
		% within managerial problems—lack of proper planning	57.70%	39.40%	45.90%
		% of total	20.40%	25.40%	45.90%
	No	Count	60	157	217
		Expected count	76.8	140.2	217
		% within technological problems—lack of technological skills	27.60%	72.40%	100%
		% within managerial problems—lack of proper planning	42.30%	60.60%	54.10%
		% of total	15.00%	39.20%	54.10%
Total		Count	142	259	401
		Expected count	142	259	401
		% within technological —lack of technological skills	35.40%	64.60%	100%
		% within managerial problems—lack of proper planning	100.00%	100.00%	100%
		% of total	35.40%	64.60%	100%

Examination of motivating employees' skill (V_{4o}) with technological skills (V_0) for dependency shed light upon moderate association of the two (see Fig. 15.1). This is apparent in Table 15.4 where the association is slightly positive with not much difference if the extent of technological knowledge is less among women-owners. Plausibly V_4 involves more of human skills, therefore it is understandable that motivating employees' needs more personal immersion than technological skills. This may hold

Table 15.2 Decision-making vis-a-vis technological skills

*Technological problems—lack of technological skills * managerial problems—lack of decision-making skill cross-tabulation*

			Managerial problems—lack of decision-making skill		*Total*
			Yes	*No*	
Technological problems—lack of technological skills	Yes	Count	76	108	184
		Expected count	51.9	132.1	184
		% within technological problems—lack of technological skills	41.30%	58.70%	100.00%
		% within managerial problems—lack of decision-making skill	67.30%	37.50%	45.90%
		% of total	19.00%	26.90%	45.90%
	No	Count	37	180	217
		Expected count	61.1	155.9	217
		% within technological problems—lack of technological skills	17.10%	82.90%	100.00%
		% within managerial problems—lack of decision-making skill	32.70%	62.50%	54.10%
		% of total	9.20%	44.90%	54.10%
Total		Count	113	288	401
		Expected count	113	288	401
		% within technological problems—lack of technological skills	28.20%	71.80%	100.00%
		% within managerial problems—lack of decision-making skill	100.00%	100.00%	100.00%
		% of total	28.20%	71.80%	100.00%

untrue in remote operations as remote operations in a business rely highly on ICT, but, because present context encompasses MSMEs which mostly exhibit small, home based, one location enterprises (see Sect. 15.4.2) or enterprises which does not have remote operations, we may infer this logic.

A dependence/independence analysis of controlling skills (V_5) with technological skills (V_0) reports dependency of V_5 on V_0 with strong

Table 15.3 Managerial communication vis-a-vis technological skills

*Technological problems—lack of technological skills * managerial problems—lack of communication skill cross-tabulation*

			Managerial problems—lack of communication skill		*Total*
			Yes	*No*	
Technological problems—lack of technological skills	Yes	Count	68	116	184
		Expected count	50	134	184
		% within technological problems—lack of technological skills	37.00%	63.00%	100.00%
		% within managerial problems—lack of communication skill	62.40%	39.70%	45.90%
		% of total	17.00%	28.90%	45.90%
	No	Count	41	176	217
		Expected count	59	158	217
		% within technological problems—lack of technological skills	18.90%	81.10%	100.00%
		% within managerial problems—lack of communication skill	37.60%	60.30%	54.10%
		% of total	10.20%	43.90%	54.10%
Total		Count	109	292	401
		Expected count	109	292	401
		% within technological problems—lack of technological skills	27.20%	72.80%	100.00%
		% within managerial problems—lack of communication skill	100.00%	100.00%	100.00%
		% of total	27.20%	72.80%	100.00%

and acceptable association (see Fig. 15.1). Table 15.5 brings forth the positive association between V_5 and V_0 depicting better controlling skills with better technological knowledge. Having discussed technologies of ubiquitous computing (see Sect. 15.2.2.1) which observes the development of easy-to-use technologies and their connection to communication networks blurring the gap between physical spaces and electronic spaces (Cascio & Montealegre, 2016), above depiction seems becoming stronger

Table 15.4 Managerial motivational skill vis-a-vis technological skill

*Technological problems—lack of technological skills * managerial problems—lack of motivation to employees cross-tabulation*

			Managerial problems—lack of motivation to employees		*Total*
			Yes	*No*	
Technological problems—lack of technological skills	Yes	Count	51	133	184
		Expected count	40.4	143.6	184
		% within technological problems—lack of technological skills	27.70%	72.30%	100.00%
		% within managerial problems—lack of motivation to employees	58.00%	42.50%	45.90%
		% of total	12.70%	33.20%	45.90%
	No	Count	37	180	217
		Expected count	47.6	169.4	217
		% within technological problems—lack of technological skills	17.10%	82.90%	100.00%
		% within managerial problems—lack of motivation to employees	42.00%	57.50%	54.10%
		% of total	9.20%	44.90%	54.10%
Total		Count	88	313	401
		Expected count	88	313	401
		% within technological problems—lack of technological skills	21.90%	78.10%	100.00%
		% within managerial problems—lack of motivation to employees	100.00%	100.00%	100.00%
		% of total	21.90%	78.10%	100.00%

with ICT skills ingrained in women entrepreneurs through training and better ICT entrepreneurial ecosystem.

Table 15.5 Managerial control vis-a-vis technological skills

*Technological problems—lack of technological skills * managerial problems—lack of control cross-tabulation*

			Managerial problems—lack of control		Total
			Yes	*No*	
Technological problems—lack of technological skills	Yes	Count	71	113	184
		Expected count	51.4	132.6	184
		% within technological problems—lack of technological skills	38.60%	61.40%	100.00%
		% within managerial problems—lack of control	63.40%	39.10%	45.90%
		% of total	17.70%	28.20%	45.90%
	No	Count	41	176	217
		Expected count	60.6	156.4	217
		% within technological problems—lack of technological skills	18.90%	81.10%	100.00%
		% within managerial problems—lack of control	36.60%	60.90%	54.10%
		% of total	10.20%	43.90%	54.10%
Total		Count	112	289	401
		Expected count	112	289	401
		% within technological problems—lack of technological skills	27.90%	72.10%	100.00%
		% within managerial problems—lack of control	100.00%	100.00%	100.00%
		% of total	27.90%	72.10%	100.00%

15.6 Implication and Suggestions

The output of the study shows that ICT usage (69.3%) and knowledge of ICT skills (54.1%) among women entrepreneurs is an encouraging trend in Gujarat, as compared with the result of other studies done around emerging markets (Shah, 2013). This reflects that women can outperform in business if she is given proper direction of utilizing ICT and related skills in her day to managerial functions.

Nevertheless, women are still abstained from access of technical know-how and mainstream technologies in their business set-up in comparison with their male counterparts (Shah, 2013; SPF, 2017). It is this area of lacuna that the following suggestions derived from this chapter can be appropriate for policy makers.

Bottom-up globalization and balancing it with top-down globalization—Global players generally go for convenient markets and are therefore unable to harness the opportunities available in other upcoming economies. This is problematic as globalization will benefit certain select market protagonists, global giants and governments rather than benefiting the whole society, referred to as a top-down activity (Samli, 2009). In contrast, when the global players pay equal attention to the bottom tiers of the global economy, a holistic advancement can be achieved, termed as bottom-up globalization (Samli, 2008).

The increased prevalence of small, scattered and sole businesses in emerging economies call for the implementation of bottom-up globalization with an adequate balance of the top-down globalization. This will ensure easy access of robust and better technologies to women entrepreneurs and enable better management practices.

Leveraging mobile-based entrepreneurship programmes (SPF, 2017)—Study based on emerging economies similar to the current study present a remarkable image of the success of women entrepreneurs' usage of ICT in day to day business operations in the form of smartphones, laptops and other devices. This is an important piece of information to government and international aiding agencies, for them to initiate mobile-based entrepreneurship development programmes to enable flexible learning to women entrepreneurs. Connectedness to mentors *via* these programmes can create leapfrogging effect on their managerial and related business skills.

Networking and Mentoring interventions—A mobile application that is developed for women entrepreneurs as networking and mentoring solutions builds an opportunity to create social capital and support. Studies suggest that there is positive relation between mentoring and career advancement and women entrepreneurs experience improved career advancement if she receives career support from a female mentor (Kariv, 2013; Singh, 2017). This implies policymakers to spread more words of success for ICT usage by women entrepreneurs so that when these able and successful women entrepreneurs' mentor others in their network, they emphasize upon ICT imperativeness in business practice.

SMS-based interventions (SPF, 2017)—Digitization has been the prime propaganda of Indian government, however internet accessibility is questionable in many places. Also, faced with lack of money, substantial section of entrepreneurs tends to go with basic mobile devices. This is an opportunity for government and NGOs to make mobile users attain access in the form of SMS.

Mobile-based interventions are more accessible to women *via* smartphones that assure flexibility learning for women entrepreneurs than laptop or any other form of ICT devices for networking and other business-related solutions. Beyond this, radio, TV and print media also has great potential.

Street plays by university/college students or NGO's for building awareness—It is observed that women in Gujarat are highly aware of events like business exhibition, targeted business fairs, the facilities of *haat*,[2] etc. that extend space solutions to women entrepreneurs. These can be a target place where university/college students or NGO's can perform street plays projecting day to day business-related management solutions with the help of accessible ICT devices. This will be specifically constructive to those 30.7% of small business women in this study (see Sect. 15.4.2) who do not make use of ICT in their business operations.

15.7 Conclusion

The ICT landscape has evolved in a steadfast manner in the recent years, with increased accessibility of the internet, mobile phones and other new opportunities that include business process outsourcing models. In sync with the evolving landscape, the barriers women face in the use, access and implementation of ICT needs to be recognized with further inputs to reduce the gap in the use of ICT. This will empower women and address the issue of reducing gender disparities in an ecosystem of growth of ICT. Hence, programmes for growth of women entrepreneurs can be made successful when they address specific gendered vulnerabilities of women (Seth, 2009; Samantroy & Tomar, 2018). Investments are required in

[2] Gujarat has one haat each in Ahmedabad, Surat and Bhuj that is developed under Urban Haat Scheme, sponsored (70:30) by Government of India. Intention is to make urban market accessible to handloom and handicrafts artisans.

ICT and in learning and acquiring knowledge about ICT so that the business venture can be kept up and running. More so, investments on the lines of innovation make a positive impact in generating substantial firm growth.

Along-with knowledge and use and application of ICT, changes will also occur. These changes bring about varied sets of different knowledge and capability needs for the owner that will further push boundaries of learning and incorporation of ICT and related skills. This will also push them to be risk takers and dabble in technology and its related aspects.

An assimilation of the emerging technologies and novel innovations is shaped not only by products and features but is based on how users (entrepreneurs) use it, innovate with it, participate in its regulation, and adjust to it that provides the path ahead for facing future challenges.

References

Akoglu, H. (2018). User's guide to correlation coefficients. *Turkish Journal of Emergency Medicines, 18*(3), 91–93. https://doi.org/10.1016/j.tjem.2018.08.001. Retrieved December 26, 2019, from https://www.ncbi.nlm.nih.gov/pmc/articles/PMC6107969/.

Alderete, M. (2015). Does digital proximity between countries impact entrepreneurship? *Info: The Journal of Policy, Regulation and Strategy for Telecommunications, Information and Media, 17*(5), 46–65. https://doi.org/10.1108/info-03-2015-0020.

Alshubiri, F., Jamil, S. A., & Elheddad, M. (2019). The impact of ICT on financial development: Empirical evidence from the Gulf Cooperation Council countries. *International Journal of Engineering Business Management, 11*, 1847979019870670.

APEC Policy Partnership on Women and the Economy. (November 2018). *Case studies of successful women entrepreneurs in the ICT industry in 21 APEC economies*. https://www.apec.org/-/media/APEC/Publications/2018/12/Case-Studies-of-Successful-Women-Enterpreneurs-in-the-ICT-Industry-in-21-APEC-Economies/218_PPWE_Case-Studies-of-Successful-Women-Enterpreneurs-in-the-ICT-Industry-in-21-APEC-Economies.pdf.

Auramo, J., et al. (2005). The roles of information technology in supply chain management. Proceedings of the 17th Annual NOFOMA Conference, Copenhagen, Denmark, June 9–10, pp. 1–16.

Avgerou, C. (2008). Information systems in developing countries: A critical research review. *The Journal of Information Technology, 23*, 133–146.

Bernardt, Y., & Muller, R. (2000). *Determinants of firm size: A survey of literature*. Zoetermeer: EIM Small Business Research and Consultancy. Available at: http://ondernemerschap.panteia.nl/pdf-ez/h199913.pdf.

Bosma, N., De Wit, G., & Carree, M. (2003). *Modelling entrepreneurship* (Tinbergen Institute Discussion Paper, TI-2003–014/3). Rotterdam: Tinbergen Institute.

Bramann J. U. (2017). Building ICT entrepreneurship ecosystems in resource-scarce contexts: Learnings from Kenya's "Silicon Savannah". In B. Ndemo & T. Weiss (Eds.), *Digital Kenya: Palgrave studies of entrepreneurship in Africa*. London: Palgrave Macmillan. Retrieved December 27, 2019, from https://link.springer.com/chapter/10.1057/978–1-137-57878-5_8.

Brynjolfsson, E., Hitt, L. M., & Bresnahan, T. F. (2002). Information technology, workplace organisation, and the demand of skilled labor: Firm-level evidence. *Quarterly Journal of Economics, 117,* 339–376.

Carayannis, E., Popescu, D., Sipp, C., & Stewart, M. (2006). Technological learning for entrepreneurial development (TL4ED) in the knowledge economy (KE): Case studies and lessons learned. *Technovation, 26*(4), 419–443.

Carroll, S., & Gillen, D. (1987). Are the classical management functions useful in describing managerial work? *The Academy of Management Review, 12*(1), 38–51. Retrieved from www.jstor.org/stable/257992.

Cascio, W. F., & Montealegre, R. (2016). How technology is changing work and organizations. *Annual Review of Organizational Psychology and Organizational Behavior, 3,* 349–375. https://doi.org/10.1146/annurev-orgpsych-041015-062352.

Caskey, C. (1972). The four functions of management. *Journal (American Water Works Association), 64*(6), 361–366. Retrieved from www.jstor.org/stable/41266737.

Clement, R. W. (1992). Functions, roles and behaviors: Teaching the managerial job. *Journal of Managerial Issues, 43*(3), 438–446. Retrieved from www.jstor.org/stable/40603948.

Deborah, A. E., Wilhelmina, S., Oyelana, A. A., & Ibrahim, S. I. (2015). Challenges faced by women entrepreneurs and strategies adopted by women entrepreneurs to ensure small business success in Nkonkobe Municipality, South Africa. *Journal of Economics, 6*(1), 37–49.

Energy, N. (2010). *SMEs, entrepreneurship and innovation*. OECD Studies on SMEs and Entrepreneurship. Retrieved December 27, 2019, from http://rosted.nu/attachments/File/2010/SMEs_Entrepreneurship_and_Innovation_2010.pdf.

Feller, A., Shunk, D., & Callarman, T. (2006). Value chains versus supply chains. *BP Trends*, 1–7. Retrieved December 27, 2019, from https://www.bptrends.com/publicationfiles/03-06-ART-ValueChains-SupplyChains-Feller.pdf.

Ghosh, S. (1980). Technological change and workers' participation in management. *Indian Journal of Industrial Relations, 15*(4), 599–603. Retrieved from www.jstor.org/stable/27768585.

Golson, J. P. (1977). The impact of technological change on organization management. In *Proceedings of the 15th Annual Southeast Regional Conference (ACM-SE 15)* (pp. 293–299). New York, NY, USA: ACM. https://doi.org/10.1145/1795396.1795437. Retrieved from https://dl.acm.org/citation.cfm?id=1795437.

Isenberg, D. (2011). *The entrepreneurship ecosystem strategy as a new paradigm for economic policy: Principles for cultivating entrepreneurship.* Presentation at the Institute of International and European Affairs. Wellesley: Babson.

Islam, N. (2016). The use of information and communication technology (ICT) and business management: Contemporary issues and challenges. *SSRN Electronic Journal*. https://doi.org/10.2139/ssrn.2856262.

Junare, S. O., & Singh, R. (2016a). Technological understanding and usage vis-à-vis knowledge of government schemes—A study of women entrepreneurs of selected cities of Gujarat. *Amity Journal of Entrepreneurship, 1*(1), 71–85.

Junare, S. O., & Singh, R. (2016b, April 24). An analysis of technological practice among women entrepreneurs of different entrepreneurial avenues in selected cities of Gujarat. In *Proceedings of 53rd IRF International Conference*, Pune (India). Available at: http://www.digitalxplore.org/up_proc/pdf/223-146174102481-89.pdf.

Kariv, D. (2013). *Female entrepreneurship and the new venture creation*. New York: Routledge. https://doi.org/10.4324/9780203140987.

Kot, S. (2018). Sustainable supply chain management in small and medium enterprises. *Sustainability, 10*(4), 1143. Retrieved December 27, 2019, from https://www.mdpi.com/2071-1050/10/4/1143/htm

Kumar, D., & Rajeev, P. V. (2016). Value chain: A conceptual framework. *International Journal of Engineering and Management Sciences, 7*(1), 74–77. Retrieved from http://accioneduca.org/admin/archivos/clases/material/value-chain_1564001043.pdf.

Kushwaha, G. S. (2011). Competitive advantage through information and communication technology (ICT) enabled supply chain management practices. *International Journal of Enterprise Computing and Business Systems, 1*(2). ISSN (Online): 2230–8849.

Lazear, E. P. (May, 2004). Balanced skills and entrepreneurship. *The American Economic Review, 94*(2), 208–211.

Leduc, S., Guilbert, L., & Vallery, G. (2015). Impact of ICTs on leadership practices: Representations and actions. *Leadership & Organization Development Journal, 36*(4). https://doi.org/10.1108/lodj-07-2013-0090.

Locust, V. Y. (2018). *Strategies used by women to secure SBA's 8(a) and 504 loan financing*. Unpublished thesis, Walden University. Retrieved from https://scholarworks.waldenu.edu/cgi/viewcontent.cgi?article=6777&context=dissertations.

Madanda, A., Kabonesa, C., & Bantebya-Kyomuhendo, G. (2007). Challenges to women's empowerment through ICTs: The case of Makerere University. *Agenda: Empowering Women for Gender Equity, 21*(71), 81–88. Retrieved from www.jstor.org/stable/27739247.

Martínez, I., & Nguyen, T. (2014). *Using information and communication technology to support women's entrepreneurship in Central and West Asia*. Manila: Asian Development Bank. Retrieved from https://digitalcommons.ilr.cornell.edu/cgi/viewcontent.cgi?article=1380&context=intl.

Newton, K. (2001). *Management skills for small business*. Retrieved December 27, 2019, from https://www.ic.gc.ca/eic/site/061.nsf/vwapj/mngtsklls_e.pdf/$FILE/mngtsklls_e.pdf.

Niu, Y. (2010). *The impact of information technology on supply chain performance: A knowledge management perspective*. Unpublished Doctoral thesis, University of North Carolina at Charlotte, Charlotte. Retrieved December 27, 2019, from http://libres.uncg.edu/ir/uncc/f/Niu_uncc_0694D_10092.pdf.

NSTEDB. (2013). *Fuelling entrepreneurship—The story of technological business incubation in India*. Retrieved from http://www.nstedb.com/booklet.pdf.

NSTEDB. (n.d.). *Developing eco system for knowledge to wealth creation*. Retrieved from http://www.nstedb.com/Developing-Eco.pdf.

Papulová, Z., & Mokroš, M. (2007). Importance of managerial skills and knowledge in management for small entrepreneurs. *E-leader, Prague*, 1–8. Retrieved December 27, 2019, from https://www.g-casa.com/PDF/Papulova-Mokros.pdf.

Prljić, S., Vučeković, M., & Vujačić, S. (2015). The importance of information and communication technologies in the development of women entrepreneurship. *Journal of Women's Entrepreneurship and Education, 3–4,* 65–76.

Samantroy, E., & Tomar, J. S. (2018). Women entrepreneurship in India: Evidences from economic censuses. *Social Change, 48*(2), 1–20. Retrieved June 17, 2019, from https://www.academia.edu/37143630/Women_Entrepreneurship_in_India_Evidence_from_Economic_Censuses.

Samli, C. A. (2008). *Globalization from the bottom up*. New York: Springer.

Samli, C. A. (2009). *International entrepreneurship—Innovative solutions for a fragile planet* (p. 112). New York: Springer.

Sasakawa Peace Foundation and Dalberg Global Development Advisors. (2017). *Advancing women's empowerment: Growing women's entrepreneurship through ICT in Southeast Asia*.

Seth, A. (2009). *Entrepreneurship and E-business development for women*. New Delhi: ALP Books.

Shah, H. (2013). *Creating an enabling environment for women's entrepreneurship in India* (Development Papers No. 1304). United Nations Economic and Social Commission for Asia and the Pacific (UN ESCAP), South and South-West Asia Office. South and South-West Asia Office.

Shavazi, A., Abzari, M., & Mohammadzadeh, A. (2009). A research in relationship between ICT and SCM. *Engineering and Technology, 50*, 92–101.

Singh, R. (2017). *Problems and prospects of women entrepreneurship with special reference to MSMEs in the state of Gujarat*. Unpublished doctoral thesis, Gujarat Technological University, Gujarat, India. Retrieved from https://www.gtu.ac.in/uploads/Thesis129990992024.pdf.

Singh, R. (2019). A beginner's guide to descriptive research: Dilemmas expected while researching women entrepreneurship in an Indian context. *Sage research methods cases*. https://doi.org/10.4135/9781526493767. Retrieved June 10, 2019, from http://methods.sagepub.com/case/beginners-guide-descriptive-research-dilemmas-women-entrepreneurship-india.

Singh, R., & Sebastian, T. (2018). Familial legacies: A study on *Gujarati* women and family entrepreneurship. *Journal of Global Entrepreneurship and Research, 8*, 5. https://doi.org/10.1186/s40497-018-0090-x.

Spanos, Y. E., Prastacos, G. P., & Poulymenakou, A. (2002). The relationship between information and communication technologies adoption and management. *Information & Management, 39*, 659–675.

SPSS Tutorials. (n.d.). *Cramer's V: What and why?* Retrieved December 26, 2019, from https://www.spss-tutorials.com/cramers-v-what-and-why/.

Subashini R., Rita S., & Vivek M. (2012). The role of ICTs in knowledge management (KM) for organizational effectiveness. In P. V. Krishna, M. R. Babu, & E. Ariwa (Eds.), *Global Trends in Information Systems and Software Applications, ObCom 2011*. Berlin, Heidelberg: Springer. *Communications in Computer and Information Science, 270*, 542–549. Retrieved from https://link.springer.com/chapter/10.1007/978-3-642-29216-3_59.

Swissnex India Report. (2017). *India's booming digital industry*. Retrieved from https://www.swissnexindia.org/wp-content/uploads/sites/5/2017/09/ICT-Report.pdf.

Toader, E., Firtescu, B., Roman, A., & Anton, S. (2018). Impact of information and communication technology infrastructure on economic growth: An empirical assessment for the EU countries. *Sustainability, 3750*(10), 1–22.

Tseng, M. L., Wu, K. J., & Nguyen, T. T. (2011). Information technology in supply chain management: A case study. *Procedia-Social and Behavioral Sciences, 25*, 257–272.

Van der Zwan, P., Thurik, R., & Verheul, I., et al. (2016). Factors influencing the entrepreneurial engagement of opportunity and necessity entrepreneurs. *Eurasian Business Review, 6*(3), 273–295. https://doi.org/10.1007/s40821-

016-0065-1. Retrieved December 23, 2019, from https://link.springer.com/article/10.1007/s40821-016-0065-1.

Veiga, J. F., & Yanouzas, J. N. (1976). What women in management want: The ideal vs. the real. *The Academy of Management Journal, 19*(1), 137–143.

CHAPTER 16

Conclusion and Future Research Agenda

João J. M. Ferreira, Sérgio J. Teixeira and Hussain G. Rammal

Leading this edited book and interacting with technological innovation and international competitiveness academics allowed us to contact with some exciting topics and also opportunities for future research with considerable challenges.

J. J. M. Ferreira (✉)
Department of Management and Economics & NECE Research Unit in Business Sciences, University of Beira Interior, Covilhã, Portugal
e-mail: jjmf@ubi.pt

S. J. Teixeira
Higher Institute of Administration and Languages, Research Centre—ISAL, Funchal, Portugal
e-mail: sergio.teixeira@isal.pt

NECE—Research Unit in Business Sciences, Funchal, Portugal

H. G. Rammal
UTS Business School, University of Technology Sydney, Sydney, Australia
e-mail: hussain.rammal@uts.edu.au

J. J. M. Ferreira et al. (eds.), *Technological Innovation and International Competitiveness for Business Growth*, Palgrave Studies in Democracy, Innovation, and Entrepreneurship for Growth,
https://doi.org/10.1007/978-3-030-51995-7_16

Table 16.1 Topics of interest for future research agenda

Research themes	*Research topics*	*Research questions—future agenda*
Bridging technological innovation domains	Technological innovation and exports	What are the main antecedents to firm exports and innovation?
	Innovation, technology, and competitiveness	What are the main effects of export and innovation activities on firm growth?
	International growth and competitiveness	What are the main boundary conditions of technological innovation?
	World of technology	How to develop a unified approach to technology, innovation and strategy to generate competitive advantage in increasingly demanding business environments
	Drivers of international growth	What is the impact of globalisation on business growth?
	Social media competitiveness	What extent and under which conditions social media is relevant for international growth?
Dynamics of international business competitiveness	Innovation, entrepreneurship, and competitiveness	What dimensions can explaining and help in measuring the competitiveness phenomenon?
	Innovation and R&D	Is sustainability a relevant dimension to evaluating international competitiveness?
	Global competitiveness	
	Barriers to international competitiveness	
	Sustainability and competitiveness	

(continued)

In Table 16.1, we highlight the main challenges, for each one of the research themes approached in the book, that this research field faces and which are potential future lines of investigation.

Table 16.1 (continued)

Research themes	*Research topics*	*Research questions—future agenda*
Refining the technological innovation and business growth link	Technological innovation capabilities and management	Under what contexts will some recourses and capabilities explain innovation and competitiveness?
	Innovation and technology service business	How do the sector's dynamics shape management and decision-making processes?
	Service growth	How can companies explain different technological options in the same sector, but in different countries?
	Spinner innovation model	What kind of indicators explains the efficiency and performance of business and countries?
	R&D efficiency of countries	
Empirical case studies	Kaiser internet of thigs roadmap	What is the impact of innovation on global value chains?
	Steel industry's efficiency	How government policy could promote the competitiveness of business, industries and countries?
	Business growth, innovation, and internationalization—IT industry	With the advancement and proliferation of the Internet of Things, what techniques to use to analyse data and use it to boost business growth?
		How can scholars gain access to big, longitudinal datasets on technological innovation and competitiveness?

(continued)

Table 16.1 (continued)

Research themes	*Research topics*	*Research questions—future agenda*
		What methodological changes must take place for international competitiveness research to become more predictive?

16.1 Research Theme 1: Bridging Technological Innovation Domains

Today, the fields of technological innovation urgently need a unified approach. The challenges for theorists are many, as developing an approach that is generalizable in various contexts of technological innovation is not an easy research task. With this in mind, and as noted in Table 16.1, many questions can catalyze the construction of theory in the technological innovation literature. This effort is worthwhile because nowadays, much of the research focuses on micro aspects, such as those that succeed and fail, and less on macro aspects, such as the development of an integrative approach to the various elements and dimensions of analysis.

16.2 Research Theme 2: Dynamics of International Business Competitiveness

Recognizing and examining the multifaceted and dynamic nature of international business competitiveness is another central challenge for this field of research. As several of the chapters in this book demonstrate, the decisions, processes, and outcomes of international business competitiveness are influenced by several factors that interact with each other in very complex ways. Therefore, the examination of international competitiveness processes must use the approaches and methods that clarify these complexities. There appear to be various configurations for addressing the different perspectives and dynamics in international competitiveness research which, although complex, are particularly useful to the academic effort to simplify such complexities and provide greater clarity on possible generalizations of a phenomenon that is by nature multifaceted.

16.3 Research Theme 2: Refining the Technological Innovation and Business Growth Link

Studying and refining technological innovation and business growth is another challenge that still needs to be addressed. Several chapters in this book point to the need to integrate several elements, such as entrepreneur, company, industry in the development of the approach to this theme. Moreover, it is observed that such elements are hardly isolated from the organizational reality and industry contexts. These examples demonstrate how the adoption of a single approach generates incomplete and insufficient estimation models that limit the complex processes of analysis of technological innovation and business growth. Bringing a refining perspective of connection between business growth and technological innovation to the research field represents another important step in the development of the topic and helps to understand the role played by various players, at the micro and macro level, and how they interact with each other in this context. These and other paths for future research can generate interesting research questions.

16.4 Final Considerations

As reflected in the set of chapters in this book, the field of technological innovation and international competitiveness for business growth still lacks much future research.

The revision of this complex and multifaceted field of study can hardly be fully addressed in a single study and this book is no exception. Each author, in his chapter, deals with a different part of a larger body and ends with a different understanding of the phenomena. Thus, a fundamental task for scholars in this area of knowledge is the development of an approach, which offers clearly defined boundary conditions concerning actors, processes, levels of analysis, and contexts.

This book and the delimitation of the main topics of interest and research questions for future research summarized in Table 16.1 represent our contribution to the future development of this theme. As the various studies (chapters) in this work elucidate, there is significant scope for future research, especially in terms of building a more solid and eclectic approach.

However, this book represents an important step in that direction as it provides a common vision for understanding the main dimensions of technological innovation and international competitiveness for business growth. It is indeed encouraging that the vastly heterogeneous configurations discussed in this book can be aggregated.

Based on this, we hope that the topic will attract increasing attention and provide researchers with new and interesting possibilities to contribute to this fascinating field of knowledge.

Index

J. J. M. Ferreira et al. (eds.), *Technological Innovation and International Competitiveness for Business Growth*, Palgrave Studies in Democracy, Innovation, and Entrepreneurship for Growth,
https://doi.org/10.1007/978-3-030-51995-7

The manufacturer's authorised representative in the EU is Springer Nature Customer Service Centre GmbH, Europaplatz 3, 69115 Heidelberg, Germany. If you have any concerns regarding our products, please contact ProductSafety@springernature.com

Printed and bound by CPI Group (UK) Ltd, Croydon, CR0 4YY

30/09/2026

02225448-0002